Britain's
WATERWAYS
A unique insight

Contents

What to see around:

Special features

GEOprojects (UK) Ltd.
9-10 Southern Court
South Street
Reading
RG1 4QS

Tel: 0118 939 3567
Fax: 0118 959 8283

GEO projects

Coastline, rivers and canals

Waterways were vital routes for marauding invaders. Military expeditions penetrated up river and established their garrisons at the limits of navigation. Romans at Colchester and Rochester, up the Thames at Dorchester and on the Dee at Chester. The Romans even extended the natural limits of the Trent to get to Lincoln. Later Vikings entered from the sea, raided for loot and slaves, and captured and settled as far inland as Nottingham and York.

As rivers were modified to improve navigation, coastal trade penetrated further inland. Tonbridge, Norwich, Peterborough, Worcester, Burton upon Trent, Gainsborough and Newark became important inland ports. Navigation on the great rivers was mentioned in 'Magna Carta' but the vested interests of millers and fishermen slowed progress upstream.

The rapid expansion of the industrial revolution was assisted by privately funded canals until overshadowed (after fifty years) by railways and (within this century) by road improvements and new motorways financed by Government.

Canals are now recognised as a unique snapshot of pioneering British innovation, surviving from a time before cameras were invented. They now have a new lease of life as a quiet haven for wildlife, walkers and fishermen as well as for their original purpose.....navigation for all shapes and sizes of boats.

Tidal estuaries and the sea

Some say our longest river is our coastline.

John Masefield's 'Dirty British coaster with its salt cake smokestack' was only one of a long line of craft designed to hug the sea shore and take their cargoes wherever wide estuaries funnel tides deep inland.

The scouring action of the tide and the shape of the lower reaches of the river itself dictate how far inland shallow drafted coastal shipping can go. Deep rivers can be navigated many miles inland, particularly on spring tides or when the river is full of winter rainwater. On the other hand, summer flows can be so low that riverbed shallows are exposed and navigation halted.

Four rivers; the Severn, Thames, Mersey and Humber-Trent were, for centuries, the major routes inland. Worcester on the Severn, Staines on the Thames, Runcorn on the Mersey and Gainsborough on the Trent were all inland ports that grew up at tidal limits. Smaller rivers enabled Chester, Colchester, Bristol and King's Lynn to flourish when the only roads were a dilapidated Roman legacy.

Primitive tracks were so soft and rutted that heavy waggons were forced by law to fit wide rimmed wheels to spread the load. Despite this, parishes that paid for their upkeep viewed waggons as a nuisance. They damaged the tracks but did not pay. This led to Turnpikes (1700-1750).

Upriver travel

Rivers provided food and power in medieval times. Fishermen and owners of water mills threw fish traps and weirs across the flow to control the water for their use. However, one of the promises of the Magna Carta (1215) was that the Great Rivers of the Kingdom were to be open to all men.

Authority to 'improve navigation' was passed from Parliament to 'commissions' of local citizens. Initially the work involved clearing obstructions such as fish traps and weeds. Later more positive improvements were undertaken, generally starting where the tidal influence was weakest.

Clearing towpaths alongside the river eased the labour of gangs of men hauling on ropes attached to boats' bows, 'bowhauling'. Wider horsepaths followed. Short 'cuts' or canals bypassed difficult shallows or bends. Constant depth of water in both summer and winter was ensured by impounding the stream behind small dams or weirs; the top of which set the depth of water on the upstream side.

Until locks were invented, downstream movement was achieved by 'shooting' the rapid water flow over a partially open weir and upstream by a huge effort pulling the boat with rope and winches against the same partial waterfall. Rivers were thus improved step by step but navigation 'improvements' always led to arguments between mill owners and boatmen.

'Pound locks' were the break through. Introduced on the Thames to get from Burcot up to Oxford (1635), they meant that the volume and depth of water above a miller's weir could be retained at the same time as vessels made their way up stream. Locks became commonplace. River navigation served inland ports further and further upstream on the Wey (1663), the Ouse (1689), the Kennet (1723), the Avon (1727), the Mersey (1736), the Medway (1750), the Nene (1761), the Ure (1775), the Trent (1801) and later, the Severn (1858).

Despite these improvements some present day cities (eg Birmingham) were a series of landlocked villages with little reason for people to travel between the valleys where they lived. When they did, people went on horseback and goods went by 'trains' of pack horses. Many tracks were muddy in summer and impassable in winter. Wide drovers' trails delivered herds of sheep, cattle and tar-footed geese long distances to market towns.

The main routes stayed on hill sides and ridges as far as possible. River crossings were by ferry or ford; some place names have survived for hundreds of years, for example Guildford, Wallingford, Wilden Ferry. Bridges were only built across rivers and streams when the banks were close enough to be spanned by the engineering skills of the time. They tended to be far up stream eg Radcot on the Thames (AD958 and 1787) and only wide enough for two pack horses to pass, eg Gee Cross near Manchester.

Canal system

The first modern British canal was built when a scheme for controlling the Sankey Brook between St Helens

and the Mersey at Warrington was abandoned in 1757. Instead an 8 mile long canal was built alongside the brook following the principles of locks and weirs that had been used to bypass an obstruction on the River Exe in 1567.

A second canal originated within coal mines at Worsley near Manchester which incorporated a system of underground drainage waterways. Coal was already being loaded directly into primitive narrow boats at the coal face and floated out to the surface on water swept along by the mines' drainage channels. The Duke of Bridgewater, who owned the mines, had the idea that, if the channel were extended to Manchester coal could be directly unloaded.

The six mile Bridgewater Canal between Worsley and Castleford in Manchester was opened in 1765. The new canal **crossed over the River** Irwell on a stone aqueduct at Barton. This caused such a sensation that it became an instant 'tourist attraction'.

Eleven years later the Duke extended his canal to the River Mersey close to the tidal limit at Runcorn. Manchester was then linked to Liverpool estuary by a reliable waterway with only one flight of locks where the canal stepped down to the river. This presented severe commercial competition to the variable water flows on the Mersey and Irwell Navigation.

The next canals to be built were those of the **Grand Cross** with the aim of interconnecting the navigable reaches of the four great rivers of England and Wales:- **Staffs & Worcs Canal** (1772) leading from River Severn, **Trent and Mersey Canal** (1777) connecting the Humber to the Mersey, and the **Oxford Canal** (1790) leading to the Thames, all joining up around Birmingham.

A disjointed network of turnpike roads presented no serious competition to these canals, and the first railway (Stockton and Darlington, 1825) was not even under discussion. **Over 35 new canals** were promoted in Parliament 1792-1794, the years of **canal mania**.

The Sankey Canal was built with swing bridges to allow the masts of Mersey flats to remain rigged on their way up-stream to St. Helens. When the first passenger railway was built between Liverpool and Manchester it was forced to give the neccessary mast clearance over the navigation by means of a huge embankment leading up to a tall viaduct still in use today at Earlestown.

Success

Once canals began to connect with each other and the river navigations traffic became more than a local affair. Trade increased and, for a while, some companies began to pay dividends way above the maximum interest (5%) then paid on savings.

Sankey Brook Navigation paid up to 20% (1772). For 40 years the Oxford Canal Company paid over 20% to shareholders and sometimes achieved 33% (1824-1826). More common were the dividends of 4%-5% which the railway companies guaranteed to existing shareholders when they began to 'buy out' the canals as unwelcome competition.

Predatory railways

Canals were a prime way of moving coal and heavy materials for all kinds of construction. eg limestone chippings, timber, boulders. Some Acts of Parliament authorising canals required them to move materials for repair of roads at no charge. Railways required heavy construction materials in great quantities and as a result were often constructed alongside the canal, (eg the Great Western Railway to Bristol) and, like turkeys voting for Christmas, many canal companies carried their maximum tonnages at the time of railway construction.

Railway companies always set their termini close to canal termini, eg Paddington in London, Castlefield in Manchester. As soon as railways opened they were able to under cut canal rates to attract business. Canal companies struggled, bargees were expected to take such a large cut in their money that they could no longer afford to keep their families in houses on the bank. Living aboard in tiny cabins became the norm for long distance carrying.

By the railway age Birmingham had an intricate network of canals serving hundreds of factories. Railway companies were content to transfer goods to boats for the last leg of the journey. Boats within Birmingham did not travel far and were only used on a day-by-day basis. These 'day-boats' did not have cabins for the crews' families.

Railway companies purchased canal companies. Sometimes with a promise to run the two systems together, but sometimes specifically to make use of existing tunnels.

The third longest canal tunnel at Strood in Kent (1824, 12 000 feet) was closed and converted to rail. The longest canal tunnel (through the Pennines at Standedge (1811, 16 000 feet) was used to help create a railway tunnel alongside. Side passages were built at regular intervals giving access to the working faces digging the rail tunnel alongside. When opened, smoke from passing steam trains overwhelmed many canal crew members.

Two world wars

Carrying on the canal system was faced with extra competition after the First World War. Men had learnt to drive army lorries and cheap surplus vehicles thronged a road system built for horses and carts. Again under cutting of rates took place. Lorries could travel door to door and were generally off loaded by the labourers at factory yards before they did boats.

During the Second World War canals were part of the strategy. The Kennet and Avon was fortified as some sort of 'Maginot Line'. The improved Grand Union was used to relieve the railways from the

When the forests of England had been cut down for fuel coal came from Newcastle to London and on ships like these. Loading was directly into the ship's hold from waggons held high by huge wooden scaffolding known as 'staithes'. The earliest tramways led from pit heads to such loading arrangements.

Newcastle pit owners objected in Parliament to new canal proposals, especially where they enabled coal to be delivered from inland pits to 'their' markets in London.

carrying of coal, steel and cement and boatmen were augmented with emergency, all female crews - the celebrated 'idle women'.

Revival

Post war all transport was nationalised. Road and rail were 'flavour of the month', waterways were mere adjuncts to docks and waterborne trade faded. The *coup-de-grace* was a very severe frost in 1963 which left boats and their cargoes frozen and immobile in iced up canals for three months.

Narrow boats did not only carry coal. For example, on the Regents Canal in London, corpses for burial in Kensal Green Cemetery and Sunday School outings into the countryside around Uxbridge were also carried. Crowds of children benefited and I know of no loss of life although, nowadays, a special licience would be needed for more than 12 passengers.

However, a bunch of enthusiasts, inspired by a book written as war broke out and published immediately afterwards, formed an early environmental pressure group and started to campaign against public and political indifference. The fledgling Inland Waterways Association (IWA) used direct action (Stratford Canal 1947, Standedge 1948, Dudley 1959), exhibitions

(Heals 1948), media events (Market Harborough 1950), parliamentary battles (1956) and public campaigns (1968 Act) to press its cause. It encouraged the stewardship of the National Trust (Stratford 1960, Wey Navigation 1964) and even intended to bid at auction (Basingstoke 1947).

Meanwhile, the first independent trusts and restoration societies were set up (eg River Avon 1952) and volunteers got organised nationally (1970) to achieve the physical restoration of navigations at little cost to 'authority' (celebrated after 25 years by a 'Big Dig' on the Wilts and Berks Canal 1995, 10 000 volunteers). More recently these efforts have been matched by major grants from Lottery funds.

'Pleasure seekers'

Under the slogan 'The fastest way of slowing down' there is now an industry employing thousands caring for all kinds of pleasure boating. Hire boats, trip boats, electric boats, etc, carry people using the water to retreat from a world dominated by ever faster machines. Canoeists, oarsmen, fishermen, towpath walkers and ramblers or just passers-by, do their own thing and share the delights of sitting at picnic sites, restaurants and pubs overlooking water, made more relaxing by the sight of boats floating by.

In the nineties the IWA, whilst continuing to lobby responsible bodies, has turned its attention to the small 'characteristic details' which distinguish between individual canals and which stem from differing designers, their growing engineering confidence and the increasing financial confidence of canal shareholders. They seek to 'preserve the fast disappearing artifacts and structures which make our waterways a historic record unique in the world'. After visiting some of the places suggested in this book you may come to agree with their recent Chairman, Audrey Smith, who claimed our waterways are 'an enormous piece of living liquid history'.

The National Waterways Network

About this book

The maps in this book are drawn to three scales:-
waterways 1: 350 000 (Broads and BCN 1: 250 000)
short strolls 1: 15 000
whole system 1: 700 000 (Scotland 1: 825 000)
Starting overleaf the directory lists all the **waterways of Britain** in *alphabetical order.* Included are 55
individual **waterway maps** at a common scale of *1: 350 000 (except BCN p12 and Broads p16 at 1: 250 000).*
Beside each map there is a **short description** of the waterway giving **dates** of the first improvements, names of
the **engineers** responsible, **location** details and **statistics**. A selection of **waterway features** for each is
described, followed by general *directions for finding them* from a major road or motorway junction. **Local
boat trips** and **tourist information centres** are given *(plus contact telephone numbers)*. The page number for
each of these waterways is **located on the key map** opposite.

Twenty one **short strolls** at a scale of **1: 15 000** demonstrate where waterways can be found close to a popular
tourist attraction and explore different aspects of life alongside water - birds, flora, boat types, industrial
archaeology, early engineering. These are **located on the key map** opposite, listed on the contents page and
can be found on the green-edged pages in the directory close to the waterway concerned.

Comprehensive coverage of the **whole system** is given in the **regional maps** at the end of the book with
England and Wales at **1: 700 000** and Scotland at **1: 825 000**.

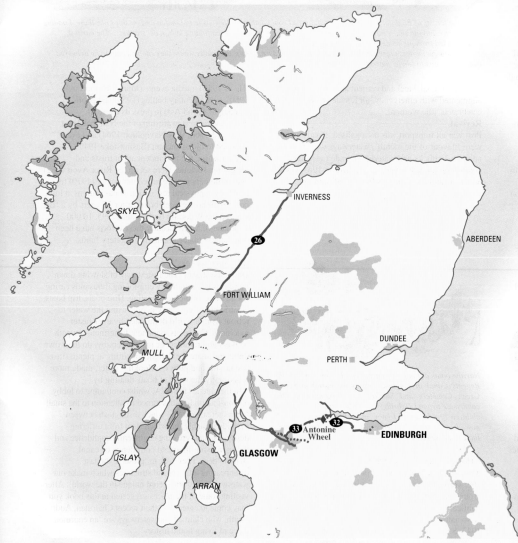

Waterway spotting
(a quick guide)

Existing waterways are fairly evident on the
ground but derelict canals can be exceedingly
difficult to find. Their alignments may be shown
on old maps of the area but you may not have
access to these. In that event field exploration is
what is required.

Waterway spotting is a complex activity but
there are often obvious, and sometimes not so
obvious, clues if you look carefully. Spotting the
local waterway can be just as much fun as
spotting 'Eddie Stobart' lorries with their
distinctive canal-style lettering.

Road signs indicating hump back bridges,
water's edge and 'beware ducks' are
useful, as are pub signs which retain such old
names as The Ferryman, The Wherry, Navigation
Inn, The Barge, Lime Kilns, The Shroppy Fly.

Street names such as Water Lane, Weir Road,
River View, Canal Way, Quay Street or Potato
Wharf tend to give the game away. More obscure
names including words such as causeway, mill,
marsh, mead, meadow, lammas, hythe and staithe
can also help.

When standing on a slope, the river is likely to
be downhill. A canal, however, can be either
above or below you, although it would have
been built to try and stay at a consistent level for
long stretches. So, if you have glimpsed it
nearby, look for the continuation at about the
same contour.

Often, if you know a waterway is nearby, this
extra detective work will give final confirmation.
If you are sure of your approach, and all else
fails, see if a local resident knows the
whereabouts of his nearest waterway...
... but not everybody does!!

Navigating

Motorsport navigators instruct their drivers and
read the signs. Your map reader will see road
signs, mostly in white lettering on coloured
backgrounds. Blue backgrounds on motorways,
green on trunk roads will help you along, but
signs naming the forgotten villages that are
beside waterway features are often the little white
ones with black writing. If you are lucky, as you
get closer, the sought after name might also
appear on special brown 'tourist' signs.

The waterway features described in the
Directory pages of this book end with a suggested
'approach' from a nearby major road or motorway
junction. The suggestions will rarely be the *only
possible* approach and *not necessarily the shortest
or the quickest* but will involve *as few twists and
turns* as possible. Experienced navigators might
then, knowing where the site is, choose a different
route of their own.

Waterway features are to be found all over
the country. It is easiest to approach them by
boat or car. To get to the sites of the suggested
'short strolls' it is also generally feasible to
arrive by bus or train. Ordnance Survey
Landranger map references are given to help
pinpoint the locations.

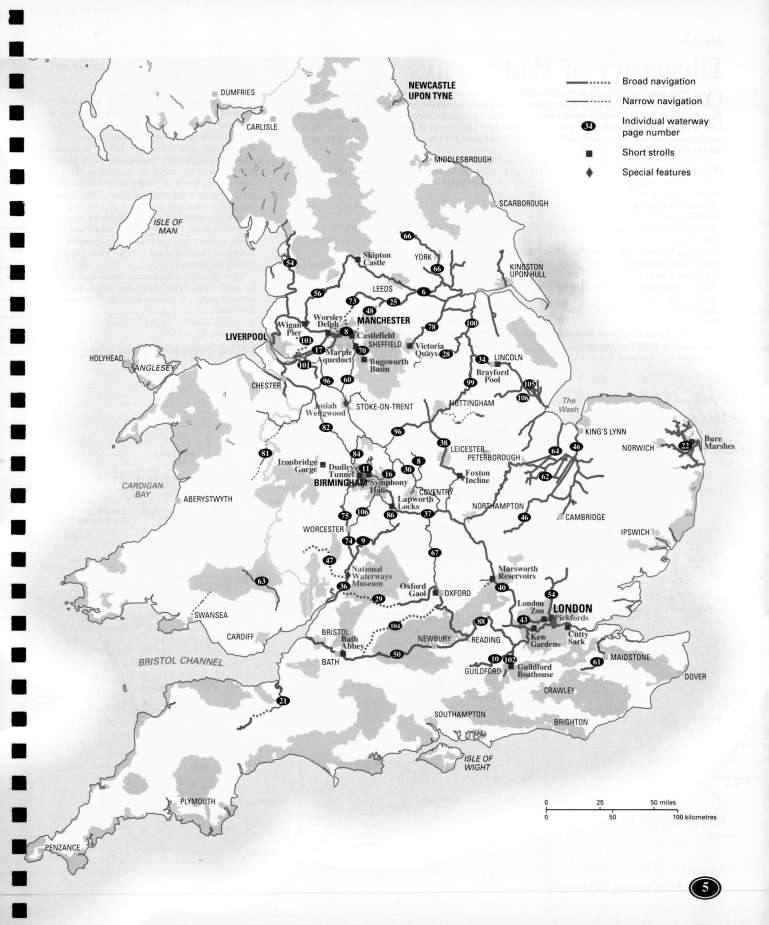

Broad navigation ······

Narrow navigation - - -

🅓 Individual waterway page number

■ Short strolls

◆ Special features

DUMFRIES

CARLISLE

NEWCASTLE UPON TYNE

MIDDLESBROUGH

SCARBOROUGH

ISLE OF MAN

KINGSTON UPON HULL

66

York

66

Skipton Castle

54

56

LEEDS

73 25 6

48

Worsley Delph MANCHESTER

78 100

Wigan Pier 8

101 Castlefield SHEFFIELD

17 Marple 70 Victoria Quays 28

101 Aqueduct Bugsworth Basin 34 LINCOLN

HOLYHEAD *ANGLESEY* 96 60 Brayford Pool

105

CHESTER 99 106

Josiah Wedgwood STOKE-ON-TRENT NOTTINGHAM

82 96 *The Wash*

81 38 LEICESTER KING'S LYNN NORWICH 22 *Bure Marshes*

84 Ironbridge Gorge Dudley Tunnel 8 PETERBOROUGH

CARDIGAN BAY 11 30 Foxton Incline 64 46

ABERYSTWYTH BIRMINGHAM 16 Symphony Hall COVENTRY 62

Lapworth Locks NORTHAMPTON 46 CAMBRIDGE

75 106 86 37 IPSWICH

WORCESTER 74 9 67 Marsworth Reservoirs

47 40 54

63 National Waterways Museum Oxford Gaol OXFORD London Zoo LONDON

SWANSEA 36 29 43 Pickfords

CARDIFF 104 NEWBURY 88 READING Kew Gardens Cutty Sark

BRISTOL Bath Abbey 50 10 102 Guildford 61 MAIDSTONE

BATH GUILDFORD Boathouse CRAWLEY DOVER

BRISTOL CHANNEL 21 SOUTHAMPTON BRIGHTON

ISLE OF WIGHT

PLYMOUTH

PENZANCE

0		25		50 miles

0	50		100 kilometres

Directory of Waterways

Over 3000 miles of canals and rivers interconnect with each other to create a network the size of the motorway system... and, better than motorways, they penetrate to the centre of almost every major city. They were built and improved by uncoordinated individual companies, concerned with individual towns. Like all individuals they each have their eccentricities. They continue to be known by their 'given' names and this directory lists every one in alphabetical order with enlarged entries and location maps for some 46 links in the system.

Aberdare Canal	**114** C4
Abercynon to Aberdare	
Aberdeenshire Canal	**123** E2
Aberdeen to Inverurie	
Adelphi Canal	**119** D4
Adelphi Works, Calow to near Staveley	
Adur, River	**113** D3

Shoreham-by-Sea to Shermanby Place (**East Adur**) and to Bines Green (**West Adur**)
11⅛ miles, 0 locks
Includes: **Baybridge Canal** West Grinstead to Bines Green
Environment Agency, Southern Region
Tel: 01903 820692

Southwick Canal (Shoreham Harbour)	**113** D4

Shoreham-by-Sea to Portslade-by-Sea
Shoreham Port Authority Tel: 01273 592613

Aike Beck (Lockington Navigation)	**119** E2
River Hull to Lockington Landing	

Aire and Calder Navigation
119 D2-D3

Opened: Wakefield 1699, Leeds 1702
Engineers: Hadley, Smeaton, Jessop, Rennie, Telford, Leather
Trent Falls to River Lock (Leeds) and to Flood Lock (Wakefield)
44 miles, 12 wide locks plus Wakefield Branch 7 miles, 4 wide locks

Not all waterways can carry commercial craft of 700 tons inland for 70 miles. The Aire and Calder here shows how water can provide cheap and environmentally-friendly transport of bulk goods through locks up to 22 feet wide and 200 feet long!!

These two rivers have been steadily improved since the first works allowed 15 ton river keels to go upstream beyond the weir at Knottingley Mill (1700) which formed the (then) tidal limit. Subsequently, enlarged to allow 150 ton boats, long, straight cuts were made to bypass problems where the rivers were too narrow or too tortuous. The company reinforced and raised the banks along most of the Aire and made completely artificial cuts first to Selby and then to Goole. It also relieved York Corporation of the responsibility for channel improvements on the Lower Ouse (1884) from Goole to where the Ouse ceases its independent existence (Trent Falls) and joins the River Trent to become the Humber.

This is definitely a commercial waterway; it even has traffic lights on the locks. Large cargo vessels, some sea going, still penetrate to Goole, Ferrybridge and Leeds.

Management
British Waterways, Castleford Tel: 01977 554351
Calder Navigation Society Tel: 01422 823562

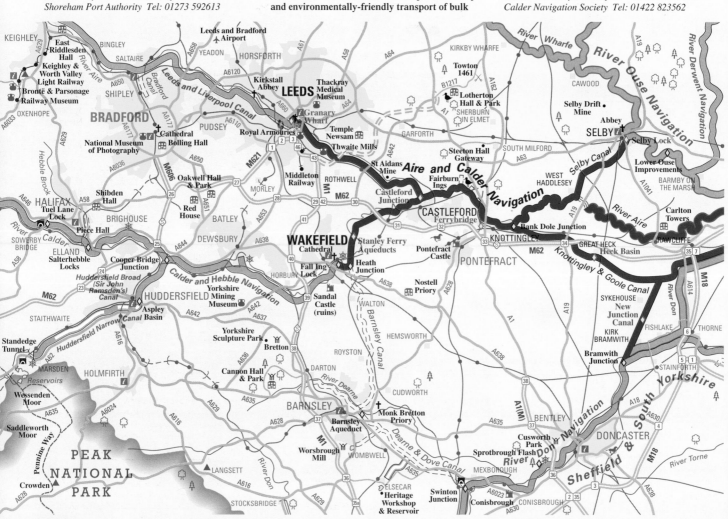

◊ **Granary Wharf: Leeds**
Found near the main rail station and from streets near Victoria Bridge, this is Leeds' answer to the better known regeneration projects of Manchester and Birmingham. Shops, a craft market, entertainment and a trip boat to Tetley's Yorkshire Brewery, have recently been augmented by the Royal Armouries from London.
From M621 J3 go north towards 'City Centre'.
◊ **Stanley Ferry Aqueducts** (1839 and 1981)
Iron arches carry a 180 foot wrought iron trough with metal Doric columns over the River Calder in a bold, confident construction typical of the Victorian age. Parallel is a second aqueduct in concrete (1981) built with stronger sides to resist the knocks of larger 700 ton commercial boats.
Approach from M62 J30. Use A642 going south and turn right towards Altofts.
◊ **Castleford Junction**
The senior Aire and junior Calder join at Castleford. Both river courses have been straightened and at the confluence, a weir and flood lock handle any excess water flowing off the hills. The result is a difficult 'four way' junction with traffic lights, sharp bends and cross currents. A wider Aire then takes traffic towards the tidal Ouse and the inland sea ports of Selby and Goole.
Approach from M62 J32. Use A656 going north.

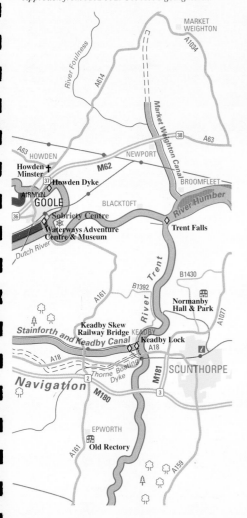

Leeds waterfront is undergoing major transformation. The Royal Armouries Museum is able to display over 8000 exhibits in its new waterside building.

◊ **Ferrybridge**
Vehicles on the Great North Road once paid a toll to pass over the stone arches of a bridge now devoted only to people. The central navigation arch is awkwardly placed for huge cargo boats and requires a high level of skill when the Aire is full after rain.
Lean on the parapet. All manner of vessels will pass below ... pleasure craft sensibly avoiding arguments with gravel barges or 600 ton oil tankers ... and, uniquely, the three unit 'pans' of coal being pushed towards the massive hoist which unloads each 150 ton 'pan' in less than 10 minutes... over a million tonnes a year are delivered to the power stations which dominate the landscape for miles around.
Approach from M62 J33. Use A1 going north.
◊ **Selby Lock**
Outlet of the controlled canal onto the ravages of the Tidal Ouse and thus only operated when the lock keeper is present and the levels are good.
Approach from M62 J34. Use A19 going north.
◊ **New Junction Canal** (1905)
Absolutely straight for five and a half miles, this canal was the last to be built in Britain. A shared enterprise with the Sheffield and South Yorkshire Navigation, it allowed the coal mines around the River Don to send trains of 'Tom Puddings' to the port at Goole.
Faced with competition from the railways, the company's engineer, W.H. Bartholomew (1831-1919), saw how specially designed square 'compartment boats' or 'tubs' of 35 tons capacity could be controlled in 'water-trains' pushed in front of or hauled behind a strong steam tug. Each tub could be filled in 20 minutes and could be emptied even quicker by a hoist picking it out of the water and tipping directly into a ship's hold. After initial testing (1862) the main locks were lengthened to 215 feet, thus taking 17 tubs and the tug at one pass. A huge trade in coal using such 'trains' developed. They were brought down to Goole and the coal tipped one tub at a time into sea going colliers. Over 1000 'Tom Puddings' were built.
Approach from M18 J6. Use A614, turn immediately west towards Fishlake / Braithwaite.
◊ **Sobriety Centre and Tom Puddings** (1865-1986)
Outside Goole, sandwiched between Vermuyden's Dutch River (a 350 year old drainage cut) and the Knottingley and Goole Canal (1826), is the 'Sobriety Waterways Adventure Centre and Museum'. Here the use of 'Tom Puddings' is explained, and a remaining hoist on the South Dock nearby shows the scale of the former operation.
Approach from M62 J36. Use A166 going south.

◊ **Goole**
A town built by the Company for the Company.
A company housing estate (1830s), now demolished, formed the beginnings of the town which became independent of the company 80 years later and a formal borough only in 1933.
The calm water of the Port protected good transfer between river barges and sea going ships from the turbulent waters of the tidal Ouse. As trade expanded (1820-1842) eight docks were created.
Amazingly, you are allowed into the working area. Take care for your safety by listening out for trucks and staying between the lines!
Approach from M62 J36. Use A166 going south.

✺ **Boat Trips**
Leeds *Inspiration 2000* Tel: 0113 242 3731
Goole *Sobriety* Tel: 01405 768730

📖 **Suggested Guide Book**
Keith Noble *West Yorkshire Waterway Guide*
Calder Navigation Society, 1992

ℹ️ **Tourist Information**
Leeds Tel: 0113 242 5242
Selby Tel: 01757 703263
Wakefield Tel: 01924 305000 / 305001

Main Line Goole Docks to Leeds Bridge (includes **Knottingley and Goole Canal** Goole Docks to Knottingley and **Brotherton Branch, Fairburn Canal and Stainland's Canal**)
River Aire Section River Ouse Navigation to West Haddlesey
Barnsley Canal Heath Junction to Barnby Basin
Dewsbury Old Cut Calder and Hebble Navigation to Savile Town Wharf, Dewsbury
New Junction Canal Aire and Calder Navigation to Bramwith Junction
Selby Section Selby to Bank Dole Junction (includes **Selby Canal** Selby to West Haddesley)
Wakefield Section Castleford Junction to Fall Ing Lock

....

Aire, River - see **Aire and Calder Navigation**
Alde, River   117 E3
Orford to Snape Bridge
88 miles, 0 locks
Suffolk Coastal District Council, Woodbridge Tel: 01394 383789
Ancholme, River   119 E3
Ferriby Sluice to Bishopbridge
19 miles, 2 locks
Environment Agency, Lincoln Tel: 01522 513100
Andover Canal   112 B3
Redbridge to Andover
Southampton Canal Society Tel: 023 8086 0384
Ant, River - see **The Broads**
Arun Navigation   112 C3
Houghton Bridge to Newbridge. Now part of River Arun and Wey and Arun Canal navigations.
Environment Agency, Worthing Tel: 01903 820692
Wey and Arun Canal Trust Tel: 01903 753099
Arun, River   112 C4-C3
Littlehampton to Pallingham
Little Hampton Harbour Board (Littlehampton to Arundel Bridge). Littlehampton: 01903 721215
Environment Agency (Arundel Bridge to Pallingham), Worthing Tel: 01903 820692

Ashby-de-la-Zouch Canal 115 E1-F2

Opened: 1804
Engineers: Whitworth, Jessop, Newbold
22 miles, 0 locks
Marston Junction to Moira

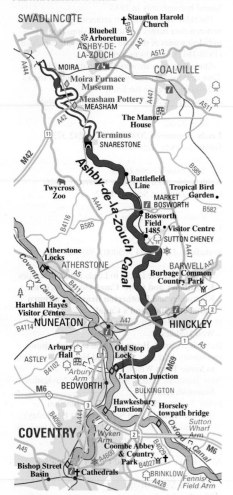

'Moira Cut' meanders through gently rolling
countryside. Away from motorways and dual
carriageways, it even avoids almost every village
on the way. Absolutely without slopes, the towpath
follows this broad canal for 22 lock free miles
along a single contour at 300 feet. Hedges and reed
lined banks create a wildlife corridor harbouring
many species, eg dragonfly, heron, kingfisher.

Early (1781) designs were to link Burton upon
Trent to the coal and limestone deposits at Ashby
Would and onwards to the recently completed (1769)
Coventry Canal. Over 20 years later it opened for 30
miles between Coventry Canal and a scatter of
tramways serving into the coalfields but failed to
arrive at Burton and missed Ashby by 5 miles.

The coalfields were extensive and produced the
highest quality coal until the Donisthorpe pit closed.
For over 150 years it was carried by water to London
markets. Subsidence undermined the canal leading to
successive breaches and closures of the northern

extremity in 1918, 1944, 1957 and 1966. The London
Midland and Scottish Railway Company could not
give the canal away... the Coventry Canal Company
refused the offer.

Restoration plans attracted Lottery support in 1997
but a little local difficulty jeopardised the project for
a time.

Management and Restoration
British Waterways, Alrewas Tel: 01283 790236
Ashby Canal Restoration Project Tel: 01530 273956
Ashby Canal Association Tel: 01455 614816

◊ **Moira Furnace** (Tel: 01283 224667)
Currently under restoration, a massive brick structure
with its own (dry) wharf arm directly below. The
blast furnace was finished the year the canal opened
and operated for 8 years. The excellent coal became
highly prized in London and was thus worth more as
coal than when used to create iron. The foundry
continued for 40 years and limekilns for 150 years.
Industrial heritage trail and parkland.
From M42 J11, use A444 / B5003, going north-east.

◊ **Measham Pottery**
Supplied to order, including personalised inscriptions,
from Mrs Brown's canalside shop in Measham but
made 5 miles away in Church Gresley. Salt glazed,
generally brown, earthenware jugs, jars, chamber
pots, kettles and, most famously, the tea pots treasured
as 'best' by many a boatwoman. Oldest 1792; others
celebrate Queen Victoria's Diamond Jubilee (1879)
and Edward VII's coronation (1902). Buy a modern
replica to support the canal restoration project.
Approach from M42 J11. Use B5006 going north.

◊ **Snarestone**
Limit of navigation (since 1967) is in an open field
just beyond a short (250 yard) wide beam tunnel.
From M69 J1, use A5 / A444 / B4116 going north-east.

✵ **Boat Trips**
Sutton Wharf *Rose* Tel: 0378 734073

ℹ **Tourist Information**
Ashby-de-la-Zouch Tel: 01530 411767
Hinkley Tel: 01455 635106
Nuneaton Tel: 024 7634 7006

Ashton Canal 118 C3

Opened: 1796
Engineer: Brown
Dukinfield Junction with the Peak Forest Canal to
Ducie Junction with the Rochdale Canal.
6 miles, 18 narrow locks

An early success of the canal restoration movement,
this thoroughly urban canal climbs west-east to
Ashton-under-Lyne on the edge of the Manchester
conurbation. The free labour of gangs of canal
enthusiasts in 1968 (600 volunteers) and 1972
(1000 volunteers) kick started the remedial works.

Twenty five years after the Bridgewater Canal was
opened to Castlefield, two canals were promoted
eastwards to the industries of Huddersfield and the
limestone quarries of Peak Forest. Typical of the
fragmented processes of the Canal Mania years, there
was a separate Act (1792) for the 6 miles of the
Manchester and Ashton-under-Lyne Canal and its 11
miles of branches.

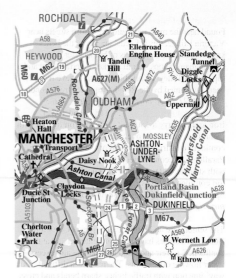

The Huddersfield Narrow and the Peak Forest Canal
link with the Ashton around the Portland Basin and
all three were finally opened at practically the same
time (1800). Trade was further boosted when the
Cromford and High Peak Railway and Macclesfield
Canal funnelled extra trade into the Peak Forest Canal
(1831). However, the coming of the railways reduced
trade and the canal sold out to the competition (1848).

Restoration was promoted to create a vital link in
the 100 mile 'Cheshire Ring' (1968) when hundreds
of lorry loads of rubbish were collected from the
canal bed, dry since it had sprung a leak in 1964.

Management
British Waterways, Marple Tel: 0161 427 1079

◊ **Portland Basin: Dukinfield Junction**
Every year Tameside Canals Festival is held where
three canals meet over the River Tame. A 'Heritage
Centre' including an industrial museum is nearing
completion (1999) inside the restored Portland
warehouse which burnt down (1972).
Approach from M67 J3. Use A627 going north.

✵ **Boat Trips**
Denton *Ashton Packetboat (horsedrawn)*
Tel: 0161 320 8338
Ashton *Greater Manchester* Tel: 0161 339 1332

ℹ **Tourist Information**
Ashton-under-Lyne Tel: 0161 343 4343
Manchester Tel: 0161 234 3157 / 3158

• •

Avon (Bristol) Navigation
- see **Avon (Somerset) Navigation**
Avon (Hampshire) Navigation　　　**112 A4-B3**
Christchurch to Salisbury
Avon (Somerset) Navigation　　　**111 E1**
Avonmouth to Bath. Includes **Avon (Bristol)
Navigation** Avonmouth to Hanham Lock
24 miles, 9 locks
*Bristol City Docks (Avonmouth to Hanham Lock),
Bristol Tel: 01179 264797*
*British Waterways (Hanham Lock to Bath),
Devizes Tel: 01380 722859*

Avon Navigation 115 E3

Improved: 1639, 1751, 1965, 1974
Engineers: Sandys, Yarrenton, Perrott
Tewkesbury to Stratford-upon-Avon
44 miles, 17 wide locks

Stratford-upon-Avon is central to a wandering river that flows through the rich fruit-growing areas of the Vale of Evesham and is overlooked by Brendon Hill and the Cotswolds.

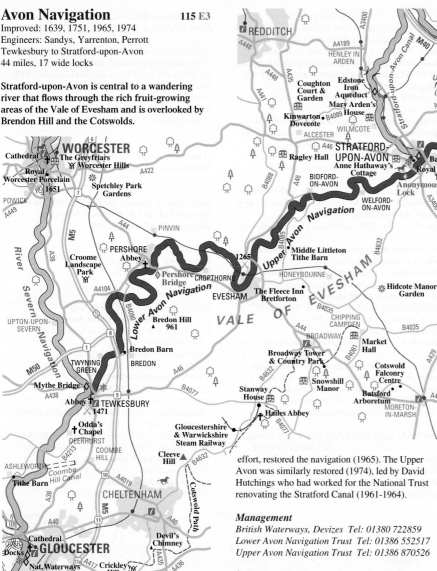

Strong personalities dominate this navigation. At the start, over 350 years ago, William Sandys of Fladbury personnally designed, financed and operated improvements that saw 30 ton barges passing the 13 locks between Tewkesbury and Stratford (1639).

Later (1751) confused ownership of the navigation rights were resolved into two parts; Lower Avon and Upper Avon, divided at Workman Bridge, Evesham.

Lower Avon passed to the Perrott family who then leased it to the Worcester and Birmingham Canal (1830-1872).

Upper Avon was neglected by Lord Windsor then bankrupted William James before it was leased (1842) by the Stratford Canal and eventually bought out by the railway company (1842).

After 100 years (1949) Douglas Barwell purchased the Lower Avon, formed a Trust which, over the next 16 years, helped by huge, unprecedented volunteer effort, restored the navigation (1965). The Upper Avon was similarly restored (1974), led by David Hutchings who had worked for the National Trust renovating the Stratford Canal (1961-1964).

Management

British Waterways, Devizes Tel: 01380 722859
Lower Avon Navigation Trust Tel: 01386 552517
Upper Avon Navigation Trust Tel: 01386 870526

◊ **Pershore Bridge**
Actually two bridges. One stone built (1300s), the other in early concrete (1928). The old bridge can hold back floodwater so much that it becomes a strong running weir in winter.
Approach from M5 J7. Use A44 going south-east.
◊ **Anonymous Lock**
Upper Avon restoration was helped by many people. George Billington, Robert Aickman and Colin P. Witter are all commemorated by having locks named after them but this lock, the last to be completed, was different. So many anonymous donations had been made to help with the construction of the locks and weirs of the Upper Avon that a plaque has been installed here to commemorate them. Footpaths on both sides of the river lead downstream from the A4390 bridge and are linked by footbridges at Weir Brake.
Approach from M40 J15. Use A46 / A422 going south and east onto A4390.
◊ **Leam Link**
The River Avon is navigable beyond Stratford to the

Red House. Further upstream it passes under the Grand Union Canal into the River Leam valley between the two parts of Leamington Spa. To the west of the town there is an opportunity to connect with the canal. Such connection would bring added interest and visitor spend to Leamington by creating a short circular route... returning to Stratford by the Lower Stratford Canal. Enthusiasts promoting this line are well aware of the wildlife interest and expect to create improvements to the habitats along the way.
Approach from M40 J15. Use A445 / A425 going east.

i Tourist Information

Tewkesbury Tel: 01684 295027
Evesham Tel: 01386 446944
Stratford-upon-Avon Tel: 01789 293127
Warwick Tel: 01926 492212

River Avon at Tewkesbury

Basingstoke Canal 112 C2

Open: 1794-1930, reopened 1991
Engineers: Parker, Jessop. Contractor: Pinkerton
Woodham Junction on the Wey to terminus at
Greywell Tunnel
31 miles, 29 wide locks

Walk the towing path of this canal. Lush vegetation
and clear water attracts a rich wildlife including
20 types of dragonfly, over 100 species of water
plants and many heavyweight fish. Part of the
3700 foot Greywell Tunnel has collapsed (1932)
but now has squatters: 12 000 bats, including the
world's largest colony of Natterer's Bat.

After 28 locks in nine miles there are almost 20
miles of canal summit winding gently through
heathland and pineforests interrupted only by a
single lock at Ash.

When opened the canal extended for 37 miles, had
a long tunnel, a deep cutting and a high embankment,
all built by the picks, shovels and wheelbarrows of
navvies in only six years (1788-1794). The Act had
been obtained 10 years before but the American War
of Independence had led to a lack of capital and a
lack of confidence.

Huge capital costs and lack of through traffic meant
that the company never paid dividends. Since it was
officially bankrupt (1866) it has changed hands
twelve times. A.J. Harmsworth was carter, bargeman
and finally owner (1922-1947). Soon after his death it
was auctioned for £6000, but restoration only really
started after two County Councils (Surrey and
Hampshire) compulsorily purchased it as a public
amenity (1974). Many hours of volunteer labour over
14 years and almost continuous use of steam dredger
'Perseverance' were required before reopening (1991).

Movements of boats are electronically monitored to
ensure the water does not stagnate and that the
wildlife is not excessively disturbed. Problems of
water supply to the summit often lead to the closure
of the link with the River Wey, thus disconnecting
the Basingstoke from all other waterways.

Management and Restoration
Basingstoke Canal Authority Tel: 01252 370073
Surrey and Hampshire Canal Society
Tel: 01483 721710

◊ **Greywell Tunnel** (1794-1932)
Present navigational terminus is at the eastern portal.
Long term restoration of the final 5 miles is deferred
because 5 species of bats have made their home here.
Efforts are concentrating on improving the horse path
over the hill and a partially filled isolated length into
Basingstoke itself.
Approach from M3 J5. Use A287 going south.

◊ **Crookham Wharf**
One of ten wharves, now available as car park and
access point to the canal. Follow the towpath east; the
third bridge was built for agricultural carts, now for
people only, and is the last remaining swing bridge.
From M3 J5, use A287 going east; turn north.

◊ **Eelmoor Flash**
One of many alongside the canal, this flash is close to
Farnborough Military Airfield and was a landing strip
for early sea plane trials (1913).
From M3 J4. Use A321 / A325 / A323 going south-west.

◊ **Ash Embankment and Blackwater Aqueduct**
The 3000 foot embankment over the Blackwater
Valley was constructed of the spoil from Deepcut
cutting nearby. A dramatic breach (1968) reduced the
chance that the then owners would restore the canal.
One of the newest canal aqueducts in the country
has been constructed here so that a 'Relief road'
(A331) could pass underneath the restored
embankment (1995).
From M3 J4. Use A331 / A323 going south then east.

◊ **Ash Vale Barge Yard**
One of the few modest boatyards left on the entire
system, this cheaply built, corrugated iron shed was
operated as a barge building and repair business
(1918-1935) by Alexander Harmsworth as adjunct
to his carrying trade. He even purchased the canal
itself (1922).
From M3 J4, use A331 / B3411 to Ash Vale Station.

◊ **Mytchett Canal Centre** (Tel: 01252 370073)
Home of the Basingstoke Canal Authority. Many
activities start here. Boating, rowing, caravanning and
camping, adventure playground and a canal exhibition
explaining the history, restoration and wildlife habitats

are all available for a small fee.
From M3 J4. Use A331 / B3012 going south.

◊ **Deepcut Locks and Cutting**
Fourteen locks raise the canal 100 feet in only two
miles achieving practically the summit level. It then
maintains this level by passing into a cutting 3000
foot long, which is up to 70 feet deep. Thus the
canal moves secretly through an area secured
mainly for military use.
Approach from M3 J3. Use A322 / A324 going south.

❋ **Boat Trips**
Winchfield *John Pinkerton* Tel: 01252 622758
Mytchett *Two 12-seaters* Tel: 01252 370073

📖 *Suggested Guide Book*
Dieter Jebens: *Guide to the Basingstoke Canal*
Basingstoke Canal Authority and Surrey and
Hampshire Canal Society, 1996

ℹ️ *Tourist Information*
Basingstoke Tel: 01256 817618
Fleet Tel: 01252 811151

• •

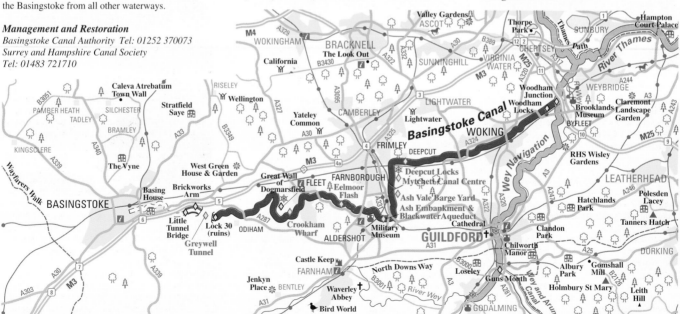

Birmingham Canal Navigations (BCN) 115 E2

Opened: 1769-1863
Engineers: Brindley, Smeaton, Dadford, Pitt, Telford
Over 100 miles, lots of narrow locks at the edges

BCN might have a forbiddingly long industrial history and cover an enormously large area but a surprising number of towpath walks are semi-rural or tree-lined suburban. Even within the heartlands of the City and Black Country, where housing and offices now flourish instead of industry, improvements have left an excellent example of what, in administrator's jargon, might be called a 'leisure resource'.

1768: The formation of the Company
Every full moon, the Lunar Society (1765-1790) met in Birmingham. Small in numbers, it consisted of inventors, pioneering scientists and engineers from around Birmingham. They noted (1776) that the first long distance canals linking the Severn with Trent and Mersey did not intend to connect to Birmingham. To ensure the connection was made the Society helped form a separate Birmingham Canal Company.

A typical Brindley-designed contour canal resulted. It 'wormed' **north** past most of the existing towns and coal mines on the plateau: Oldbury, Tipton, Bilson, Wednesbury to Wolverhampton. After a year (1769) the main line was open to Wednesbury coal mines and local traffic mushroomed. Three years later (1772) the second half to Wolverhampton and the 21 locks descending to the Staffs and Worcs at Aldersley were finished.

Birmingham was now connected to the potteries at Burslem and ports at Hull (via the Trent at Derby) and at Bristol (via the Severn at Stourport). Business was excellent... almost to capacity!

Over the next 20 years other companies proposed descents from the Birmingham plateau to the expanding waterway system. Due **west** via Dudley and Stourbridge, due **east** via Castle Bromwich and Tamworth, **south-west** via Tardebigge and Worcester and towards the **south-east** via Warwick and Braunston........... *The Company did not like this !!*

Company lobbies against canals from the west
Lord Dudley's bill (1775) for a line from Rowley Hills to the Staffs and Worcs at Stourton was thrown out of Parliament due to lobbying by the Company. The following year two separate bills were passed for separate canals north and south from the Black Delph near Brierley Hill but the Company forced the inclusion of high compensation tolls for themselves. The descent from Rowley Hills was soon completed (1779) but the last two miles to Lord Dudley's limestone quarries and colliery was mainly through a tunnel (9462 feet overall) and took a further Act (1785) and seven years before it was open (1792).

After this the fourth longest tunnel of the system at Lappal (11 385 feet) was built as part of the 10 mile Dudley No 2 canal to Selly Oak, connecting with the new Worcester and Birmingham (1798). This was also expensive to build and was plagued by mining subsidence. Nevertheless, the Dudley resisted becoming part of the BCN for 50 years, only joining under the threat of railway competition (1846).

The last few yards of the original Birmingham Canal (1769) have been transformed into the centrepiece of the modern regeneration of Broad Street (1992-1999). The footbridge from the waterbus stop leads up across the water to Brindley Place ... an area of entertainment and new offices. The glass doors of the covered mall leading to Centenary Square and serving the many conference halls of the International Convention Centre are to the right of the picture.

Company forces amalgamation to the east
The Company tried to promote its own project to the west to form a route to London via Coventry and Oxford but, when defeated (see page 16), proposed amalgamation with the Birmingham and Fazeley Company (1784). The two companies then (1794) formed the Birmingham Canal Navigations (BCN).

Company forces problems in the south-west
The Company defeated two bills for the Worcester and Birmingham in Parliament (1786 and 1790). A bill was finally passed at the next try (1791) but the Company made life very difficult for the new canal by insisting that physical connection with their waters could not be made between the two termini at Gas Street Basin. Thus, the builders of the new canal had the expense of finding water for their summit and the carriers had the expense of double-handling goods across the 7 foot wide spit of land between the canals - still known as the Worcester Bar.

Company agrees south-east route to London
Two canals were promoted from Warwick: to the Birmingham Co's Digbeth Branch (1793) and to the Oxford Co's pound between Napton and Braunston (1794). Together they were designed to link with the Grand Junction's direct line from Braunston to London (Brentford) which at the time was under construction (finished in 1800 except for Blisworth tunnel). This became the 'upper road' from London.

Birmingham levels
The canal between Birmingham and Wolverhampton was built at two major levels. The original Brindley main line (1768) looped round the 453' contour and went on to Wolverhampton twenty feet higher (473').

There was a short summit at Smethwick (491') which Smeaton later (1790) lengthened and reduced in height to the 'Wolverhampton' level (473').

Later still (1799) a short branch down to Ryders Green was extended to Walsall and established a third major level (408').

When congestion at locks and problems with water supply got really bad (1824) Telford was called in. He proposed radical (and expensive) improvements which would cut journey times by two hours.

A new straight Main Line *with a towing path on each side* was built for seven miles at the Gas Street Basin level (453'). It bypassed many Brindley loops and removed the Smethwick summit with a cutting 71' deep. Telford also bypassed what is now called the Wednesbury Oak Loop by wide-bore Coseley tunnel.

Factories over a wide area were served by branches with their own set of locks achieving other levels eg Oldbury (Crows 511'), Essington (527'). One climbed Tat Bank to collect water from Rotton Park.

'More canals than Venice'
In the mid 1800s industry flourished, Farmer's Bridge locks to the east and Dudley tunnel to the west could not cope with expanding traffic. Extra canals (east) were built along the Tame valley from the Walsall level to Salford Junction and extended to Camp Hill locks on the Grand Junction (1844). Canal routes (west) were duplicated by Netherton tunnel. Result by 1858: a longer network than in Venice.

Railway control
BCN subscribed to a railway to Birmingham up the Stour valley (1846) and, in return for underwriting its dividend (at 4%), welcomed London and Birmingham

Railway Company nominees into its management.

At that time the canals provided an intricate network of local 'sidings' serving almost every potential industrial customer, most of whom already had a wharf or private basin. The railway companies, therefore, constructed over 40 'transfer stations' alongside canals to give themselves access to these customers. The biggest at Wolverhampton, Great Bridge, Tipton, Bloomfield and Hawne have been demolished. Only Chillington and Hockley Park remain.

Full control of canal management was only triggered (1874) when canals failed to earn the 4% dividend.

Inland Waterways Association Festival at Windmill End

However, canals complemented the long distance railways, rather than competed against, and so investment continued till 1858, eg the huge gas lit, wide-bore Netherton tunnel (9081 feet), Tame Valley canal and further branches to Hednesford (Cannock Extension), Bentley and Rushall. Even at the turn of the century (1905) most BCN traffic was local (journeys finished within a day) and less than 20% transferring to rail.

Decline and Regeneration
Decline came in the 1930s depression. At the same time motor lorries began to give door-to-door service. Indifference or nationalisation (1948) reduced maintenance so that boats could not carry full loads over the shallows. A 3 month freeze (winter 1963) stopped movement altogether and boats were scrapped. Birmingham industrial canals had nothing to offer a growing leisure industry in boating.

Another recession (1989) left Birmingham with many derelict buildings. In the town centre planners proposed (1992) an axis of rejuvenated public squares around which new development could cluster. It ends in a bridge over the canal halfway between Old Turn Junction and Gas Street Basin. Stunning new buildings nearby include Symphony Hall, an International Convention Centre, The

National Indoor Arena and a Sea-Life Centre. In 1995 an American charity awarded the Waterfront an international award. People throng the area; visits by boat are welcomed, and are fun.

Management and Restoration
British Waterways, Tipton Tel: 0121 506 1300
British Waterways (Farmer's Bridge Junction to Minworth Bottom Lock), Bilston Tel: 01902 409010
British Waterways (Minworth Bottom Lock to Whittington), Alrewas Tel: 01283 790236
Birmingham Canal Navigations Society, Membership Secretary, 37 Chestnut Close, Handacre, Rugeley, Staffs WS15 4TN
Http://www.bcn-society.demon.co.uk
Coombeswood Canal Trust Tel: 0121 550 1355
Dudley Canal Trust Tel: 01384 236275
Lapal Canal Trust, Public Relations Officer Tel: 01772 746914
Lichfield and Hatherton Canals Restoration Trust Tel: 01543 262466

◊ **Windmill End: Cobb's Engine House**
For 100 years Cobb's Engine House (1831-1930) drew water from underground coal seams and pumped it into the canal partway along Lord Dudley's lock free No 2 Canal. Built originally (1793) to compete with the BCN main lines on the other side of the hill, after amalgamation (1846) the double towpath Netherton Tunnel was built (1858) joining the two together, thus creating this junction. Location for the Inland Waterways Association Annual Festivals in 1991 and 1996.
From M5 J3, go north A456 / A459 to Halesowen Rd.

◊ **Wolverhampton Locks** (21 rising 132 feet)
Wolverhampton is only twenty feet higher than Central Birmingham and the early canal made good business with 'shuttle services' around the plateau. This major engineering feat was the first link with the national canal network and is now a joggers paradise ... passing fields, parklands, Dunstall Park Race Course and ending next to the ruined brick stables at Aldersley Junction.
Approach from M54 J2. Use A449 going south.

◊ **Chasewater Reservoir** (1800)
The Wyrley and Essington started out buying water from the BCN, built this reservoir and then made good business selling water to other companies. Now a nature reserve rich in bird life, it forms a major feature of the Chasewater Leisure Park.
Approach from M6 J12. Use A5 going east.

◊ **Ogley Junction** (1797-1954)
Anglesey Bridge Marina is at the end of the 16 mile summit level of the Wyrley and Essington Canal main line and at the beginning of its 7 mile, 30 lock descent past Lichfield to the Coventry Canal at Huddlesford. A Restoration Trust (1988) aims to restore this link and has improved sections around Darnforn Lane and Fossway Lane.
From M6 J12, use A5 / A452 / B4155 going east.

◊ **Engine Arm**
Water was back-pumped from the Birmingham to the Wolverhampton levels by a huge steam engine (1779), the water running into the Old Main Line along this arm. An underground feeder channel from Rotton Park reservoir was added (1826) and then Telford had to build his cast iron aqueduct across his new main line (1829).

The Galton Valley Canal Heritage Centre has such an engine and other relics of the canal age.
From M5 J1, go south-east, using A4168 / A4252 / A457.

◊ **Soho House**
Matthew Boulton was the financial muscle behind James Watt's patented steam engines. They kept their monopoly going for 30 years and supplied many huge pumps to canal companies throughout the country. He lived here (1766-1809) next to his factory and was host to many meetings of the Lunar Society. Now a Birmingham museum.
From M5 J1, use A41 going south to Soho Avenue.

⚓ **Boat Trips**
International Conference Centre Waterbus and Sherborne Wharf *Jericho, Saint Catherine, Euphrates Packet* Tel: 0121 455 6163
Oxley Moor *Stafford* Tel: 01902 789522

📖 **Suggested Guide Book**
Micheal Pearson *Canal City* J M Pearson & Son, 1998

ℹ️ **Tourist Information**
Birmingham Tel: 0121 693 6300
Convention Centre Tel: 0121 643 2514
Dudley Tel: 01384 812830
NEC Tel: 0121 780 4321
Wolverhampton Tel: 01902 312051

Important Branches:
Bentley Canal
Walsall Canal (Anson Branch) to Wednesfield Junction
Includes: **Neachells Branch**
Birmingham Canal
Gas Street Basin to Aldersley Junction
New Main Line includes: **Dixons Branch, Dunkirk Branch, Gower Branch, Newhall Branch, Roway Branch**
Old Main Line includes: **Cape Arm, Engine Branch, Houghton Arm, Oldbury Loop, Old Summit Level, Oozzells Street Loop, Rotton Park Loop, Soho Loop, Tipton Green Branch, Titford Canal, Wednesbury Oak Loop**
Birmingham and Fazeley Canal - see p16
Dudley No 1 Canal
Delph Junction to Tipton Junction
Includes: **Pensnett Canal, Two Lock Line**
Dudley No 2 Canal
Selly Oak Junction to Park Head Junction
Includes: **Grazebrook Branch, Lord Wards Canal, Netherton Tunnel Branch, Withymoor Branch**
Walsall Canal
Riders Green Junction to Walsall Town Wharf
Includes: **Anson Branch, Bilston Branch, Danks Branch, Gospel Oak Branch, Haines Branch, Lower Ocker Hill Branch, Monwy Branch, Walsall Junction Canal, Whitehall Branch, Willenhall Branch**
Wednesbury Old Canal
Horseley Fields Junction to Huddlesford Junction
Includes: **Ridgacre Branch**
Wyrley and Essington Canal
Horseley Fields Junction to Huddlesford Junction
Includes: **Anglesey Branch, Birchills Branch, Cannock Extension Canal, Churchbridge Branch, Hatherton Branch, Daw End Branch, Essington Branch, Vernons Branch, Gilpins Arm, Lord Hays Branch, Rushall Canal, Sandhills Branch, Short Heath Branch, Sneyd Branch, Wyrley Bank Branch, Wyrley Branch**

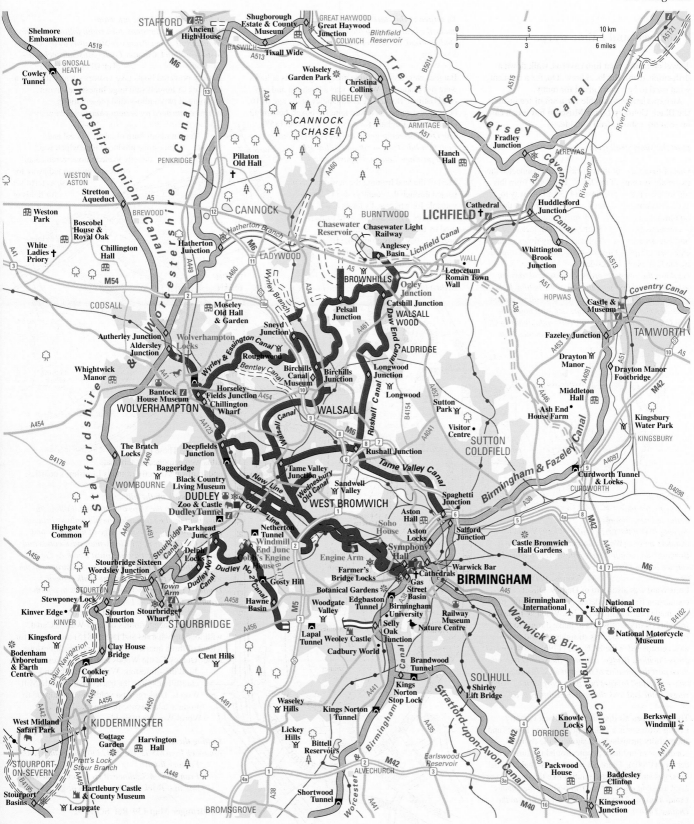

Dudley Tunnel
Two levels and a time warp.

Travel on trams, float into caverns, walk down a drift-mine, drink the local brew. Do, for a moment, what used to be a daily grind for many.

All experiences available for a small fee inside the Black Country *Living* Museum but much can be seen on a short stroll outside.

Start the short stroll from:-

1 Three Locks at Factory Road
One of many sets of three locks which connected the two main systems of the BCN. The water from this top lock is on the same level (473') all the way to Wolverhampton (5 miles) and the water from the bottom lock is on level 453' to Birmingham (8 miles). As business became brisk these original locks became bottlenecks and were duplicated many times… the extra set at Tipton Green is now infilled and fronted by the houses of 'Lockside'.
Go down this towpath, cross to the second towpath using the small bridge at the tail of the bottom lock (lifted clear of the ground at one end to allow the tow ropes through). Down the slope and turn half right into Coppice Street. After 50 yards, right again up Old Cross Street onto the towpath beside Fountain Inn.

Walk south following the blue bullnose brick copings and curving line of the first canal of the BCN which wanders on this (Wolverhampton) level towards Birmingham for a further 9 miles. From the bend you can see across to:-

2 Lord Ward's Canal (755 yards; 1778)
Lord Ward was also Lord of Dudley. Direct canal connection from his underground quarry to the BCN was made near Pitchfork Bridge. When he tunnelled from his quarry westwards to make a route to the River Severn the line was straightened and a stop lock constructed at the BCN end (1796). *Go along and cross Pitchfork Bridge, return by the second towpath to go past the remains of this stop lock. Continue under two road bridges and past short term mooring rings. At the end look through the railings at a:-*

3 Gas-lit street lamp
The main open air display of the Black Country Living Museum is a village of re-erected houses and shops, fully furnished and showing the living conditions of ordinary people around the turn of the century (1900s). There are sweet shops, bakers, coal fires, gas stoves and gas mantles like the one you see. *Look straight ahead at the trip boats of the Dudley Canal Trust and beyond to see the entrance to the Dudley Tunnel.*

To return to the start of this short stroll, go back under the bridge, go up the ramp and turn left along Dudley Road, cross over and turn right into Castle Street to:-

4 William Perry's Statue on Tipton Green
Bargees were a competitive group, arguments at locks were not unknown. William was a boatman and son of a boatman. Backed by Lord Dudley at the age of 16, he started a career as a bare knuckle boxer, becoming champion of England for seven years (1850-1857). *Use Owen Street to get to the towpath in front of Fountain Inn. Turn north and follow the canal past new houses. Opposite are:-*

5 Malthouse Stables
Most of the land fronting the new canal as it passed through the countryside (1772) was valuable for wharves, factories and warehouses. These stables were formerly used by the horses that pulled narrow boats and day boats around the BCN. They are now a base for canoes, a trip boat, moorings and a boatyard.
Return to **1** **Three Locks.**

A long walk inside the museum
From **3** *go up the steps, turn right, follow the Tipton Road uphill. The entrance is 500 yards away. Once inside the Black Country Living Museum seek out:-*

6 Dudley Tunnel Trips (Tel: 0121 520 5321)
Battery powered boats take visitors silently through a complex of tunnels into huge limestone caverns, stopping at two audio-visual presentations.
Not recommended for serious claustrophobics.

7 Lord Dudley's Lime Kilns (1842)
A continuous burn of layers of coal and limestone produced lime which was directly loaded into covered canal boats and transported away for use as fertiliser for fields or mortar for buildings. These huge kilns were supplied by tub boats and tramways directly from his Lordship's quarries.

A longer walk up the hill
From **3** *go up the steps and turn left. Follow the pavement up the hill, under the old railway bridge, then up the footpath on the edge of the woods and along Castle Mill Road. Go further, past woods and houses, then turn left down Forest Road. At the bottom there is a small car park at an entrance to the woods. This is part of Limestone Walk (one of Dudley's Countryside Walks) and leads to a path around a safety fence. Look down on :-*

8 Castle Mill Basin (over 80 feet below)
Early quarry face terminus of Lord Ward's Canal, with loading wharves and later (1815) tunnels ran for a total of three quarters of a mile under the limestone under Dudley Castle Woods and Wren's Nest Hill.
Find the Limestone Walk waymarks and carefully explore the tracks inside Castle Mill Woods. Underground voids have collapsed to produce a landscape pockmarked like a World War I battlefield.

Getting there:
Approach from M5 J2. Use A4123 to Dudley then A4037.
P   *Factory Road*
⇌   *From Tipton Station exit right across the canal and into Brick Kiln Street. Join at* **1**.

Landranger Map 139 Ref *SO 95 92*

Symphony Hall
Canalside bars, bistros and restaurants.

Lying at the heart of 15 miles of towpath improved by the Birmingham Inner City Partnership (1982 onwards), people now enjoy an area which spearheaded regeneration in the City.

Start the stroll from:-
1 Centenary Square
As befits a European city, car free Birmingham is on a grand scale. Victoria Square, dominated by the Town Hall, New Street surrounded by shops and cinemas and Centenary Square, overlooked by the Repertory Theatre and Symphony Hall, are huge spaces full with hurrying citizens and wandering visitors. *Go down the glazed mall of the ICC mall (only closed at night 23.30 - 07.00). At the canalside reach the:-*
2 Waterbus stop
Passenger boats stop here, The Fiddle and Bone, Sherbourne Wharf and Gas Street Basin, to give short round trips daily. *Go up steps ⚠ over a footbridge, turn left and, looking down on the canal, pass bars and restaurants and arrive at Broad Street. (Alternative route: up the curving ramp on the right past the crèche and across the next bridge). Cross Broad Street and half-right down Gas Street. This left hand pavement follows the high wall designed to keep the underworld of wandering bargees apart from the upright citizenry that they served. Behind it lies:-*
3 Worcester Bar: Gas Street Basin
Seven feet of pavement, now used as moorings by a variety of narrowboats, kept the waters of the BCN separate from the waters of the newcomer Worcester and Birmingham Canal Company (1769). Goods destined for the River Severn at Worcester or the Stratford-upon-Avon Canal had to be double-handled for 46 years until the narrow stop lock was inserted (1815). *Go through the hole-in-the-wall, down the slope and left along the towpath, back under the frequently widened Broad Street (mind your head) and onward past 24 hour moorings to:-*

4 Old Turn Junction: Heart of the system
The hulks of the National Indoor Arena and the Sea-Life Centre dominate this turn. In its heyday the ramped bridges helped horses across the canals in all directions. More recently pleasure narrowboats from all points of the compass pass below them and moor up around this turn. The Birmingham and Fazeley Canal comes in from the right, the Oozells Street Loop enters from the left. BCN goes straight on to Smethwick and Wolverhampton. *To return to the start at 1, go up the bridge ahead, turn left down onto the towpath, left again and go towards the BT tower to the top lock of:-*
5 Old Thirteen: Farmer's Bridge Locks (80 feet)
Once the busiest locks on the entire system, they were worked for seven days a week and, after installation of some of the earliest gas lighting in the country, for twenty four hours a day. *Cross the footbridge onto the side of Cambrian Wharf and, overlooking the canal, follow the terrace of 'James Brindley Walk', turn up past 'Cambridge House' across Cambridge Street, past 'Baskerville House' to 1 Centenary Square.*

A small detour from 2 Waterbus stop *pass over the bridge but turn half-right to the:-*
6 Dancing Fountains
Floodlit at night, Brindley Square is overlooked by a continental-style café. The Ikon Gallery and Crescent Theatre are nearby. *Go beyond, seek out the Viva fitness centre and return to* **4 Old Turn Junction.**

A long walk
From 5 Old Thirteen *continue down to the end of Farmer's Bridge flight via the BT 'tunnel' and Canning Walk. At Aston Junction (1799) ignore the further locks, turn right over a typical Horseley Iron Works cast iron overbridge to go down past the locks of the Digbeth Branch Canal to:-*
7 Digbeth Basin and Warwick Bar
Outside Digbeth Basin lies Warwick Bar... a stop lock at the beginning of the Grand Union Canal's direct route to London. *Climb out of the forgotten world of industrial canals and use Fazeley Street to return to the pedestrian shopping streets around New Street and, at its end, Victoria Square. Enjoy the City itself from 1 Centenary Square.*

Follow the stream of people north, through the glass doors of Paradise Forum to the City Library and Chamberlain Square. Downhill, behind the Town Hall is Victoria Square and the start of New Street shops.

Getting there:
Approach from M5 J1. Use A41 / A4540 to National Indoor Arena (NIA).
🅿 *National Indoor Arena. Join at 4.*
♿ *Orange Badge parking at Cambridge Street. Join at 1.*
🚆 *New Street Station exit turn west / left into New Street / Victoria Square. Join at 1.*

Landranger Map 139 Ref SP 36 06

15

Birmingham & Fazeley Canal

115 E2

Opened: 1789
Engineer: Smeaton
Farmer's Bridge Junction to Fazeley Junction plus
extension to Whittington Brook
15 miles, 38 narrow locks plus 5 miles, 0 locks

Until recently, this was a 'private' industrial world behind high walls with three long flights of locks (Farmer's Bridge, Aston and Curdworth) coping with a steep descent from Gas Street Basin at the end of the Birmingham Canal to the Coventry Canal at Fazeley.

This canal was the first of Birmingham's re-generation schemes (1984). Farmer's Bridge Locks were cleaned up, lit and landscaped. Towpath accesses were created through the walls. Resurfaced towpaths now attract families on weekend strolls and relaxing workers on weekday lunchtimes.

The Birmingham and Fazeley Canal Company made waterways history. Even before they started to seek approval for their scheme to build a canal to Fazeley they gained uncharacteristic cooperation from three other independent companies (1782). Known as the 'Coleshill Agreement', incomplete canals were to be finished and some long distance routes established.

The **Trent and Mersey Co.**, which had already (1777) linked these two rivers at Fradley, agreed to 'go halves' with the Birmingham and Fazeley on financing a missing link from Fradley to Fazeley. **Coventry Canal Co.** agreed to finish its canal from Atherstone as far as Fazeley, and **Oxford Canal Co.**, which had already built a canal from Coventry as far as Banbury, agreed to complete its intended route to the Thames at Oxford. Thus the system around Fazeley

was to be connected to London markets.

Within 8 years all four companies had fulfilled their promises and Fazeley became a busy entrance to Birmingham. A prosperous Birmingham Canal Company understood the benefits of such progress and, after the Birmingham and Fazeley had obtained their Act (1783), proposed an amalgamation (1784) to form the Birmingham Canal Navigations (1794).

Management

British Waterways (Farmer's Bridge Junction to Minworth Bottom Lock), Bilston Tel: 01902 409010
British Waterways (Minworth Bottom Lock to Whittington), Alrewas Tel: 01283 790236

◊ **Fazeley Junction**
The great and good of Tamworth insisted that canals be routed in the fields at the edge of their town boundary. The company created wharves and formed a junction with the Coventry at the point where it served the old Roman Road (Watling Street: A5). 44 years later a fugitive from striking workers in Lancashire diverted the local stream and created a series of water-powered factories to mass produce calico. The multi-storey mill buildings still stand alongside the canal. Go walkabout.
Approach from M42 J10. Use A5 going north-west.

◊ **Drayton Manor Footbridge**
Spiral stairs encased in tiny Gothic towers hold up the footbridge itself. Much photographed.
From M42 J9, use A446 / A4091 going north.

◊ **Curdworth Tunnel and Locks**
Tunnel approaches are in cutting; the eleven locks are set in wide expanses of fields and gravel pits. Some worked out pits have been improved to create the 30 lakes of the Kingsbury Water Park.
Approach from M42 J9. Use A4097 going west.

◊ **Under Spaghetti Junction**
A38(M) Aston Expressway into Birmingham from

the M6 is only one of six main roads connected by the many twisting slip roads that give rise to the name Spaghetti Junction. Most are on stilts and in the wasteland below is a four way canal junction (Salford Junction) that has existed here for 150 years.
Approach from M6 J6. Use A38 going south-west into city and turn left into B4132 over the canal.

◊ **Digbeth Branch and Basins**
Turn south for London! Many towpath bridges over arms to former factory basins lead down, through six locks and a tunnel, to Digbeth Basin, and joined by the Warwick and Birmingham (1799). A second warehouse of Fellows, Morton and Clayton (1935) marks the start of the 147 mile Grand Union Canal Walk to London.
From Birmingham Inner Ring Road (A4540), use A47 going west, turn immediately left and left again.

◊ **Farmer's Bridge and Aston Lock flights**
Farmer's Bridge and Aston Locks take the canal down 150 feet in less than three miles. Only the second connection to the canals serving the rest of the country, the flight was provided with gas light for night working and worked 24 hours a day, 7 days a week. The Farmer's Bridge flight was, for 50 years, the busiest flight on the system.

This was a serious a bottle-neck. Hemmed in by factory walls, the locks could not be duplicated and were eventually bypassed completely (1844) by the 8 mile Tame Valley Canal which connected to the Birmingham and Fazeley at the bottom of the hill at Salford Junction.
Birmingham Inner Ring Road (A4540) follow 'NIA'.

ℹ Tourist Information
Birmingham Tel: 0121 693 6300
Lichfield Tel: 01543 252109
Tamworth Tel: 01827 709581

• •

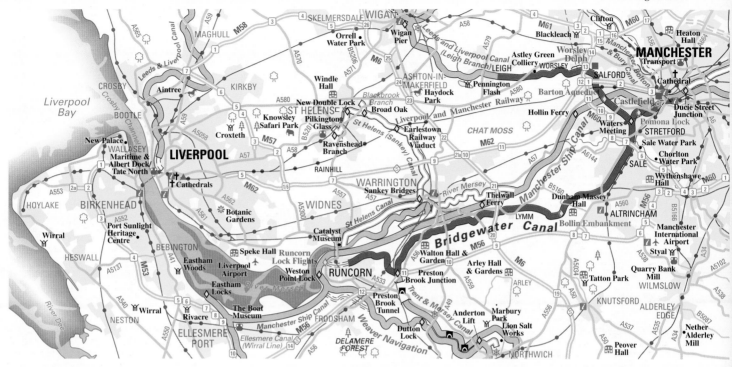

Bridgewater Canal   118 B4-C3

Opened: Stretford 1762, Castlefield 1765,
Runcorn 1773
Engineers: Gilbert, Brindley, Morris
Worsley to Castlefield
Branches to :
- Trent and Mersey at Preston Brook
- Liverpool and Leeds at Leigh
- Manchester Ship Canal at Pomona Lock
- Runcorn and Western Canal (down locks)
- Hollins Ferry

40 miles, 0 locks

Walkers looking for variety below their feet can become bored hereabouts. The Bridgewater is as flat as a pancake for 34 miles.

The towpath moves along the edge of the Cheshire Plain, gently crosses the Bollin Valley and overlooks the River Mersey. Within Greater Manchester it passes through pleasant suburbs and crosses the waters of the River Irwell as they run down the biggest canal in the country. A short length passes through some industrial areas which the canal itself stimulated, but even here the towpath is being improved and promoted as being 'In Brindley's Footsteps'.

Canals were nothing new to the Duke of Bridgewater. He owned several inside his mine in Worsley which had been carting coal to villages nearby for 350 years. He had seen Government financed canals in France (Canal Du Midi: opened 1681) and had been aware of improvements locally, to Weaver River (1732) and Sankey Brook (1757).

What was new was his ambition to build an above-ground canal across a valley and carry canal water over river water. Engineering skills were based on knowledge gained from mills powered by wind or water and from quarrying stone or mining slate and coal. They were primitive by today's standards but our motorway embankments rely on the experience gained when engineers built our railways... and many railway engineers learnt their trade on canals.

The Duke's agent, John Gilbert, was project manager and his engineer was the millwright James Brindley who had already surveyed a canal to extend the Trent upstream from Derby into the Potteries (1758).

Not only did they design the 600 foot long sandstone faced Barton Aqueduct spanning the Mersey and Irwell Navigation on three large arches but they achieved the construction of the first ten miles of a broad canal, including long embankments up to 40 feet high *in less than two years*.

Allowing for inflation, the Duke first spent his personal fortune and then ran up about £20 million of personal debts on his canal. He borrowed from whoever he could; even his tenants and landowners from whom he purchased land. City financiers were thin on the ground in 1760 and the 'hair-brained scheme' was such a novelty no one could tell if it was going to make money or not.

As it turned out the Duke's canal was joining two fast growing centres of the industrial revolution. Canals were more reliable than rivers and they easily took business from pack horses and carts. Eventually money to repay his debts came from an income variously estimated (correcting for inflation) at between £4 million and £6 million a year.

After he died his trustees bought the Mersey and Irwell Navigation, they tripled the carriage rates on both systems and, thereby, made the creation of railways worth the investment.

Non profit Management
Manchester Ship Canal Company, Manchester
Tel: 0161 888 8200

◊ **Runcorn Lock Flights**
Eventually two flights of 10 locks each were needed to cope with the traffic between the river and canal. The canal currently ends at 'Waterloo Bridge' which stood at the beginning of both flights. Passengers from the Duke's 'Packetboats' alighted here and, with porters carrying their bags, walked down the flight to the waiting sailing boats for the onward trip to Liverpool. At present the locks are filled in but a waymarked walk is proposed.
From M56 J11, use A56 / A558 / Town Centre.

◊ **Bollin Embankment**
A breach forced a two year closure of the canal (1971), but it has since been repaired with *proper concrete!*
Approach from M56 J7/8. Use A56 going west.

◊ **Barton Aqueduct** (1761-1893)
The size of the original arches can be appreciated as the facing stones of one arch are re-erected alongside the B5230 as it passes under the canal.
Approach from M60 J10. Use dual carriageway north, past the shopping centre and north again at the roundabout; cross the ship canal into B5230.

◊ **Pomona Lock**
Built to replace Hulme Lock flight (1997) this is the modern way to access the River Irwell north to the Mark Addy and south to Salford Quays.
From M6 J12 to M602 go east to A5063. Use A5063 going south to A56 going north-east.

✸ ***Boat Trips***
Castlefield *Castlefield* Tel: 0161 748 2680

ℹ ***Tourist Information***
Altrincham Tel: 0161 912 5931
Manchester Tel: 0161 234 3157 / 3158

Castlefield

Sandstone cliffs, railway viaducts and multiple wharves.

A traffic free wander around the southern extremity of Old Deansgate where the 'Duke of Bridgewater's' privately financed canal came to the River Medlock (1765) and set the scene for the Industrial Revolution in Manchester.

Start the stroll from:-

1 Knott Mill Bridge

Brindley widened and deepened the river downstream to create his terminal basin and the first two bay warehouse.

This was the Romans' ford, where the River Medlock powered a mill before hitting the sandstone cliffs which protected Mancenium's Castle. Until the 1800s the castle site was an undisturbed field, crossed only by railway viaducts and the Rochdale Canal. *After looking over the parapet, pass into Castlefield, down across the open area, through an arch to arrive at:-*

2 Grocers Warehouse

Warehouses were built all around the terminus. The Grocers being an early example (1789-1960), recently partially reconstructed. The 'Knott Mill Packet Station' nearby provided a boarding point for comfortable high speed journeys to Runcorn, Worsley, Wigan and Liverpool.

Initially, coal was unloaded in the open on the river bank of the Medlock and dragged up to Castle Street. Brindley then tunnelled into the cliff (1771) so that boats could be manoeuvred under a 22 foot lift shaft which took boxes of coal directly from them to the surface at Castle Street. A water wheel powered the wooden hoist (till 1805), driven by the flow of the River Medlock.

Look around. Castlefield Management have set plaques and interpretive panels all over the place. Cross the footbridge, turn right in front of the prize winning Quay Bar, follow the wharf edge and over the small lifting bridge to:-

3 Merchants Bridge

Modern engineering that has arrived many years after the last merchant left the area, but a vantage point to see:-

- **Lock No 92** on the Rochdale Canal. Despite it not being in his ownership the Duke extracted tolls from everything passing!

- **The Middle Warehouse** the one with two huge arches where the barges entered to unload in the dry. Now home to a radio station.

- **Three Victorian cast iron railway viaducts** used by trains from 'Knott Mill and Deansgate' station plus the Metrolink tram from Altrincham and Salford Quays (in the south) through the city centre to Piccadilly and Bury (in the north).

- **The Merchants Company's warehouse** (with two slightly smaller arches). Renovated after a fire, the wooden structure with fire resistant crosswalls has been retained: now offices.

To return to the start at **1** *cross* **3** Merchants Bridge *into Catalan Square, go over the stone bridge, turn past* **Lock 92** *onto the Rochdale Canal. From the Rochdale Canal towpath (eastwards), the first access upwards is:-*

4 Castle Street Access Slope

On the *north* side of Castle Street. *Either go left along Castle Street to return to* **1** *or cross to the south where* △ *steps lead down past all levels of the partially reconstructed* **2** Grocers Warehouse. *Look at the interior. At the bottom, turn left to return to* **1**.

A longer walk back to **4** Castle Street

From **3** Merchants Bridge *go further along the cobbled towing path on the slate wharf (southern) side, past the restored entrance to 'The New Basin' and cross the canal. Use the* △ *steps over the footbridge to:-*

5 Potato Wharf

Staple diet of Mancunians. Specialist wholesalers would unload the barges onto waggons and carts for delivery around the city. Other wharves were named for their use as termini for timber, slate and coal. *Follow the trees and cross the top of the arm. Within the forecourt of 'The Visions Centre,' a Millennium Community Project, there is:-*

6 Giants Basin

Huge 'plughole' without a plug. Water from the Medlock flows through the whole Castlefield area and out through this massive drain. Brindley built a clover leaf structure, replaced by this circular stone sluice (1809). Two outlets drain into the Medlock (the other coming from Knott Mill). *Look across the road and through the railings to see them. Pass up the road, or, go with the water, in front of the YHA building to the Castlefield Hotel and:-*

7 Events Arena

Events throughout the year, the arena overlooks twin canal arms formerly under the

'Staffordshire' Warehouse. Visitor Centre staffed with helpful people and plenty to read (0161 834 4026). Visiting narrowboats often tie up here.

Return in front of the white canopies, over the metal footbridge under the three huge railway viaducts to Catalan Square close to **3** Merchants Bridge. *The stone bridge at* **Lock 92** *on the Rochdale Canal leads to a narrow towpath, an access slope up to* **4** *and across Chester Road to* **1**.

A longer walk to Bridgewater Hall

From **4** Castle Street *use the northern access slope to the Rochdale Canal, turn right, away from Castlefield, and start a journey in the enclosed world of urban canals.*

First an extended bridge under Deansgate leads to Lock 91 and 90. Then pass the arches of thousands of bricks. These are the structure of the undercroft to the G MEX Exhibition Centre, formerly Central Station. Another bridge (Albion) and 150 yards leads to Lock 89 and the junction with the:-

8 Salford and Irwell Junction Canal (1839)

A subterranean canal from here to the River Irwell, built to bypass tolls at Lock 92.

For guided walks 'Under the city streets' book ahead at Tourist Information Centres.

Cross over from the towpath (developers promised this new pedestrian bridge in 1997)

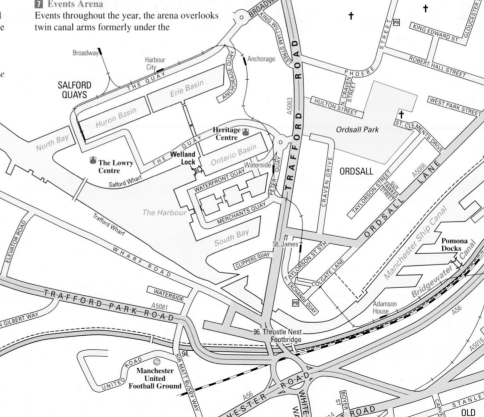

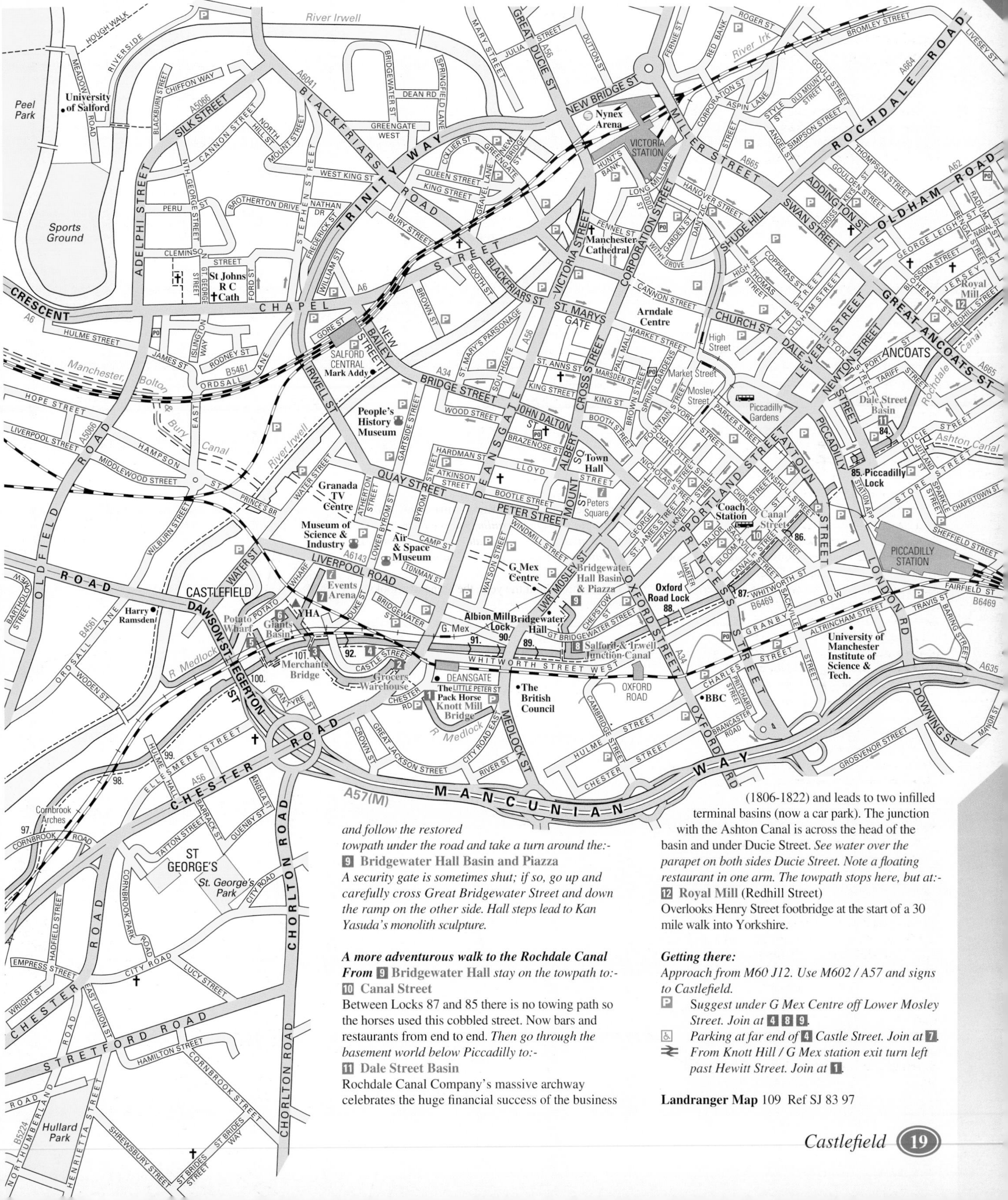

(map of Castlefield / Manchester with numerous street labels)

Body text:

and follow the restored
towpath under the road and take a turn around the:-

9 Bridgewater Hall Basin and Piazza
A security gate is sometimes shut; if so, go up and carefully cross Great Bridgewater Street and down the ramp on the other side. Hall steps lead to Kan Yasuda's monolith sculpture.

A more adventurous walk to the Rochdale Canal
From **9** **Bridgewater Hall** *stay on the towpath to:-*
10 Canal Street
Between Locks 87 and 85 there is no towing path so the horses used this cobbled street. Now bars and restaurants from end to end. *Then go through the basement world below Piccadilly to:-*
11 Dale Street Basin
Rochdale Canal Company's massive archway celebrates the huge financial success of the business

(1806-1822) and leads to two infilled terminal basins (now a car park). The junction with the Ashton Canal is across the head of the basin and under Ducie Street. *See water over the parapet on both sides Ducie Street. Note a floating restaurant in one arm. The towpath stops here, but at:-*
12 Royal Mill (Redhill Street)
Overlooks Henry Street footbridge at the start of a 30 mile walk into Yorkshire.

Getting there:
Approach from M60 J12. Use M602 / A57 and signs to Castlefield.
P *Suggest under G Mex Centre off Lower Mosley Street. Join in at* **4 8 9**.
Parking at far end of **4** *Castle Street. Join at* **7**.
From Knott Hill / G Mex station exit turn left past Hewitt Street. Join at **1**.

Landranger Map 109 Ref SJ 83 97

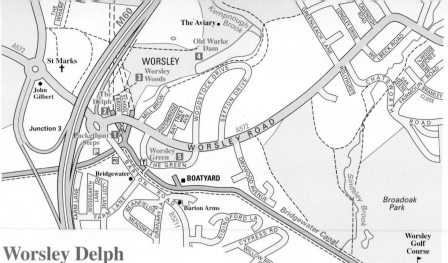

Worsley Delph
A double first. First canal and first passanger railway.

An unexpected village of half-timbered houses, green spaces and industrial relics. This was the cradle of the modern canal system. By 1774 the Duke of Bridgewater brought coal to the surface by floating it out on the mines' drainage system and sent it to Manchester in broad beam barges.

Start the stroll from:-
1 Packetboat Steps
Packetboats were built narrower than normal, hauled by more than one horse and provided the swiftest, most comfortable travel of the day. The bollards at the foot of the steps held the boat for boarding. The red brick building behind you (1770) accommodated passengers awaiting the service, was extended (1850) by Lord Egerton in the black and white mock-Tudor style which now appears all around. Cost of travelling 'steerage' in 1850 to *Patricroft* was 'one penny', *Castlefield* 'tuppence', 'Best Cabin' luxury a penny extra, refreshments served!

Stand on **1** *Packetboat Steps*
- *look right*, under the road bridge and motorway junction 13, the canal will take you exactly 46 miles to Liverpool Docks, via Leigh and Wigan.
- *look left,* under the road bridge, the canal gives direct access to more than 46 miles of coal seams on four levels with underground inclined planes connecting the upper two levels.
- *in front,* there are eight broad gauge lock free miles to Castlefield in Manchester and 30 miles at this level

to the Runcorn Gap on the tidal River Mersey (where the canal dropped 80 feet through ten locks to the river). *Go left up over the 26 planks of the 'alphabet' footbridge and across the road. From the bridge over the canal arm, look into the:-*
2 Ochre red water of The Delph
Two exits from the underground canals of the coal mine can be seen. Against the left hand cliff face lies a half sunk 'starvationer' (boats that carried coal out from the mine). *Follow the footpath right, round into School Brow with railings protecting from 'Thin ice'. Climb up into:-*
3 Worsley Woods
Bluebell woods are over the warren of tunnels that produced coal since 1376.
Alternatively go direct to:-
4 Old Warke Dam *by remaining on the A572 road and turning up Mill Brow. Return to the A572 road, go left a few yards and cross the road to:-*
5 Worsley Green
The amenity society has designed interpretation boards all around the village, giving directions and a little history. As they will tell you, this green, in days gone by, was black with industrial activity.
Follow directions on the boards.

These stones are all that were left after the Manchester Ship Canal had demolished Brindley's bold aqueduct.
A wonder of the waterways in its time (1762-1892) and such a tourist attraction that Josiah Wedgwood placed its picture on a plate of the 952-piece dinner service that he manufactured for Queen Charlotte of Russia (The Frog Service 1774).
*   The stones have been re-assembled alongside the B5230 as it passes under the canal. They previously formed the arch within the original embankment over the same roadway.*

A longer walk to **9** Barton Swing Aqueduct
From **5** Worsley Green *Go down the gentle slope of the green to the canal and cross the bridge (1901), turn left onto the towpath. Walk 1½ miles to:-*
6 Patricroft Railway Bridge
George Stephenson's **first** passanger railway had its **first** crossing of the Duke's **first** Canal on this substantial embankment (1830).
A further mile along the towpath you reach:-
7 Aqueduct Gardens
Quiet havens on the north bank of the Ship Canal. Gardens everywhere. Alongside the towpath, down below alongside the very wide embankment, and ⚠ down further steps alongside the vast waterway. *From the Ship Canal go up ⚠ steps to road level and cross the:-*
8 Barton Swing Bridge
Like the 'wonder-of-the-waterways' aqueduct; crossing at the higher level, this bridge also swings parallel to the shore when big ships need to pass to Salford. *There is no towpath across the canal aqueduct; use this bridge. Look downstream at the Barton High Level Motorway Bridge (M60), built so high to allow big ships below. Maybe you will see one pass. At the southern end of the bridge turn left up a cobbled driveway to join the fishermen trying their luck. Enter the:-*
9 Barton Swing Aqueduct and the 'Black Cage'
Questions of modern day public safety require these railings. Look through them to Edward Leader-William's 235 foot long, 1450 ton swing aqueduct which replaced (1893) Brindley's original three arches. See the typical 'standby crane' ready to lift the nearby stop planks into place in case the sliding / swinging joint fails and water starts cascading from the Bridgewater into the Ship Canal.

Getting there:
Approach from M60 J3. Use B5211 south.
P *Suggest on right immediately beyond the roundabout. Join at* **1**.
♿ *As above. Join at* **1**.
🚆 *From Patricroft station exit turn west. Join at* **6**.

Landranger Map 109
Ref SJ 74 00

Bridgwater and Taunton Canal
111 E2

(Grand Western Canal 111 D2 and River Parrett 111 E1)
Opened: 1827-1904, 1985
Engineer: Hollinsworth
Bridgwater Docks, off the River Parrett to Taunton (links to Grand Western Canal and River Tone)
14½ miles, 6 wide locks

Flora and fauna abound alongside these south-west waterways. A wild river system and three lengths of calm water are well worth the overland journey from the connected system.

The tide rushes into the River Parrett and its tributaries to such an extent that it remains a river little used by boats. Upstream of Oath Tidal Sluice the river is managed to maintain a constant water table in the huge Somerset Levels.

Three isolated canals are in water and are managed to provide a different environment from most canals of the connected system. The **Grand Western** is owned by Devon County Council who encourage canoes, rowing and horsedrawn boats. No powered craft are allowed, except electric boats.

The **Bridgwater and Taunton** has three slipways for launching powered trailer boats and a new marina built around the old docks. A further isolated navigation for small craft was restored by the then Water Authority at the **Westport Canal.**

Bridgwater was a major port with lock connection from the docks to the fiercely tidal River Parrett. There were schemes to bypass these docks and join Bristol to Taunton and on to Exeter, thus avoiding Land's End (1796-1811). But the Grand Western Canal and the Bridgwater and Taunton Canal, running west and east of Taunton (where they once joined each other at Firepool Lock) were the only bits built.

First to open was an 11 mile lock free level fit for barges from Tiverton as far as Lowdwells (1814). Later a lock free extension to Taunton was opened (1838) but only for small tub boats which could fit the seven boat lifts and climb the inclined plane.

The second was built from the Bridgwater Docks upstream to Taunton, bypassing the river Tone (1827). This led to arguments with conservators… resolved when the canal bought them out (1832).

Management and Restoration
British Waterways, Govilon Tel: 01873 830328
Somerset Inland Waterways Society
Tel: 01278 652681

◊ Maunsel Locks: Somerset Space Walk
The Sun, centre of the solar system, is found near this only remaining lock cottage… now a picnic area and base for walking. The Sun model and all the other planets of the solar system are to the same scale and are set the correct (same-scale) distance apart along the towpath to both the north and south.

Pluto is the furthest planet. Find it 6.8 miles away at either the Bridgwater canal teminus or Taunton canal terminus.
From M5 J25. Use A361 going north; brown signs.

◊ Grand Western Canal Country Park
A major linear park, includes picnic areas, course fishing, circular walks, rowing boat hire and moorhens, coots, heron, kingfisher, swans, water iris and water lilies. Base for a horsedrawn barge.
From M5 J27, go west on A361; then brown signs.

⚓ Boat Trips
Tiverton *Tivertonian (horsedrawn)* Tel: 01884 253345
Taunton *Olive Rose* Tel: 01823 444630
Bridgwater *Peggotytom, Ladypeggy*
Tel: 01278 451523

📖 Suggested Guide Book
Jean Hall, Joy Yeates *West Country Waterway Heritage* printed by Profile Printers, 1997

ℹ️ Tourist Information
Bridgwater Tel: 01278 427652 (seasonal)
Taunton Tel: 01823 336344
Tiverton Tel: 01884 255827

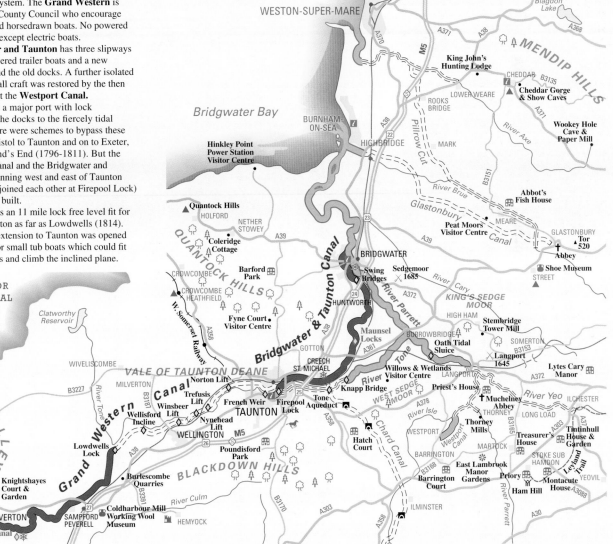

The Broads   117 E2

Myriad lakes and five slow flowing rivers
From the sea at Great Yarmouth and Lowestoft to
Norwich, Beccles and inland villages
125 miles, 0 locks
River Ant to Dilham Staithe: 8 miles
River Bure to Coltishall Lock: 32 miles
River Chet to Loddon Water Mill: 4 miles
River Thurne to Catfield Common: 16 miles
River Waveney to Geldeston Lock: 17 miles

Roughly two thirds of all the holidays taken on our
waterways use over 2500 miles of interconnected
rivers and canals. The other third takes place
within these Norfolk and Suffolk Broads.

Open sky, distant horizons, reed swamps, village
'staithes', waterside pubs and car inaccessible
backwaters make water-borne exploration very
rewarding.

Competition between wildlife in the fens and
marshes and human activity, eg sailing, walking,
canoeing, windsurfing, etc, is intense. The Broads
Authority provides much needed management to
achieve balance between conservation, recreation
and navigation.

Five rivers wander through marshland to an eroding
coast. Formerly, peat was dug from behind the
riverbanks to supply the hearths of Norwich (1000s -
1400s). The diggings were abandoned then became
flooded and formed 'The Broads'. Some are silting
up and slowly returning to mixed woodland via
reedbeds, fen and carr.

Huge pumps harnessed the wind to drain the peat
which then became rich farmland but also shrank.
About a third of the Authority's area is below sea
level. Only riverbanks stop flooding of the area.
Strict speed restrictions for boats are enforced as
banks could be undermined by their wash. Wind-
encouraged tides sweeping in from the North Sea
have been known to break through (1953).

Management
The Broads Authority Tel: 01603 610734
Great Yarmouth Port Authority Tel: 01493 335500
The Broads Society Tel: 01493 700344
Norfolk Windmills Trust Tel: 01603 222705

◊ **Norwich Cathedral: Pull Ferry**
Norman cathedral built of Caen stone from France.
The stone was brought up the Broads' rivers and then
floated along a side channel leading to the building
site. A depression in the Cathedral Close fields and
an impression in the river bank show the line.
*Approach from A147 / A1242 junction. Walk north
on the western riverbank.*
◊ **Norwich Boom Towers**
On either side of the River Yare. A chain suspended
between these towers was only lowered to let cargo
vessels out of Norwich Port after they had paid their
harbour dues (1000-1989).
*Approach from A47 / A416 junction. Go north-west
using A417 until it crosses River Wensum.*
◊ **Reedham Chain Ferry**
The only vehicle crossing of the Yare between A47
bridge at Norwich and the Breydon Bridge at Great
Yarmouth. A few cars at a time are ferried across by
hauling on a chain laid across the bed of the river.
Approach from A47 / A1064 junction. Go into Acle

then south using B1140 to its end.
◊ **Oulton Broad** (130 acres upstream of Mutford Lock)
Home to the oldest power boat club in the country.
Power boat racing can be seen most summer
Thursdays. Water sport schools abound. Windsurfing,
canoeing, sailing are all available.
See from A146 / A4117 junction outside Lowestoft.
◊ **Berney Arms Mill** (Tel: 01493 700605)
Tallest (70 feet) drainage mill in full working order.
Wide views from the seventh floor, windmill exhibition.
*Approach by train: park at Reedham or Great
Yarmouth. Walk 1 mile from station.*
◊ **Breydon Water**
Remains of a river estuary. Very shallow except in
the dredged channel. Fast running tidal stream enters
from Great Yarmouth.
*Approach from A47 western bypass at Great
Yarmouth. Walk along the southern banks.*
◊ **Hickling Broad** (Norfolk Wildlife Trust)
Coot, moorhen, butterflies in abundance can be viewed
from the water trail boat trip on a replica reed lighter.
Together with nearby Horsey Mere it makes a huge
area devoted primarily to wildlife.
*Approach from A149 / A1062 junction at Potter
Heigham. Use A149 going north, look right.*

*Some trading Wherries were swept out in the summer and
pioneer Victorian city-dwellers camped in their holds for
holidays. Earnest Collins had a fleet of fully fitted Wherries
'to sleep ten persons comfortably' and yachts with 'the
most reliable skippers and attendants..(who).. are steady,
clean and obliging'. He appointed H. Blake & Co. of 10
Basinghall Street, London E.C. to act as his agent. This is
part of the first catalogue cover (1908).*

◊ **Potter Heigham Bridge**
700 year old Bridge with limited clearance under the
central arch. 17 miles upstream from the sea, this is
where an understanding of tides is essential. A pilot
assists hire boats through as tidal movement can be
two feet on a nominal seven feet.
Approach from A149 / A1062 junction. Turn south.
◊ **Briggate Lock**
Derelict lock upstream of the bridge. It shows the
size of the Norfolk wherries that used this eight mile
canal up to North Walsham.
From A149 / A1151 junction, use A149 going north.
◊ **How Hill: Ludham**
Major educational centre (1983) with access around
the estate showing 'Broads in microcosm'- reed, sedge,
carr, marshman's thatched cottage, clear open water
and marsh meadows. Three restored windpumps can
be visited - Turf Fen, Boardmans and Clayrack. Also

'Electric Eel' water trail boat (Tel: 01692 678763).
*Approach from A147 / A1062 junction, Potter
Heigham. Use A1062 going west.*

✱ **Boat Trips**
Acle Bridge *Mermaid Cruises* Tel: 01493 728876
Great Yarmouth *The Golden Galleon*
Tel: 01494 750643
Hoveton *Broadland Craft* Tel: 01603 782207
Norwich *Southern River Steamers*
Tel: 01603 624051
Oulton Broad *Waveney River Tours*
Tel: 01502 574903
Potter Heigham *Herbert Woods* Tel: 01692 670711
Stalham *Stalham Water Tours* Tel: 01692 670530
Wroxham *Broads Tours* Tel: 01603 782207

⚓ **Electric Boats** (day hire)
Hoveton *Fineway Cruisers* Tel: 01603 782309
Ludham Bridge *Ludham Bridge Services*
Tel: 01692 630486
Potter Heigham *Herbert Woods and Phoenix Fleet*
Tel: 01692 670711 / 460
Ranworth *Granary Stores* Tel: 01603 270432
Wroxham *Broads Tours* Tel: 01603 782207

⚓ **Wherry Hire**
Albion Tel: 01603 505 815
Olive, Norada, Hathor Tel: 01603 782470
White Moth Tel: 01692 631330

🚲 **Broads Bike Hire** Tel: 01603 782281
Acle Bridge, Gays Staithe, Hickling Staithe, Hoveton,
Ludham Bridge, Reedham Quay, Sutton Staithe and
Thurne Staithe

ℹ **Broads Information** *(Easter-October)*
Beccles Tel: 01502 713196
Great Yarmouth Tel: 01493 332095
Hoveton Tel: 01603 782281
How Hill Tel: 01692 678763
Potter Heigham Tel: 01692 670779
Ranworth Tel: 01603 270453

ℹ **Tourist Information**
Great Yarmouth Tel: 01493 842195
Lowestoft Tel: 01502 523000
Norwich Tel: 01603 666071

Ant, River River Bure to Wayford Bridge
    Includes **North Walsham and Dilham Canal**
    Wayford Bridge to Antingham and **Barton Broad**
Bure, River Great Yarmouth to Coltishall
Bure (Aylsham) Navigation
    Coltishall to Aylsham
Chet, River River Yare to Loddon
Norwich and Lowestoft Navigation
    Lowestoft to Norwich. Includes part of **River Yare**,
    Haddiscoe New Cut, part of **River Waverney**,
    Oulton Broad and **Lake Lothing**
Thurne, River River Bure to West Somerton
    Links to **Hickling Broad** and **Horsey Mere**
Waverney, River Breydon Water to Bungay
    Includes **Bungay Navigation** Geldeston to Bungay
    See also **Norwich and Lowestoft Navigation** (above)
Wensum, River River Yare to Norwich City
Yare, River Gorleston-on-Sea to River
    Wensum at Norwich. Includes **Breydon Water**
    See also **Norwich and Lowestoft Navigation**

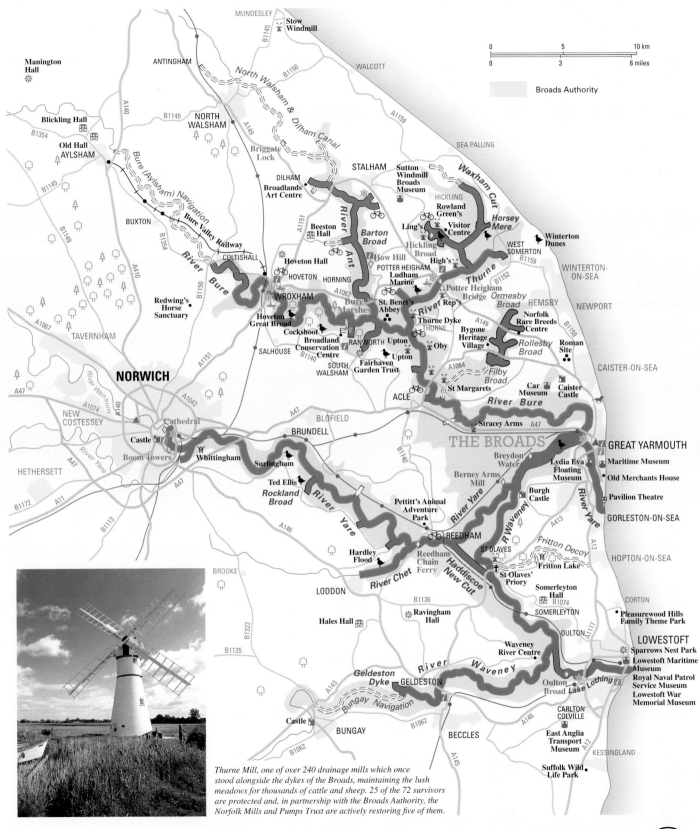

Thurne Mill, one of over 240 drainage mills which once stood alongside the dykes of the Broads, maintaining the lush meadows for thousands of cattle and sheep. 25 of the 72 survivors are protected and, in partnership with the Broads Authority, the Norfolk Mills and Pumps Trust are actively restoring five of them.

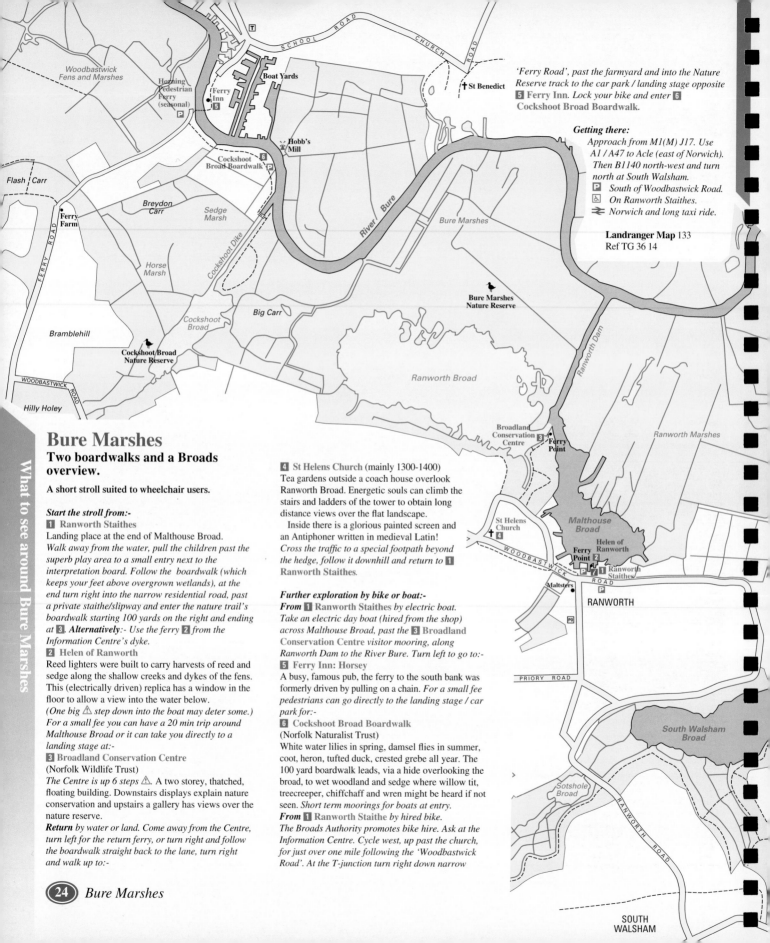

'Ferry Road', past the farmyard and into the Nature Reserve track to the car park / landing stage opposite **5** Ferry Inn. *Lock your bike and enter* **6** Cockshoot Broad Boardwalk.

Getting there:
Approach from M1(M) J17. Use A1 / A47 to Acle (east of Norwich). Then B1140 north-west and turn north at South Walsham.
P *South of Woodbastwick Road.*
On Ranworth Staithes.
Norwich and long taxi ride.

Landranger Map 133
Ref TG 36 14

Bure Marshes
Two boardwalks and a Broads overview.

A short stroll suited to wheelchair users.

Start the stroll from:-
1 **Ranworth Staithes**
Landing place at the end of Malthouse Broad. *Walk away from the water, pull the children past the superb play area to a small entry next to the interpretation board. Follow the boardwalk (which keeps your feet above overgrown wetlands), at the end turn right into the narrow residential road, past a private staithe/slipway and enter the nature trail's boardwalk starting 100 yards on the right and ending at* **3**. **Alternatively**:- *Use the ferry* **2** *from the Information Centre's dyke.*

2 **Helen of Ranworth**
Reed lighters were built to carry harvests of reed and sedge along the shallow creeks and dykes of the fens. This (electrically driven) replica has a window in the floor to allow a view into the water below.
(One big ⚠ step down into the boat may deter some.) For a small fee you can have a 20 min trip around Malthouse Broad or it can take you directly to a landing stage at:-

3 **Broadland Conservation Centre**
(Norfolk Wildlife Trust)
The Centre is up 6 steps ⚠. A two storey, thatched, floating building. Downstairs displays explain nature conservation and upstairs a gallery has views over the nature reserve.
Return *by water or land. Come away from the Centre, turn left for the return ferry, or turn right and follow the boardwalk straight back to the lane, turn right and walk up to:-*

4 **St Helens Church** (mainly 1300-1400)
Tea gardens outside a coach house overlook Ranworth Broad. Energetic souls can climb the stairs and ladders of the tower to obtain long distance views over the flat landscape.
Inside there is a glorious painted screen and an Antiphoner written in medieval Latin! *Cross the traffic to a special footpath beyond the hedge, follow it downhill and return to* **1** **Ranworth Staithes.**

Further exploration by bike or boat:-
From **1** **Ranworth Staithes** *by electric boat. Take an electric day boat (hired from the shop) across Malthouse Broad, past the* **3** **Broadland Conservation Centre** *visitor mooring, along Ranworth Dam to the River Bure. Turn left to go to:-*
5 **Ferry Inn: Horsey**
A busy, famous pub, the ferry to the south bank was formerly driven by pulling on a chain. *For a small fee pedestrians can go directly to the landing stage / car park for:-*
6 **Cockshoot Broad Boardwalk**
(Norfolk Naturalist Trust)
White water lilies in spring, damsel flies in summer, coot, heron, tufted duck, crested grebe all year. The 100 yard boardwalk leads, via a hide overlooking the broad, to wet woodland and sedge where willow tit, treecreeper, chiffchaff and wren might be heard if not seen. *Short term moorings for boats at entry.*
From **1** **Ranworth Staithe** *by hired bike. The Broads Authority promotes bike hire. Ask at the Information Centre. Cycle west, up past the church, for just over one mile following the 'Woodbastwick Road'. At the T-junction turn right down narrow*

Brown's Canal   **111 E1**
River Bure to North Drain near Glastonbury
Brue, River   **111 E1**
Sea to Glastonbury Canal near Highbridge and
Pillrow Cut to Glastonbury
Buckingham Canal (Old Stratford Arm and Buckingham Arm) - see **Grand Union Canal**
Bude Canal Bude to Blagdonmoor   **110 B2-C2**
  Druxton Branch Red Post Junction to Druxton
  Virworthy Branch Brendon Moor Junction to
Tamar Lake
Bude Canal Society, Tel:01288 354736
Bungay Navigation - see **The Broads**
Bure (Aylsham) Navigation - see **The Broads**
Bure, River - see **The Broads**
Burnturk Canals   **123 D4**
Kingskettle to colliery near Burnturk
Burwell Lode - see **Reach Lode**

Caistor Canal   **119 E3**
River Ancholme to Moortown

Calder and Hebble Navigation
118 C3 - 119 D3

Opened: Brighouse 1764, Sowerby Bridge 1770
Engineers: Smeaton, Eyes, Brindley, Holt, Carr
Fall Ing Junction to Sowerby Bridge terminus
21½ miles, 26 wide locks, 8 flood-control structures

Travelling at the bottom of an ever narrowing valley up towards Norland Moor, the navigation-cum-canal plays bib and tuck with the river from which it gets its name.

After the Aire and Calder Navigation had improved the lower reaches of the Calder to Wakefield (1699) this waterway was promoted to extend navigation even further. Originally it consisted of a riverside horse path and short cuts around river difficulties.

On the Calder and Hebble, a unique arrangement has the 'spindles' underground. A handspike is pushed into a horizontal capstan roller that lifts a rack which opens the paddle. The handspike is made of hardwood about three inches by two inches, which was standard equipment on Yorkshire Keels before ever canal locks came to these rivers.

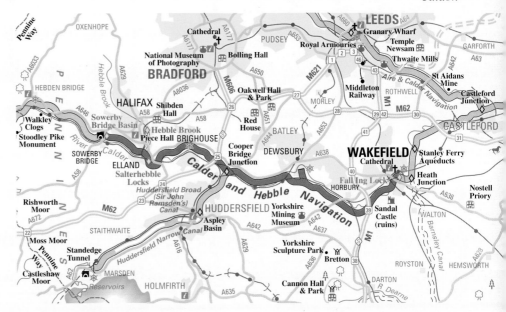

Over the years further improvements were made so that it became more a canal than a river navigation. A drawback was the early decision to construct only short locks for keels (14' x 57'), which hampered later through navigation.

Management
British Waterways, Castleford Tel: 01977 554351
Calder Navigation Society Tel: 01422 823562

◇ **Sowerby Bridge Basin**
Always a transhipment basin, firstly from packhorses on the Halifax-Rochdale turnpike (1770-1798) then between the 70' Rochdale Canal boats and the shorter 57' Calder boats.
Approach from M62 J22. Use A6172 going north.
◇ **Salterhebble Locks**
Early locks were swept away by floods. Now three twisting locks set in the Calderdale landscape lead up to the canal junction towards Halifax. Under the

Working Locks
Locks are like big steps, most allow you to go up or down by about eight feet or so. The technical term is 'pound lock'. They consist of a walled chamber with doors either end into which boats fit snugly like a hand in a glove. Boats are lifted on the rush of water let into the chamber from the higher level or they are lowered by emptying the water out of the other end into the canal below.
Water is let into the chamber in one of two ways. The simplest is to have a small 'shutter' in the lock door itself but a safer way is for the water to have a separate conduit from the canal which ends up feeding water into the chamber from underneath. The flow is then controlled by an underground shutter and does not splash so much. When they are made these shutters look like 'paddles', which is their correct name.
It takes a huge effort to move the paddles against the pressure of water and so the rod controlling the paddle generally has some gearing which ends in a spindle. On most canals the spindle is turned by a crew member using a removable cranked handle.

road, beyond the bottom lock, the towpath has its own horse tunnel. Electrically operated guillotine bottom gates were installed after road widening.
Approach from M62 J22. Use A6172 going north.
◇ **Hebble Brook to Halifax**
Hebble Brook falls away from Halifax down a steep valley and has had powered textile mills since the 1500s. When the improved Calder navigation arrived at the wharf at the bottom (1767) goods were delivered by horsedrawn carts. Later (1828) a short branch canal with 14 locks climbed 100 feet back up the hill to arrive at a new basin close to the heart of Halifax woollen trade … Piece Hall.
The 'Hebble Trail' footpath now follows the brook and the abandoned canal up the steep valley.
From M62 J24, use A629 / A646 going north-west.
◇ **Fall Ing Lock: Wakefield Flood Lock**
Two locks are needed to control the cascades of variable mountain water that can swell the River Calder. Boaters need care when passing into the Wakefield Branch of the Aire and Calder navigation as the Fall Ings lock is deep (16 feet) and long (130 feet) with large paddles which can create turbulence - a treat for the critical gaze of gongoozlers.
Approach from M1 J38. Use A636 going north.

✳ *Boat Trips*
Brighouse Basin *Waylon* Tel: 01484 713424
Dewsbury *Calder Lady* Tel: 01924 467976
Shepley Bridge *Marina* Tel: 01924 491872
Saville Tel: 01924 402652 / 201880

📖 *Suggested Guide Book*
Keith Noble and society members: *West Yorkshire Waterway Guide* Calder Navigation Society, 1992

ℹ️ *Tourist Information*
Halifax Tel: 01422 368725
Huddersfield Tel: 01484 223200
Wakefield Tel: 01924 305000 / 305001

Caldon Canal - see **Trent and Mersey**

Caledonian Canal   122 B3-C1

Opened: 1822-1843, 1847
Engineers: Watt, Rennie, Telford, Jessop
Loch Linnhe to Moray Firth
20 miles, 29 wide locks

The Great Glen, overlooked by Ben Nevis and set in the heart of the Highlands, consists of three lochs surrounded by a few original natural forests of oak, birch and ash and new afforestation (1930-1960) by the Forestry Commission. Best seen in June when the immigrant rhododendrons bloom, there are ten waymarked forest walks varying in length from ½ mile to 4¼ miles and in difficulty from flat to steep. There is also an 80 mile cycle route, waymarked through forest tracks, minor roads and along canal towpaths, except where one of the 12 stages uses the A82!!

The Caledonian Canal connects the lochs with short sections of man made waterway, linking to sea water at the northern and southern ends.

The Jacobite rebellion (1745) encouraged the London Government to consider improvements to Scottish Highland infrastructure and war with France (1793) gave added emphasis to the strategic advantage of a sea to sea waterway through the Great Glen.

Unlike most waterways it was financed publicly. The water catchment to the small summit Loch Oich was so vast that water supply has never been a problem. Telford grouped his locks, over two thirds of them built as staircases... doubles at Corpach and Laggan, quadruple at Muirtown; Fort Augustus has five and a massive eight-lock 'Neptune's Staircase' at Banavie, dropping down towards Loch Linnhe and the Sea of the Hebrides. They were huge by the canal standards of the day, 160 feet long and 36 feet wide; all the bridges along the route were swing or pivot bridges with unlimited headroom. There are also two sea locks and the Dochgarroch regulating lock onto Loch Dochfour.

Although used by pleasure passenger boats from the start (1822-1939) and as expected by Moray Firth fishermen crossing between coasts, it finally fulfilled its strategic role in two World Wars. Mines were transported to the North Sea (1918) and East Coast bases victualled (1945).

Management
British Waterways, Inverness Tel: 01463 233140

◊ **Sea Locks**
Operated in rhythm with the tides. Normally open 4 hours either side of high water during duty hours.
Corpach Sea Lock Tel: 01397 772249
From A82 at Fort William, use A830 going west.
Clachnaharry Sea Lock Tel: 01463 713869
From A9 at Inverness, Use A82 / A862, going west.
◊ **Neptune's Staircase** (64' rise, 1500' run)
Narrow staircases at Foxton and Watford and the wide five lock staircase at Bingley are insignificant by comparison with this set of eight, each chamber constructed large enough for sea going fishing craft (150' long and 35' wide). Before addition of hydraulics these huge gates needed 126 turns of a capstan to the fully open position. One remains.
From A82 at Fort William, use A830 going north.
◊ **Loch Lochy**
500' deep and 11 miles long, this loch was raised 12 feet to make simple water connections at either end. Levels vary depending on rainfall. Major flooding was averted (1834) by quick action of lock keepers and sailors, since when extra lock gates have been added.
Use A82 between Spean Bridge and Laggan.
◊ **Leitirfearn Forest Nature Reserve Walk**
A railway ran from Fort William to Fort Augustus. This walk follows the dismantled line through ash and elm woodland and is complemented by General Wade's Military Road alongside the water.
From A82 east of Laggan: Great Glen Water Park.
◊ **Loch Oich**
Telford dredged a channel down a pair of shallow lochs to create this summit to the canal. Probably the earliest use of a steam powered bucket dredger.
Approach from A82 around Invergarry.
◊ **Falls of Foyers**
Britain's first hydroelectric scheme (1896-1967) powered an aluminium smelter, using the drop of these falls (lower 90 feet and upper 30 feet).
Approach from B862 Fort Augustus, following General Wade's narrow road with passing places.
◊ **Old Bridge: Invermoriston**
One of Telford's thousand bridges, built when he was engineer to the Highland Commissioners (1802-1819). Now pedestrian only; the River Moriston flows

underneath and tumbles down through a series of waterfalls into Loch Ness.
Approach from A82 / A887 junction.
◊ **Loch Ness**
Mountains slope steeply down 1000 feet below the water level, 24 miles long and gouged out by accelerated glaciers during the ice age, Loch Ness has more water in it than all the water bodies of England and Wales put together. It has caught the imagination ever since a new road (1933) opened up the shoreline to passers by and a London surgeon purported to take a photograph of a 4 foot neck rising out of the water.

Reports of 'sightings' (1960, 1979, 1987 and 1994) of the 'monster' have attracted the watchful eyes of enthusiasts and well equipped expeditions. Two exhibitions in Drumnadrochit, the 'Original' and the 'Official', attempt to persuade visitors of the truth of the legend.
◊ **John Cobb Memorial**
His world water speed record attempt (1952) ended in disaster for John and his boat (*Crusader*).
On the A82 at the lake shore: Lower Lenie.
◊ **Urquhart Castle**
Enduring image of Loch Ness. Robert the Bruce fought for it in the Wars of Independence, Jacobites laid siege (1689) and it became this ruin when blown up to prevent occupation by rebels.
On the A82 at Strone Point.

※ **Boat Trips**
Fort Augustus *Royal Scot, Royal Princess*
Tel: 01320 366221
Drumnadrochit *Deep-Scan* Tel: 01456 450218 (monster exhibition)
Nessie Hunter Tel: 01456 450395 (Ness Cruises)
Fort William *Souterslass* Tel: 01397 703919

📖 **Suggested Guide Book**
Anthony Burton *The Caledonian Canal* Aurum Press, 1998

ℹ️ **Tourist Information**
Fort William Tel: 01397 703781
Fort Augustus Tel: 01320 366367
Inverness Tel: 01463 234353

Sea Lock into Loch Linnhe at Corpach Basin: Ben Nevis beyond

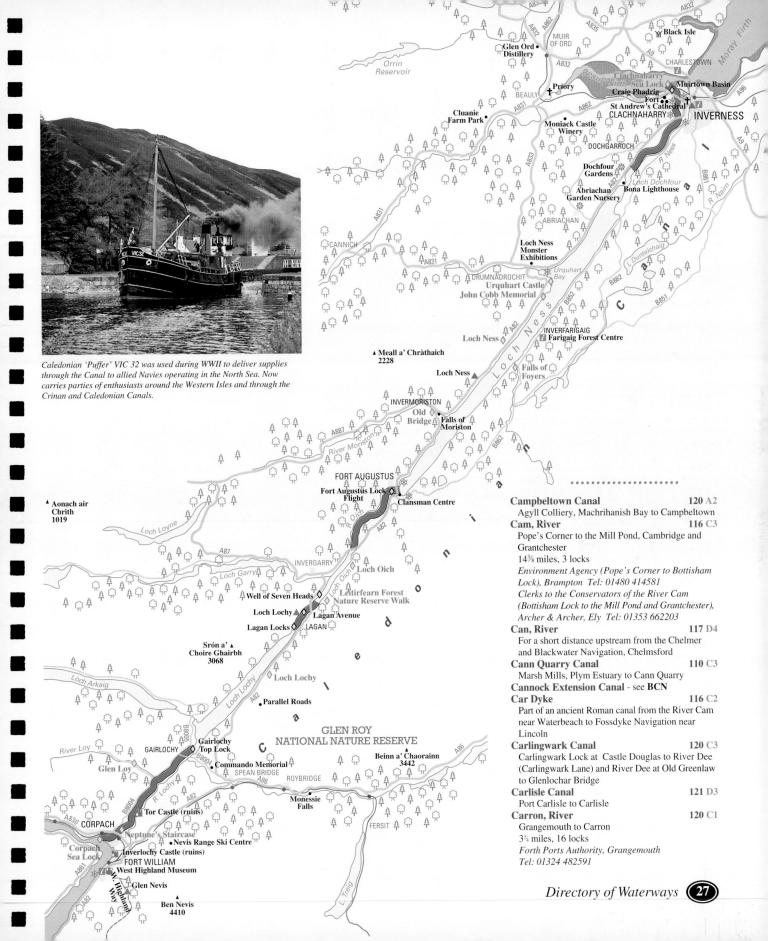

Caledonian 'Puffer' VIC 32 was used during WWII to deliver supplies through the Canal to allied Navies operating in the North Sea. Now carries parties of enthusiasts around the Western Isles and through the Crinan and Caledonian Canals.

Orrin Reservoir

Glen Ord Distillery

MUIR OF ORD

Black Isle

CHARLESTOWN

Moray Firth

Clachnaharry Sea Lock

Muirtown Basin

Craig Phadrig Fort

Priory

BEAULY

St Andrew's Cathedral

CLACHNAHARRY

INVERNESS

Cluanie Farm Park

Moniack Castle Winery

DOCHGARROCH

R. Ness

R. Nairn

Dochfour Gardens

Abriachan Garden Nursery

Bona Lighthouse

Loch Dochfour

CANNICH

ABRIACHAN

L. Duntelchaig

Loch Ness Monster Exhibitions

Urquhart Bay

DRUMNADROCHIT

Urquhart Castle

John Cobb Memorial

Loch Ness

INVERFARIGAIG

Farigaig Forest Centre

Loch Ness

▲ Meall a' Chràthaich 2228

Loch Ness ▲

Falls of Foyers

INVERMORISTON

Old Bridge

Falls of Moriston

River Moriston

FORT AUGUSTUS

Fort Augustus Lock Flight

Clansman Centre

R. Oich

▲ Aonach air Chrith 1019

Loch Loyne

INVERGARRY

Loch Garry

Loch Oich

Letterfearn Forest Nature Reserve Walk

Well of Seven Heads

Loch Lochy

Lagan Avenue

Lagan Locks

LAGAN

Srón a' Choire Ghairbh 3068

Loch Arkaig

Loch Lochy

Loch Lochy

Parallel Roads

Beinn a' Chaorainn 3442

GLEN ROY NATIONAL NATURE RESERVE

ROYBRIDGE

FERSIT

River Loy

Gairlochy Top Lock

GAIRLOCHY

Glen Loy

Commando Memorial

SPEAN BRIDGE

Monessie Falls

R. Lochy

Tor Castle (ruins)

CORPACH

Neptune's Staircase

Nevis Range Ski Centre

Corpach Sea Lock

Inverlochy Castle (ruins)

FORT WILLIAM

West Highland Museum

Glen Nevis

W. Highland Way

Ben Nevis 4410

L. Treig

Campbeltown Canal **120 A2**
Agyll Colliery, Machrihanish Bay to Campbeltown

Cam, River **116 C3**
Pope's Corner to the Mill Pond, Cambridge and Grantchester
14⅜ miles, 3 locks
Environment Agency (Pope's Corner to Bottisham Lock), Brampton Tel: 01480 414581
Clerks to the Conservators of the River Cam (Bottisham Lock to the Mill Pond and Grantchester), Archer & Archer, Ely Tel: 01353 662203

Can, River **117 D4**
For a short distance upstream from the Chelmer and Blackwater Navigation, Chelmsford

Cann Quarry Canal **110 C3**
Marsh Mills, Plym Estuary to Cann Quarry

Cannock Extension Canal - see **BCN**

Car Dyke **116 C2**
Part of an ancient Roman canal from the River Cam near Waterbeach to Fossdyke Navigation near Lincoln

Carlingwark Canal **120 C3**
Carlingwark Lock at Castle Douglas to River Dee (Carlingwark Lane) and River Dee at Old Greenlaw to Glenlochar Bridge

Carlisle Canal **121 D3**
Port Carlisle to Carlisle

Carron, River **120 C1**
Grangemouth to Carron
3¾ miles, 16 locks
Forth Ports Authority, Grangemouth
Tel: 01324 482591

Cart Navigation   **120 B1**
River Clyde to Paisley
Paisley Canal and Waterways Society
Iain Morrison, 19 Greenhill Crescent, Elderslie,
Johnstone PA5 9AW

Cassington Cut   **115 F4**
River Thames to near Eynsham

Chard Canal   **111 E2**
Creech St Michael to Chard

Charnwood Forest Line (Leicester Navigation)
- see **Grand Union Canal**

Chelmer and Blackwater Navigation   **113 E1**
Heybridge Basin to Chelmsford Basin
13¾ miles, 13 locks
The Company of the Proprietors of the Chelmer
and Blackwater Navigation Ltd, Little Baddow
Tel: 01245 412025

Chester Canal (later part of **Ellesmere and
Chester Canal**) - see **Shropshire Union Canal**

Chesterfield Canal   119 D4-E3
Opened: 1777
Engineers: Varley, Brindley, Henshall
West Stockwith Junction with tidal Trent navigable
to Worksop, 26 miles; 16 narrow locks under active
restoration for 20 miles; 49 narrow locks from near
Norwood summit tunnel down to Chesterfield.

**Occasionally diverting around obstacles, the
Cuckoo Way nevertheless allows walkers to follow
the rural calm of this canal through meadows and
woods for 45 miles to Chesterfield.**

At first aimed at Gainsborough, the eventual line of
this canal crossed two watersheds and meandered
down two valleys. Although all early canals had tried
to avoid construction costs of locks (and time penalty
for boats) by sticking closely to a single contour,
Brindley grasped the engineering challenge of
designing two long flights of locks and the longest
tunnel of its day, notwithstanding Harecastle on the

Trent and Mersey. Pressure from other canal projects
led him to delegate the supervision to John Varley as
Resident Engineer. Brindley's death (1772) led to
five years of changing contractors and supervisors to
complete the canal before the money ran out.

Management and Restoration
British Waterways, Newark Tel: 01636 704481
Chesterfield Canal Trust, Tel: 01246 855601

◊ **West Stockwith** (lock open 7 hours each tide)
High concentration required of boat captains to
understand the tidal currents across the mouth of this
lock. The Basin provides respite from the tides for all
manner of river craft.
From M18 J1, use A631 east / A161 north.

◊ **Drakeholes Tunnel** (under Cuckoo Hill)
Like most navigations in Yorkshire, this tunnel (462
feet) is wide beamed to take Trent keels, as were six
locks to Retford, narrowboats only thereafter.
From A1(M) J34. Use A614 / A631 going east.

◊ **Whitsunday Pie Lock: Retford**
So called after the huge pie cooked by a farmer's
wife for the navvies to celebrate its completion.
Approach from A1 at Ranby. Use A620 going east.

◊ **Giants Staircase** (22 locks in one mile)
Two lock flights at Thorpe and Turnerwood above
Shireoaks have only 200 yards between them. Four
staircase locks are in water: 2 double and 2 treble.
Approach from M1 J31. Use A57 going east.

◊ **Rother Link**
The 1771 Act kept river and canal apart. It forbade
any stream in the watershed feeding the River Rother
(and therefore the Don) from being used to supply
the canal. This proposed new link to the non tidal
Don navigation would join up to the expanding non
tidal Pennine canal system.

✵ *Boat Trips*
Retford *The Norwood Packet* Tel: 01246 812313
Chesterfield *The John Varley* Tel: 01246 274077

▥ *Suggested Guide Book*
Christine Richardson, John Lower *A Walkers' and*
Boaters' Guide to the Chesterfield Canal and Cuckoo
Way Hallamshire Press, 1994

ℹ *Tourist Information*
Retford Tel: 01777 860780
Worksop Tel: 01909 501148
Chesterfield Tel: 01246 345777

• •

Chet, River - see **The Broads**

Chichester Canal   **112 C4**
Birdham Pool to Chichester now known as
Chichester Canal
- see also **Portsmouth and Arundel Canal**
4½ miles, 1 lock
The Chichester Canal Society
Tel: 01243 671051

Cinderford Canal   **115 D4**
Cinderford ironworks to Broadmoor near Steam
Mills

Clay Dike   **116 C1**
South Forty Foot Drain to Kyme Eau

Clyde, River   **120 B1**
Greenock to Cambuslang
29½ miles, 0 locks
Clyde Ports, Glasgow Tel: 0141 221 8733

Cod Beck (unfinished)   **119 D1**
Swale Navigation to Thirsk

Colne, River   **117 E4**
Sea to East Bridge, Colchester
11 miles, 0 locks
The Harbour Master, Wivenhoe Tel: 01206 827316

Compstall Navigation   **118 C3**
Compstall to Etherow near Marple

Coombe Hill Canal   **115 D3**
River Severn to Coombe Hill
2¾ miles, 2 locks

Copperhouse Canal - see **Hayle Canal**

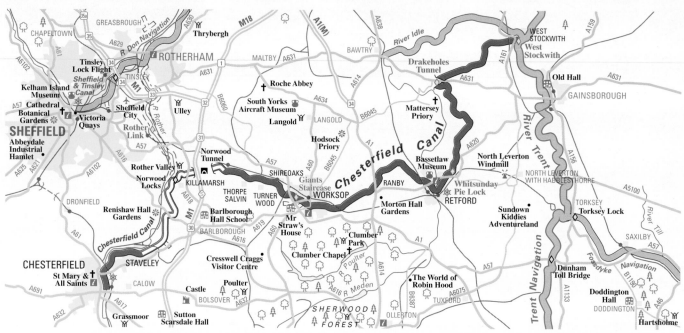

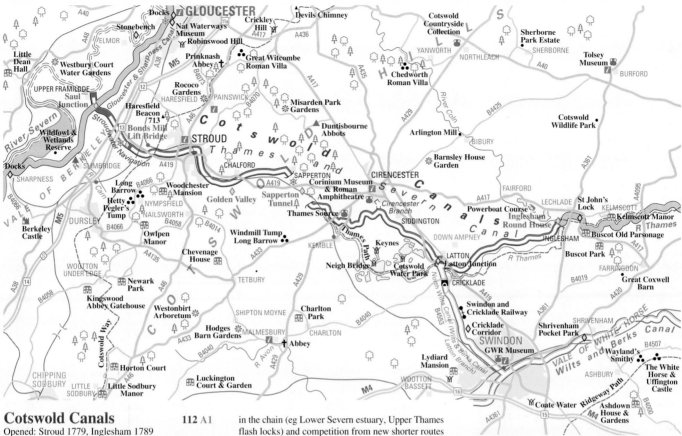

Cotswold Canals   112 **A1**

Opened: Stroud 1779, Inglesham 1789
Engineers: Hore, Dadford, Yeoman, Whitworth, Clowes
Stroudwater Navigation
Upper Framilode to Stroud (8 miles, 13 wide locks)
Thames and Severn Canal
Stroud to Inglesham (28¾ miles, 44 narrow locks)
Cirencester Branch (1½ miles, 0 locks)

Cotswold Canal Trust, with help from public authorities and local organisations, is seeking to re-open this link through beautiful countryside between the Rivers Severn and Thames. Already there are many towpath sections where landowners permit a relaxing walk alongside water and others where volunteers keep undergrowth away from picnic sites and towpath.

After earlier Acts (1730, 1759) had suffered from mill owner difficulties, wide beamed Severn Trows (16 feet) arrived at Stroud only four years after the Bridgewater Canal arrived in Manchester (1779) and made huge profits carrying coal to mills and cloth to wider markets. Thames and Severn Canal was 16 feet wide as far as Brimscombe Inland Port (now an industrial estate) then through 28 narrower locks (13 feet) up the steep Golden Valley to the longest tunnel of its time (1789) which emerged close to the source of the Thames at Thames Head.

Implementing earlier ideas for a waterway linking Bristol to London (1662-1668), it was potentially the final link in a 250 mile chain of waterways from the fast growing Midlands to London. Its profitability was hampered by lack of improvements in other links

in the chain (eg Lower Severn estuary, Upper Thames flash locks) and competition from new shorter routes via the Oxford Canal (225 miles) and Grand Union Canal (140 miles). Viability was further undermined by difficulties with water supply.

The company was rescued, first by a consortium of other canal companies (1893-1901) and then by Gloucestershire County Council (until 1927 and 1933). Now declared a Conservation Area along most of its length, recent road building has allowed for full restoration by incorporating 'hidden bridges' eg bypasses at Stroud (1987) and Latton (1997).

Restoration

Cotswold Canals Trust Tel: 01285 643440
Http://www.cotswoldcanals.mcmail.com

◊ **Saul Junction**
Waterway crossroads with the Gloucester and Sharpness Ship Canal (1827). A short section of the Stroudwater is navigable, boats are moored and the towpath a pleasant walk.
From M5 J13, use A38 / B4071 going north.

◊ **Bonds Mill Lift Bridge and Gun Turret**
Reinforced glass fibre lift bridge (1994), strong enough for the lorries of the Industrial Estate, is guarded by a World War II gun turret.
From M5 J13, use A419 going east. Beyond a roundabout find Blunder Lock car park. Walk east.

◊ **Golden Valley: Chalford Round House**
Autumnal leaves explain the nickname for this part of the River Frome which is known here as the 'Black Gutter'. 20 locks climb the valley, keeping the canal out of the river flood plain and away from former

millponds and weirs. One of the surviving drum shaped lengthman's houses can be seen from the A419 at Chalford.
Approach from M5 J13, use A419 going east.

◊ **Sapperton Tunnel: Coates Portal** (11 450 feet)
Winter water often allows a trip boat to enter this portal from King's Reach (King George III visited in 1788). The tunnel bore is up to 200 feet below ground and passes through solid limestone caverns and brick lined fullers earth. Both portals are now restored (Coates 1977, Daneway 1996).
Approach from M5 J13. Use A419 going east. Turn right for Coates and right towards Tarlton.

◊ **Inglesham Round House**
At the Thames limit of navigation for powered craft stands the Canal Companies Round House marking the former junction with the Thames and its Path.
Approach from M4 J15. Use A419/A361 going north to Lechlade and then the Thames Path.

✱ *Boat Trips*
Eastingham, Stroud Tel: 01453 545042 *(summer only)*
Sapperton Tunnel Tel: 01452 741302 *(winter only)*

📖 *Suggested Guide Book*
Richard Attwood, David Jowett *A Guide to the Cotswold Canals* Cotswold Canal Trust, 1997

ℹ️ *Tourist Information*
Stroud Tel: 01453 765768
Cirencester Tel: 01285 654180

Cottenham Lode	**116** C3
Old West River to Cottenham	
Counter Wash Drain	**116** C3
Welches Dam to Mepal	

Environment Agency, Brampton
Tel: 01480 414581

Coventry Canal   115 E2

Opened: Atherstone 1771, the whole 1790
Engineers: Brindley, Yeoman, Lingard
Fradley Junction to Coventry terminus
27 miles, 13 narrow locks: 4 miles, 0 locks

Skirting the Birmingham plateau on its eastern side, the Coventry is now a rural canal. Colliery spoil heaps have disappeared under grass and even the towpath into the city is improved with modern day sculptures to enliven the scene.

Bishop Street Basin, Coventry

When the Trent and Mersey Canal had connected those two rivers and the Severn had been linked to it at Great Haywood (1777) all businesses alongside still lacked connection to a huge London population. The weak link in the chain was the Coventry which had a reasonable business moving coal around the Midlands but no capital left to build extra lengths of canal. The company promoting a canal from Birmingham to Fazeley offered (1782) to build some of the Coventry's line (Fazeley-Fradley) if the Coventry did the rest (Atherstone-Fazeley). When all was done (1790) the Coventry bought back some of their line. Birmingham and Fazeley did not number their bridges and to this day those without numbers show the part they retained. (Fazeley-Whittington).

Management
British Waterways, Alrewas Tel: 01283 790236
Coventry Canal Society Tel: 024 7661 1198

◊ **Huddlesford Junction**
Turn west for Chasewater! Not yet maybe but this line of moorings marks the end of 10 miles of canal restoration which could increase visitors to Lichfield, Brownhills and the National Forest around Cannock. It needs restoration of 30 locks and a short length of new canal in open country (2 miles, 8 locks) to join with eight locks leading down to the Staffordshire and Worcestershire Canal and thus create one side of a one week cruising 'golden triangle' via Great Haywood and Fradley.
Approach from M42 J10. Use A5 / A51 going north. Turn right to Whittington

◊ **Atherstone Locks** (11 rising 80 feet)
The only locks (bar two at Glascote) on the Coventry. They pass down from this Georgian market town into the countryside of the Anker valley. Medieval football can be seen on Shrove Tuesday.
Approach from M42 J10. Use A5 going south-east.

◊ **Hartshill Yard** (British Waterways)
Example of careful stewardship of run-of-the-mill buildings which allows us to understand working methods in the horse and cart era.
Approach from M42 J10. Use A5 going south-east and turn right beyond Atherstone.

◊ **Marston Junction**
Pivot point of 52 miles of relaxing lock free boating. 8 miles from the Atherstone flight, 8 miles from Coventry terminus, 21 miles from Snarestone and, if you discount the Oxford Canal's single stop lock at Hawkesbury, 20 miles from the Hillmorton flight.
Approach from M6 J3. Use B4113 to Bedworth.

◊ **Sutton Stop** (Hawkesbury Junction)
Mr Sutton and his sons were lock keepers here in the 1800s but the junction and gauging lock had only been opened up (1785) after 14 years of argument between the Coventry and Oxford canal companies.

Tariffs were charged by the distance travelled. The Oxford had tried to make a connection close to Sir Roger Newdigate's Griff Collieries to the north but, to start with, the Coventry only allowed a junction at Longford. This meant boatmen had to travel for two useless miles and pay extra fees. The 'Greyhound' pub now overlooks the basin and watery hairpin bend formed when the spit of land between the canals was removed. The old Oxford line can just be seen in the undergrowth.
Approach from M6 J3. Turn off into B4113 and north under the motorway, then right into Blacksmith Rd.

◊ **Cash's Hundreds**
Three storey weavers' houses built around a large square. In the centre, a steam engine supplied power to a pulley shaft running along the whole length of the roof of each terrace. The third storey of each individual house gave good daylight onto the looms. Joseph Cash started the engine each morning but the weavers themselves decided whether to work. No goods, no pay! The square was never complete but

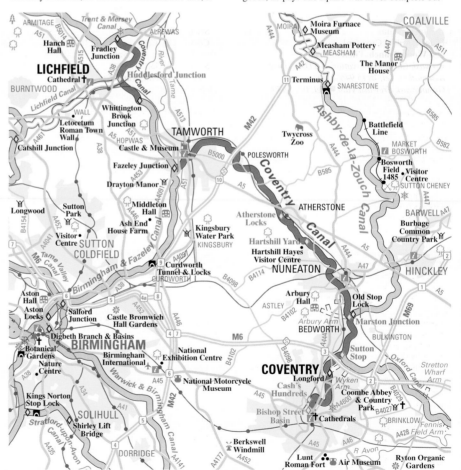

37 houses now provide the basis for apartments.
Approach from M6 J3. Use A444 to J1 on the City Centre Ring Road. Then north on B4098 (J9) for 200 yards. turn right (east).
◊ **Bishop Street Basin: Coventry**
With footbridge access to the city centre over a wide inner ring road, the terminal basin has been restored (1984) and old warehouses (1914) now do duty as offices. The canal society looks after one of the original weighbridges (1769).
Approach from M6 J3. Use A444 into the city, turn right at the inner ring road.

※ **Boat Trips**
Coventry *Coventrian* Tel: 024 7625 8864

ℹ **Tourist Information**
Coventry Tel: 024 7683 2303
Lichfield Tel: 01543 252109
Tamworth Tel: 01827 311222

•••••••••••••••••••••••••••••••••

Crake, River   118 A1
River Leven to Penny Bridge
Cray, River
- see **Dartford and Crayford Navigation**
Crinan Canal   120 A1
Crinan to Ardrishaig
9 miles, 15 wide locks
British Waterways, Lochgilphead
Tel: 01546 603210
Cromford Canal   116 A1
Langley Mill to Cromford
Lea Wood Branch, Pinxton Branch
Erewash Canal Preservation and Development Association Tel: 0115 946 4479
Groundwork Erewash Valley Tel: 0115 949 0235
Crouch, River   113 E1
Sea to Battlesbridge
17½ miles, 0 locks
Crouch Harbour Authority, Burnham-on-Crouch
Tel: 01903 820692
Croydon Canal   113 D2
Grand Surrey Canal to Croydon
Cuckmere, River   113 D4
Sea to Alfriston
Environment Agency, Worthing Tel: 01903 820692
Cyfarthfa Canal   114 C4
Canaid Brook to Cyfarthfa

Dartford and Crayford Navigation   113 D2
River Thames to Dartford
River Cray Branch to Crayford
2¾ miles, 1 lock
Port of London Authority Tel: 020 8265 2656
Dart, River   111 D3
Sea to Totnes
10¼ miles, 0 locks
Dart Harbour Authority, Dartmouth
Tel: 01803 832337
Dearne and Dove Canal   119 D3
Swinton Junction to Barnsley Canal
Elsecar Branch, Worsbrough Branch
Barnsley Canal Group Tel: 01909 565225
Deben, River   117 E3
Felixstowe Ferry to Woodbridge
11 miles, 0 locks
Suffolk Coastal District Council, Woodbridge
Tel: 01394 383789

Sutton Stop: Hawkesbury Junction between the Oxford and Coventry Canals. Manhandling of laden boats was frequently required. Robert Longden photograph (late 1960s) from A Canal People, Sonia Rolt, Sutton Publishing, Stroud 1997.

Dee (Flintshire), River   118 A4-B4
Sea to Farndon
Chester City Council Tel: 01224 325681
Dee (Dumfries and Galloway), River 120 C3
Sea to New Galloway
- see also **Carlingwark Canal**
Derby Canal   115 F1
Swarkestone to Sandiacre
Little Eaton Branch, Phoenix Branch to River Derwent in Derby, **Swarkestone Branch**
Derby and Sandiacre Canal Society
Tel: 0115 939 5592
Derwent (Cumbria), River   120 C4
Workington to Cockermouth
Derwent (Derbyshire), River   115 E1-F1
Derwent Mouth to Derby
Derwent (Yorkshire) Navigation   119 D2-E1
Barmby-on-the-Marsh to Yedingham
Environment Agency, Leeds Tel: 0113 244 0191
Dewsbury Old Cut
- see **Aire & Calder Navigation**
Dick Brook   115 D2
River Severn to Astley
Doctor's Canal   114 C4
Dynea to Treforest
Don Navigation, River
- see **Sheffield and South Yorkshire Navigation**
Don, River   119 D3
Goole to Fishlake
Includes **Dutch River** Goole to New Bridge
12¼ miles, 0 locks
Navigable Sections: *British Waterways, Doncaster Tel: 01302 340610*
Donnington Wood Canal   115 D1
Wombridge Canal, Donnington Wood to Pave Lane
Dorset and Somerset Canal   111 F1
Frome to Nettlebridge
Dorset and Somerset Canal Study Group
Tel: 01761 434618

Douglas Navigation   118 B3
Ribble Estuary to Wigan
11¼ miles, 8 locks
Dovey (Dyfi), River   114 B2
Sea to Cemmaes Road
Driffield Navigation   119 E2
Aike to Driffield
Corps Landing Branch, Foston Mills Branch, Frodingham Beck
11 miles, 6 locks
The Driffield Navigation, 70 Middle Street South, Driffield, East Yorkshire YO25 7QF
Driffield Navigation Amenities Association,
Tel: 01377 252412
Droitwich (Barge) Canal   115 D2
Hawford to Droitwich
5¾ miles, 8 locks
Droitwich Junction Canal   115 E2
Droitwich to Hanbury Wharf
Droitwich Canals Trust Ltd, Tel: 01905 774225
Dudley No 1 Canal - see **BCN**
Dudley No 2 Canal - see **BCN**
Dutch River - see **River Don**

Earl of Ashburnham's Canal   114 A4
Sea to Ffrwd
Bowser's (Coal) Level
Earn, River   123 D4
River Tay to Bridge of Earn
6 miles, 0 locks
Port of Dundee Ltd (Buddon Ness to Balmerino), Dundee Tel: 01382 224121
Perthshire and Kinross Unitary Authority (Balmerino to Perth), Perth
Tel: 01738 624056
Eden, River   121 D3
Solway Firth to Carlisle

Edinburgh

Edinburgh and Glasgow
Union Canal
120 C1 - 121 D1

Opened: 1822
Engineers: Baird, Telford
Falkirk to Lochrin Basin, Edinburgh
30 lock free miles, 1 filled in lock ladder, 3 aqueducts, 1 tunnel

Thirty miles of level towpath making spectacular river crossings of Almond (5 arch aqueduct 420' x 76' high) Avon (12 arches 810' long x 86' high), and Water of Leith (8 arches 500' x 75' high).

Thirty two years after the Forth and Clyde Canal was open Baird designed a contour canal from central Edinburgh to join up to it at the top of the existing 16 lock flight leading down to Grangemouth.

Management and Restoration
British Waterways, Glasgow Tel: 0141 332 6936
Scottish Inland Waterways Assoc. Tel: 0131 443 2533
Linlithgow Union Canal Society Tel: 01506 671215
Website: http://www.millenniumlink.org.uk

◊ **Millennium Link: Interchange Wheel**
Replacement for the filled in, 11 lock ladder (1933). A new length of Union Canal will tunnel (700 feet) under the Antonine Wall then leap across a new aqueduct (600 feet) to meet the interchange wheel.
Approach from M80 J4. Use A803 going east.
◊ **Falkirk Tunnel** (2800 feet)
A handrail protects towpath walkers inside this unlit tunnel, Scotland's oldest. Torches recommended!
From M80 J4. Use A803 east / B8028 south.
◊ **Avon Aqueduct**
12 arch structure is the second largest in Britain, 2½ miles to the west of Linlithgow.
From M9 J4, use A801 going south, B825 east.

◊ **Linlithgow Loch**
Lochside circular footpath has classic views of Linlithgow Palace and is only a half mile walk from the free Canal Museum at Manse Road Basin. (Walk through the town, past St Michael's Church to join just south of the railway station.)
Approach from M9 J4. Use A803 going east, B9080.
◊ **Wester Hailes** (One mile blockage)
3 miles from the Edinburgh terminus. This blockage will be one of the final efforts of the lottery project.
(Currently you have to follow the pavements of residential roads; ask for Calder Crescent, Calder Grove, Murrayburn Drive, Hallesland Road and Park to Tesco's and Dumbryden Road). From M8 J1, use A71 / B701 signposted to Calder Crescent.
◊ **Leamington Lift Bridge**
'Four-poster' lift bridge at the entrance to Lochrin Basin was formerly located at Fountainbridge.
Approach from M8 J1. Use A71 City Centre (east).

⚓ **Boat Trips**
Ratho *Pride of Belhaven, Pride of Union,* Ratho
Princess Tel: 0131 333 1320
Linlithgow *Victoria, St Magdalene* (electric)
Tel: 01506 842123

⚓ **Community Boat**
Ratho, Falkirk *Seagull* Tel: 0131 229 1789

ℹ **Tourist Information**
Falkirk Tel: 01324 620244
Linlithgow Tel: 01506 844600
Edinburgh Tel: 0131 473 3800

· ·

Ellesmere Canal (later part of **Ellesmere and Chester Canal**) - see **Shropshire Union Canal**
Ellesmere and Chester Canal - see **Shropshire Union Canal**

Ely Ouse - see **Great Ouse Navigation**
Emmet's Canal   **118 C2**
Blue Hills to Emmet's Foundry near Birkinshaw
Erewash Canal - see **Grand Union Canal**
Exe, River   **111 D2**
Exmouth to Topsham and King's Arms Sluice (Exeter Canal Basin) to Exe Bridge, Exeter
Exeter City Council, Exeter Tel: 01392 274306
Exeter & Crediton Navigation (unfinished) **111 D2**
Exe Bridge for half a mile north
Exeter Ship Canal   **111 D2**
Turf Lock to Exeter
5¼ miles, 2 wide locks
Exeter City Council, Exeter Tel: 01392 274306

Fairburn Canal - see **Aire & Calder Navigation**
Falloch, River   **122 C4**
Loch Lomond to Inverarnon Canal
Fal, River   **110 B4**
Sea to Truro River
Truro Harbour Office, Truro Tel: 01872 72130
Farcet River or Pig Water
- see **Middle Level Navigations**
Fleet Canal   **113 D2**
River Thames to Holborn Bridge
Fletcher's Canal   **118 B3**
Clifton Junction to Fletcher's Collieries, Clifton
2¾ miles, 0 locks
Forth and Cart Junction Canal   **120 B1**
River Clyde to Forth and Clyde Canal, Whitecrook

Forth and Clyde Canal   120 B1-C1
Opened: Kirkintilloch 1773, Glasgow 1777, Bowling 1790
Engineers: Smeaton, Mackey, Whitworth
25 miles upstream of Edinburgh on the Carron at Grangemouth to 10 miles downstream of Glasgow on the Clyde
Branch to Glasgow, linked to Monkland Canal
36 miles, 39 wide locks mainly in the major flights dropping to the estuaries from Glasgow and Falkirk

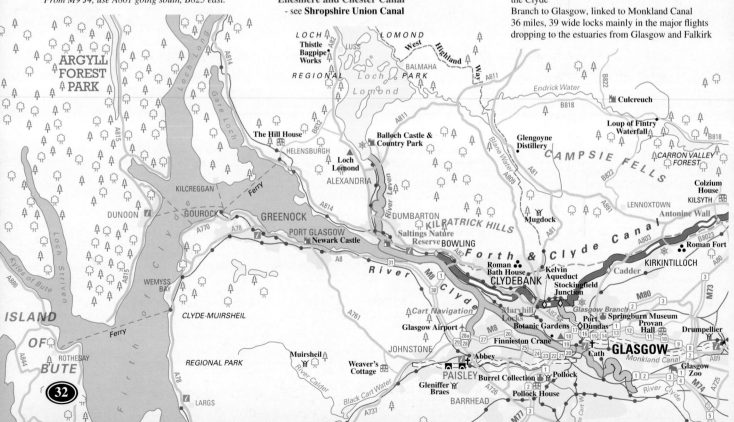

Assistance from the lottery is providing almost half the costs of recovering from the decision (1963) to close this canal which halted regular sea-to-sea passage of herring fishingboats and many pleasure craft.

The canal is wider and deeper than most, having locks big enough for small sea going craft (68 feet long x 20 feet wide). All major roads that cross it once permitted full mast headroom by using rolling or swing bridges and the minor roads used two leaf bascules. Many are to be renovated although modern masts will need adjustment.

In days of sail it was tempting to contemplate avoiding the trip around the Hebrides that had sunk the Spanish Armada. King Charles thought to make the connection for his warships (1650) and the final section from Glasgow to the Clyde was finished with the help of a Government loan (1784).

The company owed much to the energy of its chief shareholder, Lord Dundas, who lived in London but whose estates surrounded the eastern end at Falkirk and Grangemouth. He encouraged many pioneering experiments. *Charlotte Dundas,* the first steam driven narrowboat (1788), pulled two other loaded narrowboats on a windy day (1803) from Lock 20 for 20 miles in 6 hours. *Comet,* the first commercial steamboat (1812), and *Vulcan,* the first iron hulled passenger boat (1818). *Cyclops,* a New Orleans style paddle boat (1830). They even tried hauling by a bank mounted locomotive for 1 mile above Lock 16 (1839).

Following trials on the Paisley Canal super-narrow 'swiftboats' (pulled for 2 miles at a time by changing pairs of horses) were introduced (1831) and halved the journey time to Glasgow.

Passenger services ran four times a day and even (1841) included nightly 'sleeper' services. They only

Trip boat 'Victoria' at Linlithgow Manse Basin

stopped when railways bought out the service (1849).

The wide beamed Clyde 'puffers' were preceded by excursion steamers named after 'Queens', introduced by James Aitkin & Co. (1893), and lasted for over 40 years (1939).

Management and Restoration

British Waterways, Glasgow Tel: 0141 332 6936
Scottish Inland Waterways Assoc. Tel: 0131 443 2533
Forth and Clyde Canal Society Tel: 0141 776 3812
Forth and Clyde Canal Community Project
Tel: 0141 332 9115 ext 19
Website: http://www.linnet.co.uk/lucs

◊ **Saltings Nature Reserve: Bowling**
Flooded grasslands near the Bowling Basin and harbour. Noted for orchids, excellent level footpaths and a living willow sculpture.
From M8 J30, use M898 / A82 going north-west and A814 east.

◊ **Maryhill Locks**
Five locks run up to a stone built Lock 20 which leads onto the 16 mile summit pound. Four arch massive stone aqueduct over River Kelvin (400' x 70' high), bascule bridges, dry dock and the beginning of the Glasgow branch to Port Dundas.
Approach from M8 J17. Use A18 going north.

◊ **Cadder**
Burke and Hare, bodysnatchers, used the canal for a fast getaway from churchyards that provided their source material. Cadder still has an empty grave.
Approach from M8 J15. Use A803 going north.

◊ **Antonine Wall: Kilsyth**
Forts were built along the wall by the Romans. Canalside remains are at Twechar, Barhill and Kilsyth. Long stretches of the wall are still visible and parts form links in local walks.
From M73 J3, use A80 / B802 going north.

◊ **Lock 16: Port Downie** (Union Inn)
'Shelter' at the end of a 30 mile, practically lock free run from Glasgow. Passengers from the 'swiftboats' changed to early stagecoaches to Edinburgh. Later, when the Union Canal's new 11 lock flight came down from their single 30 mile level, they walked the flight as this was quicker than waiting for the boat to work the locks.
Approach from M80 J4. Use A803 going east.

✱ **Boat Trips**
Kirkintilloch *Gypsy Princess, Janet Telford, Ferry Queen* Tel: 0141 772 1620

✱ **Community Boat**
Glasgow *Nolly Barge* Tel: 0141 336 7859

ℹ **Tourist Information**
Glasgow Tel: 0141 204 4400
Falkirk Tel: 01324 620244

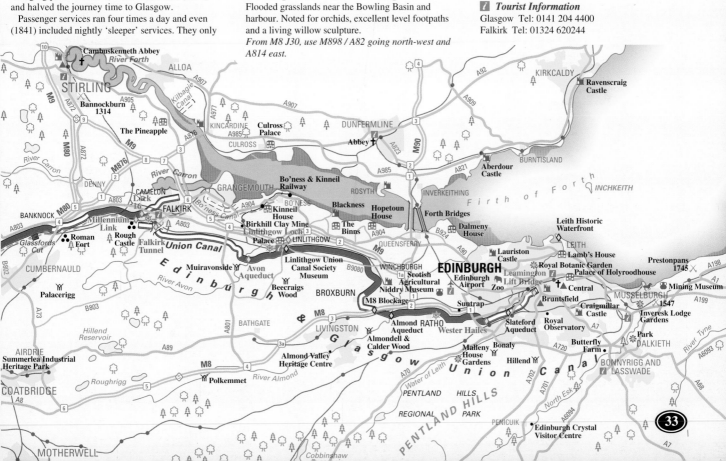

Forth and Clyde
Antonine Wheel

Close to the Roman Fort at Roughcastle and also to the best preserved section of the Antonine Wall, a type of 'Ferris Wheel for Boats' is destined to become the Eighth Wonder of the Waterways.

It will be the only change in level along 69 miles of Lowland Canals between Glasgow and Edinburgh.

Two balanced pairs of boat caissons are suspended from a pair of structural wheels. At the beginning of each cycle each pair will be at the level of one of the canals whilst boats enter and leave. The tiny motors will then turn the precisely balanced wheels through 180° and, when each pair has come to rest roughly 15 minutes later, the boats will be let out at the other canal level.

This magnificent structure, which will give foot passengers and cyclists the same panoramic views offered to boats, is a modern day substitute for the 11 lock flight between the Union and Forth and Clyde Canals (filled in 1933).

Lowland Canals: 'Unlocking the Future'
This was the subtitle of the British Waterways successful bid to the Millennium Commission for funds to match those already pledged from the many partnership organisations. These include Scottish Enterprise and European Union, commercial organisations and local authorities along the route of the two historic canals.

After many nail biting negotiations, the reopening of these deep and wide canals will create a waterway route running from City to City and Sea to Sea.

These dimensions allow Northern European boats to make the journey. 900 a year already cross

Scotland's other coast to coast canal... the Caledonian Canal.

Many people live close to the route and many visitors will come. Over 7 million visits are already made along the unimproved towpath, and over 10 million a year are expected when the job is done.

The project is expected to generate over 4000 jobs and will have cost approximately £78 million when it is substantially completed in Easter 2001.

Further information available from:-
Millennium Linkline Tel: 0345 952000
http://www.millenniumlink.org.uk

Forth, River   **120** C1
Sea to Stirling
14½ miles, 0 locks
Forth Ports Authority, Grangemouth
Tel: 01324 482591

Forty Foot River (Vermuyden's Drain)
- see **Middle Level Navigations**

Foss Navigation   **119** D2
York to Sherrif Hutton
1¼ miles, 1 lock
City of York Tel: 01904 613161

Fossdyke Navigation   **119** E4
Opened: AD90, improved 1121, 1675, 1744
Engineers: Romans, Henry I, Scribo, Jessop
Torksey Junction to Brayford Pool, Lincoln
11 miles, 1 wide lock

Plain and straight with retention banks on either side, the damp towpath makes cycling tiresome and walking a matter of exercise.

The Romans brought supplies up the Trent and across the Lincolnshire plain along this oldest artificial navigation in Britian. The cut also acts as drainage dyke for the surrounding fenlands.

Management and Restoration
British Waterways, Newark Tel: 01636 704481
Restoration Society Tel: 01606 862411

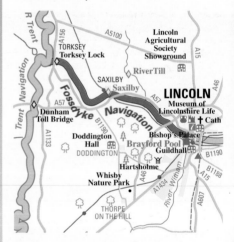

◊ **Saxilby**
The significant event on a journey along Fossdyke. Banks protect vast acreages of agricultural fenland on the approach to this isolated town. The broad waterway flows between formal and informal services connected by a metal-trellis footbridge repositioned (1987), from railway lines at Newark.
From A1 / A57 junction at Markham, use A57 west.

◊ **River Till**
The canalised river Till provides the navigable route from Odder to Lincoln, although the Romans may have chosen a slightly different line. The river drains the surrounding fens, fine in summer but adds to the interest of navigation on rainy winter days.
From A1 / A57 junction at Markham, use A57 west.

i **Tourist Information**
Lincoln Tel: 01522 529828

Lincoln: Brayford Pool
Swans, shops on a bridge and a 700 year old port.

Hill top castle walls and cathedral towers dominate Brayford Pool. Forty miles from the sea and once a destination for Roman galleys and Viking longships, the pool is close to the markets and shopping streets of the lower city and the setting for a new University.

Start the short stroll from:-
1 Five seats overlook the water at the western end of the pool close to the Wigford Way road bridge.
Sitting here
- look left, boats in the marina, University Buildings (1996)
- look right, Royal William IV pub, a trip boat boarding point and the long poolside walk of Brayford Wharf North
Go up onto the pavement of the road bridge, cross the river and back under the road. Walk (east) away from the pool. Push past the Solicitors' building and follow the railings to:-

2 High Bridge aka Glory Hole
Trouble was, the hole was not big enough to allow keels from the Yorkshire navigations through towards Boston. The single span Norman bridge was also shallow underneath. Jessop solved the problem. The archway was underpinned (1795) and dredging keeps 3-4 feet of water below. Half timbered Tudor shops still line the bridge.
Steps ⚠ lead up to the High Street Shops. Turn left to see:-

3 Stonebow
The southern gate to the medieval city on the hill (1400s). With the Guildhall above, this archway leads up to Steep Hill, Bailgate and specialist shops, the Cathedral (1072), Lincoln Castle (1068), built on the site of a Roman fortress (AD54) and containing an original copy of **Magna Carta**, plus the Bishop's Old Palace and The Lawn.
Cross High Street and go down to join the swans at the 'Waterside'. There is ramp access to the south bank. Alternatively there are steps ⚠ to the north bank. Shops face the navigation from both sides. The banks are formed with huge stone edges and chains to hold onto if you fall in. Cross the new cast iron bridge to:-

4 Central Markets
Daily open and covered markets originally supplied with farm produce direct from barges at the riverside.
Enter pedestrianised Sincil Street, go clockwise around the market buildings, past the Tourist Information Centre into Cornhill Square (1879).

Return to **1 Five seats** *by crossing High Street again, passing through the square around St Benedicts and out at the end into the pedestrian underpass below Wigford Way.*

A longer walk around the Pool
Start from **1 Five seats** *walk south along Brayford Wharf East and turn right along the southern shore of:-*
5 Brayford Pool
Romans excavated a natural lake to create this inland port at the end of their canal from Torksey on the River Trent, thus connecting to their garrison at York (AD 90 - AD 600). Danes used this canal (Fossdyke) to invade the city, and set up one of their five 'burghs' extracting Danegeld from the natives.

Lincoln was once (1200s) England's fourth largest port.

In the 1700s and 1800s barges carried all manner of goods from Boston and the Wash to the Trent and Mersey Canal, rivers in Yorkshire and thus the rest of the waterways system. The pool was fronted with grain warehouses, maltsters, breweries and mills.

Carrying stopped on the Witham (1952) and Fossdyke (1972) but now, after a new trust cleared over 20 sunken boats from the pool, it is acquiring a new lease of life.
Pass in front of the Canoe Club, the University buildings, Marina Health Club and The Hogshead pub to long steps ⚠ up to the new high level road bridge. Use this bridge to cross over Fossdyke and turn right at the end into Brayford Wharf North and return along the waterside to the Royal William IV pub and **1 Five seats.**

Getting there:
Approach from A1 at Newark. Use A46 / A1434 / A15 going north-east.
P *Over the bus station. Join at* **4** *.*
♿ *Around Brayford Wharf North*
⇌ *From the station exit go to the High Street. Turn north into pedestrian area. Join at* **2** *.*

Landranger Map 121 **Ref SK 97 71**

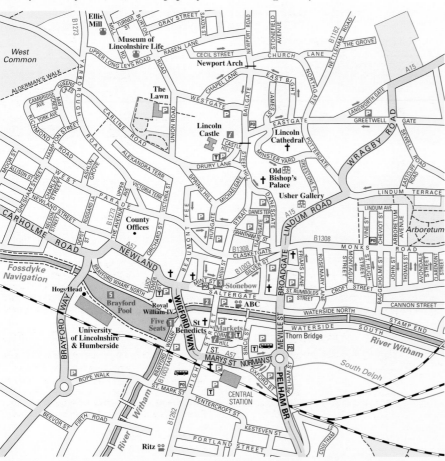

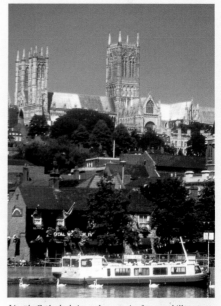

Lincoln Cathedral sits at the summit of a steep hill overlooking Brayford Pool.

Fowey, River   **110 B3**
Sea to Lostwithiel
7 miles, 0 locks
Fowey Harbour Commissioners, Fowey
Tel: 01726 832471

Frome, River   **111 F3**
Poole Harbour to Wareham
7¾ miles, 0 locks
Environment Agency, Worthing Tel: 01903 820692

Galton's Canal   **111 E1**
River Brue to North Drain

General Warde's Canal (Dafen)   **114 B4**
Llwynhendy to Dafen Pill

General Warde's Canal (Yspitty)   **114 B4**
Yspitty to Bynea

Giant's Grave and Briton Ferry Canal
- see **Neath Canal**

Gibson's (Tattershall) Canal
- see **Horncastle Navigation**

Gipping, River
- see **Ipswich and Stowmarket Navigation**

Glamorganshire Canal   **114 C4**
Cardiff to Merthyr Tydfil

Glan-y-Wern Canal   **114 B4**
Red Jacket Pill (River Neath) to Glan-y-Wern
(Crymlyn Bog) Later part incorporated into **Red
Jacket Canal** and then **Tennant Canal**
- see **Tennant Canal**

Glasgow, Paisley and Johnstone   **120 B1**
(or Ardrossan) Canal Port Eglinton to Johnstone
Paisley Canal and Waterways Society,
Iain Morrison (Sec), 19 Greenhill Crescent,
Elderslie, Johnstone PA5 9AW

Glastonbury Canal   **111 E1**
Highbridge to Glastonbury
Somerset Inland Waterways Society
Tel: 01278 652681

Glen Navigation, River   **117 C2**
Greatford to River Welland
11½ miles, 0 locks
Environment Agency, Lincoln Tel: 01522 513100

Gloucester and Sharpness Canal
     115 D4
(formerly **Gloucester and Berkeley Ship Canal**)
Opened: 1827
Engineers: Clowes, Mylne, Dadford
Sharpness Tidal Basin to Gloucester Docks
16 miles, wide tidal locks at each end

**Built to bypass the tortuous meanders of the tidal
reaches of the River Severn. Only finished after
two injections of public money, it allows ships of
600 tons to a pass from the pilotage of the
estuary, bypass the tidal reaches of the River
Severn and arrive at Gloucester Docks or
upstream at Tewkesbury.**

Management
Gloucester Docks Tel: 01452 318000
Sharpness Harbourmaster Tel: 01453 811644

◊ **Gloucester Docks** (Tours Tel: 01452 311190)
Locks on the upstream side of the main basin hold
the water in the dock at constant level for tall ships
and boats of all kinds. Fifteen warehouses around
three basins and two dry docks are silent witness to
the former huge trade of this inland port. Cafes,
restaurants and bars, compete for attention with
museums celebrating soldiering, advertising and
packaging... and for the story of waterways. The
National Waterway Museum.
*Approach from M5 J11. Use A40 west, follow the
brown 'Historic Docks' tourist signs.*

◊ **Duck Decoy**
Food for 19th Century tables was provided by wild
ducks that migrated to these wetlands. They were
caught by a duck decoy set in woodlands close to
the line of the canal. The coming of the canal
reduced its effectiveness and it has now been moved
to assist in research in the Slimbridge Wildfowl and
Wetlands Reserve. (Tel: 01453 890333)
Approach from M5 J14. Use A38 going north.

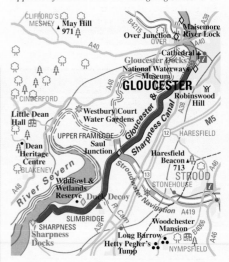

◊ **Sharpness Docks**
Two tidal basins where ships could await the right
tide levels before venturing into the estuary. The
second (1874) was built to take larger vessels
almost 50 years after the first was opened (1827).
    Magnificent views across the wide expanses of the
Severn estuary.
From M5 J14, use A38 / B4066 going north.

ℹ **Tourist Information**
Gloucester Tel: 01452 421188
Stroud Tel: 01453 765768

• •

National Waterways Museum

Gloucester Docks: National Waterways Museum
in the **Llanthony Warehouse** and **Barge Basin.**
Only closed on Christmas Day, displays include full size
exhibits on three floors, stables, blacksmiths workshop,
forge, engine house and a vast selection from the British
Waterways National Collection. Café, bookshop and
children's corner with waterplay area, model locks etc.
    Outside the warehouse special events show how
ropes, railways, cranes and horses were used on the
waterways. In the basin is a huge steam dredger and
examples of many types of older tugs, barges, leisure
and pleasure craft including an experiment to make
narrowboats of concrete!
    Go aboard some of them and, if you want a short ride,
Queen Boadicia II was a little ship that went to Dunkirk
and is now doing duty as a trip boat from outside the
Vining Warehouse.
    A visit could take all day!

Exhibits in the museum

Getting there
*Llanthony Warehouse is at the southern end of
Gloucester Docks. To get there:-*
*By Car: Approach from M5 J11. Use A40 west to St
Oswalds Road just before the Bridge over the river.
Turn south along the Quay and follow the brown
tourist signs 'Historic Docks' to the main entrance on
Southgate Street. Car Parks are inside.*
*By Train or Bus: These stations are together.
From either, walk towards the Cathedral Tower,
down Northgate Street, cross the centre of the Roman
city into Southgate Street.
The main entrance is just to the south.*
Museum Information Tel: 01452 318054
Gloucester Docks Events Tel: 01452 311190

Grand Union Canal 115 E2-112 D2

Created by merger: 1920
167 miles, over 166 locks
Brentford to Birmingham and Langley Mill

The main route of the Grand Union runs through lush valleys and past attractive market towns. A fully restored towing path (1993) provides a long gentle alternative to fell walking. The main slopes are from Brentford (3 feet) up to Tring Cutting (395 feet) in 33 miles and from Warwick (190 feet) towards Kingswood (337 feet) in 7 miles. Smaller climbs are required over the tops of the two tunnels, neither of which are wide enough to include a path.

The Grand Union Canal is a waterway of many parts. Its oldest parts are wide navigations up the Rivers Soar and Erewash to Loughborough, Leicester and Heanor. Its wide central spine was built as the Grand Junction Canal (1800, 1805) from Braunston to the tidal Thames in London.

Connecting Canals from Wedover (1799), Buckingham (1801), Weedon Barracks (1804), Market Harborough (1814), Northampton (1815), Aylesbury (1815), City of London (1816), East end of London (with the Lee Navigation 1830) and Slough (1882), eventually joined up various positions along its length. The most ambitious of these was the (Old) Grand Union from Foxton to Norton designed to link the northern system of river navigations to the central spine and its connecting canals.

Not all the connecting canals joined the company merger spearheaded by the Chairman of London's Regents Canal, Sir W.H. Curtis. Those that did underwent a vigorous overhaul which included Government sponsored reconstruction of the line

from Braunston to Birmingham (1934) to take the same wide beamed boats that could already travel from London to Braunston.

It was a bold decision, defeated in part, by the bottlenecks at Blisworth Tunnel (9000 feet long) and Braunston Tunnel (6000 feet long), which could accommodate wide beamed boats, but not two going in opposite directions.

Warwick Canals (1799) 115 E2-F2

Open: 1799, 1800
Engineers: Bull, Felkin, Witton, Handley

Warwick and Birmingham
Digbeth Junction to Warwick
23 miles, 32 narrow locks since widened, 1 tunnel
Warwick and Napton
14 miles, 25 narrow locks since widened
Warwick to the Oxford Canal at Napton

These narrow canals promoted at about the same time (1793/4). They joined end-to-end at Budbrook in Warwick, linking Birmingham via Digbeth to the end of the Grand Junction Canal at Braunston via a piece of the Oxford Canal.

Most of the post-merger reconstruction money was spent (1932) changing these canals and their locks into state-of-the art canals capable of taking big barges each of which could carry the equivalent of two modern lorries (70 tons), although the design idea was for 100 tons.

◊ **Fellows Morton and Clayton's Warehouse**
Birmingham depot of the carrying firm (1837-1949) which shunned coal traffic in favour of general merchandise. Known as 'Joshers' after Mr Fellows, the firm once owned over 200 boats.
Approach from A45 / A435 junction, going north-west.
◊ **Knowle Locks** (42 feet rise)
Side ponds and remains of the earlier narrow locks can be seen alongside the first wide locks going south.
Approach from M42 J5. Use A4141 east.

Hatton Lock Flight

◊ **Kingswood Junction**
Short tree lined branch to the Stratford-upon-Avon Canal.
Approach from M42 J4. Use A3400 going south.
◊ **Shrewley Tunnel** (1300 feet)
Horses had their own underpass below the village of Shrewley Common. Now used by walkers.
Approach from M42 J5. Use A4141 east.
◊ **Hatton Lock Flight** (146 feet rise)
21 locks climb out of Warwick, built wide and strong with paddle gear hidden in silver capsules. A long haul for push chairs, it is a major achievement for boaters.
Approach from M40 J15. Use A46 & A4177 going west.
◊ **Stockton Lock Flight** (54 feet rise)
An eerie collection of overgrown, abandoned works alongside the canal once used the local Blue Lias Limestone to make lime fertiliser and cement. A modern works continues the trade but uses lorries for deliveries.
Approach from M6 J1. Use A426 going south.
◊ **Napton Junction**
Long distance boats using the stretch from here to Braunston paid exorbitant tolls to the owners, the Oxford Canal Company, and for many years kept them in sufficient dividends to fend off alien control by railways.
From M45 / B4429 junction. Use A45 south-east.

ℹ️ ***Tourist Information***
Leamington Spa Tel: 01926 311470
Birmingham NEC Tel: 0121 780 4321
Kenilworth Tel: 01926 852595

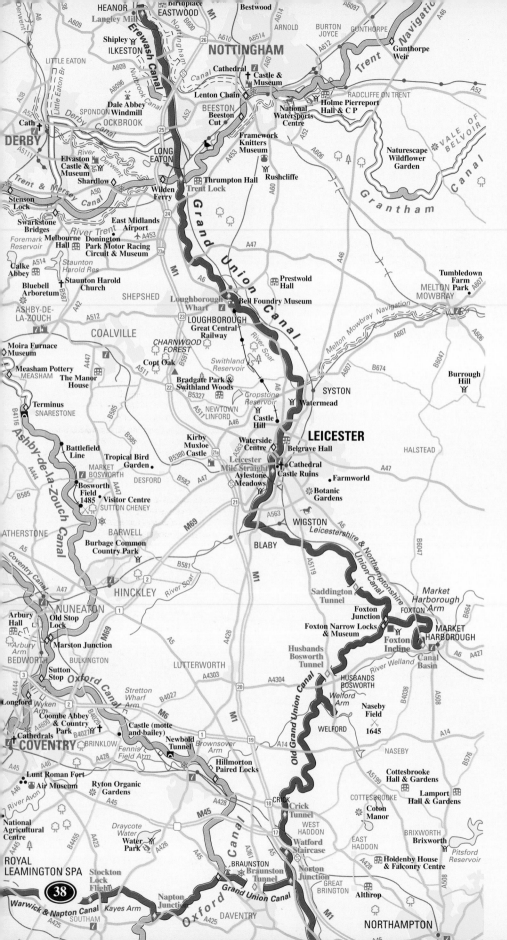

Erewash Canal and Soar River Navigation
119 D4

Opened: 1778, 1780, 1794, 1797, 1809-1932
Engineers: Smith, Varley, Jessop, Staveley
From the Trent to Market Harborough

Erewash Canal
From the Trent to Langley Mill
11 miles, 15 wide locks
Soar River Navigation
From the Trent to Loughborough and Leicester
16 miles, 11 wide locks
Leicestershire and Northamptonshire Union Canal
From Leicester to Market Harborough
34 miles, 24 wide locks, 1 tunnel

Early improvements to the River Soar (1776) took broad barges from the Trent as far as Loughborough and later works (1794) allowed them to reach Leicester. Navigation was extended by the construction of a wide canal to Market Harborough 15 years later (1809).

◊ **Langley Mill: Great Northern Basin**
Head of the Erewash Canal, foot of the Cromford Canal and formerly terminus of the Nottingham Canal, this basin was closed (1962), protested (1968), adopted (1972) and restored (1983). Thank the Erewash Canal Preservation and Development Association for that.
Approach from M1 J26. Use A610 going north-west.
◊ **Trent Lock**
Outlet onto a crossroads of water, complicated by a turbulant River Trent flowing over Thrumpton Weir.
Approach from M1 J25. Use B6002 / B6540 going south.

◊ **Loughborough Wharf and Chain Bridge**
Passing upstream of the wharf without paying tolls was prevented by a heavy chain put under the bridge at night.
Approach from M1 J23. Use A512 going east.
◊ **Leicester Mile Straight**
City-owned, tree-lined, flood-relief channel at the start of Leicestershire and Northamptonshire Union Canal.
Approach from M1 J22. Use A50 going south-east.
◊ **Saddington Tunnel**
Boats and bats share the gloom for 2600 feet.
From M69 and M1 J21. Use A563 / A6 going south.
◊ **Market Harborough Canal Basin** (1809)
With the support of Mr Peter Scott (Director of the Severn Wildfowl Trust), under the chairmanship of Robert Aickman and with LTC Rolt as its Secretary, the fledgeling Inland Waterways Association held its first (1950) 'Festival and Rally of Boats' to 'advance the cause of the waterways' in this basin. The event was held in conjunction with the Market Harborough Urban District Council and ration books had to be carried. The Docks and Inland Waterways Executive (unusually) passed boats at a 'single toll for the return journey'!!

The IWA returned here (1996) with another rally, this time celebrating its 50th anniversary. Today (1999) the warehouses and wharves are the subject of a waterside regeneration scheme, typical of many around the system.

Old Grand Union   115 F2

Opened: 1814
Engineers: Telford, Barnes, Bevan
From Norton Junction to Foxton Junction
23 miles, 17 narrow locks, 2 wide tunnels

A union between the wide waters of the Grand Junction and the river navigations reaching to Market Harborough was a splended vision. Unfortunately, economies were made when the Old Grand Union Canal was built which have proved to be the Achilles heel of the whole inland waterways system ever since. Designed as a wide canal with two wide tunnels on its long summit pound, the economies were made at each end. In the south, seven narrow locks up the Watford flight include a four lock staircase and in the north the ten lock flight at Foxton was also built to narrowboat dimensions. These two bottlenecks are all that presently stand in the way of heavily loaded barges travelling from Tilbury on the Thames to Hull on the Humber or Yorkshire towns such as Leeds, Wakefield, Goole and York.

◊ **Husbands Bosworth Tunnel** (3500 feet)
Approach from M1 J20. Use A4304 going east.
◊ **Crick Tunnel** (4580 feet)
Quicksands were discovered on the original alignment and the tunnel repositioned. Despite this it was opened on time.
Approach from M1 J18. Use A428 going east.
◊ **Watford Staircase**
On the long distance footpath known as Jurassic Way, a 7 lock flight (rebuilt 1902) up to the 20 mile summit pound is in a rural setting but with roaring roads nearby. Four staircase locks with side ponds are the centrepiece.
From M1 J18. Use A5, Watling Way, go west / south.

ℹ️ Tourist Information
Derby Tel: 01332 255802
Nottingham Tel: 0115 915 5330
Loughborough Tel: 01509 218113
Market Harborough Tel: 01858 821270

The Steamboat Inn at Trent Lock

Foxton Incline
Engineering design ahead of its time.

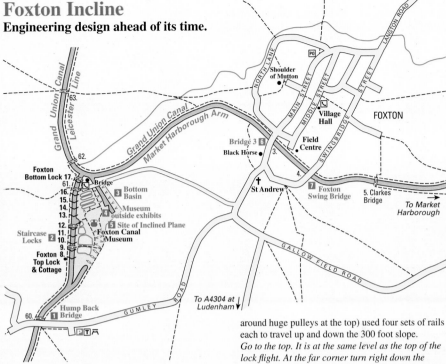

An independent tree lined footpath leads away from the County Council's picnic site to:-

1 Hump Back Bridge (Gumley Road)
Narrow tarmac crosses over the canal, but people have a wooden alternative (1974).
Go under the road, cross the footbridge to the main towpath. Turn north to the lock cottage and the:-
2 Staircase Locks
Special locks, where the tall bottom gates of the first lock are also the top gates of the second lock, and so on. Foxton has two five lock staircases.
*Go down past both staircases. Pass under Bridge 61 and continue to renovated Bridge 62. Turn across the bridge and head towards Market Harborough.
After 50 yards look across; under the brick bridge you can see boats floating (at the lowest level) on:-*
3 Bottom Basin of the Inclined Plane
Caissons of the inclined plane (80' x 15' x 5'deep) travelled down the steep tree covered slope on your right, dipped into this basin, opened their hydraulic doors and let the boats out onto the Leicestershire and Northamptonshire Union Canal. *Remember this view.
Go back across Bridge 62, across Lock 17 and up onto Bridge 61. Look over the parapet to see the double-height gates in close-up. Turn back past the pub and, just before the bottom basin, turn right up the slope to see:-*
4 Museum outside exhibits
Tipper trucks, ice breaker, stop lock gates and other large items each have a note attached. *Follow the slope past the side ponds of the locks, pass to the left of the stop lock gates and continue climbing onto the:-*
5 Site of the Inclined Plane (1900-1911)
You are halfway up a steady gradient of one in four, which once carried eight sets of railway lines (GWR broad gauge type). Two caissons (balancing each other

around huge pulleys at the top) used four sets of rails each to travel up and down the 300 foot slope.
Go to the top. It is at the same level as the top of the lock flight. At the far corner turn right down the sloping path, right again, and enter a renovated boiler house (excellent museum: small fee). All will now be revealed by models and video!
Alternatively, *go to the right of the stop lock gates at* **4***, follow the easier path to the museum.*

To return to the start at **1** *Bridge 60 cross the footbridge above the 'meeting place' pound to regain the main towpath and turn left... (no steps).
Alternatively, go past the museum back up the ⚠️ steps to* **5** *Site of the Inclined Plane, bear right by the old barge and follow the path crossing between the ponds (stunning views) to cross the footbridge at Lock 9 and regain the towpath, turn south to* **1** *Hump Back Bridge.*

A longer walk:-
Go from the towpath opposite **3** *and continue to:-*
6 Bridge 3: Foxton Village
Opposite is the former village wharf and forge.
To explore the village go up, left into Main Street, quickly right into Middle Street and, halfway down on the right, go through a gate and down an alleyway to Swingbridge Street. Turn right again, past 'The Old Manse' and Foxton Lodge up to this canal which once carved the village in two and find:-
7 Foxton Swing Bridge
Last version of the movable bridge to give access to the church further up the hill. *Continue left to other bridges connecting with other footpaths to explore the countryside, or right to return to* **3**

Getting there:
Approach from M1 J20. Use A4304 going east. Turn north at Lubenham, follow the brown signs.
🅿 *County Council Car Park, Gumley Road.*

Landranger Map 141 Ref SP 69 89

Marsworth Reservoirs
Huge nature reserves, broad and narrow canals.

A stroll around the start of the Aylesbury Arm of the Grand Union, (½ mile) or three waymarked walks (up to 6 miles) around man made reservoirs that attract many migrant birds to their reed beds.

Start the stroll from-
1 Lock 39 (counting from the Midlands)
Lock 39 is served by a large car park. It is bottom of a flight of seven, easing the canal down from Bulbourne at the end of the Tring cutting (summit level). A typical broad lock, it can take one barge from the Thames or a pair of narrow boats side by side. When opened (as the Grand Junction Canal) narrow boats were expected to travel in pairs, thus making full use of the locking water drawn down from the nearby reservoirs. Later, in 1838, the Canal became so busy that a narrow lock was built alongside every broad lock, thus reducing the bottleneck effect for single boats moving alone. Look for the remains of this second lock, and the second arch to the road bridge that was built at the same time.

2 Bridge 132
Overlooks Lock 39. Hump backed over the wide canal, it has no pavements and the road is so narrow that it has to be controlled by traffic lights. The Lower Iknield Way uses this bridge. Cross with care.
There are two towing paths. Go down beside the White Lion pub onto the south bank, past the moored narrowboats, and keep left into:-

3 Marsworth Junction
At the end of a canal that failed to get to the intended destination on the Thames at Abingdon. It made it as far as Aylesbury.

4 Locks 1 and 2
These narrow locks are the first of another flight of seven which complete the drop into the Vale of Aylesbury. These are so close together that the bottom gates of the first are double height and are the same pieces of wood as the top gates of the second, known as a 'staircase'. If a boat is about to enter, wait and see the fun!
Return to the start at **1 Lock 39** *by going up onto the cart track bridge and follow Watery Lane to the B489 road and the two pubs. Pay a visit to the* **5 British Waterways Offices** *across the canal or:-*

A longer walk would start:-
From **1 Lock 39** *Walk uphill towards Lock 40. At the* **6 Information Board** *you can take one of three trails waymarked by British Waterways around their four huge reservoirs built as part of the Grand Junction Canal in the early 1800s.*
   Water comes from natural springs and from the streams off the Chiltern Hills, it is pumped up by the **7 Tringford Pumping Station** into the Wendover Arm at the level of the canal summit. It is then drawn down by the lockful with every boat passing, either north-bound towards Fenny Stratford or south-bound towards Berkhamsted.

ℹ Tourist Information
Berkhampsted *Tel: 01442 877638*
British Waterways **5** - on site *Tel: 01442 825938*

Getting there:
🚗 Approach from M1 J5. Use A505 west to Dunstable then B489 towards Tring.
🅿 Opposite the White Lion.
🚉 Tring and a long towpath.

Landranger Map 165 Ref SP 92 14

Grand Junction Canal   115 F3-112 C1
Opened: 1800
Engineers: Jessop, Barnes
Braunston on the Oxford to River Thames at Brentford
93 miles, 101 locks in all

Long distance carrying business from Birmingham boomed on the Oxford Canal the minute it opened onto the Thames allowing boats to reach London (1790).
   A more direct route to London was possible but it involved crossing hills near Daventry, the River Ouse at Wolverton and the Chilterns at Tring. Proprietors of the Grand Junction Canal took up the challenge (1793). Only four years later goods were flowing along the broad beamed 93 mile route, despite having to load and reload from barges onto a temporary double track horse tramway around Blisworth Tunnel (till 1805).

◊ **Braunston Tunnel** (6126 feet)
The footpath over the top is marked by the ventilation shafts which give air and drip water onto boats below. Limitations of early survey techniques have left this tunnel with a double kink half way through.
From M45 / B4429 junction. Use A45 going south.
◊ **Rotherthorpe Lock Flight**
Fourteen narrow locks within two miles, with long views over Northampton. This route links the canal system with the River Nene, Peterborough and the system of Fenland waterways leading to Cambridge. Country lanes between Gayton, Milton Malsor and Rotherthorpe villages give access to the towpath.
Approach from M1 J15a. Use A43 north and double back left at the first roundabout into a small lane.
◊ **Blisworth Tunnel** (9168 feet)
At present (1999) the longest navigable tunnel in Britian, it proved very troublesome to build. Flooding halted initial construction and a new alignment was chosen. Work did not start until two years after revenue was flowing from the rest of the line. It took 3 years to finish. For over 60 years boats moved by 'legging it' through the tunnel. Then for 60 years a steam tug pulled trains of boats through. Most boats then became self propelled. It collapsed again and had to be rebuilt (1984) with circular concrete segments bolted together... a 'spare' can be seen on the bank at the southern end.
At M1 J15, use A508 south. Turn right in under a mile.
◊ **Canal Museum: Stoke Bruerne**
Prosperous because of trade from bargees, and the long period of tunnel construction nearby, this quiet village and its lock flight now attracts gongoozlers from far away. The Canal Museum was one of the first (1963) and gives excellent insights into the 200 year story of life and work on the canals.
Approach from M1 J15. Use A508 going south.
◊ **Old Stratford Tunnel**
The Buckinham Arm linked Buckingham with the end of an earlier short 3 lock arm to Old Stratford. It is no more than a very wide bridge but, as it had no towpath, horses were unhitched and boats were 'legged' through. It, therefore, qualifed as a tunnel.
From M1 J15. Use A508 going south to A5.
◊ **Great Ouse Aqueduct** (35 feet high)
The present iron aqueduct (1811) replaced one in brick which collapsed after only 3 years (1805-8). Walkers get the best view of the engineering from the Ouse Valley Way long distance footpath below.

Map labels:
Red Lion
130.
2. Dixon's Gap-Bridge
Aylesbury Arm
British Waterways Offices   131.
4.   3.
5.   Marsworth Narrow Locks
Church Lane
Vicarage Road
MARSWORTH
To Long Marston
Wingrave Road
Watery Lane
Marsworth Junction
To Pitstone
Locks 1. & 2.
Bridge 132.
White Lion
STARTOP'S END
Anglers Retreat
Lock 39.
Tea Rooms
Grand Union Canal
40.   41.
Marsworth Locks   44.
42.   43.   45.
Wendover Arm
Startop's End Reservoir
Nature Reserve
Marsworth Reservoir
WILSTONE GREEN
B489 Lower Icknield Way
TRINGFORD
Cemetery
Wilstone Reservoir
Tringford Reservoir
Abandoned Canal
Little Tring Road
Tringford Road
Gamnel Bridge
TRING WHARF
Bulbourne Road
B488
LITTLE TRING
7 Tringford Pumping Station
Wendover Arm
To Tring
To Tring

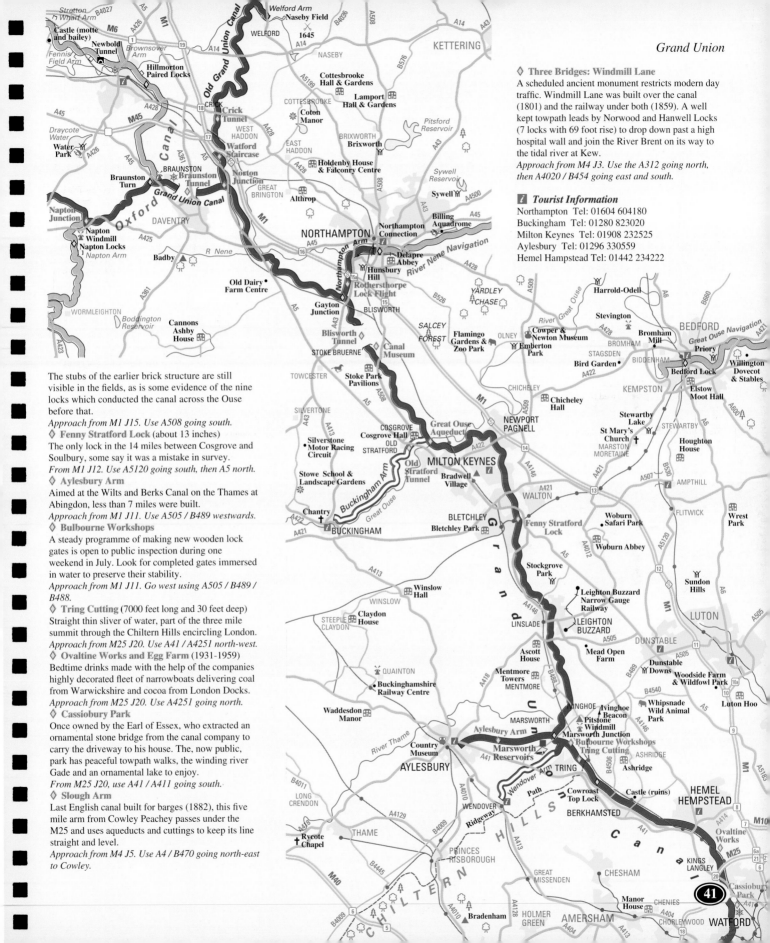

◇ **Three Bridges: Windmill Lane**
A scheduled ancient monument restricts modern day traffic. Windmill Lane was built over the canal (1801) and the railway under both (1859). A well kept towpath leads by Norwood and Hanwell Locks (7 locks with 69 foot rise) to drop down past a high hospital wall and join the River Brent on its way to the tidal river at Kew.
Approach from M4 J3. Use the A312 going north, then A4020 / B454 going east and south.

ℹ *Tourist Information*
Northampton Tel: 01604 604180
Buckingham Tel: 01280 823020
Milton Keynes Tel: 01908 232525
Aylesbury Tel: 01296 330559
Hemel Hampstead Tel: 01442 234222

The stubs of the earlier brick structure are still visible in the fields, as is some evidence of the nine locks which conducted the canal across the Ouse before that.
Approach from M1 J15. Use A508 going south.
◇ **Fenny Stratford Lock** (about 13 inches)
The only lock in the 14 miles between Cosgrove and Soulbury, some say it was a mistake in survey.
From M1 J12. Use A5120 going south, then A5 north.
◇ **Aylesbury Arm**
Aimed at the Wilts and Berks Canal on the Thames at Abingdon, less than 7 miles were built.
Approach from M1 J11. Use A505 / B489 westwards.
◇ **Bulbourne Workshops**
A steady programme of making new wooden lock gates is open to public inspection during one weekend in July. Look for completed gates immersed in water to preserve their stability.
Approach from M1 J11. Go west using A505 / B489 / B488.
◇ **Tring Cutting** (7000 feet long and 30 feet deep)
Straight thin sliver of water, part of the three mile summit through the Chiltern Hills encircling London.
Approach from M25 J20. Use A41 / A4251 north-west.
◇ **Ovaltine Works and Egg Farm** (1931-1959)
Bedtime drinks made with the help of the companies highly decorated fleet of narrowboats delivering coal from Warwickshire and cocoa from London Docks.
Approach from M25 J20. Use A4251 going north.
◇ **Cassiobury Park**
Once owned by the Earl of Essex, who extracted an ornamental stone bridge from the canal company to carry the driveway to his house. The, now public, park has peaceful towpath walks, the winding river Gade and an ornamental lake to enjoy.
From M25 J20, use A41 / A411 going south.
◇ **Slough Arm**
Last English canal built for barges (1882), this five mile arm from Cowley Peachey passes under the M25 and uses aqueducts and cuttings to keep its line straight and level.
Approach from M4 J5. Use A4 / B470 going north-east to Cowley.

Pickfords
Pioneer Canal Carriers (1786-1847).

Over 200 years ago, Pickfords grouped small packets and large parcels into wicker 'panniers' or 'hampers' and sent them by 'fly-boats', long distance canal boats moving day and night to a regular timetable. The hampers were delivered to new wharves constructed wherever canals crossed older Roman roads or the newer turnpikes. They were forwarded to clients by Pickfords own vans '*on springs and guarded*'.

The company used whatever transport route gave best service to their customers and kept a tally of the location of every packet in their care… in much the same way as present day courier services such as DHL or UPS.

Their operation became one of the most famous and reliable on the canals, even promising ' *if the canals be stopped by Frost, or any other impediment, every Attention will be paid to have the Goods forwarded by Land*'.

Early days
Pickfords started the carrying business (1630) in a small way around Poynton in Cheshire using packhorses in 'caravans' of forty or fifty at a time. Later they used broad wheeled, heavy waggons between London and Manchester (1756) and then matched the speed of stagecoaches with their 'Fly Wagon' powered by up to four horses, which carried parcels between Manchester and London in only four and a half days (1772)!

Their first canal services
A canal route towards London opened (1777) when the three tunnels on the Trent and Mersey Canal near Runcorn were finished. These linked with the Bridgewater Canal, to give a continuous waterway from Manchester to a canal / road interchange at Shardlow near Burton upon Trent, and thence by the Great North Road to London.

In an uncertain world, Pickford's management decided to actually own the means of transport and bought Henshall & Co., a firm that had pioneered services along the Trent and Mersey Canal (1786). Put together with their earlier purchase of the road carrying business of William Bass of Burton upon Trent (who then concentrated on beer production), it formed an integrated system for Pickford's small containers to be carried into London.

Expansion of canal carrying
By the Coleshill Agreement (1782) canal companies undertook to create a continuous waterway route from the Trent and Mersey Canal into London. Pickfords then set about negotiating special toll rates for itself (1788), even before the route was finished (1790).

For almost 60 years narrowboats then provided their major Manchester to London trunk service, initially via Oxford and the Thames (1790) then along the Grand Junction to Paddington (1805).

This was achieved by negotiating priority at locks... up to 50 boats carried a single diamond on their prow to indicate this concession. They were also licenced to travel by night. The regular run at one time was quicker by a whole day than competing services by road.

Final delivery of goods was by Pickfords own vehicles from wharves along the canals to Leeds, Congleton, Macclesfield, Sheffield, Huddersfield and Halifax whilst coastal boats from Liverpool took goods for delivery to 'Ireland, North Wales, Isle of Man and the West of Scotland'.

Pickfords soon owned 10 narrowboats (1795) and when Napoleon threatened invasion (1803) it had 28 boats to offer Government for troop movement. By the time a new partner, Joseph Baxendale, joined the firm (1817) they had 80 boats and 64 wharves / depots eg Polesworth (opened 1789), Castlefield (1794), Blisworth (1796), Paddington (1801), Braunston (1805) and Pickford boats had been in the inaugural flotilla of the Grand Junction Canal (1814).

Railway services
However, as railways, in their turn, began to link into a national network, Pickfords reviewed their commitment to canals. Joseph Baxendale spent 127 days travelling over 4000 miles by specially equipped narrowboat, coach and posthorse (1835).

He decided to anticipate a huge railway business by creating canal / road / rail distribution depots in London, integrated with the Regents Canal. Short canal arms were built into warehouse basements, both in the storage complex built by Pickfords itself (Camden, 1841), and the Liverpool and Birmingham Railway's building on the bank opposite.

These well laid plans were then undermined. The Grand Junction Railway started charging such 'exorbitant' rates for Pickfords' 'hampers' that Pickfords instigated a long legal battle, winning all their court cases but finally losing in Parliament (1840-1844). Despite this loss Pickfords continued to cooperate with the Liverpool and Birmingham Railway but three years later the two railway companies merged and independent carriers were shut out for good (1847).

Sale of the narrowboat fleet
Always the pragmatists, Pickfords decided to cast their lot with the railways. They ceased to offer independent long distance services and became collection and delivery agents from the new railway termini. They increased their road vehicle numbers and sold their fleet of over 100 narrowboats to the Grand Junction Canal Company who set up a subsidiary company especially to buy them (1847). After 29 years this new company was faced with large compensation claims because a gunpowder cargo exploded in Regents Park, London (1874). As a result, it withdrew from carrying and its boats, including Pickfords' fleet, were passed on to many different combinations of the descendants of Joshua Fellows and Fredrick Morton, trading firstly as London and Staffordshire Carrying Co. (1876), then as Fellows, Morton and Co. (1879), and finally Fellows Morton and Clayton Ltd (FMC:1890-1949).

THOMAS & MATTHEW PICKFORD,
Carriers by Land & Canal to the North of England
RECEIVE GOODS AT

The CASTLE INN, Wood Street, Cheapside;
The CANAL WAREHOUSE, Fore Street, Cripplegate;
Their Whares, Paddington;

Whence their FLY-BOATS set out daily
DIRECT FOR

MANCHESTER, LIVERPOOL, DERBY, LEICESTER, OXFORD, BIRMINGHAM, WORCESTER.

Which convey Goods for all Towns, Places and Wharfs on the line of the Canals or contiguous thereto, and generally for LANCASHIRE, YORKSHIRE, CHESHIRE, DERBYSHIRE, STAFFORDSHIRE, SHROPSHIRE, WARWICKSHIRE, WORCESTERSHIRE, HEREFORDSHIRE, OXFORDSHIRE, NOTTINGHAMSHIRE, LEICESTERSHIRE, NORTHAMPTONSHIRE, BUCKINGHAMSHIRE, BEDFORDSHIRE, HERTFORDSHIRE.

From LIVERPOOL
Goods are forwarded by the regular Brokers to IRELAND, and ISLE of MAN, and Coastwise to NORTH WALES, North of LANCASHIRE, WESTMORELAND, CUMBERLAND and West of SCOTLAND.

In case of Goods not being consigned to a Broker, they will be delivered at the Owners risk to those usually employed.

CARAVANS
On Springs and guarded, for the conveyance of Goods only, from the CASTLE INN, WOOD STRREET, every Evening at Six o'Clock, through LOUGHBOROUGH, DERBY, ASBOURNE, LEEK, MACCLESFIELD, STOCKPORT, in 96 Hours to MANCHESTER, whence Goods are immediately forwarded to LIVERPOOL, WARRINGTON, WIGAN, PRESTON, LANCASTER, and all Parts of LANCASHIRE.

CARAVANS
Every Evening through NORTHAMPTON and HARBOROUGH, in 18 hours to LEICESTER, which convey Goods for NOTTINGHAM, MANSFIELD, CHESTERFIELD, and SHEFFIELD.

By these Conveyances, THOMAS & MATTHEW PICKFORD hold themselves responsible for Goods committed to their care according to the Notice and conditions subjoined, which are publicly exhibited at their Offices and Warehouses, where they receive Goods.

WAGGONS as usual.

Thomas and Matthew Pickford's London poster (circa 1801) promises to 'hold themselves responsible for Goods committed to their care' and alongside gave a list of 223 place names which were 'TOWNS and WHARFS. For which, and Places adjacent thereto, Goods are received by THOMAS & MATTHEW PICKFORD'.

Paddington Arm (1801) and Regents Canal (1820) and Hertford Union (1820)

113 D2

Paddington Arm (1801)
From Bulls Bridge to Paddington Basin
13 miles, 0 locks
Regents Canal (1802)
From Little Venice to Limehouse Basin
8 miles, 12 wide locks, 2 tunnels
Engineers: Whitworth, Nash, Telford

A partnership between London Boroughs and British Waterways (The London Canal Conference) has a lottery assisted programme of improving all the facilities along this corridor into the heart of London.

Paddington Arm turns east at Bulls Bridge and stretches lock-free into London. It stopped in fields on the edge of town where new warehouses were laid out around a terminal basin 30 years before the Great Western Railway was thought about.

The Regents Canal picks up from near Paddington Basin and drives through the City of London down to an improved Limehouse Basin in Docklands. Together they form the central part of a very long urban walk, linking the open areas of the Colne Valley and the Lee Valley Regional Parks.

Management and Support
British Waterways Tel: 020 7286 6101
Grand Union Canal Society Tel: 020 8841 3788
Website: http://www.ian .wilson4@which.net

◊ **Bulls Bridge Junction**
Start of Paddington Arm. Supermarket and car park have been built on the site of major workshops and basin where boats 'waited for orders'.
From M4 J3, use A312 going north.
◊ **Little Venice**
The *Architectural Review* first published (1949) Eric De Mare's book '*The Canals of England*' where he suggested 'Paddington Basin has great inherent possiblities as England's *Little Venice*'. The basin is yet to come into its own but the Regency houses around Warwick Avenue have acquired the name.
From A5 / A40(M), use Edgware Road going north.
◊ **Islington Tunnel** (2880 feet: 1820)
Brass plaques set in the pavement lead walkers over a tunnel without a towpath. Originally barges were 'legged' through but a steam tug was installed (1826-1934) which towed barges by pulling itself along a chain laid underwater.
Most craft nowadays are self propelled.
Approach from A1 / B515 junction: The Angel. Walk north and east into Duncan Street.
◊ **Hertford Union Canal**
Sir George Duckett financed 1¼ miles of canal to connect the Regents Canal at Limehouse Basin directly to the Lee Navigation (and thus to his Stort Navigation) in order to avoid tidal Thames waters. Sold to Regents Canal 1857.
From A102(M). Use A102 / A11 / A1205 north to Old Ford.
◊ **Limehouse Basin**
Originally a ship basin with a large lock to the tidal Thames, it has been reduced in size by a major road running underwater to the Docklands developments.
Approach from A1203 / A13. Use Narrow Street / Limehouse Causeway.

Regents Canal was an immediate success (1820). It was the only connection between the rapidly expanding network of docks of the Port of London and the vast system of inland canals. Short river based shuttle services to and from private wharves and basins in the City plus narrowboat services deep into the nation (direct from 'over-the-side' unloading of ocean going ships) made this a very congested stretch of water. Many sorts of vessel used the wide paired locks in uneasy combination... overloaded lighters and barges from the docks sometimes got stuck in the bridge holes and ruined the timetables of long distance narrowboats.

✴ **Boat Trips**
Little Venice *Jason* Tel: 020 7286 3428
Jenny Wren Tel: 020 7485 4433
Camden *Waterbuses* Tel: 020 7482 2550
Cassio Wharf *Arcturus* Tel: 01438 714528
Cowley *Pisces, Gemini* Tel: 01895 440017

📖 **Suggested Guide Book**
Anthony Burton, Neil Curtis *Grand Union Canal Walk* Aurum Press, 1993

ℹ **Tourist Information**
Discover Islington Tel: 020 7278 8787
London Tourist Board Tel: 0839 123456
Hounslow Tel: 020 8572 8279

Grand Union

London Zoo

200 year old Ice Store, landing stages, two tunnels and broad beam locks.

London Zoo's private landing stage is served all summer by converted traditional working narrowboats which run at hourly intervals from both Little Venice and Camden Market.
(Get a combined Zoo / Waterbus ticket).

Two 'Short strolls' are suggested.

If you have all day, do both and the bit between. They are linked by a 'Longer walk' from Little Venice that meets the Camden Market stroll at **8** *London Zoological Gardens. Walk one way along the whole length and you could return to your start using a* **canal waterbus** *or one of the many tube stations.*

Start the stroll around 'Little Venice' from:-

1 **Rembrandt Gardens**
Amsterdam is Westminster's twin city. These gardens were named (1975) in their honour. *Enter from Warwick Avenue, down the slope and follow the path to a small gate. Go through, stop at the water. To the left, a path leads under a bridge, past green lawns and quiet fishermen towards, but with no access (1999), to:-*

2 **Paddington Basin** (1801)
34 years before Brunel engineered his railway, goods were sent from here to Southall, Maidenhead, Reading, Bath and Bristol, but by broad gauge boat instead of broad gauge railway. *Return to the gardens. Circle right along the narrow tree lined waters edge to view:-* (children can view from inside the garden railings)

3 **Browning Island**
Named for Robert, who lived in Warwick Crescent (1862-1889). *Re-enter the garden. Turn up into Warwick Avenue, circle left across the canal and down into Blomfield Road. Follow the railings and stop at a gate opposite number 42. Then either cross the canal by Westbourne Terrace Road Bridge (note 'Paddington Borough 1900') or, if the gate is open, step down to:-*

4 **Broad Beamed Barges**
Restaurant, Puppet Theatre, Art Gallery, Coffee Shop and information centre all serve you from on the water. *At the foot of the steps go right, under the generous canopy, cross the canal by a narrow 'turnover bridge'. Once across, go down the slope and sharp left onto the towpath, passing back under the roadbridge to:-*

5 **The Toll House:** London Canals Office Boats from Central London to the Midlands paid their toll while held in this narrow throat of water. Stop gates almost hidden in the canal wall allowed full control if necessary. *Circling left go up the slope at the beginning of the moored boats into Delamere Terrace and, at the end, cross into Warwick Crescent. Go either -* **straight on,** *where railings overlook the water and a gate at the end allows access to the Waterbus services:-*
or return to the start at **1** *Rembrandt Gardens by turning left and across the canal using the 'turnover bridge' and go eastwards along the level towpath past* **4** *Barges. Go under Warwick Avenue Bridge, left up onto Blomfield Road and left again.*

For a longer walk to **8** London Zoo, go from:-

1 **Rembrandt Gardens** *pass the residential boats moored alongside Maida Avenue. At the top, turn left, pass in front of the café with tables overlooking the entrance to:-*

6 **Maida Hill Tunnel**
No towing path for 272 yards. Horses had to walk over the top. *Do the same by carefully crossing the A5, Edgware Road, into the calm of Aberdeen Place. At the far end pass 'Crockers Folly' into a small un-named passage to the right of Elmton Court. At the end rejoin the canal as it emerges from the tunnel. Stay on the pavement above the water and follow the railings as far as Lisson Grove, cross carefully and regain the towpath by taking the slope down on the left of the Victorian office.* (Alternatively, at the tunnel exit use ⚠ steep steps). *The next long section of canal is hidden away from Lisson Green and goes through Regent's Park in a lush green cutting. Just before the zoo, go under:-*

7 **Blow-up Bridge** (Macclesfield Road)
Gunpowder was a frequent cargo because transport by water meant fewer bumps! But an onboard spark ignited one such load just as it passed below this bridge (1874). It was rebuilt, but supports were misplaced. Grooves worn in the Doric columns by over 50 years of rubbing by towropes, now appear on both sides!
Continue to opposite:-

8 **London Zoological Gardens**
36 acres, 8000 species. Some of the enclosures come close to the water. Lord Snowdon's Aviary is one of the more spectacular. Narrowboats stop at this landing stage to let *those with tickets* into the zoo.

44 *London Zoo*

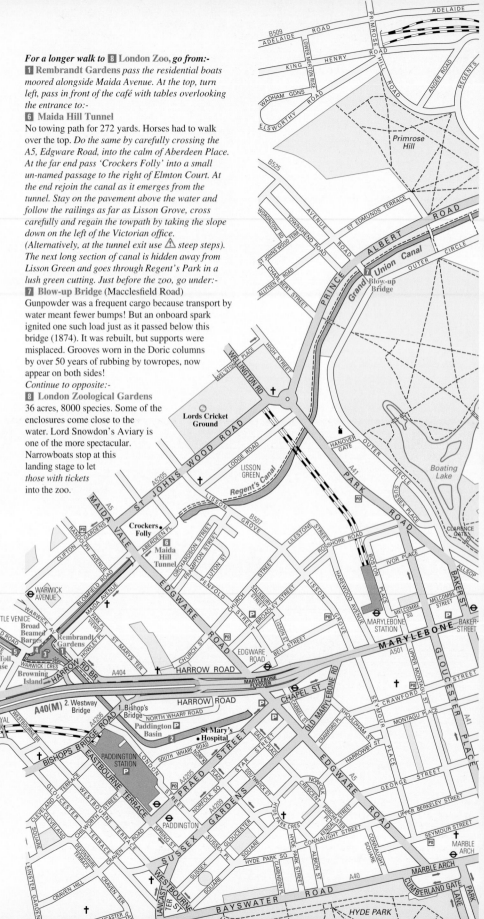

Grand Union

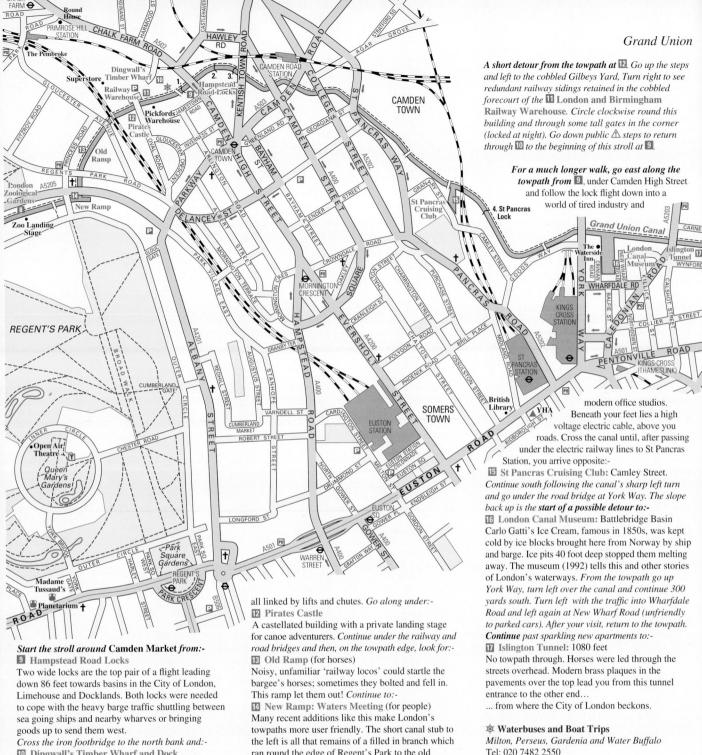

A short detour from the towpath at **12**. *Go up the steps and left to the cobbled Gilbeys Yard, Turn right to see redundant railway sidings retained in the cobbled forecourt of the* **11** **London and Birmingham Railway Warehouse**. *Circle clockwise round this building and through some tall gates in the corner (locked at night). Go down public* ⚠ *steps to return through* **10** *to the beginning of this stroll at* **9**.

For a much longer walk, go east along the towpath from **9**, *under Camden High Street and follow the lock flight down into a world of tired industry and* modern office studios. Beneath your feet lies a high voltage electric cable, above you roads. Cross the canal until, after passing under the electric railway lines to St Pancras Station, you arrive opposite:-

15 **St Pancras Cruising Club**: Camley Street. *Continue south following the canal's sharp left turn and go under the road bridge at York Way. The slope back up is the start of a possible detour to:-*

16 **London Canal Museum**: Battlebridge Basin Carlo Gatti's Ice Cream, famous in 1850s, was kept cold by ice blocks brought here from Norway by ship and barge. Ice pits 40 foot deep stopped them melting away. The museum (1992) tells this and other stories of London's waterways. *From the towpath go up York Way, turn left over the canal and continue 300 yards south. Turn left with the traffic into Wharfdale Road and left again at New Wharf Road (unfriendly to parked cars). After your visit, return to the towpath.*
Continue past sparkling new apartments to:-

17 **Islington Tunnel**: 1080 feet
No towpath through. Horses were led through the streets overhead. Modern brass plaques in the pavements over the top lead you from this tunnel entrance to the other end…

… from where the City of London beckons.

✳ **Waterbuses and Boat Trips**
Milton, Perseus, Gardenia and Water Buffalo
Tel: 020 7482 2550
Jasons Trip Tel: 020 7286 3428
Jenny Wren Tel: 020 7485 4433

Getting there:
Approach from M25 J16. Use M40 going east and A40 / A40(M) West. Way. Use public transport. Many tube stations serve the area.

Landranger Map 176 Ref TQ 26 81

Start the stroll around Camden Market *from:-*
9 **Hampstead Road Locks**
Two wide locks are the top pair of a flight leading down 86 feet towards basins in the City of London, Limehouse and Docklands. Both locks were needed to cope with the heavy barge traffic shuttling between sea going ships and nearby wharves or bringing goods up to send them west.
Cross the iron footbridge to the north bank and:-
10 **Dingwall's Timber Wharf and Dock**
Now the waterbus terminus and a seven day market with outside stalls at weekends. *A little further along the towpath, it rises up and you can look down on canal water as it enters the basement level of:-*
11 **London and Birmingham Railway Warehouse**
Now converted to 'The Interchange' offices. The basement of this preserved warehouse used to be served by canal barges, the ground floor by railway wagons and the upper floors were used for storage,

all linked by lifts and chutes. *Go along under:-*
12 **Pirates Castle**
A castellated building with a private landing stage for canoe adventurers. *Continue under the railway and road bridges and then, on the towpath edge, look for:-*
13 **Old Ramp** (for horses)
Noisy, unfamiliar 'railway locos' could startle the bargee's horses; sometimes they bolted and fell in. This ramp let them out! *Continue to:-*
14 **New Ramp: Waters Meeting** (for people)
Many recent additions like this make London's towpaths more user friendly. The short canal stub to the left is all that remains of a filled in branch which ran round the edge of Regent's Park to the old Cumberland Market. *To link up with the 'longer walk' from Little Venice follow the towpath (sharp right) to* **8** *opposite London Zoological Gardens.*
To return to the start at **9**, *retrace your steps* along the towpath (maybe including the slight detour noted below), or **alternatively**, *cross into Regents Park Road, up past Primrose Hill and some shops. Over the railway bridge, turn right into Chalk Farm Road to find* **10** **Markets** *and* **9** **Hampstead Road Locks**

Grand Western Canal
- see **Bridgwater and Taunton Canal**

Grantham Canal   **116 B1**
West Bridgford to Grantham
British Waterways, Nottingham Tel: 0115 946 1017
Grantham Canal Restoration Society
Tel: 0115 953 1153
Grantham Navigation Association, Philip Johns
(Membership Services), 19 Coniston Road, Cropwell
Bishop, Nottingham NG12 3BJ

Greasbrough (Park Gate) Canal   **119 D3**
River Dun Navigation to Greasbrough Ings
Newbiggin Branch

Great Ouse Navigation
        116 C3 - 117 D2
Opened: 1904, 1978.
Engineers: Vermuyden, Rennie, Telford
The Wash to Bedford
75 miles, 16 wide locks via Hundred Foot Drain

**Draining a huge catchment from Northamptonshire,
down through the flat landscape of the Fens to the
racing tides coming up from the Wash, this
navigation has always been hampered by the need
for flood control. It gives entry to the Middle Levels
and connects the rivers Wissey, Lark, Little Ouse
and the Cam up to Cambridge.**

Nature changed its own mind then man tried to
modify the result. The early outlet to the Wash via
Upware and Wisbech changed naturally to pass more
directly north. Lynn became the fifth port of the
Kingdom (1204) with a tidal flow reaching inland for
almost 50 miles. Upstream of St Ives was then
improved almost to Bedford (1635). Civil War raged
around the wetlands of the Fens, bridges over the river
were fortified and afterwards Lynn was renamed Kings
Lynn (1685). The final reach to Bedford Town was
only achieved a century later (1720). Vermuyden had
drained the Fens, creating a 20 mile straight cut below
Earith (1637) which he later duplicated (1651) with
another half a mile away and a Hundred Foot wide.

His first Denver Sluice succumbed to nature (1713)
and was then rebuilt with a lock alongside (1750).
Tides and silt still gave problems. A series of short

cuts around meanders were built at Eau Brink (1821),
Littleport (1830) and another sluice at Brownhills
(1837) but railway competition reduced income and,
therefore, maintenance. After a short life as a private
navigation (1893-1904) the river was reopened to
Eaton Socon (1939) and Bedford (1978) after the
efforts of the Great Ouse River Authority and Great
Ouse Restoration Society.

Management and Society
Environment Agency, Brampton Tel: 01480 414581
Environmental Agency, Bedford Tel: 01234 262622
*Great Ouse Boating Association, St John's House,
High Street, Huntingdon.*

◊ **Denver Tidal Sluice**
One of the largest structures on the waterways, it
stands at a 'Clapham Junction' of rivers, drains and
flood relief channels. A channel to the east collects
water for the Black Dyke pumphouse delivering
water over 12 miles away. Entry to Salters Lode for
the Fens requires lock keepers advice and respect for
the tidal river. (Tel: 01366 382013)
*From A47 / A1101 junction, use A1101 / A1122
going south-east; look south of Downham Market.*

◊ **Ely Island**
Inhabited before fen drainage, this is the only hard
ground for miles around. Oliver Cromwell was here!
From M11 J14, use A14 / A142 going north.

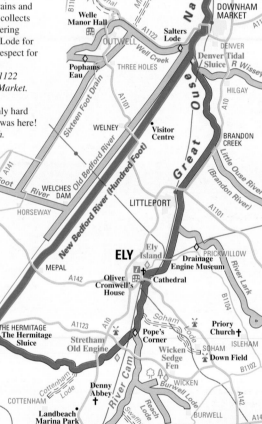

◊ **Stretham Old Engine**

Hero of a breach in a river bank (1919), this steam beam engine lifted 120 tons of water an hour for 47 days until a repair was made. Now supplemented by diesel (1924) and electric (1956) pumps, the tall chimney marks the place for summer visitors.
From M11 J13 / 14, use A10 north / A1123 west.

◊ **Wicken Sedge Fen**

Knowledge of the idiosyncrasies of deep marsh and variable water levels was a good defence against strangers. Evidence of early habitation is preserved in this 'Site of Scientific Interest'.
Approach from M11 J14. Use A14 / A10 going north-east, then A1123 east.

◊ **Earith Reach**

Tidal currents coming up the Hundred Foot Drain (New Bedford River) are still felt on two miles of the main river between Brownhills Staunch and The Hermitage Sluice either side of Earith.
From M11 J14, use A14 / B1050, going north to A1123.

◊ **Godmanchester Bridges**

Replacing (1332) a Roman fording point, the stone bridge across the Ouse had a chapel at one end. The Causeway leading to the stone bridge looks across the Mill Pond to Holme Meadows, with foreground of a Chinese style footbridge leading to lock island.
From M11 J13 / 14 use A14 north.

◊ **Bedford Lock**

No moorings upstream of here. An island close to Russell Park. Footbridges across the river, lake, bandstand, weirs and moorings, available since re opening (1978).
Approach from M1 J13. Use A421 / A6 going north.

❊ *Boat Trips*

Cambridge *Georgina* Tel 01223 500333

▣ *Suggested Guide Book*

Great Ouse Boating Association *Two guides: Cam & Lower Ouse and Upper River* Imray Laurie Norie and Wilson, 1996

ⓘ *Tourist Information*

King's Lynn Tel: 01553 763044
Ely Tel: 01353 662062
Bedford Tel: 01234 215226
Huntingon Tel: 01480 388588

. . . .

Grosvenor Canal   **113 D2**
River Thames to Grosvenor Basin
½ mile, 1 lock

Hackney Canal   **111 D3**
River Teign to near Kingsteignton

Haddiscoe New Cut - see **The Broads**
Halesworth Navigation
- see **Blyth (Halesworth) Navigation**

Hamble, River   **112 B4**
Southampton Water to Botley
7½ miles, 0 locks
*Hamble Harbour Masters Office, Warsash
Tel: 01489 576387*

The Haven (River Witham)   **116 C1**
The Wash to Boston
Port of Boston Ltd Tel: 01205 362328

Hayle (Copperhouse) Canal   **110 A4**
River Hayle to Copperhouse Foundry

Hedon Haven River Humber to Hedon **119 E3**

Herefordshire and Gloucestershire Canal   115 D3

Opened: Ledbury 1798, Hereford 1845
Engineers: Henshall, Clowes, Whitworth, Ballard
Junction with River Severn at Over to Hereford
34 miles, 22 narrow locks, 3 tunnels

Rolling countryside provides an attractive setting for a restoration supported by Local Authorities and already in water for the enjoyment of walkers at one site in each county.

A canal which exhausted itself financially by the need to construct Oxenhall Tunnel and thus had to obtain its funds through two Acts (1791, 1839). After a railway takeover, the canal bed from Over to Ledbury was changed to a railway (1881) and was itself then abandoned (1964).

Management and Restoration
*Herefordshire and Gloucestershire Canal Trust
Tel: 01452 332900*

◊ **Roman Road: Hereford**
After a celebrated decision by a planning inspector, this rebuilt road has a bridge over the dry bed of the restoration line… 32 miles from the nearest point of the connected canal system at Over.
Approach from M50 J2. Use A417 / A4103 going west to A465 roundabout.

◊ **Skew Bridge: Monkhide**
Built as an unnecessary engineering showpiece. Restoration assisted (1988) by the Waterways Recovery Group, it crosses the canal water at a 30 degree angle to the towpath, probably the most

extreme in the country. A mile in water.
Approach from M5 J7. Use A44 / A4103 going south-west. South of A4103 just beyond A417 junction.

◊ **Oxenhall Tunnel (6575 feet)**
Mile and a half towpath walk between tunnel entrance and restored lock cottage.
Approach from M50 J3, use B4221 going east. Turn north to Oxenhall.

◊ **Over Junction: Gloucester**
Two miles downstream of Upper Parting on River Severn. Active restoration of the first length of canal above the junction has started (1998) as part of a residential development in the grounds of a former hospital site. After 6 years of negotiation, volunteers have undertaken to complete excavations, build wharf walls and weirs within a very tight schedule.
From M5 J11, use A40 west to A40 / A417 junction. Modern crossing of River Severn, has Telford's Stone Bridge on the south, the canal to the north.

ⓘ *Tourist Information*
Hereford Tel: 01432 268430
Ledbury Tel: 01531 636147
Newent Tel: 01531 822468
Gloucester Tel: 01452 421188

. . . .

Hertford Union Canal - see **Grand Union Canal**
Hopkin's Canal   **114 B4**
Yspitty to near Bryn Carnafon
Horncastle Navigation   **117 C1**
River Witham to Horncastle. Includes:
   Tattershall Canal River Witham to Tattershall
Huddersfield Broad Canal
- see **Huddersfield Narrow Canal**

Horsepower

Some aero-engines are equivalent to 2000 horsepower, but when canals were first designed both Smeaton and Telford famously worked out that the power of a real horse depended critically on how it was applied. They found that eight packhorses were needed to carry one ton, a cart horse could pull two tons but a boatman's horse could haul over fifteen times as much. A 'payload' up to 30 tons along a waterway was common which meant that one narrowboat was equivalent to 250 packhorses.

Engineering for horses

Boats should go along a canal. A perfect pull is only possible directly down the middle of the canal but, in practice, the boat tends to move towards the towpath where the horse is. The nearest a horse can get to a direct pull is to be as far ahead of the boat as possible. Power transfer was therefore through a rope of huge length, generally of cotton.

A horse would not give a continuously steady pull and when it eased off, unless boatmen were lucky or careful, the rope collapsed into a tangled skein. All canal engineers knew this. Many construction details that can still be seen on today's canals are a particular shape because of the help the boatman and his horse needed.

Snagging of towropes

If a long rope suddenly caught on anything, tree stump, rough stone, bridge arch or hand-rail... it spelt disaster for the boat, its cargo and sometimes killed the horse by jerking him into the water.

Long ropes would tend to cut sharp corners, for example, where the canal suddenly widened after a bridge or at a junction between canals. Vertical rollers were sometimes erected to ease the passage of the rope (*as in the picture on the left*). At other bridge holes this was not done and the wet towrope, full of stone dust from the towpath, wore deep notches in the brickwork arch.

Sometimes a 'smooth' cast iron angle might be bolted to protect the arch and, although iron is more resistant to abrasion from rope, the enormous tension still left deep scars (*as in the silhouette on the right*).

Engineers built bridge parapets of smooth rounded coping stones or bull nosed bricks and any handrails or walls that came between the boat and horse were tapered away into the ground to eliminate snagging (*as in the picture on the left*).

A video of this and other skills in working horsedrawn boats is available from the Friends of the National Waterways Museum Tel: 01452 318054.

Boats don't have brakes

To slow down or stop, you cannot put a horse into reverse. Wooden bollards are the answer. The cotton towrope is given one or two loose turns around a bank side post and then pulled tight. Friction between the wood and rope can act to slow up to 30 tons weight of boat as it runs past. The rope is weakened and the post is worn, resulting in posts with sculpted waistlines, the remains of which can still be seen all around the system.

❀ *Quiet travel on horsedrawn trip boats*
Foxton *Vixen* Tel: 0116 279 2285
Guide Bridge *Maria* Tel: 0160 320 8338
Godalming *Iona* Tel: 01483 414938
Hebden Bridge *Sara Siddons* Tel: 01422 845557
Llanfrynach *Dragon's Tail* Tel: 01874 665382
Llangollen *William Jessop, James Brindley*
Tel: 01978 860702
Newbury *Kennet Valley* Tel: 01635 44154
Tiverton *Tivertonian* Tel: 01884 253345

Huddersfield

Huddersfield Narrow Canal
and Sir John Ramsden's Canal   118 C3
(Huddersfield Broad)
Opened: broad 1774, narrow 1797-1811
Engineers: Whitworth, Holt, Brown, Outram
Dukinfield Junction to Cooper Bridge
Narrow: 20 miles, two tunnels and 74 locks
32 locks west of Standedge Tunnel: 42 to the east

Short but steep, rising into glorious Pennine moorland with many reservoirs and swathes of National Trust land. Walkers can already enjoy most of this soon-to-be-restored canal and many features are already worth a visit by car or train. Trip boats already offer time on the water and through boating is expected by December 2000!

The massive Standedge Tunnel took ages to build (1794-1811) and nearly bankrupted the company. Locks from the west up the Tame valley were open after three years (1797), as were those from the east up the Colne valley. Traffic started. Packhorses took transhipped goods on the turnpike over the top of the tunnel for fourteen years. Transhipment was also needed when narrowboats met the relatively short length of Sir John Ramsden's Canal. It was designed for the Calder keels... which were only 57 feet long and, therefore, the locks, though broader than required, were *too short* to take the standard 70 foot narrowboats. Double handling pushed up costs and reduced canal revenue... even before the Huddersfield and Manchester Railway bought it out.

Management and Restoration
British Waterways, Castleford Tel: 01977 554351
Huddersfield Canal Company Tel: 0161 339 1332
Huddersfield Canal Society Tel: 0161 339 1332
Website: http://www.hcanals.demon.co.uk

◊ **Tameside Canoe Trail**
Steps up from the rapids on the river below Scout Tunnel (615' long: closed 1999), allow canoeists to return upstream by the placid waters of the canal.
Approach from M67 J4. Use A57 / A6018 / A635 going north.
◊ **Uppermill Stepping Stones**
Earliest section to be restored (1987). Trip boat, the Brownhill Visitor Centre and an Annual Canals Festival all use this section. Saddleworth Railway Viaduct forms an elegant backdrop to a wildlife park and picnic area accessed from the canal by stepping stones across the river.
From M62 J22, use A672 / A6052 going south.
◊ **Diggle Locks: 24W-30W**
Sophisticated high speed locks (1811). A short flight where all the controls (balance beams and paddle gear) are on the same bank. The opposite bank is free of obstructions, thus allowing the towing line to remain fixed to the boat. Rapid progress was possible, even by an unaided single handed boatman.
From M62 J22, use A672 / A6052 / A670 going south.
◊ **Standedge Tunnel** (17 000 feet, ⅓ bare rock)
(638 feet below ground, 645 feet above sea level) Marsden Moor, with it's reservoirs and clough is crossed by the Pennine Way, the Chester-York Roman Road, packhorse trails and three turnpikes, all of which can be followed today. The canal tunnel (1811-1944) preceeded three railway tunnels, took 16 years to construct and now needs £5 million to clear

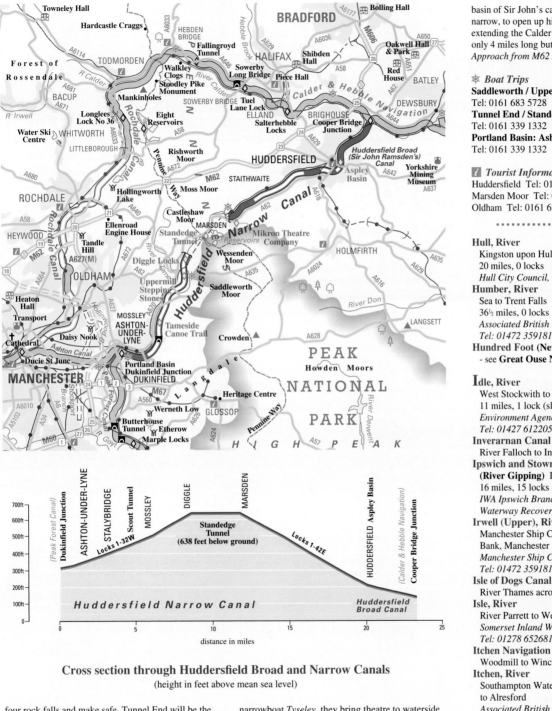

Cross section through Huddersfield Broad and Narrow Canals
(height in feet above mean sea level)

basin of Sir John's canal. Built (1774), before the narrow, to open up his lands in Huddersfield by extending the Calder and Hebble into the town, it is only 4 miles long but has nine broad locks.
Approach from M62 J24. Use A629 going south.

⚓ *Boat Trips*
Saddleworth / Uppermill *Pennine Moonraker*
Tel: 0161 683 5728
Tunnel End / Standedge *Pioneer, Oldham Otter*
Tel: 0161 339 1332
Portland Basin: Ashton *Greater Manchester*
Tel: 0161 339 1332

ℹ️ *Tourist Information*
Huddersfield Tel: 01484 223200
Marsden Moor Tel: 01484 847016
Oldham Tel: 0161 627 1024

••••••••••••••••••••••••••••••••••••

Hull, River 119 E2
Kingston upon Hull to Aike Beck
20 miles, 0 locks
Hull City Council, Tel: 01482 613385
Humber, River 119 E3
Sea to Trent Falls
36½ miles, 0 locks
Associated British Ports, Grimsby
Tel: 01472 359181
Hundred Foot (New Bedford River)
- see **Great Ouse Navigation**

Idle, River 119 D3
West Stockwith to Bawtry
11 miles, 1 lock (sluice gate at West Stockwith)
Environment Agency, Gainsborough
Tel: 01427 612205
Inverarnan Canal 122 B4
River Falloch to Inverarnon
Ipswich and Stowmarket Navigation 117 E3
(River Gipping) Ipswich to Stowmarket
16 miles, 15 locks
IWA Ipswich Branch Tel: 01449 721988
Waterway Recovery Group Tel: 020 7586 2556
Irwell (Upper), River 118 C3
Manchester Ship Canal, Manchester to Hunt's
Bank, Manchester
Manchester Ship Canal Co, Eastham
Tel: 01472 359181
Isle of Dogs Canal 113 D2
River Thames across Isle of Dogs
Isle, River 111 E2
River Parrett to Westport Canal
Somerset Inland Waterways Society
Tel: 01278 652681
Itchen Navigation 112 B3
Woodmill to Winchester
Itchen, River 112 B3
Southampton Water to Woodmill and Winchester
to Alresford
Associated British Ports, Southampton
Tel: 01703 330022
Ivelchester (Ilchester) and Langport Navigation
Langport to Pill Bridge, Ilchester 111 E1
Somerset Inland Waterways Society
Tel: 01278 652681
Ivel (Bedfordshire) Navigation 116 C3
Tempsford to Shefford
Includes **Shefford Canal**

four rock falls and make safe. Tunnel End will be the start point for 'The Standedge Experience', electric boat (Tel: 0161 339 1332) taking visitors into the tunnel itself.
Approach from M62 J22. Use A672 / A6052 / A62, go south then north to Marsden.
◊ **Mikron Theatre Company** (Tel: 01484 843701)
The most famous of several groups of players who tour the waterways system. Travelling aboard

narrowboat *Tyseley*, they bring theatre to waterside pubs and village halls. Original plays, often on waterway related themes, always include songs and humour. The Mechanics Institue, Marsden is their base.
Approach from M62 J22 use A672 / A6052 / A62. Go south then north.
◊ **Aspley Basin: Sir John Ramsden's Canal**
Huddersfield University is built around the terminal

Kennet and Avon Canal

111 E1 - 112 C2

Opened: 1723, 1727, 1810, 1951, reopened 1990
Engineers: Hore, Weston, Simcock, Barnes, Rennie
River navigations: Reading (Thames) to Newbury
and Bristol (Hanham Tidal Lock) to Bath
Canal: Newbury to Bath
86 miles, 106 wide locks, 1 tunnel

Everything about this waterway is on a grand
scale. Two rivers, a long broad beam canal, major
lock flights, serious pumping machinery, massive
decay, hours of volunteer restoration and now the
biggest collection of local funds to secure
assistance from the Heritage Lottery Fund will
solve leaks and enable full use of an historic asset
'for all to enjoy'.

Thames barges were travelling to Guildford on the
Wey (1651) and navigation of the Kennet was
proposed (Act of 1715) to do the same for Newbury
(138 feet above Reading but only 20 miles distant).

Against 'Luddite' style resistance organised by
the Mayor of Reading the river was dredged, short
cuts made and twenty locks installed (1724). Water
supply presented no problems so simple turf sided
locks were used... one of which remains on view.

Bath Corporation was granted powers to improve
the Avon from Bristol (1619) but it took 100 years
to overcome opposition and complete these works.

Later Charles Dundas MP called a meeting to
extend the Kennet Navigation to Hungerford but

they resolved to go the whole hog and connect the two
navigations (1788). For this connecting broad beam
canal water supply was a major problem, the short
summit pound requiring the assistance of the newly
invented steam powered beam engines to lift enough
water to keep the summit level topped up. The narrow
Avon valley upstream of Bath was also a difficult
stretch to build, requiring two major aqueducts, and it
regularly leaked more than a little. The Caen Hill flight
of 16 locks was the last section to be built (1810).
They have huge side ponds in an attempt to conserve
water but, until the new back pumps were installed
(1996), were subject to regular closures.

Management and Restoration

British Waterways, Devizes Tel: 01380 722859
Kennet and Avon Canal Trust Tel: 01380 721279

◊ **Floating Harbour: Bristol** (Jessop, 1809)
Home to Brunel's steam ship 'Great Britain' (1843).
All the boats remain floating because the lock gates
capture the water from each high tide. Previously the
40 foot tidal range had allowed ships to come inland
as far as Bristol but, as the tide retreated, they became
stranded on the mud. The tide now rushes past to
Hanham along a relief channel (1809).
*Approach from M5 J18. Use A4 going east to Bristol,
A4 / A38 junction.*

◊ **Bath Deep Lock** (Locks 8 / 9)
Road building required space so two locks were
combined into one, a massive 19 feet 5 inches deep.
From M4 J18. Use A46 / A4 / A36 going south.

◊ **Claverton Pumping Station** (1813-1952, 1976)
Amazing engineering which persuades the River Avon
to drive a pump which robs it of water to top up the
nine mile level of the canal 48 feet above. A 24 foot
wide undershot waterwheel drives two 18 foot beam
engines each delivering 9 tons of water at each
stroke! Restoration to working condition took
volunteers 8 years (1968-1976) and it can be inspected
most summer Sundays, working on selected weekends.
(Tel: 01272 867536 for details)

*Approach from M4 J18. Use A46 / A4 / A36 going
south. A small lane leads across the railway!*

◊ **Dundas Aqueduct** (1800)
Named after the first Chairman of the Kennet and
Avon Canal Company, Dundas Aqueduct is 64ft
main and two 20ft spans of Bath limestone in
Roman Doric style by John Rennie, one of two (the
other being at Avoncliff) crossing and recrossing the
Avon within 2 miles of each other. 48 feet between
water levels.
From M4 J18. Use A46 / A4 / A36 going south.

◊ **Somersetshire Coal Canal**
Followed the twisting, steep Cam Brook valley up
towards the rich Somerset Coalmines. Financially
successful despite experiments with a 54 foot deep
'Cassion' Lock (1798-1800) at Combe Hay and an
inclined plane which predate the flight of 22 locks
(1805). The 'Cassion' was a triumphant engineering
failure but, fortunately, failed to bankrupt the canal.
At the canal junction a visitor centre (1998) lurks
alongside the Brass Knocker Basin within a light
industrial estate (electric day boats available).
*From M4 J18. Use A46 / A4 / A36 going south. At the
B3108 junction turn immediately north.*

◊ **Limpley Stoke Bridge**
Start of stretch of canal that has been leaking ever
since it was opened. Stop planks at regular intervals
allow minimum waste during repairs by isolating the
exact section. Part of the current (1999) works
resolves the problem using modern materials, as has
been done over Avoncliff Aqueduct (1798).
*Approach from M4 J18. Use A46 / A4 / A363 going
south-east. Then turn west onto B3108.*

◊ **Semington Junction**
Junction with Wilts and Berks Canal leading to the
Thames at Abingdon. Small arch over entrance and
line of canal between trees is all that marks the site.
Approach from M4 J17. Use A350 going south.

◊ **Caen Hill Lock Flight** (16 rising 130 feet)
Daunting straight flight of wide locks with huge side
ponds which help to conserve water. Spectacular
central run of the 29 lock Devizes flight rising 237

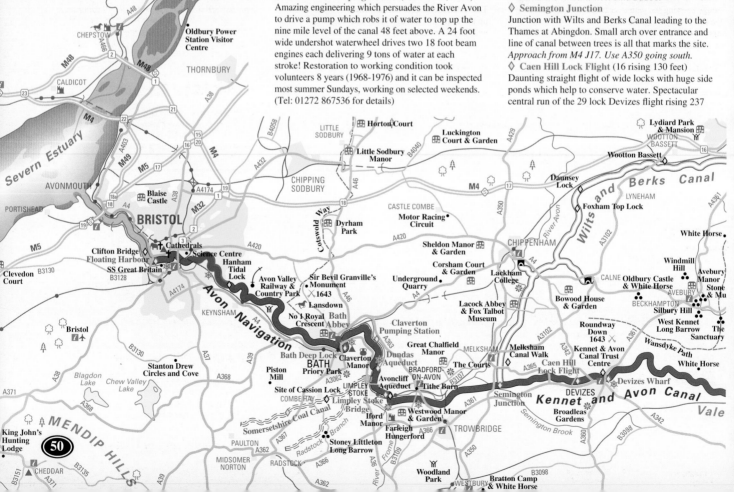

feet in 2¼ miles to reach the Long Pound at 410 feet
above sea level. Waymarked 'Discovery Trail'.
*Approach from M4 J17. Use A350 / A365 / A361
going south then east. Turn into B3101 to car park.*

◊ **Devizes Wharf** (Couch Lane)
Start of Easter Canoe Challenge to Westminster
125 miles and 77 locks away (record 90 hours).
The long timbered balcony is on the Kennet and Avon
Trust Centre. Exhibition of early history and items
found during restoration activity. Wharf Theatre.
From M4 J17, use A350 / A420 / A342 going south-east

◊ **Burbage Wharf: Bruce Tunnel**
Canalside buildings restored to domestic use.
Wooden wharf crane and towpath walk eastwards to
Bruce / Savernake Tunnel (western portal).
Approach from M4 J15. Use A346 going south.

◊ **Crofton Pumping Station** (1812-1959, 1971)
Water runs to the pumphouse from the Wilton
Reservoir and then steam driven pumps lift it into a
'leat' or channel which delivers it back to Lock 55
and the 2½ mile summit pound. Every five seconds
one ton of water is lifted 40 feet by one stroke of the
pistons! The everyday back pumping by electricity is
supplemented by regular 'Steaming' weekends.
(Tel: 01672 870300 for details)
Waymarked 'Discovery Trail' includes a windmill.
*Approach from M4 J15. Use A346 going south / A338
east towards Hungerford. Turn at East Grafton.*

◊ **Hungerford Marsh Lock**
19th Century engineering required the lock to be
exactly where a public footpath crossed the land. In
the spirit of todays Ramblers Association the local
landowner refused permission to move it. The swing
bridge carrying the path over the lock itself adds to
the complexity of operation.
*Approach from M4 J14. Use A338 south / A4. Turn
south. Short walk along towpath from town centre.*

◊ **Kintbury Wharf**
First stage of the canal was opened to here (1797).
Great Western Railway follows the canal and river
along a tree lined valley. Horsedrawn trip boat.
From M4 J14. Use A338 / A4 going south then east.

◊ **Newbury Lock** (1796)
First lock on the canal as it goes west to Bath. All 20
locks to the east were created by the Kennet
Navigation (completed 1724). Only lock in southern
England fitted with lever operated paddles at its head.
*Approach from M4 J13. Use A34 / A339 to town
centre.*

◊ **Monkey Marsh Lock: Thatcham**
Turf sided locks were normal where rivers can make
up the water lost through grass side slopes. Boats
were kept in place by staves, as evident in this working
near restoration (1990).
Waymarked 'Discovery Trail' includes
Bowdown Woods Nature Reserve and
Thatcham Reed Beds.
*Approach from M4 J13. Use A34 / A339 / A4
going south then east.*

◊ **Aldermarston Lift Bridge** (Tel: 0118 971 2868)
Hydraulic lift bridge (1984), replacing the old timber
bridge that swung over the navigation on some of the
earliest ball bearings in the country. A solid stone
bridge over the parallel river is further south-west. The
wharf has a quiet ambiance, picnic area, waymarked
'Discovery Trail' and a visitor and information centre
in a wharfinger's cottage
Approach from M4 J12. Use A4 / A340 going south

◊ **Woolwich Green Lakes** (1960)
Each side of the navigation to the west and south
of Reading are major water bodies of meadows,

Claverton Pumping Station

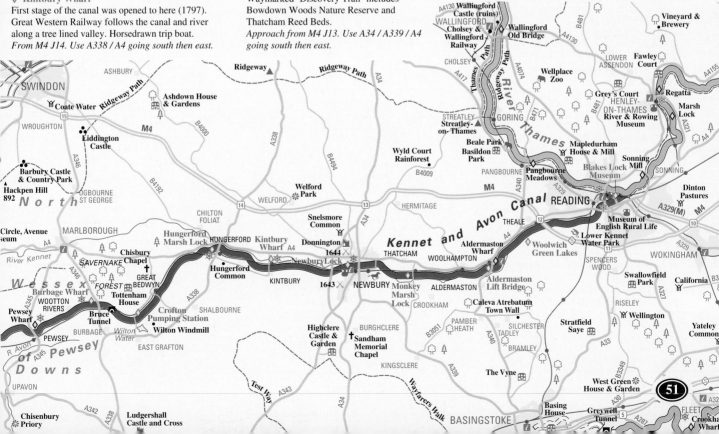

Kennet and Avon

Bath Abbey
Hot water, river and canal.

Hot Springs, Roman Baths and Georgian Circuses have for centuries attracted millions of visitors to this 'World Heritage City' on the west bank of the River Avon. But the grandest Georgian Street of all is on the opposite bank, as is the Kennet and Avon Canal which dramatically hugs the side slope of the valley.

Start the short stroll from:-

1 Abbey Church Yard and Pump Rooms
Where street entertainers of amazing quality perform to present day pilgrims. *With the Pump Rooms on your right, face the Abbey, turn right, pass down close to its south side past a square of seats in front of the Tourist Information Centre and out onto Orange Grove. Cross the road to overlook 'Parade Gardens', turn left and follow the balustrade into 'Grand Parade' which overlooks the river. Walk upstream and cross:-*

2 Pulteney Bridge (1774): Symbol of Bath
This is one of only two river bridges in England with shops on both sides. Designed by Robert Adam, it was funded by William Pulteney to open up his meadowlands on the east of the river. Just beyond the eastern end of the narrow carriageway, on the right, there are 36 busy steps winding sharply down to the 'Riverside Walk'. *West facing pub gardens overlook the river, boat trips upstream start from here and, on the left, is the Beazer Garden Maze. (Alternative ramp access to the river is available by using Grove Street almost opposite... turn back at the foot of the slope and walk under the road). Further along the walk is:-*

3 Pulteney Sluice (1972)
Opened by the Lord Mayor of London, the workings of this precursor to the Thames Barrier are clearly visible. The curved and counterbalanced sheet metal 'dam' can be swung out of the way in times of flood to allow excess water down to the sea. For a superb view of the triple-stepped weir and the renovated 'Empire Hotel' and formal Colonnade under the bus stands go up onto the 'roof'. *Continue downstream, past visiting boats, Bath Rugby Club, ice cream sellers and sandwich eating office workers to:-*

4 North Parade
Georgian ladies 'paraded' in the afternoons, much as once occured in Continental villages, to show off their finery and see who was in town. Bath also has a wide pavement South Parade, but this one has been commandeered by traffic.
Reach road level by entering the Leisure Centre Grounds and turning right up their access lane (alternatively use the twisting stair from under the bridge), pass over the river. Cross Pierrepont Street at traffic lights, down North Parade Passage past Sally Lunn's Refreshment House (1482) to:-

5 Abbey Green
Monastery Gardens enclosed the hot springs for 500 years until Henry VIII's time (1563). This remaining plane tree was probably outside the garden walls surrounded by some of Bath's few pre-Georgian buildings. Look up to the right, see the Abbey Towers.
Return to the start at **1** *Abbey Church Yard.*

A second stroll (of less than two hours):-
From **3** Pulteney Sluice. *Continue under* **4** *North Parade past the 'Pride of Bath' trip boat, along the riverside to:-*

6 Ferry Lane
A former crossing point into the medieval walled city. *Turn inland past the wall of Bath Cricket Club, under the railway bridge to a busy main road. Cross to Pulteney Gardens and, at the end, walk up the slope, follow the metal railings to arrive at:-*

7 Abbey View Lock
The last feat of Rennie's engineering was to drop the canal 74 feet to meet the navigable River Avon. This involved a steep flight of seven locks and, coupled with two pumping stations returned the lost water up to the nine mile pound.

Abbey View Lock is in the centre of the flight. Immediately uphill it has a large side pound / turning place and nearby the remaining chimney of one of the pumping stations.
Follow the towpath uphill. At the top lock note the assistance provided by the Bath Humane Society.

At the next bridge go up to the road. Cross diagonally to the end of the bridge parapet. Go down the towpath opposite new houses in front of the trip-boat wharf.

The next bridge is a 'turnover' bridge where the horses would walk up the slope, over the bridge and turn back on themselves to reach the opposite towpath. This way the towing rope did not have to be unhitched!! Do the same and follow the towpath railings under Cleveland House, the Canal Company HQ. You are now entering the cutting at:-

A graceful stepped weir (on the left of this picture) holds back the Avon and impounds the water to create a deeper reach of river which is used for boat trips and gives a natural mirror for Pulteney Bridge.

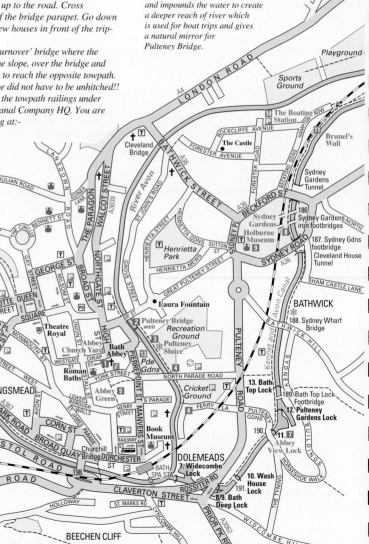

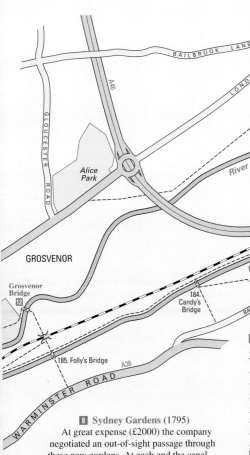

8 **Sydney Gardens** (1795)

At great expense (£2000) the company negotiated an out-of-sight passage through these new gardens. At each end the canal enters by an ornate tunnel and between is crossed by two delicate cast iron footbridges inscribed 'Anno 1800'. Between the footbridges is a short flight of steps into the Gardens. Once inside the formal layout keep straight on over Milway Bridge, go left and see how the next transport revolution was allowed through (1841)... also in a cutting but with a special garden path giving an 'Orchestra Stalls View' of the amazing steam trains going by.

To return to **2** *Pulteney Bridge exit the garden (slightly downhill from the railway), turn right down the pavement into the driveway of:-*

9 **Holburne Museum** (Tel: 01225 466669)
Stand in front of the main door. This building ends the most magnificent view of Georgian splendour in Bath... Great Pulteney Street. 100 feet wide and 1000 feet long, the street is lined by stone built four storey terraces on the axis of **2** *Pulteney Bridge.*
However, to avoid traffic, follow the driveway round to SYDNEY PLACE (carved in 6 inch high Roman lettering). Cross the road into short Sutton Street which leads into Henrietta Park. After enjoying the park go out the far end, turn left up Henrietta Street to Laura Fountain and **2** *Pulteney Bridge.*

A longer walk start from:-
9 *Holburne Museum go clockwise round the outside wall of the Gardens till you are opposite Forester Road. Go down, at the far end is a small car park serving:-*

10 **The Boating Station** (Tel: 01225 466407)
A very Victorian name for a very Victorian institution. Traditional style (some may be Victorian built!) wooden skiffs, punts and canoes can be hired onto a very calm tree lined reach of the River Avon. Spectators pay a nominal sum. Ice cream cornets, tea gardens and first floor restaurant complete the elegant ambiance. *After your stay, exit the car park, turn left, keep on left hand pavement into Beckford Gardens. At the end* ⚠ *steps up to the railway footbridge. Note:-*

11 **Brunel's Wall**
A major piece of engineering to hold the canal in place, whilst he threaded the railway along the valley side. *Go up and left along the canal towpath and then fork left down the valley side, under the railway to cross the River Avon on:-*

12 **Grosvenor Bridge**
This reach has a weir at both ends but allows trip boats an idyllic tree lined journey to Bathampton. *On the north bank turn left and cross the field as far as the Bus Depot. Pass onto London Road to catch a bus or walk back to* **1** *Abbey Church Yard.*

A small detour from **1** *Abbey Church Yard follow the short stroll to:-*
13 **Parade Gardens**
Pay a small fee, go down the steps for a choice:-
- turn left, walk down the Collonade, listen to the weir.
- turn right, walk downstream to the café under the arch.
Or rest. Use one of the canvas deck chairs to admire manicured lawns and award winning flower beds.

Getting there:
From M4 J18, use A46 / A4 going south then west.
🅿 *Suggest at Park & Ride (Lansdown from the north, Newbridge from the west). Join at* **1**.
♿ *Around Great Pulteney Street. Join at* **2**.
🚆 *From station exit follow Manvers Street northwards. Join at* **5**.

Landranger Map 172 Ref ST 74 64

---

osier beds and former gravel pits. These two are official nature reserves.
Approach from M4 J12. Use A4 going west, then turn south towards Sheffield Bottom.
◊ **Blakes Lock Museum** (Tel: 0118 939 0918)
Reading's waste water drained down towards the Thames, was treated and pumped into the Kennet close to Blakes Weir (1870). Old water driven pumps are now replaced by electric turbines. The pumphouse building displays river related Reading history alongside quiet visitor moorings. Waymarked 'Discovery Trail' includes High Bridge former wharf area and Abbey Ruins.
From M4 J11, use A33 going north, turn east on Inner Ring Road towards A329 and Gas Works Road

⚙ **Boat Trips**
Bristol
Redshank, Tower Belle Tel: 01272 268157
Flower of Bristol Tel: 01272 268157
Bath *Pride of Bath* Tel: 01225 333769
Jubilee Tel: 01980 620960
John Rennie Tel: 01225 447276
Bradford on Avon *Ladywood* Tel: 01980 620960
Monkton Combe *Patricia* Tel: 01225 722292
Devizes *Kenavon Venture* Tel: 01380 728504
Rebecca, Hannah, Rachel (special boats)
Pewsey *Dragonfly* Tel: 01980 620960
Wootton Rivers *Sarah Davey* Tel: 01703 266200
Hungerford *Rose of Hungerford* Tel: 01980 620960
Kintbury
Kennet Valley (horsedrawn) Tel: 01635 441154
Newbury *Avon* Tel: 01635 441154
Reading *Rose of Hungerford* Tel: 01189 871115

📖 **Suggested Guide Book**
Niall Allsop *The Kennet and Avon Canal* Millstream Books, 1992

ℹ **Tourist Information**
Bristol Tel: 0117 926 0767
Bath Tel: 01225 477000
Devizes Tel: 01380 729408
Marlborough Tel: 01672 513989
Newbury Tel: 01635 30267
Reading Tel: 0118 956 6226

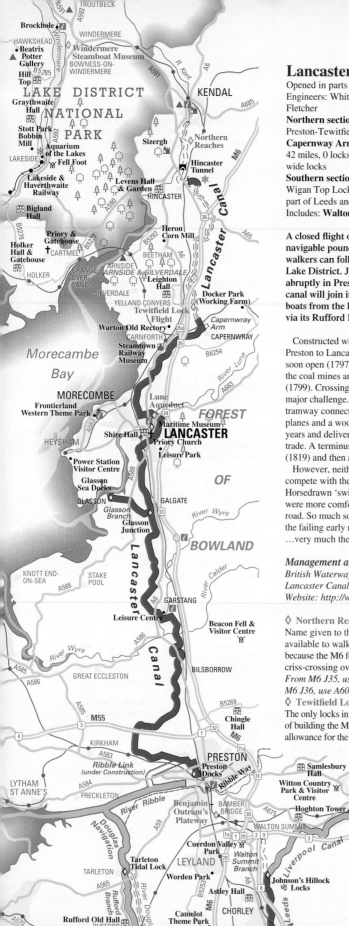

Lancaster Canal 118 B3-B1

Opened in parts 1797, 1799, 1803, 1819.
Engineers: Whitworth, Rennie, Crossley, Cartwright, Fletcher

Northern section
Preston-Tewitfield-Kendal plus **Glasson Branch and Capernway Arm**
42 miles, 0 locks: 13½ miles 8 wide locks: 2½ miles, 6 wide locks

Southern section
Wigan Top Lock to Johnson's Hillock Junction. Now part of Leeds and Liverpool Canal
Includes: **Walton Summit Branch**

A closed flight of eight locks ends the longest level navigable pound in Britain. Further to the north walkers can follow the water channel up into the Lake District. Just now, the southern end stops abruptly in Preston. Soon (2000) four miles of new canal will join it to the tidal Ribble and thus allow boats from the Leeds and Liverpool Canal to enter via its Rufford Branch and the tidal Douglas.

Constructed without locks, the 42 mile section from Preston to Lancaster and beyond to Tewitfield was soon open (1797), as was the southern 13 miles from the coal mines around Wigan to beyond Chorley (1799). Crossing the Ribble into Preston was the major challenge... so a temporary 5½ mile twin track tramway connected them (1803). Three inclined planes and a wooden trestle bridge lasted for over 60 years and delivered coal until the railways stole the trade. A terminus at Kendal was only reached later (1819) and then a branch to the sea (1826).

However, neither railways nor stage coach could compete with the Preston to Kendal passenger service. Horsedrawn 'swift boats' imported from Scotland were more comfortable than rail and twice as quick as road. So much so that, for eight years, the canal leased the failing early railway...

...very much the reverse of normal experience.

Management and Restoration
British Waterways, Wigan Tel: 01942 242239
Lancaster Canal Trust Tel: 01772 746914
Website: http://www.hillbeck.force9.co.uk.

◊ **Northern Reaches**
Name given to the length of canal up to Kendal available to walkers but currently closed to boats because the M6 followed its level line along the valley, criss-crossing over the canal six times.
From M6 J35, use A6070 to Burton-in-Kendal, and M6 J36, use A6070 to Gatebeck.

◊ **Tewitfield Lock Flight** (8 locks, 75 foot rise)
The only locks in 55 miles of canal, derelict at the time of building the M6 (1962). Already making proper allowance for the canal to the south, it proceeded to remove the lock gates and culvert the Northern Reaches.
Cinderbarrow picnic site has waymarked trails.
From M6 J35A, use A6 / A6070 going north. Turn right after crossing the motorway.

◊ **Lune Aqueduct** (1797: 664 feet)
Rennie's five arched stone masterpiece maintaining a level by crossing 60 feet over the River Lune.
From M6 J35A, use A6 going south towards Halton then follow the riverbank downstream, ie south.

◊ **Benjamin Outram's Plateway** (1803-1868)
A five mile 'temporary' link between the northern and southern sections of canal. The plateway was carried over the Ribble by a wooden trestle bridge overcoming the 222 foot level difference using three steep slopes (up to 1 in 6) worked by 'five engines' (stationary steam winding engines actuated by fire). The plateway connected Preston in the north with Johnsons Hillock to the south.

The original structure has since been replaced by a concrete bridge and enables cyclists and walkers across the river and to follow the old line for two miles, part of a scheme being created by the Local Authorities and a lottery grant (see also page 56).
From M6 J31. Use A59 west into Avenham Park.

◊ **Windermere Steamboat Museum**
Although beyond the northern reaches of the Lancaster Canal, waterway enthusiasts anywhere near Kendal should not miss the chance of visitiing this museum. When there were no roads near the lakes, Lancashire industrialists built their week-end retreats on the lakeshore, and indulged themselves by going home from the trains by steamboat.

There are many rescued examples of the type, displayed under cover but still floating on water.
Approach from M6 J36. Use A65 / A590 / A5074 going north west. Lakeshore beyond Bowness.

❋ **Boat Trips**
Crookland *Waterwitch* Tel: 01524 781604
Windermere *Teal, Tern, Swan* Tel: 01539 531118

ℹ **Tourist Information**
Brockdale Tel: 01539 446601
Kendal Tel: 01539 725758
Lancaster Tel: 01524 32878
Preston Tel: 01772 253731
Windermere Tel: 01539 446499

•••••••••••••••••••••••••••••••••••••

Lapal Canal - see BCN (Dudley No 2 Canal)
Lark, River 117 D3
Great Ouse Navigation to Bury St Edmunds
Environment Agency, Brampton Tel: 01480 414581

Lee (and Stort) Navigation 113 D1

Improved: 1424, 1430, 1577, 1767: Stort 1769, 1924
Engineers: Whittenbury, Smeaton, Yeoman
Hertford and Bishop's Stortford to the Thames at Limehouse Cut and Bow Creek
Old Ford Junction with Hertford Union (Ducketts Cut)
28 miles, 19 wide locks to Hertford; 14 miles and 15 wide locks to Bishop's Stortford

Lee Valley Regional Park Authority has worked successfully since 1967 to change the flood plain to provide a massive leisure resource for nine million people. Meadows and marshes, playing fields and lakes, nature reserves and sports facilities have been managed to give a new lease of life to the valley. An excellent footpath throughout waymarked with a 'Swan', goes as far as 'Lee Town' (modern Luton) and only floods occasionally in the tidal reaches.

Sailing, fishing for roach and bream, walking along water margins and woodland, camping and picnicking are all consciously encouraged. Wildlife

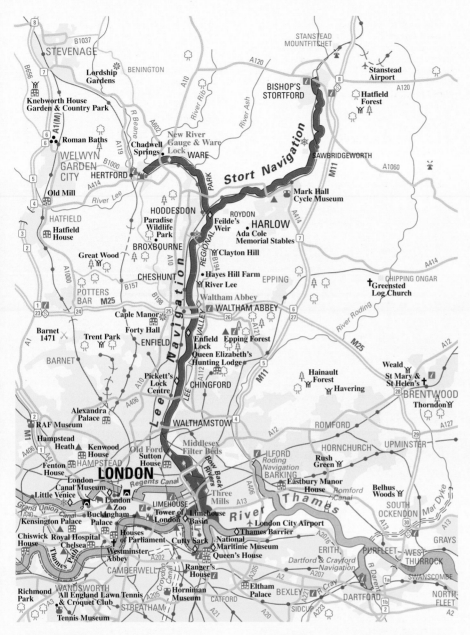

Sir George Duckett owned and canalised the Stort (1766), issuing his own money in the process. After Brick Lock on the Stort collapsed (1909) Lee Conservancy rebuilt it, paid 'five shillings' (25p) for the rest of the Stort Navigation and reopened it (1924). When carrying ended 130 ton barges could penetrate to Enfield and 100 ton barges to Hertford.

Management
British Waterways, The Toll Office, London
Tel: 020 7286 6101
Lee Valley Regional Park Authority Tel: 01992 717711

◊ **New River Gauge and Ware Lock**
The weir at New Gauge ensures River Lee only supplies an agreed volume of water to the New River water supplies. Controlled from Ware Lock.
◊ **Waltham Abbey: Royal Gunpowder Mills**
(1561-1991) Served from the Powdermill Cut, and initially a private concern, they were rationalised in 1787. The navigation carried this dangerous cargo from an internal system of canals to Woolwich Arsenal and the Naval Dockyards on the Thames. The site, damaged in War, is both a Scheduled Ancient Monument and a Site of Special Scientific Interest. It will form the heart of a Lottery supported industrial archaeology centre, planned to open in late 1999.
From M25 J26, use A121 / B194 going north.
◊ **Old Ford**
The only safe river crossing until 12th century and now the location of massive drainage outfalls, the semi-tidal lock here is at the head of a mixture of natural river courses and artificial cuts known as Bow Back Rivers, made to improve the working of the industrial area downstream as far as the Thames. It is also the home of Channel 4's studios.
From 102(M), use A102 / A11 / A115 going north.
◊ **Middlesex Filter Beds**
Increased pollution of the river from towns upstream was followed by an epidemic of cholera in London (1849). This led to the construction of massive beds to further purify London's drinking water. Operational 1849-1969, the filter beds are now a wildlife sanctuary open to the public at weekends.
From M11 J4, use A406 / A503 going west.
◊ **Three Mills: Bromley-by-Bow**
Nine mills were recorded in the Domesday Book, two tide mills are left. Clock Mill has been restored and the five storey timber framed House Mill (1776) straddles four 20 foot diameter wheels set in a 45 foot waterway. Incoming tides are held back in a lake over 50 acres in extent and 150 horsepower is then released to drive eight pairs of stones. Forbidden to grind gun-powder after 1588, the mills eventually turned to manufacturing Dutch Gin (1720-1942).
Approach from A102(M). Use A102 / A11 junction.

✽ **Boat Trips**
Broxbourne *Adventure Cruises* Tel: 01992 462085
Sawbridgeworth
Lady of Lee Valley Tel: 01279 600848
Redwatch Tel: 01277 229412

i **Tourist Information**
Hertford Tel: 01992 584322
Bishop's Stortford Tel: 01279 655831
Lee Valley Park Tel: 01992 713838

abounds. For example, the shallow waters of Hall Marsh attract redshank, tern, widgeon, and little ringed plover.

Bronze Age dugouts are witness to the long history of navigation on the relatively slow moving river system. Because it is so close to London, the valley has always been full of fiercely competing uses; for water supply, power for flour mills, as a trunk route for agricultural goods such as grain, malt and timber (even during the Plague of 1665) and a source of gravel for roads and concrete. Latterly, it has been treated as dumping ground for obnoxious trades such as slaughter houses, gunpowder and chemical industries and waste paper processing.

In 1608 London rivers were so foul King James

partially funded a 'contour' aqueduct (New River) parallel to the west bank of the river from Chadwell Springs to Islington. Concern by bargees and millowners erupted when the springs proved inadequate for the demands of Londoners and so much water was drawn from the Lee that the natural flow was lost.

Two Acts of Parliament were passed (1739, 1767) which led to replacement of primitive staunches by new cuts and modern style pound locks. Even so, water supply needs took precedence, limiting barges to 40 tons (1805). In 1902 Metropolitan Water Board took over Walthamstow reservoirs and filter beds that had been constructed from 1863 onwards and built still more reservoirs up stream at Chingford. There are now fourteen!

Leeds and Liverpool Canal

118 B2 - 119 D2

Opened: Gargrave and River Douglas (1774),
River Aire (1777), Foulridge (1796), Blackburn (1810)
Wigan Flight (1816)
Engineers: Longbotham, Brindley, Owen, Whitworth,
Clowes, Fletcher
Liverpool Docks to River Aire in Leeds.
127 miles, 93 wide locks, 2 tunnels

Arching north between the Red and White Rose Counties, this wide canal effectively provides a coast to coast waterway route. Climbing up through some of the most attractive scenery in the country spectacular locks lead to the summit on one of the lower passes across the Pennines, typified by the environs of the lock flight at Greenberfield.

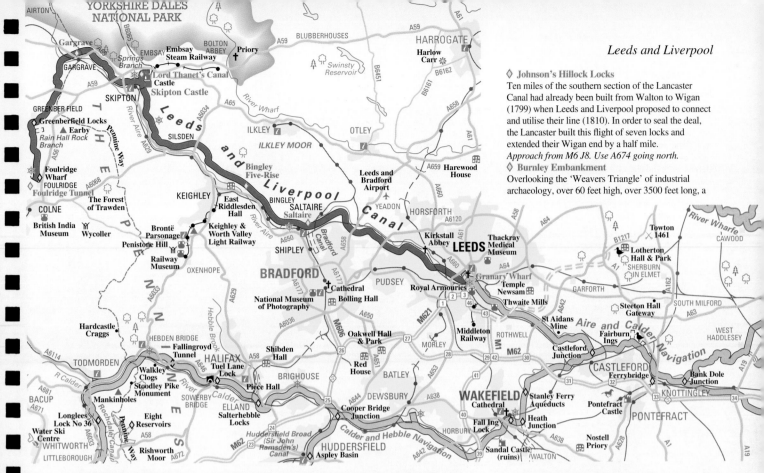

◊ **Johnson's Hillock Locks**

Ten miles of the southern section of the Lancaster Canal had already been built from Walton to Wigan (1799) when Leeds and Liverpool proposed to connect and utilise their line (1810). In order to seal the deal, the Lancaster built this flight of seven locks and extended their Wigan end by a half mile.
Approach from M6 J8. Use A674 going north.

◊ **Burnley Embankment**

Overlooking the 'Weavers Triangle' of industrial archaeology, over 60 feet high, over 3500 feet long, a major feat of engineering is now paralleled by the M65.
From M65 J12, use A6114 / A682 going south.

◊ **Foulridge Tunnel** (4900 feet)

Foulridge was the Achilles' heel of the canal. It was constructed mainly as a cut-and-cover project, took six years to build, seriously overran its budget, collapsed three times (1824, 1843, 1902) and was regularly closed in summer due to shortage of water (especially 1824, 1826). Five reservoirs, at Foulridge Lower, Barrowford, Winterburn, Rishton and Whitemoor, were built before this was solved. It was also unlucky for cows. One fell in (1912), swam the wrong way, and was only pulled out after struggling through the whole length of the tunnel. Apparently the landlord's brandy revived the animal.
From M65 J13, use A6068 / A56 going north.

◊ **Gargrave**

On the borders of Yorkshire Dales National Park twelve locks pass under the 'most picturesque route to Scotland', the Settle to Carlisle railway.
Approach from M6 J36. Use A65 going south-east.

◊ **Lord Thanet's Canal** (1797)

Privately funded, this very short branch gave access to a tramway from Lord Thanet's limestone quarries.
Approach from M6 J36. Use A65 going south-east.

◊ **Bingley Five-Rise** (5 locks rising 60 feet)

Awesome centrepiece of 5 sets of staircase locks within 5 miles of each other. In combination with 3 more staircases to the south, it was part of the bold attack on the slopes of the Pennines. There are 3 sets of *two-rise* plus 4 sets of *three-rise* plus Bingley *five-rise*, a total of 23 locks rising 155 feet over 16 miles from Kirkstall to the long pound past Skipton. *From M62 J26, use M606 / A6177 / A650 going north.*

A wide canal, 127 miles long and made suitable for Yorkshire keels (62' x 14') needing 200 bridges and 93 locks, the Leeds and Liverpool Canal was by far the most ambitious project by a single company.

First mooted at a meeting in Bradford (1766) this bold canal, the first to attempt a Pennine crossing, was somehow a relic of the Wars of the Roses. Finances were controlled by Yorkshiremen and this led to much discussion of the route to be taken through Lancashire.

It became a canal in two pieces which were not connected for 40 years. At the start two virtually lock free sections were built, one in each county… 24 miles from the River Douglas to Liverpool and 16 miles from Bingley to beyond Skipton in Yorkshire (1773). Then the valley up from Leeds to Gargrave was conquered with 'staircase' locks (1774) and connection made to the River Aire (1777).

After an 8 year delay the summit tunnel at Foulridge was tackled (opened 1796), the canal extended to Blackburn (1810) and then the final link was completed (the lock flight at Wigan:1816). Thereafter, Lancashire improvements included a link to the Bridgewater Canal (1820), lengthening locks to Liverpool (1822) and a link to the Mersey through Stanley Dock (1846).

The company was always independent of the railways, partly because their wide boats could carry twice the load of the standard 'Midlands' narrowboat.

Management and Restoration

British Waterways, (Liverpool to Greenber Field), Wigan Tel: 01942 242239
British Waterways, (Greenber Field to Leeds), Bradford Tel: 01274 611303

◊ **Merseyside Maritime Museum: Albert Dock**

On Liverpool's waterfront and within walking distance of the present day canal terminus, (¼ mile short of the original one at Pall Mall [closed: 1960]) there are five converted warehouses around Albert Dock (1846). Built for shallow draft sailing vessels, the dock is now used for floating exhibits and the warehouses contain the Maritime Museum working displays and the modern art collection of the Tate Gallery (1988).
From M6 J23, use A580 / A59 going west and south.

◊ **Aintree Canal Turn**

Sharp corner on the Grand National Race Course, five miles inland from Stanley Dock in Liverpool.
Approach from M58 J7. Use A59 going south.

◊ **Scarisbrick** (1821)

Change here for the sea side! A regular passenger service ran from industrial heartland of Manchester to meet with a stage coach from here to Southport.
Approach from M58 J3. Use A570 going north.

◊ **Burscough Junction**

Rufford Branch (1805) drops down 7 locks and replaced the earlier Douglas Navigation which had been exporting coal from Wigan for over 60 years (1741-1805). Tarleton Lock enters the tidal River Douglas and gives access to the Ribble estuary.
Approach from M6 J27. Use A5209 going west.

◊ **Wigan Flight**

Five locks from Liverpool, two locks from Runcorn and eleven locks from Lancaster; a flight of twenty one wide (14 foot) and short (60 foot) locks rises (215 feet) to meet (*and in 1851 to 'take over'*) the 13 mile southern pound of the Lancaster Canal.
Approach from M61 J6. Use A6 going north. Turn south; stop at the canal bridge beyond Aspull.

Wigan Pier

Warehouses, waterside gardens and a 70 ton flywheel.

Two Georges (Formby and Orwell) are celebrated in a classic recreation of times gone by. Canal side buildings and the towpath form an island of calm in the centre of a one way traffic system. Single payment is inclusive of a trip on the water, but there is much to see free of charge.

Start the stroll by standing at the:-
1 Waterbus Stop
The canal carried imports of raw cotton bales from Liverpool Docks and locally mined coal for the engine. All grades of yarn were exported by boat from this basin. The hoist stopped opposite the doors at each floor level.
From here look:
- *to the left for* **Trencherfield Gardens**. Well equipped kids play area and walled garden with seats.
- *straight ahead for* **The Mill at the Pier.**
Cotton warehouse adapted for jazz concerts, etc. Pier ticket holders occasionally get in free. *Go around the engine house and ask in the Tourist Information Centre:-*
- *on the right* is the **The Trencherfield Engine. House** Whistle from this 2500 horsepower original (1902) steam engine can be heard on the half-hour at the start of each demonstration run.
Here is the 70 ton / 27 foot flywheel. Thousands of spindles on the five floors of 't'mill' were powered from this single source. Cotton spinning is also explained on the hour on the ground floor as part of Wigan Pier's **all-in ticket**. For those without tickets there is a towpath joining **1** and **2**, but if

you have a ticket catch the waterbus to:-
2 The Way We Were
The Wigan Pier Theatre Company uses these displays to remind present generations of 'The Way We Were' - not always a happy life. Look for a victorian school room, a colliery disaster, the Boer War and (on the top floor) a complete pub transported from Hope Street and reconstructed by shopping centre developers. *Walk west, past full size canal artefacts displayed in the canal side gardens. Up the wide steps to:-*
3 Seven Stars Bridge
The Pub sign makes the Plough of the seven stars. *Cross the canal (but not the road), return to the towpath.*
4 Wigan Pier is 200 yards along the southern bank of the canal. Colliery Waggons were pushed to the edge of the canal and coal tipped directly into waiting boats. *Follow the towpath across the canal main line and turn left onto the metal bridge in front of:-*
5 Gibson's Terminal Warehouse
(1777, rebuilt 1984) now the Orwell Pub has twin loading bays that allowed goods to be hoisted directly from the boats to the upper floors.
Alternatively, use the main canal towpath underneath Pottery Bridge to **1 Waterbus Stop** *(Note the two sets of rollers to stop towing ropes chafing the bridge.)* The Orwell Pub and 'Way We Were' buildings were both warehouses and boats would have tied up directly under the overhanging 'cats'; the timber walkways on the canal frontage are recent additions to allow easy access.

A longer walk to **2 Whalley's Basin**
From **1 Waterbus Stop and Lock 87** *follow the towpath south (perhaps detour to the covered Dry Dock and British Waterways Depot opposite), cross the main road (Poolstock) and down to:-*
6 Lock 86

Locks are counted from Leeds (82 miles). Only 5 locks to Liverpool (35 miles). *Then go up the* **Wigan 21** *towpath via:-*
7 Whalley's Basin
Formerly a gathering spot at the end of the Ince Hall Colliery arm for boats awaiting orders. Now a bog home to wildlife.

A shorter walk would cross the new bridge over the Leigh Branch junction. Along the towpath for a short way, cross the next footbridge overlooking the:-
8 Wigan Power Station Site: Girobank
The coal fired Wigan Power Station (1948) was closed (1972) and replaced by this modern computer centre. *Turn right, follow the lower path round. At the access road turn right to cross the canal again and (at the light controlled junction) cross Poolstock (Road). Through the pavement railings is the:-*
9 River Douglas
Rising in the north, passing underground through the town and forming the old navigation from Wigan to the Ribble until the canal bypassed it to Sollom and Tarleton.
Turn to the right along the pavement, cross the canal and left onto the towpath at **6** *and return to* **1**.

Getting there:
Approach from M6 J26. Use A577 / A49 / going east.
P   *East along Wallgate, turn right into Queen Street and right again down Chapel Street. Parking at Trencherfield Mill. Join at* **1**.
From either station exit into Wallgate, walk downhill under the railway viaduct. Join at **5**.

Landranger Map 108 Ref SD 57 05

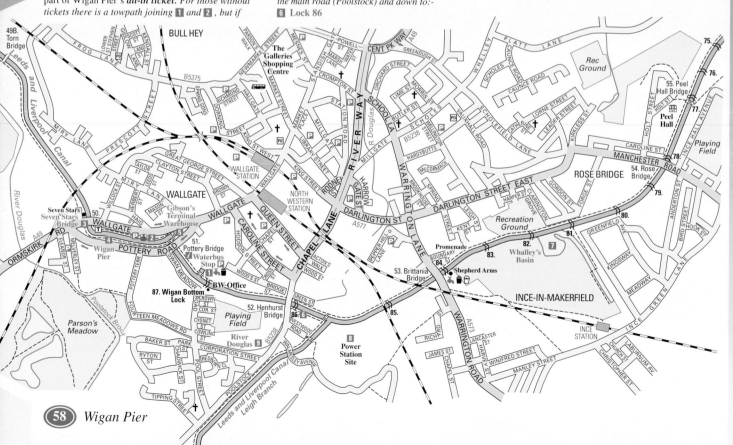

◊ **Saltaire**
The most splendid of a number of 'new towns' built by philanthropist mill owners to improve conditions for their workers. Stone built, it survives largely intact with houses, school, laundry, hospital, church but originally, no pubs. Others preceded it at *Cromford* (Richard Arkwright 1771), *Styal* (Samuel Greg 1784), *New Lanark* (Robert Owen 1800) and more locally, Copley (Edwin Ackroyd 1850). After Sir Titus Salt founded *Saltaire* (1850), *Ackroyden* (Edwin Ackroyd 1859) and *Port Sunlight* (Lever Bros. 1888) followed this more elaborate example.
From M62 J26 use M606 / A6177 / A650 northwards.

◊ **Granary Wharf: Leeds**
The canal enters the Aire and Calder Navigation at River Lock and the nearby basin is now known as Granary Wharf. Attracting crowds on summer Sundays, there is a picnic area, shops, a craft market three days a week and a trip boat to the Royal Armouries and Tetley's Brewery.
From M621 J3 or M1 J47, go to the 'City Centre'.

✿ **Boat Trips**
Leeds *Inspiration 2000* Tel: 0113 242 3731
Shipley *Apollo* Tel: 01274 595914
Skipton *Dalesman* Tel: 01756 790829
Foulridge *Marton Emperor* Tel: 01282 844033
Wigan *Kittywake* Tel: 01942 323666

ℹ️ **Tourist Information**
Liverpool Tel: 0151 708 8854
Wigan Tel: 01942 825677
Blackburn Tel: 01254 53277
Skipton Tel: 01756 792809
Bradford Tel: 01274 753678
Leeds Tel: 0113 242 5242

After the nearby colliery stopped using this wharf with its tramway tippler, boats used it as Wigan Pier.

Skipton Castle
Royalist stronghold, cobbled streets, secret canal.

Stroll around this granite *'Gateway to the Dales'* and into a deep ravine cut next to Eller Beck.

Start the stroll from:-
1 Skipton Castle Forecourt
Dominated by the Norman-French motto of the Clifford family built into the balustrade over the main gate. *Cross the graveyard of Holy Trinity Church safe from the roundabout traffic, down* ⚠ *eleven steps into Mill Bridge Road and down the hill to the bridge over Eller Beck.* **Alternatively**, *follow the narrow pavement around the outside of the churchyard (no steps). Opposite is:-*

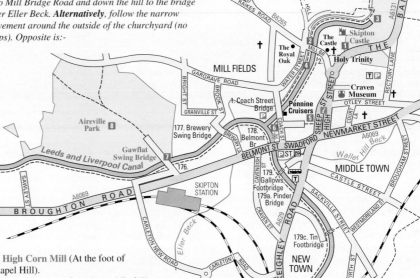

2 High Corn Mill (At the foot of Chapel Hill).
Once took its power from the rapidly falling Beck. Old millstones are let into the courtyard floor. *Go into the little, grassed open space and follow the white balustraded towpath snaking northwards away from the canal. The beck on the left is higher than the canal cut on the right. The cut is,*
3 Springs Branch or Lord Thanet's Canal. Only a thousand yards long but acts both as a moat to the castle and, until 1946, allowed limestone boats to be loaded by a metal chute (still visible) from a tramway (no longer visible) delivering from quarries further up the hill.
Keep going uphill until a short path to the left leads through a gateway into the shared driveway serving a few splendid houses. Walk away from the gate to the top of Chapel Hill, down past the Chapel and **2** High Corn Mill *to the B6265 to Grassington.*
Cross the road. A short way down Water Street is a:-
4 Single Beam Footbridge *which crosses over the beck onto the towpath! (A safer way is to join the towpath at the High Corn Mill.) From the slightly bumpy towpath look out for the sluices which controlled the flow of the beck to the, now defunct, mills further downstream. A small stream flowing energetically could power many machines.*
To return to the start at **1** *rejoin the road at the Coach Street narrow bridge and turn left into the cobbled Victoria Street, through the covered passage into* **5** Sheep Street *and left again past the market stalls into the High Street to return to* **1** Castle forecourt.

A longer walk to **8** Airville Park
From **5** Sheep Street *pass back through the passage to Victoria Square shops, cross over the (one way) Coach Street and down to:-*
6 Waterside Court and Canal Junction
Where the Springs Branch joins the main line and 50 minute wide beam boat trips can be booked.
Return to cross over the main road (A6069) and down a slope back onto the main Leeds and Liverpool Canal. Follow the towpath (for about 200 yards) past Brewery Swing Bridge.
If no boats are coming **7** Gawflat Swing Bridge *leads you up to* **8** Aireville Park *with its swimming pool, pitch and putt and children's play area.*

A second longer walk to **9** Skipton Woods
From **7** Springs Branch *follow the footpath further up the Eller Beck to the Round Dam into:-*
9 Skipton Woods *close to the old Embsey Quarry and the new A59 bypass. Return is possible via Short Lee Lane and the B6265 Grassington Road to* **2**.

Getting there:
Approach from A1(M) J47. Use A59 west.
🅿 *Suggest east of High Street. Join at* **1**.
♿ *Parking at Coach Street. Join at* **5**.
🚉 *From station exit cross road. Join at* **7**.

Landranger Map 103 Ref SD 99 52

Lichfield Canal
- see **Wryley and Essington Canal, BCN**

Limehouse Cut - see **Lee Navigation**

Linton Lock Navigation   119 D2
Widdington Ings near Newton-on-Ouse to
Swale Nab
*Clerk to the Commissioners of Linton Lock, Malton
Tel: 01653 600070*

Liskeard and Looe Union Canal   110 C3
River Looe to Moorswater

Little Ouse River (Brandon River)   117 D2
Great Ouse Navigation to Thetford
Environment Agency, Brampton Tel: 01480 414581

Little Stour River   113 F2
River Stour (Kent) to Wickhambreaux

Llangollen Canal
- see **Shropshire Union Canal**

Llansamlet Canal   114 B4
River Tawe to Llansamlet

Llechryd Canal   114 A3
River Teifi to Castle Malgwyn

Lockington Navigation - see **Aike Beck**

Looe, River   110 C3
Looe to Liskeard and Looe Union Canal

Lord Thanet's Canal
- see **Springs Branch, Leeds and Liverpool Canal**

Loughborough Navigation
- see **Grand Union Canal**

Louth Navigation   119 F3
Tetney Haven to Louth
11¾ miles, 8 wide locks (none in use)
Louth Navigation Trust Tel: 01507 607977

Lower Avon Navigation
- see **Avon (Warwickshire, Worcestershire,
Gloucestershire), River**

Lower Medway Navigation
- see **Medway Navigation**

Lugg Navigation   115 D3
River Wye to Leominster

Lydney Canal   115 D4
River Severn to Lydney Station
1 mile, 1 wide lock
Harbour Masters Office, Lydney

Macclesfield Canal   118 C4
Opened: 1831
Engineers: Telford, Crosley
Marple Junction to Hardings Wood Junction
26 miles, 12 narrow locks, 8 aqueducts, 2 swing bridges

**Starting at the summit level of the Trent & Mersey,
the 'Macc' climbs even higher and becomes the
highest level on the system (518 feet) to overlook
the Cheshire Plain and cling to the skirts of the
Pennines. Accompanied by waymarked walks, the
'Mow Cop Trail' and 'Middlewood Way', the canal
towpath presents many opportunities for short and
long distance walking, staying down near water or
climbing high up into the nearby hills with their
monuments and follies. The many connections
allow walkers and cyclists the choice of either
going round in circles or in a long straight line!**

This late canal speeded travel from Manchester to
the Potteries, Midlands and the south in two
fundamental ways. First, less distance than going via
Runcorn and not subject to delays by the operation
of the tunnels at Preston Brook and, second, it was built
after much experience of boatmen's techniques.

For example, where a lock is set close to its neighbour
it can be prepared whilst the first lock is being used.
This minimizes delay whilst waiting for locks to fill.
Telford, therefore, collected all Macclesfield's locks
into one flight and maintained a long level on each side
of them by bold "cut and fill" techniques, which gave
us eight aqueducts, high embankments and cuttings.

Post war efforts by the Chairman and members of
the North Cheshire Cruising Club (founded 1943) and
the Inland Waterways Association Second National
Rally (1953) drew attention to the lack of maintenance
and deterioration of this canal. After a campaigning
cruise met apparent sabotage (1961), the Peak Forest
Canal Society (1964) proposed a 'Cheshire Ring' of
regenerated canals (including the 'Macc') which was
finally opened after ten years' effort (1974).

Management and Restoration
*British Waterways, Red Bull Tel: 01782 785703
Macclesfield Canal Society Tel: 01625 428734
Website: http://www.ourworld.compuserve.com/
homepages/tim_boddington/macccs.htm*

◊ **Turnover Bridge: Marple**
Typical example of Telford's confident use of stone
materials in a simple graceful structure entirely suited
to its function. A horse bringing a boat into Telford's
canal from the Marple lock flight would first walk
under the bridge and then (while the boat drifted
towards the entrance to his canal) the horse would
climb *up the curving ramp*, over his canal bridge and
back down to the towpath. By then the towing rope,
although still connected to both boat and horse, would
probably be floating idly on the water. The horse
would walk on along the straight Macclesfield towing
path and pick up the strain on the rope to continue on
his way, without any of the manhandling or unhitching
of rope that might be needed with other designs.
*From M60 J27, use A626 / B6101 going south-east
or M60 J1, using A6 south to High Lane. Turn north.*

◊ **Lord Vernon's Wharf: Higher Poynton**
In the centre of a mining district which once boasted
over 70 separate establishments, this wharf was
supplied (1840-1890) from a large tramway system
around Poynton and from the Higher and Lower Canal
Pits via the Princess Incline. Flatbed bridges and
straight footpaths are relics of the coal industry.
Together with the High Lane Arm the wharf now
provides off line mooring for pleasure craft.
Approach from M60 J1. Use A6 / A523 going south.

◊ **Bosley Locks** (12 rising 118 feet)
Sole change in level between the Peak Forest Canal at
Marple, 23 miles away, and the Trent and Mersey Canal
at Hardings Wood, 9 miles away. To reduce closures for
maintenance the stone chambers are of a very solid
construction and the lock gates are heavily built.
Designed to be worked by a lock keeper and boatman
together, even the top gates of the locks are mitred.
From M6 J18, use A54 going east beyond Congleton.

◊ **Hardings Wood Junction**
Connecting with the Trent and Mersey main line just
north of the Harecastle Tunnel entrance, this junction
is a bit of a corkscrew. It takes off at the summit
level, goes parallel while two pairs of locks descend
the hill and then turns sharp north over the mainline
up the branch to meet the Macclesfield proper at Hall
Green stop lock (numbered 12½)
*Approach from M6 J16. Use A500 / A34 going east
then north to junction with A50.*

📖 *Suggested Guide Book*
Tim Boddington et al *The Macclesfield Canal*
Macclesfield Canal Society, 1998

ℹ️ *Tourist Information*
Stockport Tel: 0161 474 4444
Macclesfield Tel: 01625 504114
Congleton Tel: 01260 271095

Mackworth's Canal   114 B4
River Neath to Melyn Works near Neath
MacMurray's Canal   113 D2
River Thames to Wandsworth
Manchester Bolton and Bury Canal   118 C3
River Irwell, Manchester to Bolton
Bury Arm
British Waterways, Marple Tel: 0161 427 1079
Manchester Bolton and Bury Canal Society
Tel: 01204 844671

Manchester and Salford Junction Canal 118 C3
River Irwell, Manchester to Rochdale Canal,
Manchester
Manchester Ship Canal   118 B4-B3
Eastham to Salford
Pomona Lock Branch to Bridgewater Canal
36 miles, 5 locks
Manchester Ship Canal Company, Eastham
Tel: 0151 327 1461

Mar Dyke   113 D2
Purfleet to Bulphan Fen
Market Weighton Canal   119 E2
Weighton Lock to River Head near Market Weighton
Sir Edward Vavasour's Canal (Holme Canal)
9½ miles, 1 wide lock
Environment Agency, Leeds Tel: 0113 244 0191
Medina, River   112 B4
Cowes to Newport, Isle of Wight

Medway Navigation   113 E2-E3
Open: Yalding 1580, Tonbridge 1741
Sheerness to Allington. Allington to Tonbridge
24 miles tidal, 19 miles and 10 locks sweetwater

Separating 'Men of Kent' from 'Kentish Men' as it
flows through the 'Garden of England', the river
water meets tides and barges coming up from the
salt marshes and mud flats of the Sheerness estuary.

Allington Tidal lock is far inland and holds
water enough to allow navigation to Maidstone at
all states of the tide. Upstream there is a towpath
where walking and fishing are popular. Downstream
low tides expose the river bed and encourage an
exceptional wetland wildlife.

Every improvement to the navigation seems to have
required a separate Act of Parliament... to transport
timber and ordnance downstream for the navy (1665),
to Yalding (1740), Alyesford to Maidstone (1792), to
make Allington Flash lock (1802), to rebuild and widen
the central arches of Aylesford Bridge (1824) and to
enlarge and deepen Allington Lock (1880).

Public rights of navigation on this lively river are
sometimes curtailed in practice by the risk of
flooding from catchment rainwater and/or wind
assisted north sea tides.

Management and Restoration
Medway Ports Authority, Sheerness Tel: 01795 580003
Environmental Agency, East Malling
Tel: 01732 838858

◊ **Medway Estuary**
Where the Dutch trapped the English (1667), this
wide expanse of sheltered water is a playground for
pleasure yachts and small boats, especially at high
tide. Venue for some of the Thames Barge Races.
From M2 J2, use A228 north to Kingsnorth Pier.

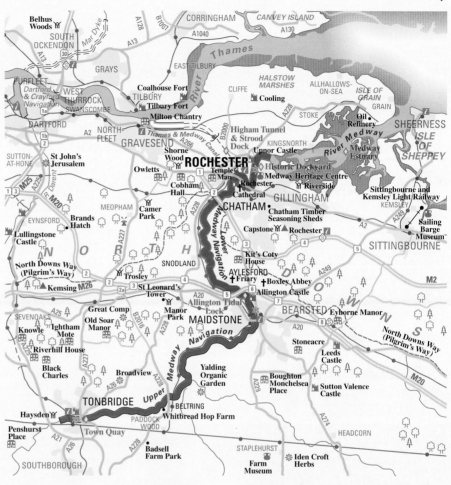

◊ **Historic Dockyard: Chatham** (1547-1984)
'The River and its appendices are..most considerable
of the kind in the world being the chief Arsenal of the
Royal Navy of Great Britain' (Daniel Defoe 1720).
Now open to non-servicemen and women. Warships
alongside, naval ordnance, working ¼ mile ropery.
Approach from M2 J3. Use A229 / A230 / A231 north.

◊ **Higham Tunnel and Strood Dock**
The generously wide Higham Tunnel (11 800 feet
long x 26 feet wide) was part of Thames and
Medway Canal (which joined the Thames seven
miles away at Gravesend). A valuable prize secured
by South Eastern Railway who purchased the canal
(1846) and within 12 months changed the canal
tunnel to a double track railway line. The tidal lock
gate to the Strood Dock remains.
Approach from M2 J2. Use A278 going north
to Strood Railway Station.

◊ **Allington Tidal Lock** (1802)
The key to the character of both halves of the river.
The riverbed regularly dries out below this huge
chamber (175 feet x 21 feet) which is accessible only
for 3 hours before high tide and 2 hours afterwards.
Approach from M20 J6. Use A229 going south.

◊ **Town Quay: Tonbridge**
Downstream of the low headroom of Great Bridge
(1775, 1887) and upstream of the last lock of the
navigation, the Quay was destination for much river

trade. Area is now host to rowing boats, a trip boat
and visiting pleasure boats.
From M26 J2a, use A25 / A227 going west and south.

✿ **Boat Trips**
Tonbridge Castle *Caxton* Tel: 01732 360630
Maidstone *Kentish Lady II* Tel: 01622 753740
Allington *Swan* Tel: 01622 752918
Chatham Dockyard *Kingswear Castle*
Tel: 01634 823800

ℹ **Tourist Information**
Rochester Tel: 01634 843666
Maidstone Tel: 01622 602169
Tonbridge Tel: 01732 770929

Melton Mowbray Navigation   116 B2
Old Junction to Melton Mowbray
Mersey and Irwell Navigation   118 B3
Hunt's Bank, Manchester to Runcorn
Mostly superseded by Manchester Ship Canal
Includes **Runcorn and Latchford Canal**
Warrington to Runcorn
Mersey, River   118 B3
Liverpool to Warrington
25¼ miles, 0 locks
Mersey Docks and Harbour Co Tel: 0151 949 6000

Middle Level Navigations   116 C3

Improved: 1631, 1651, 1810, 1844, 1874
Engineers: Popham, Vermuyden
30 miles, 8 wide locks

Main route between River Nene and Great Ouse
Navigations is the **'Middle Level Link'**
King's Dyke Stanground Sluice to Whittlesey
Whittlesey Dyke Whittlesey to Flood's Ferry
Old River Nene Flood's Ferry to Outwell
Well Creek Outwell to Salter's Lode
Bevill's Leam Angle Corner to Mere Mouth
Black Ham Drain Mere Mouth to Yaxley
Farcet River or **Pig Water** King's Dyke to Yaxley
Forty Foot River or **Vermuyden's Drain** Wells'
Bridge to Welches Dam
Middle Level Main Drain Three Holes to Well
Creek Aqueduct (no link with Well Creek)
New Dyke Nightingale's Corner to Holme
Old River Nene Mere Mouth to Flood's Ferry
Popham's Eau Old River Nene to Three Holes
Sixteen Foot River Three Holes to Forty Foot River
Twenty Foot River Angle Corner to Old River Nene

**Unique panoramas of vast skies, sunsets and storms
watch over a network of waterways where boats are
rare and coarse fishermen share the silence and
tranquillity with an abundance of wildlife.**

In the Fens drainage is king but navigation is
encouraged in the summer when retained water can
provide channels. New marinas have been
established and the locks that give access from the
Rivers Nene and Ouse have recently (1991, 1999)
been extended to take standard (72') narrowboats.

In prehistoric times huge tracts of land from the
Wash as far inland as the Great North Road consisted
largely of marshy bog. Firm foundations were in
short supply and independent, isolated Fen dwellers
built their stilt houses over the shallows or on the few
islands of harder land. Many monasteries built strong
flood defenses and 'reclaimed' local bogs from the
river delta. Then, with the patronage of the Earl of
Bedford, vast areas were subjected to systematic
drainage, thereby destroying fishing and wildfowl
resources. Dutch engineers worked for these
'Adventurers' who financed the works but had their
structures temporarily destroyed by the fiercely
independent 'Fens Tigers' (1651).

Rich residues of shrunken dark peat now make the
Fens unique. Once bog was turned into farms, land
shrank below the level of the drains and wind pumps
were needed to stop water logging. Although built in
their hundreds, they could not keep up with the
problem. Only when steam power, then diesel and
electricity was available was the problem solved (1820).

Modern sea defenses, sluices, embankments and
drains now struggle against the symptoms of global
warming and their long wide straight 'lodes' are
everywhere running to far horizons.

Management and Restoration
East Anglian Waterways Association Tel: 01354 652329
Middle Level Commissioners Tel: 01354 653232
Well Creek Trust Tel: 01945 772632

◊ **Stanground Lock and Sluice**
Main entrance from River Nene to drainage system
that contains varying depths of water depending on
season, rainfall and flood conditions. The lockkeeper
also controls the Ashline Lock at the other end of
Kings Dyke at Whittlesey.
Approach from A1(M). Use A1139 going east.
◊ **Flag Fen**
Active archeological excavations and recreated
bronze age environment. *Entrance fee.*
From Peterborough Centre, use A1139 going east.
◊ **March**
The River Nene once flowed past this market town

on one of the few islands of firm ground within the
undrained fens. Formerly both a Tudor Port and
railway town, it is the largest settlement on the levels
and has all boating facilities.
From A1 at Huntingdon, use A141 going north.
◊ **Pophams Eau** (1605)
Draining the Old Nene towards the River Ouse, this
early channel is navigable between the Sixteen Foot
Drain and a point upriver of Marmont Priory Lock.
*From A10 at Ely, use A10 / A1122 going north then
west to Nordelph.*
◊ **Well Creek** (8 miles)
Fifteen bridges criss-cross this shallow channel
between Upwell and Nordelph which was saved from
abandonment by the Well Creek Trust (1975). Delta
flows of the Nene and Ouse have both used this route
in their time and the 150' wide Middle Level Main
Drain was taken **under** Well Creek (1844).
Approach from A10 at Ely. Use A1101 going north.
◊ **Salters Lode**
Opens into the tidal Ouse whose scouring action (or
lack of it) affects the silt remaining outside the lock.
Part of the 'Clapham Junction' of waterways around
Denver Sluice 300 yards upstream.
*Approach from A10 at Ely. Use A10 / A1122 going
north then west to Denver.*

ℹ **Tourist Information**
Wisbech Tel: 01945 583263
Downham Market Tel: 01366 387440
Fenland Tourism Tel: 01775 762715

• •

Monkland Canal   120 B1
Monkland Basin, Glasgow to Woodhall near
Calderbank **Calder Branch, Dundyvan Branch,
Gartsherrie Branch, Langloan Branch**
British Waterways, Glasgow Tel: 0141 332 6936

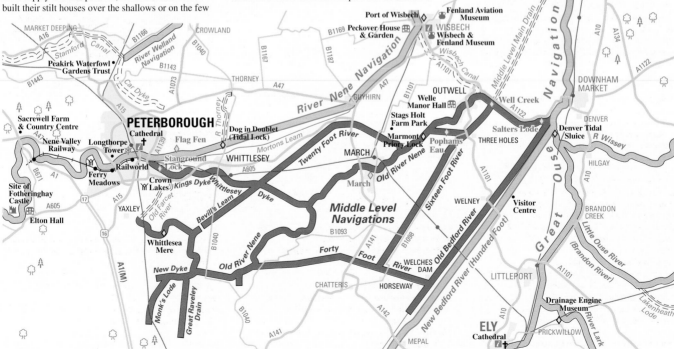

Monmouthshire and Brecon Canal
114 C3-C4

Opened: 1796, 1799, 1812-1949 and 1962, 1977
Engineers: Danford, Cartwright, Crossley
Brecon terminus to Pontymoile Junction
33 miles, 6 locks

The narrow River Usk valley runs down to Newport containing two waterways - a cascading mountain river and, high above, an isolated canal hugging the contours for 33 almost lock free miles.

This waterway has few engineering marvels but is surrounded on all sides by the spectacular Brecon Beacons National Park. Close up views of thick woodland alternate with sweeping panoramas and long mountain vistas. In many ways it is more rewarding than other, more popular, Welsh canals.

Two canals were promoted independently at the height of canal mania (1793). They both had powers to build 'feeder tramways' and the Brecknock and Abergavenny got on with tracklaying immediately, eventually owning more tramways than canal.

It joined end-to-end with the Montgomery at Pontymoile junction (1812) which thus obtained water supply from the Usk at Brecon. This became one reason for amalgamation (1865) and why it remained open long after traffic ceased (1933).

Management and Restoration
British Waterways, Govilon Tel: 01873 830328
Monmouthshire Brecon and Abergavenny Canals Trust Tel: 01446 796695

◇ **Theatre Brycheiniog**
Theatre goers overlook a spanking new (1998) terminal basin supplied by a culvert from the Usk.
From M4 J26, use A4051 / A4042 / A40 going northwest.

◇ **Tal-y-Bont Bascule Bridge**
Together with the lock at Brynich, this was a major element in the restoration (1970). Nearby remains of Bryn-Oer tram road should not be confused with a Roman road up the hill. Just to the south the B4558 is the towpath over the low Ashford Tunnel (1125ft).
Approach from M4 J26. Use A4051 / A4042 / A40 going north-west to B4558.

◇ **Llangynidr Locks**
Breathtaking scenery surrounds these locks at the head of the 25 mile lower pound and the start of an 8 mile pound to Brecon (one lock at Brynich).
Approach from M4 J26. Use A4051/A4042/A40 and B4560 going north then west.

◇ **Llangattock Wharf**
Huge cave systems (Agen Allwedd has 11 miles) remain from the days when tram roads brought limestone down to the limekilns seen on this wharf. One mile away in Crickhowell a 12 arch medieval bridge crosses the River Usk in the valley bottom.
Approach from M4 J26. Use A4051 / A4042 / A40 and B4558 going north then west.

◇ **Llanfoist Wharf: Abergavenny**
Clinging high on a narrow part of the valley, the canal here comes within a mile of its name town. The lines of old tramways rising up into the hills can be seen from many canal bridges and bits of iron track remain on the Llanfoist Wharf.
From M4 J26, use A4051/A4042/B4269 going north .

◇ **Malpas Junction**
On the outskirts of Newport, this marked the start of

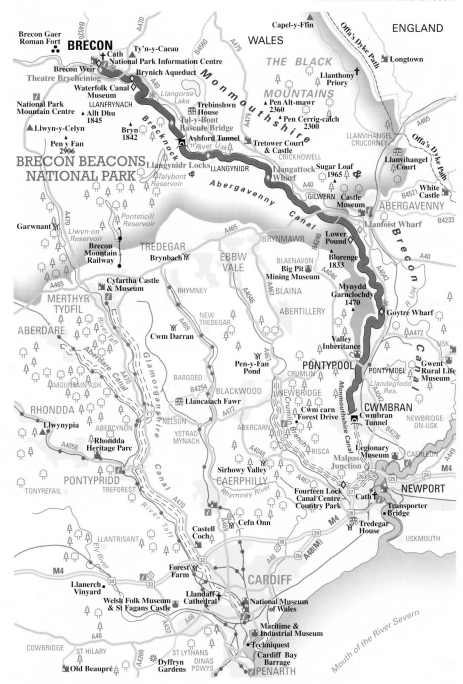

two, 11 mile arms of the Montgomery Canal. They were steeply climbing - up Ebbw Vale (32 locks: 358ft) and to Pontymoile (41 locks: 447ft).
Almost underneath M4 J26.

⚜ **Boat Trips**
Brecon *Dragonfly* Tel: 0831 685222
Llanfrynach *Dragon's Tail - horsedrawn*
Tel: 01874 665382
Goytre Wharf *The Lord William De Braose*
Tel: 01873 881069

📖 **Suggested Guide Book**
John Norris *The Brecon and Abergavenny section of the Monmouthshire and Brecon Canal* 3rd Edition, 1998

ℹ **Tourist Information**
Brecon Tel: 01874 622485
Abergavenny Tel: 01873 857588
Newport Tel: 01633 842962

Monmouthshire

Monmouthshire Canal
- see **Monmouthshire and Brecon Canal**
Montgomery Canal
- see **Shropshire Union Canal**
Morris's Canal later incorporated in
Trewyddfa Canal - see **Swansea Canal**
Muirkirk Canal
to Iron Works at Muirkirk   **120 C2**
Mundon or White House Farm Canal   **113 E1**
River Blackwater to White House Farm, Mundon

Nar, River   117 D2
King's Lynn to West Acre

Neath Canal   114 B4
Briton Ferry to Glyn-neath
Includes **Giant's Grave and Briton Ferry Canal**
Briton Ferry to Giant's Grave and **Penrhiwtyn
Canal** Giant's Grave to Penrhiwtyn
**Cnel Branch, Cowt sart Branch, Maesmarchog
Branch**
13½ miles, 19 locks
*Neath and Port Talbot Borough Council, Port Talbot
Tel: 01639 763333
Neath and Tennant Canals Preservation Society
Tel: 01792 201594*

Nene Navigation, River 116 B3-C2
Improved: 1490, 1730, 1761, 1935
Engineers: Morton, Smith
Northampton to 28 miles from The Wash
91 miles, 38 wide locks

A river in three parts: sources, middle and tidal.
Twin source streams, followed by quintessential
meanders through rich pastures with villages and
towns standing respectfully away from the banks
and, finally, severe man made engineering to drain
the waters straight out to sea.

For millennia waters from the Nene met the tides
from The Wash in a huge mosquito infested swamp.
Somewhere within the delta it joined forces with the
River Ouse to create the Wellstream to The Wash
which, from time to time, changed both course and
width. Man then started his attempts at control.

Almost 2000 years ago Romans cleared a path for
boats from Durobrivae at Peterborough to Lincoln
and towards Cambridge (Car Dyke). They are also
reputed to have made a shallow cutting north of
March to force the rivers to the sea.

A Danish king whose lands included Norway and
England created 'Knute's Dyke' (or Briggate
River) to bypass Whittlesey Mere to Floods Ferry
(1014).

Bishops then diverted the river Ouse into its
course past King's Lynn (1200s) and created a 40
foot wide channel (Mortons Leam, 1490) for the
Nene to flow to Wisbech. A Chief Justice
channelled rogue Nene waters into the Ouse near
Outwell (Pophams Eau, 1605) and Dutch engineers
finally changed the course of the Nene for good
(Vermuyden 1651). Yorkshire engineers then
constructed staunches, locks and numerous short
cuts which now bypass curving backwaters (1761).

The main channel meets the turbulant tide (1938) at
an isolated lock 30 miles from the sea next to a
small pub, 'the Dog in Doublet'.

Management
*Environment Agency: Peterborough
Tel: 01733 371811
Port of Wisbech Tel: 01945 582125
Port of Sutton Bridge Tel: 01406 351530*

◊ **Northampton Connection**
Many breweries are sited along the Nene and at
Northampton is the largest modern (1972) complex
devoted to the art… probably. It stands at the

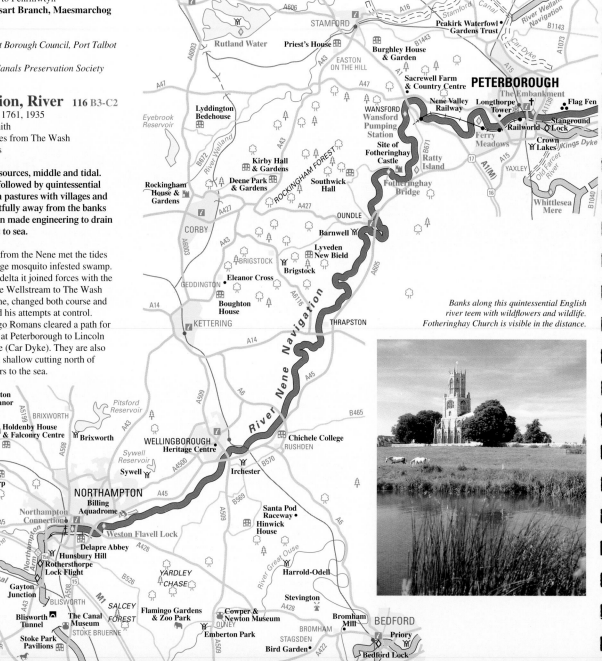

*Banks along this quintessential English
river teem with wildflowers and wildlife.
Fotheringhay Church is visible in the distance.*

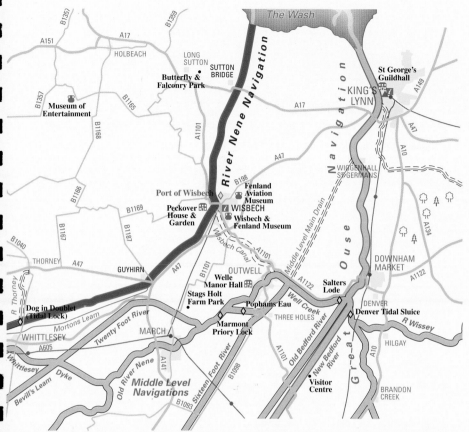

📖 *Suggested Guide Book*
David Phillips *The River Nene: From Source to Sea*
Past and Present Publishing, 1997

ℹ️ *Tourist Information*
Fens Tourism Tel: 01775 762715
Northampton Tel: 01604 622677
Peterborough Tel: 01733 452336
Wisbech Tel: 01945 583263

....

New Bedford River or Hundred Foot
 - see **Great Ouse Navigation**
New Dyke - see **Middle Level Navigations**
New Junction Canal
 - see **Aire and Calder Navigation** and **Sheffield and South Yorkshire Navigation**
Newcastle-under-Lyme Canal   118 C4
 Stoke-on-Trent to Newcastle-under-Lyme
Newcastle-under-Lyme Junction Canal 118 C4
 Newcastle-under-Lyme to Sir Nigel Gresley's Canal
Newdigate Canals   115 E2
 Coventry Canal near Marston Junction to Arbury and Seeswood Pool
Newport Pagnell Canal   116 B3
 Grand Union Canal to Newport Pagnell
Nith, River   120 C3
 Caerlaverock to Dumfries
Nocton Delph - see **River Witham**
North Drove Drain   116 C2
 From Pode Hole near Spalding
North Walsham and Dilham Canal   117 E1
 River Ant to Antingham
 2¼ miles navigable, 4 locks (none in use)
North Wilts Canal - see **Wilts & Berks Canal, Latton Branch**
Norwich and Lowestoft Navigation
 - see **The Broads**
Nottingham Canal   115 F1
 River Trent, Nottingham to Langley Mill
 Bilborough Arm, Greasley Arm, Robinett's Arm
 2½ miles, 2 locks
Nutbrook Canal   115 F1
 Stanton to Shipley

Oakham Canal   116 B2
 Melton Mowbray to Oakham
Old Bedford River   116 C2
 Great Ouse Navigation to Metal Pumping Station
 Environment Agency, Brampton Tel: 01480 414581
'Old' Grand Union Canal
 - see **Grand Union Canal**
Old West River - see **Great Ouse Navigation**
Ore, River   117 E3
 Shingle Street to Orford
 Suffolk Coastal District Council, Woodbridge Tel: 01394 383789
Orwell, River   117 E3
 Sea to Ipswich
 9½ miles, 0 locks
Ouse (Sussex), River   113 D3
 Newhaven to Hamsey Lock
 - see also **Upper Ouse Navigation**
 9½ miles, 0 locks
 Environment Agency, Worthing Tel: 01903 820692

---

confluence of the source streams and at the foot of
fifteen narrow locks which link the navigable Nene to
the Grand Union Canal. Together they make the
connection between English waterways and 2000
square miles of Fens and Cambridgeshire rivers.
From M1 J15, use A508 north to the centre.

◊ **Weston Flavell Lock**
The Environment Agency greets boaters with the first
electrically operated guillotine lock gates. There are
37 locks on the Middle Nene, not all of which yet
have this welcome, labour saving facility.
Approach from M1 J15. Use A508 / A45 north-east.

◊ **Fotheringhay Bridge**
A many arched bridge crosses the flood plain past the
lawn covered remains of a 12th century castle. Mary,
Queen of Scots, was incarcerated here for 19 years
before being beheaded (1587).
From M1 J15, use A508 / A45 / A605 going north.

◊ **Ratty Island: Elton Hall**
'There is nothing - absolutely nothing - half so much
worth doing as simply messing about in boats' was
Ratty's recommendation to Mole when first
confronted with water. Kenneth Grahame took his
inspiration for 'Wind in the Willows' from the idyllic
Nene whilst he was staying at Elton Hall.
From M1 J15, use A508 / A45 / A605 / B671 north.

◊ **Wansford Pumping Station: Rutland Water**
Lots of Nene water starts a 10 mile journey from here
to replenish the 3000 acre Rutland Water :-
a trout fishery and important wetland habitat which
was created as a water supply reservoir (1977).
Approach from A1(M) / A47 crossroads.

◊ **Ferry Meadows**
Nene Valley Steam Railway follows the river and
passes through 2500 acres of woodland and lakes
known as Nene Valley Country Park. Meadows and
backwaters alongside the river have attracted country
seekers since Victorian times.
From A1(M) J17, use A1139 / A605 going north.

◊ **The Embankment: Peterborough**
A floating pub and restaurant are two boats always
alongside these tree lined moorings close to the city
centre and its magnificent cathedral.
Approach from A1(M) J16. Use A15 going north.

◊ **Whittlesea Mere** (1851)
Before wandering about the Middle Levels the old
Nene flowed across this shallow natural lake which,
although only 5 feet deep, varied between a
summer 1600 acres and a winter 3000 acres.
During the most recent act of major land
reclamation (1851 North-Western Cut / New Dyke)
the bed revealed silverware from old inland
shipwrecks, the remains of huge log boats and a
fossilised killer whale.
From A1(M) J15, use B1043 / B660 / B1040 north-east.

◊ **Port of Wisbech**
Within 5 miles of the sea when the Domesday book
was compiled, tidal surges have flooded the area
many times (1236, 1260, 1285, 1570, 1947, 1953,
1978). Even normal tides vary by more than 15 feet
and a visit by land finds Georgian Architecture of
the North and South Brinks looking over the new
flood defence walls, with the sea 11 miles away.
From A1(M) at Wansford, use A47 going east.

Ouse (Yorkshire) Navigation

(and Ure Navigation)   119 D2-E3

Improved: 1462, 1769, 1773, 1826, 1885, 1996
Engineer: Smeaton
Trent Falls to Naburn tidal lock 38 miles, 0 locks
Naburn to Swale Nab 22 miles, 2 locks
Swale Nab to Ripon. 9½ miles, 5 locks

Towns in the upper reaches of this river system helpfully refer to the rivers in their name. Three upper river tributaries are navigable, the Swale,

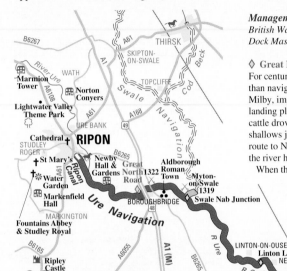

Ure and Foss. The Wharfe and Derwent join the tidal reaches but the Ouse, as such, never flows into the sea. The Ouse and Trent join together at Trent Falls and there is a change of name. They become the huge wide area of shifting sand and swirling tides that is the mighty River Humber.

York Corporation were appointed conservators of the whole system (1462) but failed to seriously concern themselves with navigation. Citizens of other towns sought to improve the tributaries under a series of Acts (1767) which, unfortunately, created a multiplicity of navigation authorities.

Works to create a lock and dam to raise Swale water levels were authorised but they had to be located on the Ure at Linton (7 miles downstream of Swale Nab - the confluence of the two rivers). This conflicted with Smeaton's designs for improvements to the Ure up to Ripon and, after a battle in

Parliament, resulted in the creation of separate 'Linton Lock Commissioners' (1770) specifically to control one short stretch of the Ure.

The Ure Navigation proper (1773) became busy with coal but was never financially successful. Bought out first by Ripon Corporation (1820) and then by the company promoting a new railway to Leeds and Thirsk (1846). Tidal reaches were eventually improved by the Aire and Calder Navigation (1885) as part of their scheme for Yorkshire keels to reach the Humber via Selby.

Management

British Waterways, Naburn Tel: 01904 728229
Dock Master Goole Tel: 01405 762691

◊ **Great North Road: Boroughbridge**
For centuries crossing the river was more important than navigating up it. The Romans inherited a ford at Milby, improved it with a bridge and established a landing place just downstream at Aldborough. Later cattle drovers encouraged their herds over the shallows just to the north and even now the land route to Northallerton and Scotland (A1(M)) crosses the river hereabouts.

When the people of Ripon sought to extend this head

of navigation by deepening the river (1766), they had to negotiate with the Duke of Newcastle to modify another structure across the river - his miller's dam.
Approach from A1(M). Use A168 / B6265 going east.

◊ **Jorvik: York**
Viking ships traded to Norway (AD 866-AD 954) until William the Conqueror laid waste to the land and established his garrison in a castle on the peninsula between the Foss and Ouse. Viking excavations and castle ruins can be seen today.
National Railway Museum Tel: 01904 621261.
From A1 / A64 junction, going east / A1036 north.

◊ **Naburn Cycle Bridge** (SUSTRAN)
Spanning the Ouse just upstream from tidal locks. Built to swing the railway out of the way of ships (1871-1973), it was only fixed (1967) after the steam driven hydraulic system had been kept in readiness 24 hours a day for 83 years (1871-1954).
From A1 / A64 junction going east / B1222 south.

◊ **Selby Bridges**
Navigation had priority in the tidal reaches. Two bridges were built on condition that they would be swung out of the way of masted vessels. A timber trestle Toll Bridge (1791-1969) which rested on early ball bearings (actually an array of cannon balls) could open within **one** minute. A bascule bridge carrying the railway (1840: replaced by the present bridge (1891-1983)) took **seven** minutes to open, later improved to **four** minutes.
From A1 / A63 junction. Use A63 east to A19.

◊ **Howden Dyke**
An extreme example of the shallow, wide course of the tidal river that exposes huge areas of grey mud banks except when there has been heavy rain upstream or the tide is in.
Visible from the M62 motorway bridge (J37-J36).

✳ **Boat Trips**
York *White Rose* Tel: 01904 628324
Castle Tel: 0836 739357
Ferry Lane Tel: 01904 704442
Goole *Sobriety* Tel: 01405 768730

📖 **Suggested Guide Book:**
Cruising Guide to the North East Waterways
Ripon Motor Boat Club, 1995

ℹ **Tourist Information**
Ripon Tel: 01765 604625
Harrogate Tel: 01423 537300
Boroughbridge Tel: 01423 323373
York Tel: 01904 621756
Selby Tel: 01757 703263

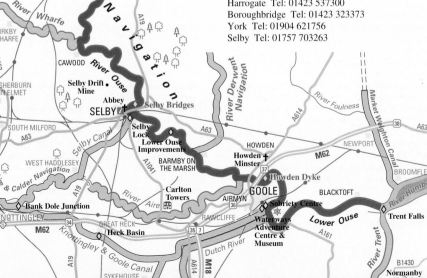

Oxford Canal
115 F2-F4

Open: Napton 1774, Banbury 1778, Oxford 1790
Engineers: Brindley, Simcock, Whitworth, Cubitt
Longford / Hawkesbury Junction to Oxford terminus
91 miles, 43 narrow locks

A canal of two parts.

Northern part, 23 miles of straightened canal broken only by a single lock flight at Hillmorton.

Southern part, 54 miles of meandering canal, climbing up eight locks in front of Napton windmill and dropping slowly down the rural Cherwell valley to the River Thames and the dreaming spires.

Dennis Watkins-Pitchford's frontispiece woodcut to Tom Rolt's seminal book 'Narrow Boat' shows a 'number one' steering into a bend on the Oxford Canal - 'home waters' for Tom's boat 'Cressy'. Without 'Cressy' he would not have written his book. Without his book, the Inland Waterways Association would not have been formed. Without the Inland Waterways Association many hundreds of miles of waterway would not be available today.

Built as a typical, early Brindley 'contour canal'. Started in 1769, it ran out of money at Banbury and was only finished to Oxford (twelve years later) as a result of a unique example of cooperation amongst canal companies; the 'Coleshill Agreement'. Changed (and cheaper) specifications were used for Banbury - Oxford section. Accommodation bridges for farmers were of the wooden 'lifting' type, bottom lock gates were only single leaf and the route even shared the bed of the River Cherwell for part of the way.

When it got to Oxford it provided the first link with London (via the Thames) and was a huge financial success, paying dividends over 20% for forty years. So much so that other companies were soon floated to steal the business by providing a shorter route for Birmingham - London traffic.

The Grand Junction Company linked Braunston to Brentford and thus completely bypassed the southern half of the Oxford. The northern half continued to prosper as part of this route to London and, when faced with competition from new canals via Warwick, was 'modernised' out of all recognition (1834). Brunel and Cubitt ironed out so many of Brindley's contour bends that they reduced the length by over 33% (36 miles to 22 miles). Business stayed brisk and, despite offers from the Grand Union, the Oxford Canal Company remained profitably independent of takeovers until nationalisation (1947).

To this day, there are two routes from Birmingham to Braunston, both similar in length and both using some part of the Oxford Canal. Duplication of the locks at Hillmorton 150 years ago (1840) are the most recent improvements on the part running north from Braunston, the five miles from Braunston to Napton widened between the wars (1935), but fifty four miles south from Napton to Oxford (1790) were never improved and remain in a 200 year time warp.

It is a significant surviving example of the way canals were constructed and made their contribution to long distance trade in the early days of the industrial revolution… a fact that should one day qualify for acknowledgement by UNESCO.

Management and Support
British Waterways, Braunston Tel: 01788 890666
Inland Waterways Association Tel: 01923 711114
Website: http://www.howco.demon.co.uk/oxbranch.htm

◊ **Sutton Stop: Hawkesbury Junction**
The original line from Longford on the Coventry Canal was shortened by opening this gap between the two canals after 14 years of argument.
Approach from M6 J3. Use B4113 going north. Turn into Black Horse Road.
◊ **Horseley Towpath Bridge**
The new towpath (1843) alongside the straightened canal required lifting over the old twisting canal route many times. The Horseley Iron Works produced a standard casting with elegant handrails, which can be seen all along the northern part of this canal.
From M6 J2. Use B4065 north. Turn right at Ansty to Nettle Hill / Hopsford Valley Aqueduct. From M1 J16 use A45 to Braunston Marina / Turn.
◊ **Newbold Tunnel** (750 feet)
Brindley went round the hill and through a shorter tunnel. Brunel went through the hill by a straight, wide tunnel with twin towing paths.
From M6 J11, use A426 south / B4112 west.
◊ **Hillmorton Paired Locks** (3 sets, rising 18ft)
Only locks on the northern Oxford, they became such a bottleneck that they were duplicated (1840).
Approach from M1 J18. Use A428 going west. Turn north under a railway embankment.
◊ **Napton Junction: Braunston Turn** (5 miles)
Largely free from road noise, this is a pivotal section in the entire waterway network. Modernised by the Grand Union Canal Company (1935) after traffic from the main Birmingham to London route had been using this tiny length for 135 years... and paying exhorbitant tolls to the Oxford Company for the privilege.
From M1 J16, use A45 going north-west / A425 west.
◊ **Napton Lock Flight**
Start of the unaltered southern part of the Oxford. Eight locks climb almost 50 feet past Napton Windmill to the summit pound. Terrific views.
From M1 J16, use A45 going north-west / A425 west.

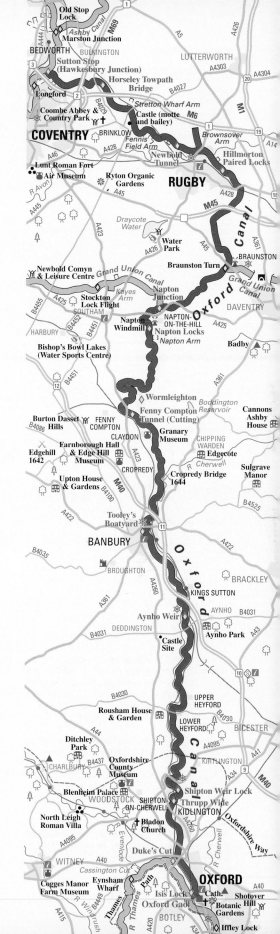

◊ **Wormleighton** (11 mile summit)
Classic Brindley. A pub-less summit pound twists and turns to such an extent that Wormleighton church tower appears at almost every point of the compass.
Approach from M40 J11. Use A423 going north.
◊ **Fenny Compton Tunnel** (1788-1870)
Eventually the roof fell in and the present day very narrow cutting is the result.
Approach from M40 J11. Use A423 going north.
◊ **Tooley's Boatyard** (1780)
Constructed during the twelve years that Banbury was the terminus. Run by the Tooley family for most of this century, it will be preserved as a working exhibit in a new museum complex.
(under construction, opening in the year 2000)
Approach from M40 J11. Use A422 going west. Near the town centre bus station.
◊ **Aynho Weir**
Long weir with towpath over, allows swollen river flows to cross the canal. Unusual diamond shaped lock is reputed to be designed like this to send more water down the canal to fill the next lock downhill at Somerton Deep Lock (12 feet).
Approach from M40 J10. Use A43 / B4100 going north. Walk the towpath south from Nell Bridge.
◊ **Shipton Weir Lock**
After flowing with the lively water of the River Cherwell from below Bakers Lock, and the canal turns into this unusual lock which takes four narrowboats side by side.
Approach from M40 J8. Use A40 / A4165 / A4260 going north-west to Shipton-on-Cherwell village, then walk the towpath north-east.
◊ **Thrupp Wide**
Temporary terminal basin whilst the rest was being constructed, provides moorings for Thrupp Canal Cruising Club. Cul-de-sac street serves stone terrace houses and a pub.
From M40 J8, use A40 / A4165 going north-west.
◊ **Duke's Cut** (1789)
Duke of Marlborough was impatient to open a route to London and made a privately funded ¼ mile cut to a backwater of the Thames, 3 miles and 6 years before the Thames link at Oxford was built.
Approach from M40 J8. Use A40 going east. Almost **under** *A34 Oxford Bypass.*
◊ **Isis Lock** (1796)
Delightfully leafy setting almost in the City Centre for wide lock built by prisoners from Oxford Gaol. River barges gained access to the canal terminus at Hythe Bridge basin. Reduced to narrow dimensions to save water.
From M4 J13, use A34 north / A420 east / City Centre.

✤ **Boat Trips**
Rugby *Rachel of Rugby* Tel: 01788 562187
Aynho *Axe* Tel: 01869 338483

📖 **Suggested Guide Book**
Micheal Pearson *Oxford and Grand Union Canal Companion* J.M. Pearson & Son Ltd., 1990

ℹ️ **Tourist Information**
Coventry Tel: 01203 832303
Rugby Tel: 01788 571813
Banbury Tel: 01295 259855
Oxford Tel: 01865 726871

Oxford Gaol
Early canal, Thames moat and castle keep.

Famous for undergraduate rowing and punting, Oxford is bounded by the water meadows of two rivers and riddled with multiple streams. There are museums and colleges in abundance and many passageways, alleyways and riverside walks.

Start this 'figure of eight' short stroll from:-
1 **Hythe Bridge and Upper Fisher Row**
Look at the waters upstream:-
- on the left: **Castle Mill Stream** off the Thames
- on the right: the final stretch of the **Oxford Canal**
- between these is the towpath, and **a semi-circular weir** allowing excess water to overflow into the river.
Turn downstream. Cross the road, follow the few steps down to the riverside walk. After 50 yards, cross the next (bus only) road and along Lower Fisher Row's waterside to:-
2 **Quaking Bridge and St George's Tower**
'Verminous dungeons' were built into Oxford's Norman (1071) castle. Developed over the years (1166-1855) and used as Oxford Gaol for centuries, modern day prisoners finally left in 1997.
Keeping on the south side of the weir for Castle Mill (1071-1930), follow the castle walls round to the end of **Paradise Street***. Cross* **Castle Street***, turn left up towards the pub. On the left of the pub are the flagstones of* **Bulwarks Lane***. Go in and keeping the garden wall to your left, find the modest door labelled:-*
3 **Canal House**
Former headquarters of the Oxford Canal Company overlooked the coal wharf and now is used as the lodgings for the Warden of St Peter's College.
Bulwarks Lane follows the original curving line of the castle outer bailey. Continue down until you can turn right. At the end of the alley is:-
4 **Old Fire Station: George Street**
Part of 24 hour Oxford. Restaurants, cinemas, a

theatre and pubs galore front this street.
Turn left down **George Street***. At the end, cross onto the northern side of* **Hythe Bridge Street** *and (going west) follow Worcester College wall. Cross over the river by* **1** **Hythe Bridge** *at the centre of this 'figure of eight' stroll. This time go upstream to the end of the terrace houses in* **Upper Fisher Row***.*
Pushing past light undergrowth, follow the ancient stone wall of Rewley Abbey (1280). the pointed arch on your left is the water gate to the abbey. (If the undergrowth is impassable the alternative is to circle clockwise following the garden wall of modern apartment blocks and use road pavements to regain the riverside walk.)
Continue until you can lean on the western parapet of the new road over Sheepwash Channel. Look down onto:-
5 **Railway Swing Bridge** (1844)
The London North Western Railway arrived in Oxford across the Sheepwash Channel at this very low level, forcing bargees to ask permission of the signalman to allow the bridge to be swung. This could only be done in accordance with the railway timetable... and thus forced significant delays on river traffic. Now fixed in the open position.
Complete your crossing of the Sheepwash Channel, then either **turn left** *and under the main railway bridge to join the Thames Path, or:-*

Return to **1** *the start by turning right and along the canal towpath between the two waterways, but first cross the cast iron bridge at:-*
6 **Isis Lock** (1796)
Built by prisoners six years after the canal arrived in Oxford, this lock was originally wide enough to allow Thames barges access to canal wharves. Since narrowed to conserve water.
Explore the covered market and university colleges or **for a much longer walk to** **6** **Iffley Lock***:-*

Punt station close to the Botanical Gardens on the River Cherwell, just below Magdalen Bridge.

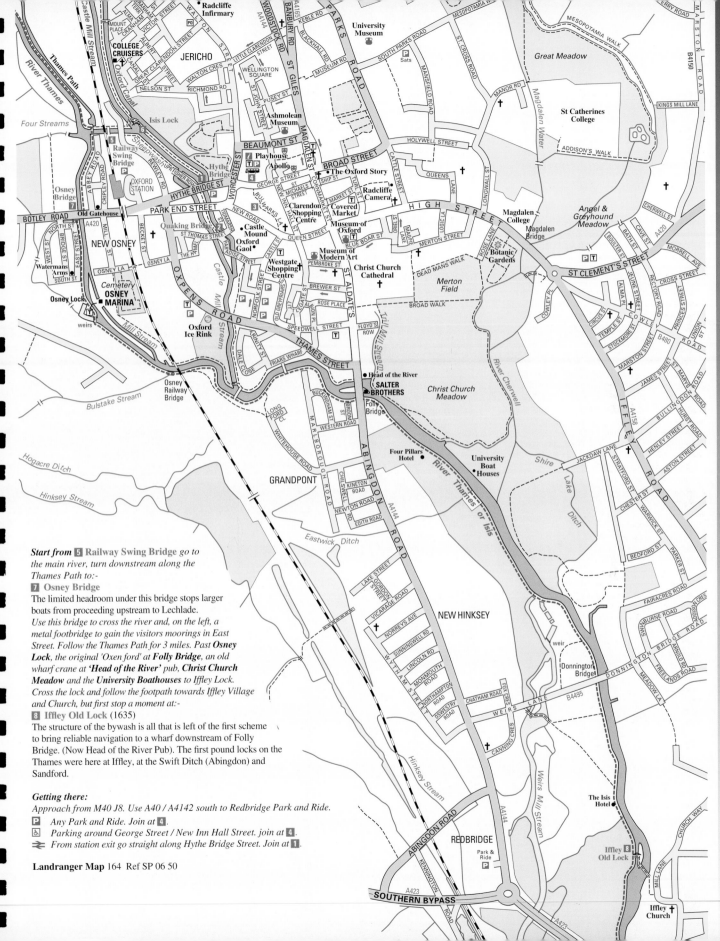

Start from **5** **Railway Swing Bridge** *go to
the main river, turn downstream along the
Thames Path to:-*

7 **Osney Bridge**

The limited headroom under this bridge stops larger
boats from proceeding upstream to Lechlade.

*Use this bridge to cross the river and, on the left, a
metal footbridge to gain the visitors moorings in East
Street. Follow the Thames Path for 3 miles. Past* **Osney
Lock***, the original 'Oxen ford' at* **Folly Bridge***, an old
wharf crane at* **'Head of the River'** *pub,* **Christ Church
Meadow** *and the* **University Boathouses** *to Iffley Lock.
Cross the lock and follow the footpath towards Iffley Village
and Church, but first stop a moment at:-*

8 **Iffley Old Lock** (1635)

The structure of the bywash is all that is left of the first scheme
to bring reliable navigation to a wharf downstream of Folly
Bridge. (Now Head of the River Pub). The first pound locks on the
Thames were here at Iffley, at the Swift Ditch (Abingdon) and
Sandford.

Getting there:

Approach from M40 J8. Use A40 / A4142 south to Redbridge Park and Ride.

P   *Any Park and Ride. Join at* **4***.*

  Parking around George Street / New Inn Hall Street. join at **4***.*

⇌   *From station exit go straight along Hythe Bridge Street. Join at* **1***.*

Landranger Map 164 Ref SP 06 50

Par Canal **110 B3**
Par to Ponts Mill
Park Gate Canal - see **Greasbrough Canal**
Parrett, River - see **Bridgwater Canal**

Peak Forest Canal 118 C3

Opened: 1800-1964, 1974
Engineers: Brown (surveyor), Outram (engineer)
Dukinfield Junction to Bugsworth Interchange
14½ miles, 16 narrow locks at Marple
3½ mile branch to Whaley Bridge Interchange

Running south from Greater Manchester, the canal towpath links with hundreds of miles of footpaths up the Goyt Valley, past reservoirs into the Peak National Park and along the High Peak Trail. Stunning scenery.

T. Brown's 'parliamentary' survey (1791) of this canal into the hills of Derbyshire had a major lock flight at Marple, another at Chapel Milton and ended with a 'railway or stone road' into the limestone of the Peak beyond Chapel-en-le-Frith.

The 'railway or stone road' is now called a 'tramway' but has never seen trams, nor was it a railway as understood today but a pioneering 'plateway'. Instead of the present day technique of flanged wheels running on I-section metal rails, waggons or carts with broad wheels were hauled along flat iron surfaces and were kept on course by L-shaped upstands on the running plates - plateways.

Originally, high level reservoirs were proposed around Chapel-en-le-Frith and The Wash but lack of water above Bugsworth (533 feet above sea level) meant that the design was adjusted so that the canal section had only one flight of locks at Marple and stopped at Bugsworth; the 'railway' section was then doubled in length to come down to meet it.

Outram, Jessop and two partners had set up an ironworks near Butterley Hall, Cromford (1792) and, therefore, Outram was familiar with the design of the new-fangled 'plateways' of which Jessop's 'Little Eaton Gangway' (1793) was one. Nevertheless the Peak Forest Canal's requirement (1794) for 5½ miles of cast rails up to the quarries at Doveholes was probably its first large order. A cheaper, temporary 'tramway' incline was also built along the future lock flight at Marple (1796) because the money authorised by the first Act of Parliament finally ran out. This allowed traffic to start moving whilst a second Act was obtained (1800). The operational delay of loading and unloading stone at Marple tramway was frustrating, and subscription money was slow in coming. So two industrialists Robert Arkwright (Cromford) and Samuel Oldknow (Marple) speeded up construction by providing capital themselves to finish the locks (1805).

The Peak Forest Canal was operated as a single unit with the Ashton Canal (1809) and this management was extended to the Macclesfield Canal when all three were acquired by the Manchester, Sheffield and Lincolnshire Railway Company (1847). Only when tolls were raised by the London and North Eastern railway (after railway amalgamation: 1923) did traffic fall away and the 'tramway' close.

Management and Restoration
British Waterways, Marple Tel: 0161 427 1079
Inland Waterways Protection Society (restoration of Bugsworth Basin) Tel: 01625 613177
British Waterways, Kidsgrove Tel: 01782 785703

◊ **Tame Aqueduct**
The Ashton Company was so pleased with the prospect of tons of limestone passing down their water to the growing chemical industries around Runcorn that they built this splendid aqueduct on the new companys line, before the Peak Act was passed!
From M67 J3, use A627 going north, until A635.
◊ **Butterhouse Tunnel** (501 feet)
Unlike Hyde Bank tunnel near Marple (where walkers follow the old horsepath over the top), this tunnel near Woodley is wide enough to take walkers through on a towpath.
From M67 J3, use A560 going south-west.
◊ **Marple Locks** (16 rising 212 feet)
Sole lock flight 1½ miles long climbs up a leafy slope at a gradient of 1 in 34.
From M60 J1, use A6 / B6171 / A626 going east.
◊ **Bugsworth Basin** (1796, 1810, 1835, 1850-1927)
(re-opened to boats by Inland Waterways Protection Society 1999)
Unique canal / tramway interchange under continuous restoration by volunteers (1968-1998). A Scheduled Ancient Monument (1977) that was partially buried by the A6 bypass (1984) but further restoration is now partially funded by European money.
From M60 J1, use A6 going south-east and turn sharp north (back on yourself) onto the B6062, immediately under a railway bridge.
◊ **Whaley Bridge**
Combs and Toddbrook Canal Reservoirs supply water to the Ashton and Macclesfield Canals as well as the Peak Forest. This fact hindered complete abandonment in the difficult years after WWII.

The branch terminus has a stone built warehouse and wharf, now used as a base for restaurant/trip boat. Its two arches, formerly for rail wagons, sit either side of a covered wharf. Within a few yards is the start of the first incline on the rail line to Cromford. Waggons were hauled up by chains powered by a horse capstan at the top of the Whaley Rise for over 125 years (1825-1952). Now a well kept footpath.
From M60 J1, use A6 going south-east.
◊ **Peak Forest Tramway** (1799-1926)
Rising 615 feet in 7½ miles, early tramway waggons were worked uphill by teams of horses and downhill mainly by controlling the force of gravity. From Bugsworth Basin a steady 1 in 70 slope led alongside Black Brook, past Whitehough to the bottom of a 1 in 7 'Inclined Plane' 512 yards long at Chapel Milton. From the marshalling yard at the top of the 'Plane' a 1 in 200 slope led past Barmoor Clough to the multiple limestone quarry sidings around Dove Holes Dale at a top level of 1158 feet above the sea.

Some parts of this alignment are buried under road improvements but others can still be seen today.
From M60 J1, use A6 going south east. A footpath follows the derelict track up from the basin.
◊ **High Peak Trail**
(Cromford and High Peak Railway: 1831-1967)
Grand Junction Canal Company proposed a canal (1810) to extend its Cromford Canal from north of Derby, past Harpur Hill near Buxton, down the Goyt valley to join the Peak Forest Canal at Whaley Bridge. Fourteen years later, and four months *before* the official opening of the Stockton and Darlington Railway, this idea was changed into 'The Cromford and High Peak Railway' (1825) with nine cable worked inclined planes substituted for the nine proposed lock flights. At first horse power was

retained along the contour alignments, gradually replaced by steam (1833-1863). It was then connected to the rest of the rail network at High Peak Junction (1853) and the Whaley Bridge spur (1857). 16 miles of the 33 mile alignment (from Hurdlow south east to Cromford Wharf) is now waymarked and maintained as the 'High Peak Trail', used by horseriders, cyclists and walkers.

Approach from M60 J1. Use A6 going south-east to A5270 south of Buxton. South of Chelmorton the A515 / A5012 runs alongside the High Peak Trail towards Wirksworth.

i Tourist Information
Stockport Tel: 0161 474 4444
Buxton Tel: 01298 73153
New Mills Tel: 01663 746904

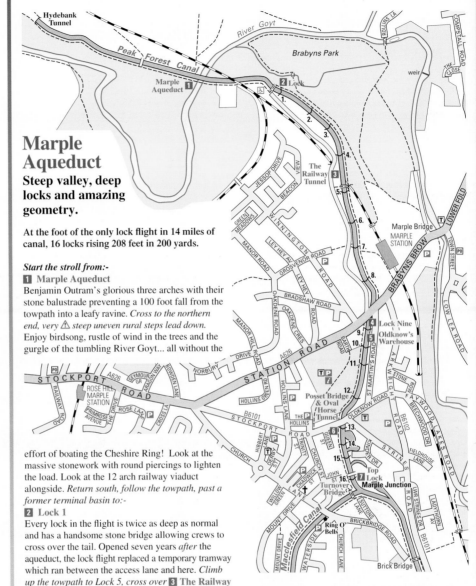

Marple Aqueduct
Steep valley, deep locks and amazing geometry.

At the foot of the only lock flight in 14 miles of canal, 16 locks rising 208 feet in 200 yards.

Start the stroll from:-
1 Marple Aqueduct
Benjamin Outram's glorious three arches with their stone balustrade preventing a 100 foot fall from the towpath into a leafy ravine. *Cross to the northern end, very ⚠ steep uneven rural steps lead down.* Enjoy birdsong, rustle of wind in the trees and the gurgle of the tumbling River Goyt... all without the effort of boating the Cheshire Ring! Look at the massive stonework with round piercings to lighten the load. Look at the 12 arch railway viaduct alongside. *Return south, follow the towpath, past a former terminal basin to:-*
2 Lock 1
Every lock in the flight is twice as deep as normal and has a handsome stone bridge allowing crews to cross over the tail. Opened seven years *after* the aqueduct, the lock flight replaced a temporary tramway which ran between the access lane and here. *Climb up the towpath to Lock 5, cross over* **3** *The Railway Tunnel and towards* **1** *Marple Aqueduct.*

A longer walk to **7** *Top Lock*
From **3** *The Railway Tunnel climb past four* **more** *locks, at the main road look for:-*
4 Horizontal roller at Lock 9 (A626)
Without this roller the parapet stone would have worn the ropes and the towing ropes would have worn the stone. *Cross the road carefully into St Martins Road to:-*
5 Oldknow's Warehouse
The main promoter of this canal built a three storey cotton warehouse to act as despatch depot for his mills 2 miles away. *After three locks you come to:-*
6 Posset Bridge and Oval Horse Tunnel (B6101)
Horses crossed under the road. *Go up the slope, definitely one way traffic! Climb* **the last** *four locks. Note the side pounds are within house gardens.*
7 Top Lock and Turnover Bridge
Top of the flight is 518 feet above sea level. The turnover bridge is a classic way for the horse to change from one side of of the Macclesfield Canal to the other without having the rope unhitched. *Try to work it out!* This handsome example was built by Thomas Telford over 30 years after the Peak Forest Canal was complete. *Follow the Macclesfield Canal towpath to Church Lane, reach the Ring O'Bells pub behind which there is a public car park overlooking the canal.*

Getting there:
Approach from M60 J1. Use A6 / B6171 / A626.
🅿 *Suggest Winnington Road or Arkwright Road. Join at* **3** *or* **6**.
♿ *Awkward turn north into tiny lane alongside canal bridge (**4**) and after many hidden 'sleeping policemen' the parking is at the end. (signpost 'Aqueduct Business Park'). Join at* **1**.
🚃 *From station exit turn right up Brabyns Brow. Join at* **4**.

Landranger Map 109 Ref SJ 95 90

Bugsworth Basin
Goyt Valley, high peak, and a 200 year old marshalling yard.

Surrounded by magnificent scenery, follow in the footsteps of a boat horse, along a towing path, through a horse tunnel, past a gauging lock and into, for me, one of the most magnificent Scheduled Ancient Monuments in Britain.

Start the stroll at:-

1 Railway Bridge (1831-1952)
These rails are where the 33 mile Cromford and High Peak Railway started up its first horse powered steep incline (*look south for 180 yards*) having collected from:-

2 Transfer Warehouse: Whaley Bridge
A three bay shed with a rail siding either side of the canal unloading bay. The Terminal Basin has a long spillway plus a narrow walkway to keep your feet dry in times of flood. *Cross the spillway, follow the waymarked Goyt and Midshire Walks along the towpath to:-*

3 Horse Underpass
As the canal main line (Ashton to Bugsworth) is opposite the branch from Whaley Bridge, there occurs a common problem of how the horse gets to the main towpath without swimming across the canal. Solved here by unhitching the rope and leading the horse **under** the canal. *Just short of the junction, a cobbled footpath goes down towards the field in the valley. at the bottom turn left, through the (possibly muddy) 'horse tunnel' under the main line. Then return up a similar steepish footpath to the main towing path. Turn left, follow the towpath westwards.*

4 Teapot Row and Gauging Stop Place
Boats settle deep in the water when loaded. The tolls payable depended on the load. One at a time a canal company employee would measure / gauge the amount of boat above the waterline and calculate the toll. Teapot Row was so called since, before environmental legislation, the tenants emptied their teapots into the canal! *Go forward, enter the largest canal / tramway interchange in Britain. There is a chain of three basins, the original (1796) is farthest away from Gauging Stop Place, then Middle Basin and the Entrance Basin is the largest and*

most recent (1840). Water is the same level in all three.

5 Horse Overpass
There are so many canal arms that a horse transfer bridge was built over them. *Emulate the horse up the ramp, across two arms and down to the wharfside. Stay down, the path goes under the road towards the original basin.*

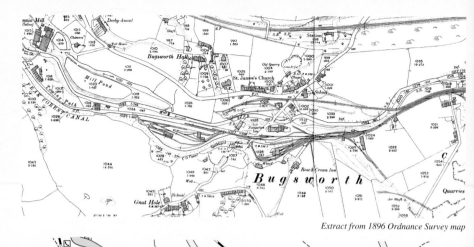

Extract from 1896 Ordnance Survey map

6 Lime Kiln Remains
Broken limestone fed into the top of a kiln, with alternate layers of burning coal, would create the high temperature (1000°C) at which stone turns into useful lime. The massive walls visible across the canal are the remains of the seven Gnat Hole kilns. Lime was taken by wheelbarrow from arches at the foot of the kiln and loaded / tipped directly into the waiting boats, then immediately covered with sheeting to keep it dry.

7 Navigation Inn
One of two pubs (the Rose and Crown disappeared when the new A6 was built, 1984) which served the needs of hundreds of boatmen, wharf labourers and

tramway workers. Now sells maps and guides to the basin, where profits assist further restoration, plus excellent food and drink.

8 Black Brook Weir
The brook was channelled along the side of its valley to make way for the Basin. It rushes over three weirs before joining the River Goyt.
Retrace your steps to **1** *along the towpath or, if you wish, join the walkers and go south across:-*

9 Silk Hill Bridge
Before the Bugsworth New Road Turnpike (B6062) this was on the main Whaley Bridge to Chinley road. *After crossing A6 go right into the 'access only' lane, up the steep hill, ⚠ down as far as the phone box, and right into a public footpath. The route down starts a bit muddy through the farmyard but has a blacktop surface for most of the way back to* **1**.

Trip and Restaurant Boat
Whaley Bridge *Judith Mary Tel: 01663 732408*

Getting there:
Approach from M60 J1. Use A6 south-east.
🅿 ♿ *Suggest end of Canal Street. Join at* **1** *or Navigation Inn. Join at* **7**.
🚉 *Hug the Jodrell Arms on the left then go down its main steps. Cross the main road straight into Bridge Street and go to* **1** *former Cromford and High Peak Railway Bridge (see the rails).*

Landranger Map 110 Ref SK 01 81

Ribble Link   118 B2
 Ribble Estuary to Preston (canalisation of Savick
 Brook) - see Lancaster Canal Map, page 54)
 Waterway Recovery Group Tel: 0161 740 2179
Ribble, River
 Sea to Preston Docks and Marina   118 B3
Ripon Canal - see **Ure Navigation**
Roach, River   113 E2
 River Crouch to near Rochford
 9¼ miles, 0 locks

Rochdale Canal   118 C3
Opened: 1804
Engineers: Brindley, Rennie, Jessop, Crosley
Sowerby Bridge to Castlefield in Manchester
33 miles, 92 wide locks, 1 very short tunnel.

**A canal which pioneered the route up the valleys on
each side of Blackstone Edge on to the magnificent
rounded slopes of the Pennine moors. Rail and
modern road followed on, but they are all packed
tightly into the available space. At present only
open from the Yorkshire end, the hope is that the
whole route will be cleared of blockages by 2000.**

 Early proposals suggested mountain streams would
supply water but downstream millowners objected to
both the first bills in Parliament (1792, 1793). When
Jessop changed the design to provide five reservoirs
on the moors, with compensation water guaranteed to
the millowners, the bill was passed (1794) but on
condition it could take Calder keels which were, by
then, arriving at Sowerby Bridge.
 It was the first of three Pennine crossings to be
completed and designed to take river craft from both
sides of the Pennines (lock size 74ft x 14ft). Payloads
of up to 70 tons of coal, grain, salt, cotton and wool
were carried around the urban areas at each end but
only a relatively small proportion of trade went
through all the locks 'over the top' (last cargo: 1937).
 The Canal was not nationalised and the private
company was inclined to develop land assets. Now
the subject of a Lottery assisted restoration project
which has the belated support of the company.

Management and Restoration
Rochdale Canal Trust Tel: 01422 844990
Rochdale Canal Society Tel: 01706 646132
Website: http://www.zen.co.uk/home/page/derek.parsons

◊ **Rochdale Nine** (Tel: 0161 236 2456)
Nine city centre locks between Castlefield and Dale
Street (former) Terminal Basin were 'saved' in the
general closure (1952) on condition that the Ashton
Canal remained open. They are used as part of the
'Cheshire Ring' (1974) on payment of dues to the
private canal company.
*Approach from A57(M). Use London Road going
north. Turn east into Ducie Street.*
◊ **M60 crossing**
Box tunnel below, towpath footbridge over. Installed
after the Canal Society held a rally (1986), a 'Big Dig'
and successfully appeared at the planning inquiry.
*Approach from M60 J19. Use A6044 / A6104 east,
then A663 going north.*
◊ **Eight Reservoirs above Littleborough**
To either side of the Pennine Way, seven high level
reservoirs supply the summit (600 feet below) with
water from 2000 acres of moorland. Water from the

Pack-horse trail, canal and railway run parallel and demonstrate the huge differences in investment needed by each.

8th (Hollingworth Lake) was pumped to the summit.
 Plenty of interesting waymarked walks. Victorian
Tourist Resort and Visitor Centre Tel: 01706 373421.
From M62 J22, use A672 north then A58 west.
◊ **Longlees Lock No 36** (Reopened 1980)
Locks were standard. Gates were interchangeable and
the constant 10 foot depth meant that exactly the same
amount of water was passed down the canal with each
lock operation. In the lock walls there are pockets for a
second set of gates for use by shorter boats but they
were never installed. At the northern end of the short
deep summit pound (600 feet above sea level) this lock
was the first restoration by the Rochdale Canal Society.
Present (1999) limit of navigation is 12 locks down the
Lancashire descent at Littleborough.
*From M62 J21 use A640 / A664 / A58 / A6033 going
north to Warland.*
◊ **Fallingroyd Tunnel**
Built without a towpath on a curving alignment, boats
were 'legged' through… still true today of the silent
horsedrawn trip-boat. Beware!

*Approach from M62 J24. Use A646 going north-west
to Mytholmroyd.*
◊ **Tuel Lane Lock** (1996: Tel: 01422 316678)
Deepest in the country (19' 6") and approached from
a new tunnel. Removal of this blockage connected
much of the Rochdale to the rest of the system.
Financed in part by European funds.
From M62 J22, use A672 going north-east

❋ *Boat Trips*
Hebden Bridge *Sara Siddons* Tel: 01422 845557
Guide Bridge *Maria* Tel: 0161 320 8338

📖 *Suggested Guide Book*
John Lower *The South Pennine Ring*
Hallamshire Press, 1988

ℹ️ *Tourist Information*
Rochdale Tel: 01706 356592
Todmorden Tel: 01706 818181
Hebden Bridge Tel: 01422 843831

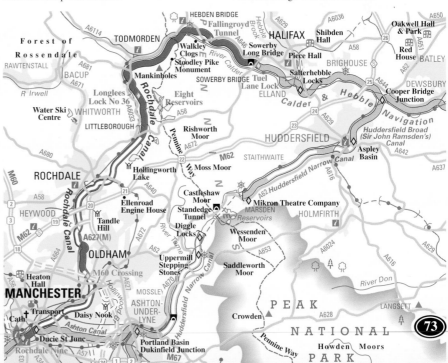

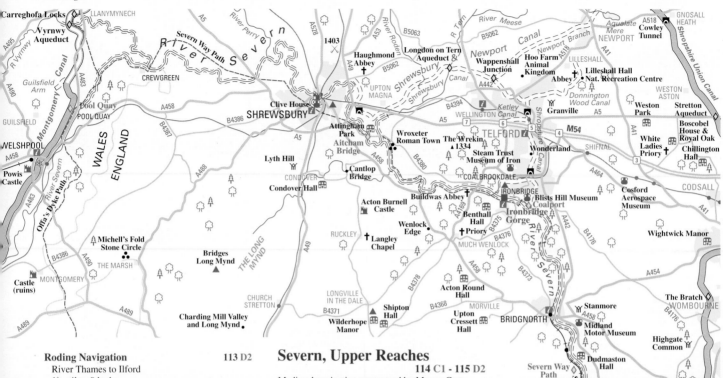

Severn, Upper Reaches

114 C1 - 115 D2

Medieval navigation guaranteed by Magna Carta
210 miles, 6 locks in the lower reaches

From its headwaters, the Severn falls 1500 feet
through forest, past hawks, kites and peregrines.
Its erratic flow has carved through limestone and
sandstone gorges and enters wide plains between
the Malvern and Cotswold Hills. It finally meanders
around mudbanks, quicksands, wetlands and other
wildlife havens in the tidal estuary.

Atlantic rain caught by the Welsh mountains
and Atlantic tides rushing up the Bristol Channel
are both fundamental to the wildness of this river.

Tidal variation can be as much as 40 feet, the
Severn Bore can send a nine foot wave up from the
river mouth, whilst every winter the weight of
Welsh water tests flood defences all the way down
the valley.

Navigable against the forces of nature as far as
Bridgnorth, Shrewsbury and sometimes Welshpool (at
Pool Quay, 1820), this waterway transported the first
fruits of the industrial revolution downstream from
Coalbrookdale to wider markets.

The creation of a path alongside such a variable river
was always a problem. Gangs of men, then horses,
hauled their way upstream, towing barges across
shallows or against floods. Paths to ease their passage
were built against strong resistance (1800-1812) but
today the Severn Way follows the wider valley, giving
side excursions up tributaries and some ascents to
ridgetop viewpoints.

Management
Environment Agency Tel: 01743 272828

◊ **Pool Quay**
Just downstream of a monastic weir, this quay only
operated in winter when flashes gave sufficient depth
to float goods downstream and gave enough water for
men to haul loaded barges upstream. When the
Montgomery Canal arrived (1797) year round trading
became possible.
Approach from M54 J7. Use A5 / A458 going west.

◊ **Aitcham Bridge** (1774, 1929)
Near Roman Virocorium, one of many stone bridges
by 'John Gwynn of Shrewsbury'.
Approach from M54 J7. Use A5 to Shrewsbury bypass.
Turn east onto B4380.

◊ **Coalport**
Coal was sent downstream from here for centuries
before the industrial revolution. At that time a third
of all coal transported by any means anywhere in the
country was carried on the Severn (1690s)
Approach from M54 J5. Use A442 going south.

◊ **Severn Way Path**
One of the longest waymarked trails in Britain, a 210
mile route runs beside the river and up onto ridgetop

viewpoints. Torrents and waterfalls around the source give way to the gentle pastures of the middle reaches and the path ends at Severn Beach on the banks of the tidal Bristol Channel.
Approach from M54 or M5.

Severn Navigation 115 D2-D3

Stourport-on-Severn to Gloucester towards the Irish Sea
42 miles of the 210 miles of river, 6 locks

When canals first arrived to the Severn (Droitwich, 1771: Staffordshire and Worcestershire, 1772) they had sophisicated expectations of the reliability of water transport. Nothing had been done except to make improvements to the banks (1797, 1800, 1804, 1809, 1812). So they attempted to obtain Parliamentary permission to improve things further (1837, 1838, 1839), but it was only when they cooperated in an Act (1842) to set up 'Severn Commissioners' that it was approved. Weirs and locks were then made, entirely funded by the Gloucester and Sharpness and Staffs and Worcs.

◊ **Stourport Basins**
Lower Mitton became a major inland port when the Staffs and Worcs Canal was refused permission to join the river at Bewdley. A broad lock and staircased narrow locks link four basins on two levels to the river and are surrounded by original warehouses.
From M5 J6, use A449 / A4025 going north-west.
◊ **Droitwich**
Romans called it Salinae and sent the salt by water. A short (5¼ mile) barge canal, the first artificial connection to the river (1771), is being restored.
Approach from M5 J5. Use A38 going south.
◊ **Diglis Basin** (Worcester)
Two wide locks up from the river at the end of the canal from Birmingham. Goods were shipped from here to London via the river. They entered the Stroudwater Navigation below Gloucester and up the 'Golden Valley' to the head of navigation on the Thames at Lechlade.
Approach from M5 J7. Use A44 going north-west.
◊ **Upton-upon-Severn**
An elegant bridge, a copper cupola atop a church tower and Georgian houses combine to give this waterfront a continental air. Once the tidal limit.
From M50 J1 use, A38 / A4104 going north.
◊ **Mythe Bridge** (1825)
One of many works by Thomas Telford when he was Surveyor of Public Works for Shropshire. Others can be seen at Montford (1792), Buildwas (1796), Bewdley (1801).
Approach from M50 J1. Use A38/A438 going south
◊ **Mills at Tewkesbury**
As a 'free river' the wiers needed by mills and fishtraps were forbidden on the Severn and were built on the tributaries instead. The Abbot's mill here dating from the 1100s is typical, as is this modern factory which, for many years, barged its products away by water.
Approach from M5 J9. Use A438 going west.
◊ **Maisemore Stream**
The most easterly of the two major flows between Upper Parting and Lower Parting. This was the hazardous route to the sea until locks and weirs controlled the water and the Gloucester and Sharpness Canal bypassed the worst of the bends and shallows (1827). Incoming tides overtop the wier at Upper Parting.
From M5 J11, use A40 going west to A417 north.

◊ **Gloucester Docks**
Llanthony Lock maintains water levels in this dock, Home to the National Waterways Museum and museums celebrating Gloucestershire military, advertising and packaging and glass.
From M5 J11, use A40 going west to A417 south.
◊ **Stonebench**
One of three favoured positions to watch the spectacle of the Severn Bore. The second highest tide in the world races up the Bristol Channel into the shallows of the river mouth and can build up to a series of waves up to six feet (2 metres) high.
Approach from M5 J13. Use A38 / B4008 going north then cross the Gloucester and Sharpness Canal on narrow roads towards Elmore.
◊ **Wildfowl and Wetlands Reserve: Slimbridge**
Sanctuary on the shallow shores for birds of many kind set up by Sir Peter Scott. Sir Peter was also Vice President of Inland Waterways Association and took part in early 'direct action' to highlight required changes in Government attitudes to our waterways (1948).
Approach from M5 J13. Use A38 going north then cross the Gloucester and Sharpness Canal on narrow roads.

※ *Boat Trips*
Stourport-on-Severn *Carvolate (1911), River King (1933), Miss Jason (1936)* Tel: 01299 871177
Gloucester *Queen Boadicea II, King Arthur* Tel: 01452 318054

ⓘ *Tourist Information: upper river*
Llanidloes Tel: 01686 412605
Newtown Tel: 01686 625580
Welshpool Tel: 01938 552580
Shrewsbury Tel: 01743 350761
Ironbridge Tel: 01952 432166
Telford Tel: 01952 291370
Bridgnorth Tel: 01746 763358

ⓘ *Tourist Information: lower river*
Bewdley Tel: 01299 404740
Kidderminster Tel: 01562 829400
Worcester Tel: 01905 726311
Upton-upon-Severn Tel: 01684 594200
Tewkesbury Tel: 01684 295027
Gloucester Tel: 01452 421188
Thornbury Tel: 01454 281638
Bristol Tel: 0117 926 0767

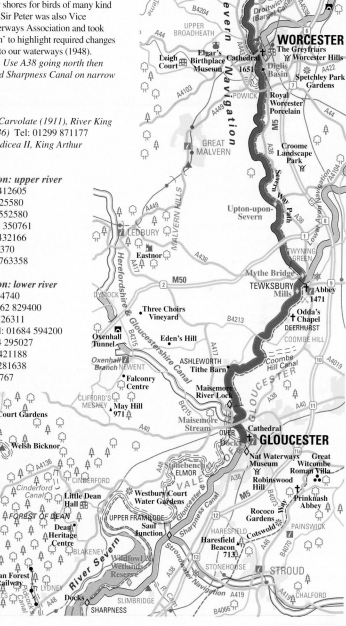

Ironbridge Gorge
The valley that changed our world.

Start the stroll from:-

1 Coalport Wharf

Terminus of ferry services from Ferry Road in Jackfield where the majority of workers lived. This riverbank allowed transhipment between the Shropshire Canal and the River Severn and served frequent river traffic. China clay was imported from Cornwall and salt glaze from Droitwich. Pottery, tobacco pipes, bricks, tiles and coal were sent downstream to Tewkesbury and Bristol. Many craft from Gloucester regularly passed upstream towards Welshpool (400 in 1758, 800 in 1808). *Stand at the far (western) end of the canal. Look up the hill to the twin tracks of:-*

2 Hay Inclined Plane (Reynolds: 1793-1894)

Tub boats of the Shropshire Canal could be floated onto wheeled cradles at the top of this 1000 foot incline and after just 3½ minutes they would be next to the River Severn wharf - 207 feet below. *In the basement of the cottage opposite is the entrance to:-*

3 Tar Tunnel (1786-1835)

A surprise awaited the miners employed to make a direct water channel link between the River Severn and underground coal. The horizontal shaft was driven into the lower coal seams at the same level as the river and after cutting 3000 feet the walls began to ooze a sticky sunstance... bitumen.

This phenomenon became a 'tourist' attraction amongst eminent scientists of the day. Boiled in tubs it became pitch and was sold as timber preservative. The tunnel was used as an air-raid shelter during World War II.

This is one of the Ironbbridge Gorge Museums... there is an entrance fee. Alternatively, purchase a 'Passport' which allows one visit to each of the Museum's nine separate sites. 'Passports' have no expiry date and can be used anytime, until all sites have been seen.

To continue the short stroll: go up △ steps onto the War Memorial Footbridge (1922), cross the river and down 25 steps △ to the Jackfield side. Turn upstream, past terrace houses to Maw & Co. Benthall Works. Go across the road at the top to:-

4 Severn Valley Way

Railway track converted to a level footpath giving glimpses through the tree of the opposite side of the heavily wooded gorge and **2 The Inclined Plane**. *Turn downstream (left) and at the end avoid the old railway platform by walking down the slope to the riverbank. Look downstream to see the:-*

5 Coalport Bridge (1818)

Thirty nine years after the first ever iron bridge was built 2 miles upstream, the original wooden bridge (1780) was replaced by this one... made of iron. *Go up to the southern end of the bridge. Start of:-*

6 Silkin Way (1977)

A waymarked path lead walkers 14 miles through the centre of Telford and beyond. This first length crosses the bridge and then follows the line built by the London North Western Railway when they used the Shropshire Canal as the route of a new railway but could not follow the geometry of **2 The Inclined Plane**.

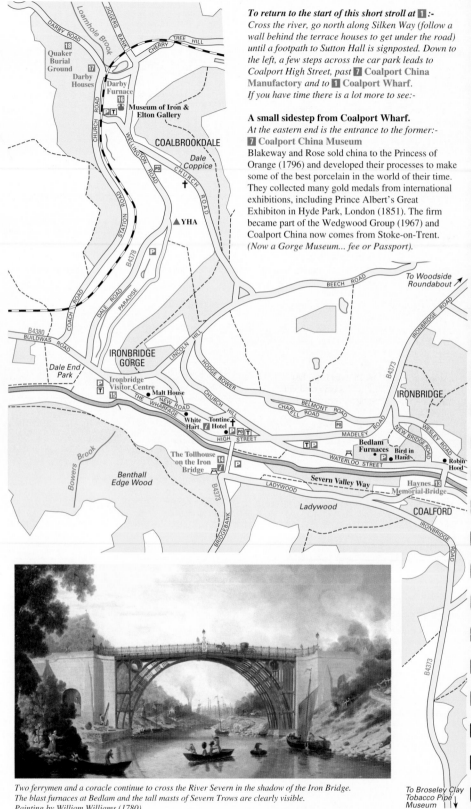

Two ferrymen and a coracle continue to cross the River Severn in the shadow of the Iron Bridge. The blast furnaces at Bedlam and the tall masts of Severn Trows are clearly visible. Painting by William Williams (1780).

To return to the start of this short stroll at 1 :-

Cross the river, go north along Silken Way (follow a wall behind the terrace houses to get under the road) until a footpath to Sutton Hall is signposted. Down to the left, a few steps across the car park leads to Coalport High Street, past **7 Coalport China Manufactory** *and to* **1 Coalport Wharf**.

If you have time there is a lot more to see:-

A small sidestep from Coalport Wharf.

At the eastern end is the entrance to the former:-

7 Coalport China Museum

Blakeway and Rose sold china to the Princess of Orange (1796) and developed their processes to make some of the best porcelain in the world of their time. They collected many gold medals from international exhibitions, including Prince Albert's Great Exhibiton in Hyde Park, London (1851). The firm became part of the Wedgwood Group (1967) and Coalport China now comes from Stoke-on-Trent. *(Now a Gorge Museum... fee or Passport).*

Or a half mile detour from 6 **Silkin Way:-**
From the Sutton Hall signpost use the Silkin Way footpath to go under the 2 *Hay Inclined Plane and continue further up the valley. Just beyond the Lee Dingle Plateway Bridge is the entrance to:-*

8 **Blists Hill Victorian Town** - one of the original sites of the Ironbridge Gorge Museum. *Website: www.vtel.co.uk/igmt.*
If you have at least two hours to spare, go inside the town (entrance fee or Passport) and look for:-

9 **Shropshire Canal**
Horses pulled tub boats along the canal and trains of waggons along the (now removed) extensive 'plateways'. They were the backbone of a system for moving heavy castings around. Canalaholics will want to walk the towpath alongside the largest single original feature within the site. Half a mile long, the canal has three locks and leads down to the River Severn by 2 **The Hay Inclined Plane.**

10 **Blist Hill Blast Furnaces**
The bellows for the 24 hour process of the blast furnaces were powered by water (1830-1912). Coal was immediately under the hill and raw iron from the furnaces was wheeled round to the forges and foundries around the Gorge. Manufacturing businessses of all sizes and types collected close by.
Further down the hill under a temporary cover is:-

11 **Severn Trow 'Spry'** (1894-1982)
Rescued from drowning and in the process of restoration, this 71' by 18' boat is the last remaining example of the flat bottomed sailing barges that once plied the Severn upstream from Gloucester.

1½ mile walk to 14 **The Iron Bridge** but you can stop short at any point! From 4 **Severn Valley Way,** go upstream and follow Salthouse Road to the:-

12 **Jackfield Tile Museum** (entrance fee or passport)
Cast iron domestic fireplaces from Coalbrookdale always had channels at the side to accommodate a selection from the huge variety of decorated tiles made in Jackfield. Victorian public buildings, such as banks, railway stations and pubs used millions of them both inside and outside their buildings. The museum has a collection of over 4000 moulds, patterns and tiles.
Continue up Severn Valley Way past:-

13 **Haynes Memorial Bridge**
The first toll free bridge across the Gorge, built by public subscription and known as the 'Free Bridge'. It was a very early example of reinforced concrete (a small portion stands on the southern bank) but it was replaced (1994) by an asymmetrical cable stay deign. It carries the B4373 which leads south to the Broseley Clay Tobacco Pipe Museum.
(Gorge Museum site - entrance fee or Passport)

Continue upstream on the Severn Valley Way.
Pass through the woods (and car park) to :-
14 **The Tollhouse on the Iron Bridge** (1779)
A toll was imposed for crossing the river, similar to ferryboat charges. To stop competition from ferries, the enabling Act of Parliamnet forbade ferry boats to operate within 1500 feet of the new structure. A marvellous advertisement for the properties of cast iron, it incurred a cost over run of 26% which was underwritten by the contractors.
There are many pleasant walks around and still four other sites to see:-

An extra mile to 18 **Quaker Burial Grounds.**
Cross the Iron Bridge to the north bank, walk upstream along The Wharfage. Call in to:-
15 **Ironbridge Visitor Centre** (fee or passport)
Superb introduction to the Gorge. Inside is a 40 foot model of the Gorge as it was in 1796 and outside are 40 minute river cruises (in spring and summer).
Cross the road, go to the bookshop on the corner of 'Paradise', climb up the steep ⚠ *slope and along the side of the valley. At the end, go north along Wellington Road and turn left down to* 16.
For a gentler alternative (through trees), continue past Dale End Park, turn right into Coach Road and at the end turn under the railway viaduct to:-
16 **Darby Furnace: Museum of Iron**
(Entrance fee or passport) Find Darby Road at the end of Coach Road. Turn left up to 17.
17 **Darby Houses** (Rose Hill and Dale House)
Owned by the ironmasters *and beyond to the:-*
18 **Quaker Burial Ground**
Includes the grave of Abraham Darby (1678-1717) who started the whole industrial expansion by using coke instead of charcoal to smelt iron ore.

Getting there:
Approach from M54 J4. Use A443 south (dual carriageway) towards Telford centre then A442 south (dual carriageway) towards Kidderminster, but continue straight on (along a narrowing road) to Castlefields Roundabout (with pit winding gear). Turn left along Castlefields Way (B4378), Madeley, left again and follow red 'Ironbridge Gorge Museum' signs to Coalport China Museum.
P *Suggest Coalport High Street. Join at* 1.
♿ *Parking as above. Join at* 1.
🚋 *From station exit catch a taxi.*

Landranger Map 127 Ref SJ 69 02

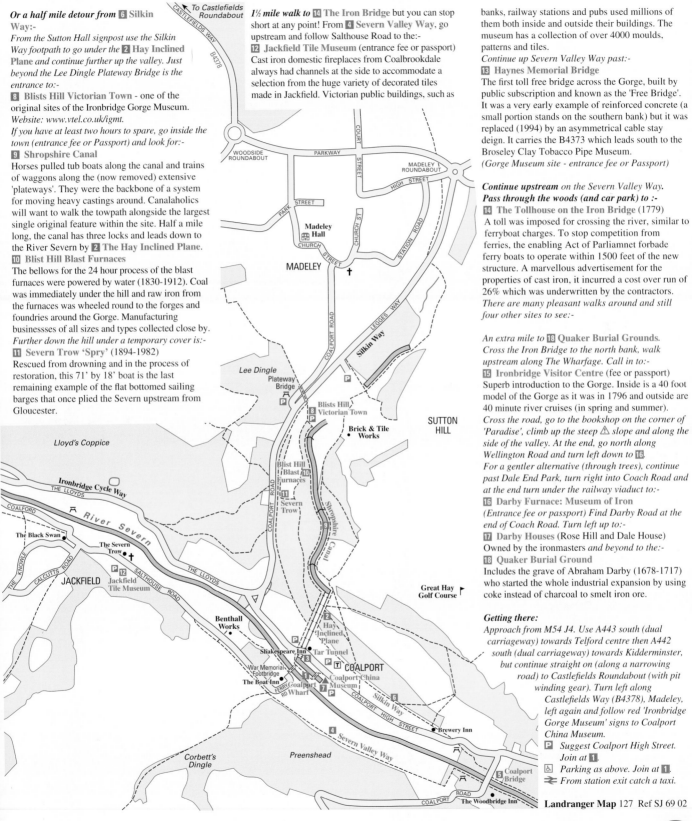

Sheffield and South Yorkshire Navigation

119 D3-E3

Improved: 1740, 1751, 1802, 1823, 1845, 1907, 1932, 1959, 1963, 1983
Engineers: Chapman, Buck, Smith, Leather
Keadby Junction to Victoria Quays, Sheffield
42¼ miles, 32 wide locks

A mix of three man made and one natural navigation. Long distance walking is possible on all three artificial cuts but only on parts of the improved river navigation.

The core of these navigations is the River Don which was navigable as far as Rotherham (1740). Schemes to link this with the hills of Sheffield were defeated twice (1704, 1721) before implementation (1819). Sheffield had boomed supplying swords, bayonets and cannon balls for the Napoleonic Wars but the end of hostilities (Battle of Waterloo 1814) reduced demand and, soon afterwards, railways took most of the trade (1838) and then control (1845).

Sheffield industrialists encouraged the formation of a separate company (1895) which survived until the first world war (1914) when many of their boats were lost carrying troops around canals in Flanders.

Huge, power operated locks have been installed recently (1983) when the navigation downstream from Doncaster for 25 miles towards Goole was modernised to be suitable for 700 tonne Eurobarges.

Management

British Waterways Tel: 01636 705584
Barnsley Canal Group Tel: 01909 565225

◇ Bramwith Junction

Waterways everywhere. Water from the tidal Don flows seamlessly onwards between floodbanks to become the Dutch River. The Stanford and Keadby Canal takes pleasure boats through many crew operated swing bridges towards the Trent. The newest canal in the country (1905, 1983) takes large cargo vessels absolutely straight through apparently automatic swing bridges to Sykehouse and the Aire and Calder Navigation.

The aqueduct taking the New Junction Canal over the Don looks incomplete. Tall guillotine gates guarding the ends seem rarely to move and one side is so low that water spills out of the canal with each passing boat.
Approach from M18 J4. Use A630 west and north to Barnby Dun and South Bramwith.

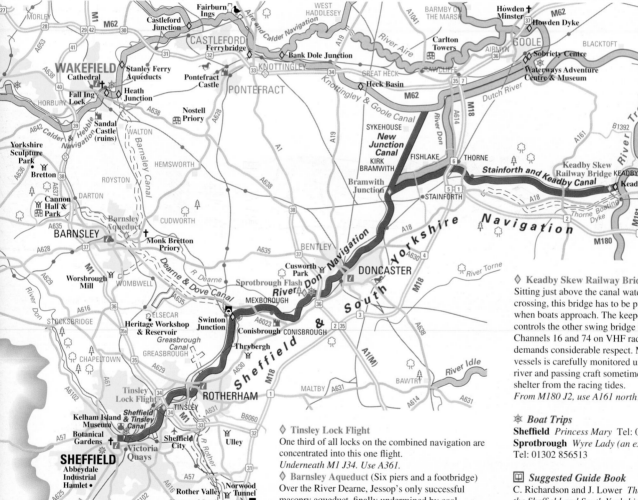

◇ Tinsley Lock Flight

One third of all locks on the combined navigation are concentrated into this one flight.
Underneath M1 J34. Use A361.

◇ Barnsley Aqueduct (Six piers and a footbridge)

Over the River Dearne, Jessop's only successful masonry aqueduct, finally undermined by coal workings.
From M1 J37, use A628 east then A61 north.

◇ Sprotbrough Flash (Tel: 01904 659570)

A Site of Special Scientific Interest in the woods just south of the lock and weir downhill from the village. Nearby is the 600 acre 'Earth Centre' devoted to sustainable development.
From A1(M) J36 a little way along A360 west.

◇ Keadby Skew Railway Bridge (1915)

Sitting just above the canal water in a kind of level crossing, this bridge has to be pulled out of the way when boats approach. The keeper of the tidal lock controls the other swing bridge (B1392) as well as Channels 16 and 74 on VHF radio. The River Trent demands considerable respect. Movement of smaller vessels is carefully monitored until they pass off the river and passing craft sometimes enter the canal to shelter from the racing tides.
From M180 J2, use A161 north/A18 east and B1392.

⚜ Boat Trips

Sheffield *Princess Mary* Tel: 0114 272 7233
Sprotbrough *Wyre Lady (an ex-Clyde ferry)*
Tel: 01302 856513

📖 Suggested Guide Book

C. Richardson and J. Lower *The Complete Guide to the Sheffield and South Yorkshire Navigation*
The Hallamshire Press, 1995

ℹ Tourist Information

Sheffield Tel: 01142 273 4611
Rotherham Tel: 01709 823611
Barnsley Tel: 01226 206757
Doncaster Tel: 01302 734309
Scunthorpe Tel: 01724 28230

Victoria Quays
Two hotels, a quiet canal and a dashing river.

Reopened (1995) as a leisure boating terminus, Sheffield Basin faces Park Square roundabout. Arches overlooking North Quay once supported a railway goods yard and now support the first hotel.

Start the stroll at the last warwhouse built on Victoria Quays:-
1 **The Straddle** (1898)
No land was left so they built over water. Grain from boats tied up below, would have been hauled up through trapdoors. After storage on four floors it was unloaded by gravity chutes to carts waiting beneath the canopies on the quay side. *Before leaving, look for the huge carp in the clear water. Then go north, pass the British Waterways office and follow the wide towpath under the:-*
2 **Wicker Viaduct** (1849)
Huge steel beams and wide stone arches once supported a Victorian railway station high over the valley and still support the recently extended and renovated second hotel (1998 : first built 1862). *Continue around the curve of the canal, to:-*

3 **'Dorothy Pax'**: Victoria Boatyard
On the far bank the sole surviving 'Humber keel' is being restored in this working boatyard. *Continue past the gentle whirr of exhaust fans from surviving industry, under bridge No 5 and, after a long straight, pass under:-*
4 **Bacon Lane Bridge**
One of two original bridges, this was the smallest and its hump back shape acted as a 'loading gauge' for the whole canal. *Turn right and go back up over the canal, down the hill to cross Effingham Road and into Stoke Street. With the wall and railings on your left follow the path down to cross:-*
5 **Washford Bridge** (1795: widened 1880)
Ancient crossing of the river Don. The door in the parapet is to allow snow to be dumped in the river. *Go left onto the waymarked 'Five Weirs Walk', follow a new river bank footpath upstream to:-*
6 **Burton Weir** at **Norfolk Bridge**
One of the five. This dam diverted water down a side channel to power factories making Sheffield steel. There are five rivers in Sheffield, power from them was the lifeblood of milling, originally of corn, (5000 mills recorded in the Domesday Book) and, latterly, for steelmaking. Nervousness about loss of water delayed the arrival of the canal (1819) until just before railways arrived (1838).

steps ⚠ to the towpath. *Turn left and retrace your route to* **Victoria Quays**.

Four longer walks:-
From **7** **Blonk Bridge** *Turn against the one way traffic flow (ie north-west), go carefully across the road junction and follow close to the iron railings of Nursery Street overlooking the River Don. At the lights turn over the river and then right into Alma Street. A little way down, on the right, is the entrance to:-*
8 **Kelham Island** (1982: Tel: 0114 272 2106)
A Bessemer Converter stands outside a fantastic tribute to Sheffield's cutlery and steelmaking skills. Little Mesters have little workshops within this museum which also houses the Don Engine (1905), built to roll armour plate up to 16" thick in 50 ton pieces. Steam driven, rated at 12 000 horse power, the engine is run up to four times every day (except on Friday and Saturday when the museum is closed).

From **4** **Bacon Lane Bridge** *continue along the towpath for miles past the sporting excellence of Don*

Valley Stadium and Sheffield Arena and the huge Meadowhall Shopping Mall at the foot of the top flight of **Tinsley Locks**. *Maybe return by Supertram or Five Weirs Walk.*

From **5** **Washford Bridge**. *Five Wiers Walk follows the valley downstream to* **Tinsley Locks.**

From in front of Victoria Quays. Park Square is straddled by pedestrian and tramway bridges. *Go up* ⚠ *steps onto the walkways over the traffic. Fork right for the Market and left to the Supertram Junction. Follow the tracks down to:-*
9 **Sheffield Supertram**: Commercial Street Stop
From here you can get to the sporting stadia, a Park and Ride or return from **Tinsley Locks.**

Getting there:
Approach from M1 J33. Use A630 / A57 south and turn right at 'Victoria Quays' traffic lights.
🅿 *Suggest North Quay Multi-storey. Join at* **1**.
♿ *North Quay (level 3). Join at* **1**.
🚃 *From station exit turn right and use footbridges over Park Square. Join at* **1**.

Landranger Map 111 Ref SK 36 87

Use Warren Street to go onto **Norfolk Bridge** *and look back at the weir. At the moment (1999) there is a missing link in the riverside walk but you can pick up the path again just under* **2** **Wicker Viaduct**. *To do this, return to the traffic lights, turn left along the pavement past the river wall and follow the bus lane until it merges into Saville Street. Some distance further along is* **2** **Wicker Viaduct**. *Find the waymark and return along the riverside to:-*
7 **Blonk Bridge**
Start of the 'Five Weirs Walk' on the 'one way' Blonk Street, just across Furnival Road from the arched entrance to **Victoria Quays.**

Alternatively, from **6** **Norfolk Bridge** turn uphill for 50 yards and left up Foley Street. Straight on at the roundabout then over the canal bridge. Turn next left into Lumley Street. After about 80 yards (at the end of the low stone wall) go down some

Sheffield and Tinsley Canal (formerly Sheffield Canal)
- see **Sheffield and South Yorkshire Navigation**
Shefford Canal - see Ivel Navigation
Shrewsbury and Newport Canal
- see **Shropshire Union Canal**
Shropshire Canal   115 D1
Donnington Wood Canal at Donnington
Wood to Coalport
Coalbrookdale Branch

*Aqueducts, tunnels and all major structures need a structural
inspection to assess maintenance requirements. Pontcysyllte
Aqueduct (below) consists of nineteen iron troughs supported
on partially hollow stone columns and it is deservedly one of
the severn wonders of the British Waterways.*
*One of the eight yearly inspections took place recently
(1998) and after stopping water at either end, British
Waterways engineers pulled the plug out... with
spectacular results.*

Shropshire Union Canal
                                    118 B4 - 115 D1
**Birmingham and Liverpool Junction Canal,
Chester Canal, Ellesmere Canal, Shrewsbury and
East Shropshire Tub Boat Canals**

The Shropshire Union Canal is a modern title
for a set of canals which were first put together by
the Shropshire Union Railways and Canal
Company (1845) which eventually owned a total
of 200 miles of canals of differing origins.
The modern names and their provenance are:-

Montgomery Canal (under restoration)
Frankton Junction to Newtown
Formerly 35 miles, 25 narrow locks
Based on the Montgomeryshire Canal with the
addition of a branch from the former Ellesmere Canal
(as far as Llanymynech).

Llangollen Canal (formerly Ellesmere Canal)
Hurleston to Llantisilio Junction
46 miles, 21 narrow locks
Based on the original alignment of the Ellesmere
Canal (before competition reduced its ambition) with
the addition of its branch from Frankton to the
Chester Canal at Hurleston.
Shropshire Union (Main Line)
Ellesmere Port to Autherley Junction
66 miles, 18 wide locks, 29 narrow locks
Based on the arrow-straight narrow Birmingham and
Liverpool Junction Canal, incorporating the wide
Chester Canal from Nantwich and the 'Wirral line', a
wide part of the Ellesmere Canal across the Wirral
Peninsula to the tidal Mersey.
Shropshire Union (Middlewich Branch)
Barbridge Junction to Middlewich
10 miles, 4 narrow locks
Chester Canal's final completion (1833) of its
original purpose of connecting the River Dee with
the Trent and Mersey Canal.

Management and Restoration
British Waterways, Ellesmere Tel: 01691 622549
Bilston Tel: 01902 409010, Norbury Tel: 01785 284253
Shropshire Union Canal Society Tel: 01626 777951
Website:
http://www.the-wharf.co.uk/canals/society/sucs.htm

Montgomeryshire Canal   114 C2-C1
Opened: 1797, 1819, 1821
Engineer: Dadford
Frankton Junction to Newtown

Another canal of two parts. The Eastern (original 1797
company) had a separate existence from the Western
part. They relied on similar traffic and were joined and
to end at Garthmyl, but such were the arguments that
the western part had to obtain its own Act of Parliament.

◊ **Freestone Lock: Newtown**
Start of a six mile journey to Berriew for canoes and
similar craft that can be carried around obstructions.
From A5 / A458 to Welshpool then use A483 north.
◊ **Pool Quay: Prince of Wales length**
Main transfer point with the River Severn. Seven
miles were restored (1980) with the help of the
Prince of Wales Committee, extended to 11 miles
when Gallows Tree Bank Bridge was restored
(1992). Narrowboat *Heulwen-Sunshine* from
Buttington Wharf (1976) and *Montgomery Canal
Cruises* from Welsh Pool Town Wharf (1992) have
been pioneers in using this restored water.
*Approach from A5 / A458 to Welshpool then use
A483 north to Pool Quay aerodrome.*
◊ **Carreghofa Locks**
Beautiful surroundings to a set of locks restored by
volunteers from the Shropshire Union Canal Society.
They were the original connection between the
Montgomeryshire (western end) and the
Llanymynech Branch of the Ellesmere.
*Approach from A5 / B4396 then find B4398 / B4393
junction west of Llanymynech.*
◊ **Maesbury Wharf**
A veritable time warp. A wharf for transhipment to
Oswestry, stables for horses and a pub for bargees.
This isolated restoration is quiet and rural (1999),
hopefully soon to change in character when linked to
Frankton Junction. Peate's Mill nearby had its own

boats (1921-1932) until they sold them when diesel lorries provided a more economical service. One of them became Tom Rolt's boat *Cressy*.
Approach from A5 / B4396; it is in the lanes north of Knockin aerodrome.

◊ **Queen's Head**
A canal milepost nearby is dedicated to Graham Palmer, founder of the Waterway Recovery Group, without whom waterways would have been lost. Next to the pub the improved A5 has a 'blind' span with sufficient headroom to allow the restored canal through... a change in official attitudes that flattened nearby bridge 76 as part of former improvements.
On A5 at junction with B5009. South of Oswestry.

◊ **1936 Breach**
A stitch-in-time would have saved a lot of restoration energy. The breach in this embankment close to the Perry Aqueduct was estimated to need £400 to repair (1936) but there was so little traffic that tolls would not have covered the expense.

Tom Rolt had not started his honeymoon voyage, *Narrow Boat* had not been written and was only published 8 years later (1944). It should not happen today... waterway societies remain vigilant.
Approach from A5 north / A495 east. Follow the towpath from the locks almost alongside the road.

Ellesmere Canal   114 C1-115 D1
(now: Llangollen Canal and part of Main Line)
Open: 1795, 1804, 1806, 1833
Engineers: Jessop, Duncombe, Denson, Turner, Telford

If a crow flying between Shrewsbury and Liverpool encountered a slight breeze from the east he might pass over Weston, Ellesmere, Llangollen, Wrexham, Chester and the Wirral Peninsula. This was the line that the Burgers of Ellesmere decided (1793) for a canal which would also connect collieries at Rauban with industries near Wrexham. A branch to limestone deposits at Llanymynech completed the idea which might eventually connect with the Montgomeryshire north from Pool Quay on the River Severn that was being proposed at the same time (1793).

They made a start on the Wirral link between the Rivers Dee and Mersey plus the more difficult bits in the middle between Chirk and Weston.

Competition, in the form of newly discovered coal nearer Chester (1800), changed their minds. They forgot the route north of Llangollen and joined up with the existing Chester Canal by branching out from Frankton down towards Nantwich (1805). Despite this change of heart they completed the two aqueducts (over the Dee and Ceirlog, 1805) and widened the feeder channel from Horseshoe Falls on the Dee near Llantisilio. These two canals were now mutually dependent and amalgamated (1827) with a view to ending their isolation by finally making the connection to Middlewich (1833).

◊ **Horseshoe Falls: Berwyn**
This perfect arc is Telford's Weir for collecting the water supply for the whole of the Shropshire Union, from Hack Green (Nantwich) to Ellesmere Port. Some of the six million gallons a day taken away also supplies the citizens of Nantwich.
Approach from M54 J7. Use A5 west to A539. On the river at Llantysilio Bridge.

◊ **Trevor Wharf / Ruabon Arm**
The iron foundry which cast the troughs for the

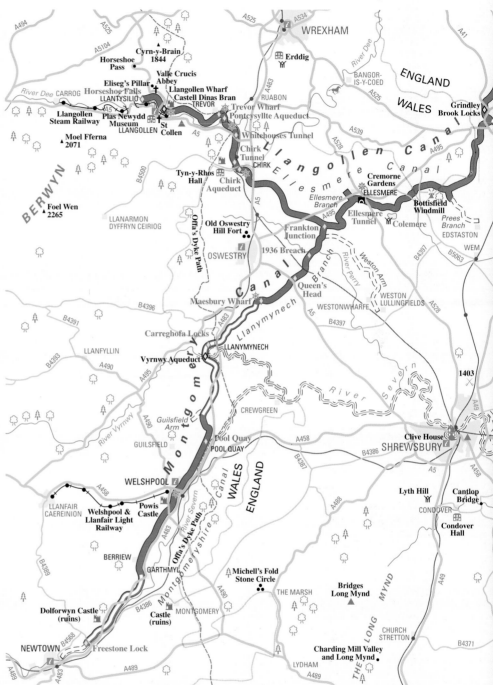

Pontcysyllte Aqueduct was served from the wharf by one of the network of tramroads also serving coal mines and limestone quarries. The wharf is now a base for hire cruisers. Horsedrawn trip boats start from Llangollen Wharf four miles further north.
Approach from M53 J12. Use A55 / A483 / A532 going south-west.

◊ **Two tunnel towpaths and two aqueducts**
Immediately south of Chirk Tunnel (1370 feet) is Chirk Aqueduct (600 feet). Whitehouses Tunnel (570

feet) is north and 2 miles further on is the aqueduct that leaves the English tongue tied (1007 feet).
Approach from M54 J7. Use A5 west and north.

Shropshire Union Canal (continued)
Birmingham and Liverpool Junction Canal, Chester Canal, Ellesmere Canal, Shrewsbury Canal.

◊ **Frankton Junction**
Leads onto the 15 mile intended Weston 'main line'

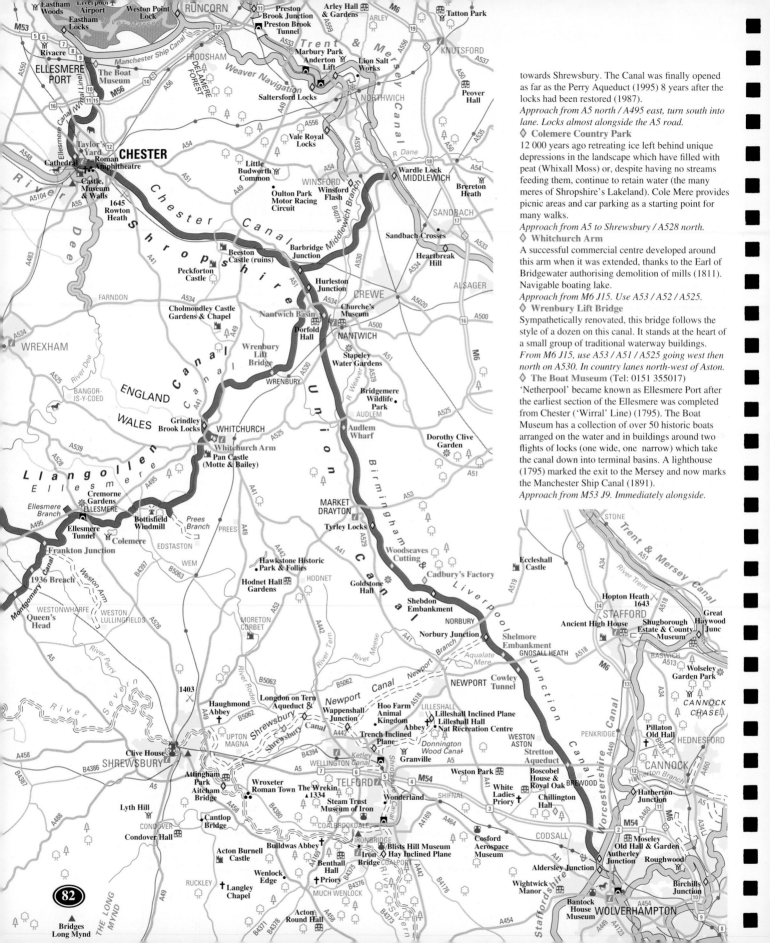

towards Shrewsbury. The Canal was finally opened as far as the Perry Aqueduct (1995) 8 years after the locks had been restored (1987).
Approach from A5 north / A495 east, turn south into lane. Locks almost alongside the A5 road.

◊ **Colemere Country Park**
12 000 years ago retreating ice left behind unique depressions in the landscape which have filled with peat (Whixall Moss) or, despite having no streams feeding them, continue to retain water (the many meres of Shropshire's Lakeland). Cole Mere provides picnic areas and car parking as a starting point for many walks.
Approach from A5 to Shrewsbury / A528 north.

◊ **Whitchurch Arm**
A successful commercial centre developed around this arm when it was extended, thanks to the Earl of Bridgewater authorising demolition of mills (1811). Navigable boating lake.
Approach from M6 J15. Use A53 / A52 / A525.

◊ **Wrenbury Lift Bridge**
Sympathetically renovated, this bridge follows the style of a dozen on this canal. It stands at the heart of a small group of traditional waterway buildings.
From M6 J15, use A53 / A51 / A525 going west then north on A530. In country lanes north-west of Aston.

◊ **The Boat Museum** (Tel: 0151 355017)
'Netherpool' became known as Ellesmere Port after the earliest section of the Ellesmere was completed from Chester ('Wirral' Line) (1795). The Boat Museum has a collection of over 50 historic boats arranged on the water and in buildings around two flights of locks (one wide, one narrow) which take the canal down into terminal basins. A lighthouse (1795) marked the exit to the Mersey and now marks the Manchester Ship Canal (1891).
Approach from M53 J9. Immediately alongside.

Chester Canal   118 B4

Opened: 1775, 1779,
Engineer: Weston
Chester to Nantwich
Branch to Middlewich

Since Roman times Chester craft could travel up the Dee as far as Holt. A wide canal was then proposed (1772) to take a parallel line to Nantwich and then turn left to the new (1770) Trent and Mersey at Middlewich. After seven years it arrived at Nantwich (1779).

It was then discouraged by the Trent and Mersey Company who were worried that traffic might leave its route to Runcorn and go to the sea via the Weaver or Dee. As the Chester Company had also run out of money it stopped at Nantwich (1779).

◊ **Taylor's Yard: Chester**
On the northern side of a two mile walk around Chester's walls there is a dramatic aeriel view onto the towpath as it slips between the sheer city walls and the canal. A curious 3 lock staircase is part of an 11 lock descent into Tower Wharf just above the short 'wide' connection to the River Dee. Around this wharf the Shropshire Union built up and maintained its own carrying fleet. When the fleet was sold (1926) Taylor's gradually took over and built up a business including building and repairing leisure craft (1935-1972).

Many specialised buildings can still be seen, including huge roof girders over a side slipway.
From M56 to A5117 / A550 west then A548 east.

◊ **Nantwich Basin**
For fifty six years the terminus of the wide Chester Canal, now filled with colourful, moored boats.
From M6 J15, use A500 / A534 going west.

Birmingham and Liverpool Junction Canal   115 D1

Opened: 1835
Engineers: Telford
Nantwich to Autherley Junction

This canal of embankments and cuttings stopped short of both Birmingham (by 12 miles) and of Liverpool (by 31 miles). It was given such a grand name because it provided a bold, straight, new 39 mile alignment which provided the missing link to make a shorter route between those cities. Compared to the route via the Trent and Mersey Canal, the journey to the Mersey was reduced by 18 miles and 40 locks.

◊ **Audlem Wharf**
Partway up a 15 lock flight, which is popular with summer Sunday gongoozlers, are an original mill and a warehouse building which have been retained but given new life.
Approach from M6 J16. Use A500 west / A529 south.

◊ **Woodseaves Cutting**
Long (4500 feet), narrow, steep sided and deep (100 feet), sometimes cut in raw red sandstone, the microclimate nurtures ferns and a slippery towpath.
Approach from M6 J15. Use A5182 / A53 / A529 south. (There are two 'Woodseaves' along this stretch).

◊ **Charlie and the Chocolate Factory (1912-1961)**
Boats each carried more than 100 milk churns collected from farms along the canal to this chocolate crumb factory at Knighton. Early steel motor boats went from here to Cadbury's canalside factories at

24 hour furnaces light up the night sky at Coalbrookdale (Bedlam Furnaces on the banks of the River Severn: Philip James de Loutherbourg 1801).
Seventy seven years after Abraham Darby had started casting pig iron using coke and twenty seven years after the Bridgewater Canal was delivering coal to Manchester, the short 8 mile Shropshire Canal was opened (1792) with branches allowing a shuttle service from the coal mines at Ketley and Donnington Wood to the blast furnaces at Blist Hill and Coalbrookdale. The Canal was small and cheap to build with the narrowest locks 6'2" and with inclined planes to overcome differences in level. The special boats were also small... mere 20 foot tubs carrying 5-8 tons each... which made them cheap to build and easy to handle on the inclined planes. When travelling between planes they were coupled together into 'trains' pulled by a single horse... up to twenty at a time along the level and four at a time through the run of locks leading to the later Shrewsbury Canal.

Bournville, Frampton-on-Severn and Blackpole. Painted in company colours with the company logo on the side, the boats were great traveling bill boards advertising the product. **Charlie** Ballinger was a latter day boatman carrying this trade and the large timber warehouse and covered loading bay is all that remains of the original **chocolate factory.**
Approach from M6 J14. Use A5013 / A519 to Woodseaves. Turn west to Knighton.

◊ **Shelmore Embankment** (1 mile x 60 feet high)
Great curving embankment near Norbury Junction, forced on the canal by Lord Anson, was the last element to be completed (1835). Constant earth slips over six years are thought to have led to Telfords death. He was 77.
From M6 J14 use A5013 going north / A519 south.

◊ **Cowley Tunnel** (240 feet)
Started life much longer (over 2000 feet) but during construction part of the roof fell in and created a raw, unlined, narrow cuttings (Gnosall Heath).
From M6 J14 go to Stafford then A518 going west.

◊ **Stretton Aqueduct: A5**
Improving Watling Street / A5 and building the 'main line' were both down to one man, Thomas Telford. Where one passes over the other he indulged in a bit of celebration... a seriously decorative design.
Approach from M6 J12. Use A5 going west.

◊ **Chillington Hall: Brewood**
Home of the Gifford family who insisted on a 'properly decorated' bridge (no 9) where the canal passed below their private driveway.
Approach from M54 J2. Use A449 going north.

◊ **Shrewsbury Canal and the Tub Boat System**
The Shropshire Union also owned an intricate network of non standard canals which served the unfolding 'Ironbridge' industrial revolution. Telford built the 11 mile lock free Shrewsbury Canal from Donnington

Wood to Shrewsbury, with a 3000 foot tunnel and a pioneering iron trough aqueduct (at Longdon-on-Tren 1796). He built it to slightly more generous dimensions than the earlier tub boat system to which he connected at Trench (eleven locks and an incline). However, this whole East Shropshire system remained isolated for 39 years until the Newport Branch from the Shropshire Union was built (1835). Soon afterwards the London North Western Railway bought them all (1857) and converted many routes to rail. The 'Hay Inclined Plane' can still be seen, others at Lilleshall (last in steam 1879) and Trench (1921) have been destroyed.
Approach from M54 J4. Use A646 / A4432 going south to Coaprt Wharf. The aqueduct will be re-erected in Ironbridge Gorge Museum.

✴ *Boat Trips*
Welshpool *Heulwen-Sunshine* Tel: 01938 552563
Severn Street Tel: 01938 553271
Maesbury Wharf *Joy, Curlew* Tel: 01691 670826
Llangollen *William Jessop, James Brindley (horse drawn)* Tel: 01978 860702
Froncysyllte Wharf *Thomas Telford (horsedrawn)* Tel: 01978 860702
Trevor Wharf Tel: 01978 823215

ℹ️ *Tourist Information*
Newtown Tel: 01686 625580
Welshpool Tel: 01938 552043
Llangollen Tel: 01978 860828
Ellesmere Tel: 01691 622981
Whitchurch Tel: 01948 664577
Chester Tel: 01244 322220
Nantwich Tel: 01270 610983
Market Drayton Tel: 01630 652139
Shrewsbury Tel: 01743 350761
Ironbridge Tel: 01952 432166

The canal and river are both forced into twists and turns by the red sandstone cliffs around Austcliff. The overhang of the 'Hanging Rock' has become less dramatic over the years as the roots of trees entering the fissures and the general passing of geological time lead to continuous erosion of the exposed rock.

Staffordshire & Worcestershire Canal   115 D2-E1

Opened: 1772
Engineers: Brindley, Henshall, Simcock, Dadford
Great Haywood to Stourport-on-Severn
46 miles, 45 narrow locks

Despite being close to the Black Country and Birmingham, this canal offers truly rural walking along two delightful river valleys, the Sow and Stour. It wriggles round the foot of Kinver Edge and then reaches down to its lifeline to the sea… the River Severn at Stourport, a small village until the canal arrived.

After the success of the privately financed Bridgewater Canal, every company wanted to reassure its shareholders that their canal would be a success by employing Brindley as their engineer.

Despite his contribution to the Trent and Mersey, this was his first canal in the central Midlands and it set the standards. His previous work had been on almost level canals with wide canals and barges. As water-use is a problem on inland summits he chose to make locks on this new canal exactly half the width of his flight to the Mersey at Runcorn and thus use half the volume of water.

He even tested his new design in his garden at Compton... inventing the ground paddle so that boats were not swamped by incoming water, and using twin gates with balance beams on the taller bottom gates to reduce the weight and wear. (Top gates do not need to be so tall and so he used a wider, but single, 'door' which was almost the same weight as each of those at the bottom.)

The canal was an immediate success, and always looked outside its line to improve canal carrying and resist railway competition. It financed the branch to Cannock (1841) and 16 locks at Churchbridge on the BCN (1863). It formed an alliance with the BCN against the railways which failed within two weeks (1844) but managed to 'rescue' the Severn Navigation from railway clutches by funding the Severn Commissioners (1856).

Luckily for us today, once it was built, the company did not invest much in improving its own line and we now see an early canal which despite the fibre optic cable beneath the towpath appears just as it was when it was opened over 225 years ago.

Management
British Waterways, Norbury Tel: 01785 284253
Staffordshire and Worcestershire Canal Society
Tel: 01902 885886
Website: http://www.users.globalnet.co.uk/~cowda/

◊ **Great Haywood Junction**
A handsome brick bridge carries the Trent and Mersey towpath over the entrance to Brindley's canal. The swiftly flowing River Trent was the first obstacle, overcome by a typical fat, squat aqueduct which makes so little fuss on the waterway it is easily missed.
Approach from M6 J14. Use A5013 / A513 going south, then A51 north.

◊ **Tixall Wide**
More an ornamental lake for the landed gentry, even the sound of the nearby railway is confined in a tunnel. Popular with kingfishers and fishermen.
Approach from M6 J14. Use A5013 / A513 going

south to Milford. Turn north.

◊ **Teddesley**
Country lane and canal are a few yards apart with a backdrop of the woodland belt planted to hide the canal from Teddesley Hall... home of one of the canal's promters. (Between Locks 40 and 41).
Approach from M6 J13. Use A449 north and turn east and 1 mile south of Acton Trussell.

◊ **Hatherton Junction**
There is no such place name. The branch was financed by the Company and named after its Chairman. It reached up into the coalfields around Cannock Chase, and may well go there again.
Approach from M6 J11. Use A460 north / A5 west to Four Crosses. Turn south.

◊ **Autherley / Aldersley Junctions**
Close to Wolverhampton racecourse and providing a cat's cradle of walks around water, Aldersley is the junction for 21 locks down from Wolverhampton.

Brindley's canal was always successful because this and other branches attracted so much traffic. Even when most traffic from Wolverhampton and Birmingham turned left at Autherley into Telford's new route to Liverpool, the Staffs and Worcs kept its finances healthy by charging a huge toll for the tiny ½ mile journey between these two junctions.
Approach from M54 J2. Use A449 south to Oxley.

◊ **The Bratch**
Best kept locks on the system (1995); when approaching these three locks look similar to the famous Bingley Five-rise staircase locks in Yorkshire ... but they are different. The white, octagonal toll house oversees three separate locks with only a few feet between them. Secret balancing reservoirs away to the side even out the flow of water as the locks are used but, even so, techniques for the boaters need adjusting and a lock keeper is on hand to help.
Approach from M5 J3. Use A456 west / A491 north. Follow A449 and turn west opposite the A463.

◊ **Stewponey Locks**
Just south of the entrance to the Stourbridge Canal, water is apparently swallowed into the ground by Brindley's circular design for an overflow weir.
From M5 J3, use A456 north / A458 west.

◊ **Stour Valley**
Carved through the red sandstone that peaks at Kinver Edge, the river and canal share a narrow valley from Wolverley to Stewponey. Raw rock cutting by chisle, pick and hammer are now covered with jungle like vegetation.
Approach from M5 J3. Use A456 west then A449 north.

◊ **Clay House Bridge: No 25**
A typical small Brindley bridge to accommodate the farmer's need to cross from field to field. This canal was created in times when *places* were as important as *cyphers*. Every bridge carries a cast iron plate with a name as well as a number. Local names with more obscure origins than this abound.

A little to the south the canal skirts underneath a spectacular 25 foot sandstone cliff face at Austcliff.
From M5 J3, use A456 south-west / A449 north. Turn west to Caunsall.

◊ **Cookley Tunnel**
Brindley's Bridgewater Canal in Lancashire had aqueducts but no tunnels. This short (195 feet) tunnel was his first and, despite being the oldest remaining on the system, it has a towpath through.
From M5 J3, use A456 south-west / A449 north.

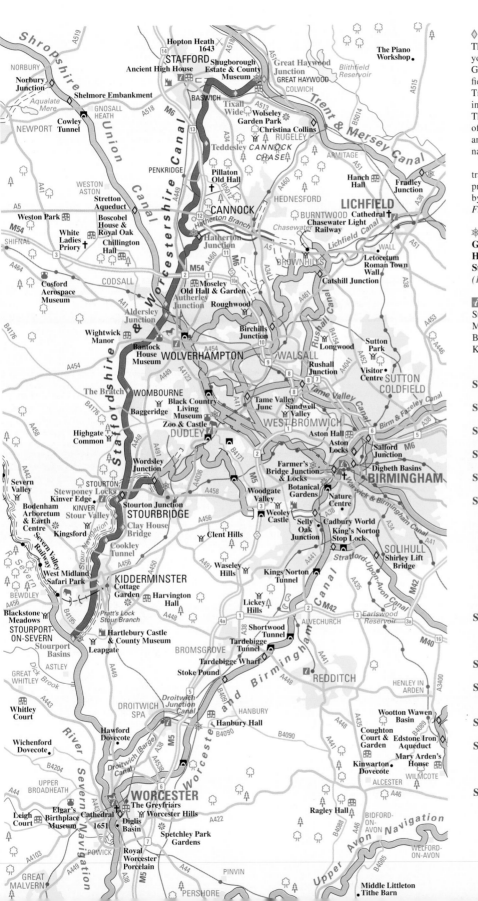

◇ **Stourport Basins**
These four basins are full of boats and a lot of what you see is unchanged since it was first built. Generously spread out across what was a farmer's field, these basins provided protection for Severn Trows from the vagaries of the river and step up in two stages to the canal, home to the narrow boat. There are two separate runs of locks; one run offers single deep locks for 16 foot wide barges and the other offers narrow staircase pairs for narrowboats.

Warehouses still remain from the busy days of transhipment into narrow boats. The most prominent is used by the local boat club and topped by a much photographed wooden clock tower. *From M5 J6, use A449 / A4025 going north-west.*

⚙ **Boat Trips**
Great Haywood *Milford Star* Tel: 01785 663728
Hatherton Branch *Calf Heath* Tel: 01902 790570
Stourport-on-Severn *Carvolate (1911), River King (1933), Miss Jason (1936)* Tel: 01299 871177

ℹ **Tourist Information**
Stafford Tel: 01785 240204
Merry Hill Tel: 01384 487911
Bewdley Tel: 01229 404740
Kidderminster Tel: 01562 829400

....

Stainforth and Keadby Canal
- see **Sheffield and South Yorkshire Navigation**
Stamford Canal
- see **River Welland Navigation**
Steeping River and Wainfleet Haven   **117 D1**
Gibraltar to Wainfleet
Stevenston Canal   **120 B2**
Saltcoats to Stevenston
Stort Navigation
- see **Lee Navigation**
Stourbridge Canal   **115 E2**
Stourton to Delph Junction
Fens Branch, Stourbridge Branch
5¾ miles, 20 narrow locks
British Waterways (Stourton to Wordsley Junction), Stafford Tel: 01785 284253
British Waterways (Wordsley Junction to Delph Junction), Bilston Tel: 01902 409010
Stourbridge Navigation Trust Tel: 01384 395216
Stourbridge Extension Canal   **115 E2**
Brockmoor Junction to Oak Farm Basin
Bromley Branch, Sandhills Branch
2 miles, 1 lock
Stour, River (Dorset)   **112 A4**
Christchurch to Iford
Stour, River (Kent)   **113 F3**
Sea to Canterbury
19¼ miles (to Fordwich), 0 locks
Stour, River Navigation (Staffordshire)   **115 D2**
Kidderminster to Stourbridge
Stour Navigation (Suffolk), River   **117 D4-E4**
Sea to Sudbury
Ballingdon Cut
25½ miles, 15 locks
Stover Canal   **111 D3**
River Teign to Teigngrace

Stratford-upon-Avon Canal

115 E2

Opened: 1803, 1816
Engineers: Snape, Clowes, Whitmore
Northern section: 12½ miles, 18 narrow locks
King's Norton Junction to Lapworth
Southern section: 13 miles, 35 narrow locks
Lapworth to River Avon at Stratford

The northern Stratford provides a level walk from outside Birmingham towards a descent into the River Avon valley and Shakespeare Country.

The southern Stratford is delightfully rural, passing through the Forest of Arden and ending in the bustling tourist centre of Stratford-upon-Avon.

This canal was doing so well after its first building phase that it nearly failed to reach Stratford.

Before the Worcester and Birmingham Canal got to the Severn at Worcester (1815) it used the Stratford as the only outlet for its Birmingham traffic going south. The northern Stratford (1803) linked King's Norton to Lapworth, from where the Grand Union (date) channelled traffic towards London.

The route was on a level from Gas Street Basin with only the one flight of locks (Lapworth). It was convenient, avoided the BCN and became very profitable. Only after considerable pressure by Stratford citizens did the southern section arrive to the River Avon (1815).

Post World War II, despite direct action campaigning by IWA members, Warwickshire County Council decided to abandon the canal because of a road problem at Wilmcote. Public outcry ensued (1959).

A national campaign, led by the IWA, eventually resulted in the National Trust leasing the canal with a promise to restore and maintain. For four years volunteer labour, defence personnel and prisoners set a cracking working pace under the leadership of David Hutchings. The first major re opening of a British canal then took place (1964) having cost the Trust less than half the County Council's estimated cost of filling it in. British Waterways then took over maintenance (1988).

Management
British Waterways, Lapworth Tel: 01564 784634
Stratford-upon-Avon Canal Society
Tel: 01608 661274

◊ **King's Norton Stop Lock**
The silhouette of huge iron frames holding up heavy wooden guillotine gates at this lock is a formidable sight. Luckily there is no longer a need to protect water between different companies and the gates remain open.
From M42 J2, use A441 going north to Pershore Road.

◊ **Brandwood Tunnel** (1056 feet)
Iron handrails inside the tunnel were used to haul boats through this short, straight tunnel whilst the horses were led over the top. The tunnel portal sports a replica of the Company Seal depicting, would you believe… William Shakespeare.
From M42 J2, use A441 going north to Pershore Road.

Broad lock linking the terminus basin of the Stratford-upon-Avon Canal with the River Avon. Multi-lingual interpretation boards explain everything. Depth of lock varies depending on how much rain is in the river.

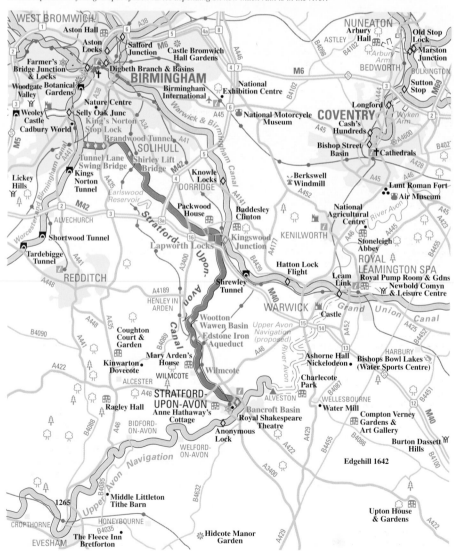

◊ **Tunnel Lane Swing Bridge**
In earlier days, when owned by the Great Western Railway, this was a drawbridge that suffered from heavy road traffic. GWR strengthened it and fixed it in place. The early campaigner for waterways, Tom Rolt, gave notice that he would exercise his statutory right of navigation with narrowboat *Cressy* (1947), and the company was obliged to unfix it and raise the deck high enough to allow passage. Many other IWA campaigners followed this lead and eventually the company installed the present bridge.
From M42 J2, use A441 going north to Pershore Road.

◊ **Shirley Lift Bridge**
Modern metal bridge carrying a busy local road. Much photographed for its slender balancing arms.
Approach from M42 J4. Use A34 north then B4102 west to Hollywood.

◊ **Kingswood Junction**
Two thirds of the way down Lapworth Locks (see short stroll alongside) a short branch under the railway viaduct links the Stratford and Grand Union. Delightful walking.
From M42 J4, use A3400 south then B4439 east.

◊ **Wootton Wawen Basin**
Terminus for a while, this basin overlooks a short span iron aqueduct over the main A34, of similar structure to Edstone Aqueduct. Watermill nearby.
Approach from M42 J4. Use A3400 going south.

◊ **Edstone Iron Aqueduct** (1813, 520 feet)
Narrow cast iron trough with low level towpath gives an odd view of passing boats. Built eight years after the similar Pontcysyllte Aqueduct in Wales, it is the longest in England.
From M42 J4, use A3400 going south to Bearley.

◊ **Wilmcote**
At the beginning of the lock flight the road leading to Mary Arden's House and the railway station crosses the canal by a new bridge. This was the bridge that road engineers did not want to build (1959) so they proposed canal closure instead. It is only here because of the successful campaign to save the canal. Such battles continue, even today.

Three groups make up a lock flight which drops down 77 feet through 11 locks from a long Preston Bagot pound which contains just the 'odd lock'.
Approach from M40 J15. Use A46 going south-west to walk up from the bottom of the flight.

◊ **Bancroft Basin: Stratford-upon-Avon**
Set within a riverside park with a wide lock connection to the Avon, this is one of the most attractive canal termini in Britain. Surrounded by flowerbeds, overlooked by the Shakespeare Memorial Theatre and the remains of a horse tramway that went as far as Moreton in Marsh.

There are many footpaths around, some following the far bank of the River Avon leading downstream to Stratford New Lock and Anonymous Lock.
From M40 J15, use A46 / A439 going south.

✵ *Boat Trips*
Stratford Basin *Countess of Evesham*
Tel: 0836 769499

📖 *Suggested Guide Book*
Stratford-upon-Avon Canal Guide Stratford-upon-Avon Canal Society

ℹ️ *Tourist Information*
Warwick Tel: 01926 492212
Stratford-upon-Avon Tel: 01789 293127

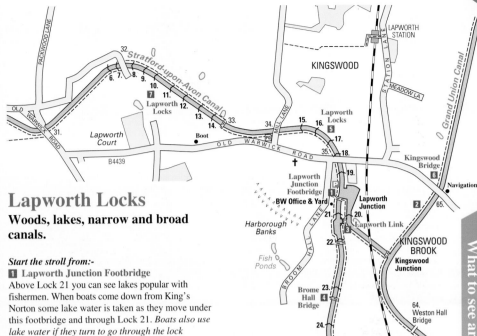

Lapworth Locks
Woods, lakes, narrow and broad canals.

Start the stroll from:-
1 **Lapworth Junction Footbridge**
Above Lock 21 you can see lakes popular with fishermen. When boats come down from King's Norton some lake water is taken as they move under this footbridge and through Lock 21. *Boats also use lake water if they turn to go through the lock connecting with:-*

2 **Grand Union Canal**
Boats passing *between* the two canals used to use both these locks, thus taking two lock-fulls of water from the lakes with each journey.
Now we have:-

3 **Lapworth Link**
This short cut, originally constructed around 1800, is now revived (1995) and thus only one lock-full is used with each pass. The water for this movement does not come the lakes, it comes from the six mile pound of the Grand Union. *Go a short way towards the Grand Union, over a modern footbridge at the head of the Lapworth Link. Turn right down behind the garden of one of Stratford Canal's standard single storey lock keepers cottages with its distinctive barrel vaulted roof. Follow the towpath further south. At the tail of Lock 23 see:-*

4 **Brome Hall Bridge**
Original cast iron split footbridge made of two identical pieces set only an inch or two apart, this is typical of the Stratford. The empty slot between each half was an advantage to the boatmen passing with horsedrawn narrowboats. The towing rope could remain attached to the horse whilst the boat was in the lock, even though the horse had moved forward to wait for the lock gates to be opened. The loose rope was simply dropped through the small gap in the bridge. Without the bridge there would have been no problem, but there would be no easy way to cross the canal either. Compare this bridge to the modern one on the restored 'Lapworth Link'; they look the same from afar but since diesel engines were invented (1920s) there is no need for the tow rope gap. *Cross the bridge turn right and go north along the towing path past the British Waterways office and shop, under the next bridge to:-*

5 **Locks 18 - 15: Lapworth Locks**
These locks (and the next group, 14 - 6) are so close that there is hardly room for the water to settle before spilling over into the next level down.

Lock 16 has a waterfall from the widened canal above, which slows when the lock is filling up. At **Lock 15** a locked frame holds some long strong planks ready for use in an emergency. Repairs may be needed down hill of this point, or the canal might spring a leak. Water up hill needs to be held back by making a temporary dam. The planks are shaped so they fit across the canal just above the lock gates and can be lowered one by one into the steel channels visible either side. *Pass under hump back bridge (34), turn sharp left up the slope and along Mill Lane to the local shops at the road junction. Turn left, back towards Bridge 35. Regain the towpath and **return to the start of the stroll at 1**.*

A longer walk from **3** *Lapworth Link.*
Go west under the railway. At the towpath bridge, turn left to follow **2** *Grand Union to:-*

6 **Kingswood Bridge**
The Grand Union is plenty wide enough for two barges to pass except at bridges like this. Barges have to take turns but, with care, two narrowboats can pass. *Use the road to return to Stratford-upon-Avon Canal Bridge 35. Regain the towpath and continue up the canal, past:-*

7 **Locks 14 - 6: Lapworth Locks**
More narrow locks of the Stratford Canal. *At the beginning of this section and after seven locks there are 'turnover bridges' transferring the towpath from side to side. Go beyond Lock 6, up onto the road bridge (31), turn left and return to 1.*

Getting there:
Approach from M42 J4. Use A3400 / B4439 south-east.
🅿️♿ *Between Broom Hall Lane and the canal. Join at 1.*
🚆 *From the station cross to the west of the line. Go to Mill Lane and turn left. Join at 5.*

Landranger Map 139 Ref SP 18 70

Stroudwater Navigation - see **Cotswold Canals**

Swaffham Bulbeck Lode   **117** D3
   River Cam to Swaffham Bulbeck

Swale Navigation (unfinished)   **119** D1
   Swale Nab to Morton-on-Swale

Swansea Canal   **114** B4
   Swansea to Hen-neuadd near Abercraf
   Includes: **Trewyddfa Canal** 1¾ miles Landore to
   Fforest **Cilybebyll Branch, Pontardawe Branch,**
   Ynysgedwyn Branch, Ystalyfera Branch
   16 miles, 36 narrow locks
   British Waterways, Govilon Tel: 01873 830328
   Swansea Canal Society   Tel: 01792 864637

Tamar Manure Navigation   **110** C3
   Morwellham to Newbridge near Gunnislake

Tamar, River   **110** C3
   Plymouth to Morwellham

Tame Valley Canal - see **BCN**

Tattershall Canal - see **Horncastle Navigation**

Tavistock Canal   **110** C3
   Morwellham to Tavistock
   Mill Hill Branch
   Morwellham and Tamar Valley Trust, Tavistock
   Tel: 01822 832766

Tay, River   **123** D4
   Sea to Perth
   31 miles, 0 locks
   (Buddon Ness to Balmerino) Port of Dundee Ltd
   Tel: 01382 224121
   (Balmerino to Perth) Perthshire and Kinross
   Unitary Authority Tel: 01738 624056

Tees, River   **121** F4
   Sea to Fardeanside Ford
   24 miles, 0 locks
   Tees Barrage Ltd, Cleveland Tel: 01642 633273

Teifi, River   **114** A3
   Sea to Llechryd

Teign, River   **111** D3
   Sea to Newton Abbot

Teme, River   **115** D3
   River Severn to Powick Bridge

Tennant Canal   **114** B4
   Port Tennant, Swansea to Aberdulais
   Includes part of **Glan-y-Wern Canal** (which was

Old Father Thames... statue to so much prosperity.
Agriculture, a reservoir of eels and salmon, endless power
for watermills and a major ships anchorage.

later incorporated into Red Jacket Canal), and
whole of **Red Jacket Canal** Red Jacket Pill to Port
Tennant **Six Branches**
8½ miles, 2 narrow locks
Neath and Port Talbot Borough Council, Port Talbot
Tel: 01639 763333
Neath and Tennant Canals Preservation Society
Tel: 01792 201594

Tern, River   **115** D1
   River Severn to Upton Forge

Thames and Medway Canal   **113** E2
   Gravesend to Frindsbury
   Thames and Medway Canal Association
   Tel: 01474 362861

Thames and Severn Canal
   - see **Cotswold Canals**

Thames, River   112 A2-113 E2

Improved: 1635, 1777, 1795, 1803.
Navigable from Cricklade - Inglesham to Sea
125 miles, 45 locks

A National Trail leads past wide flood plains west of
Oxford, passes ancient habitations when it cuts
through the Downs and then by lush meadows to
wharves and docks of the biggest market in the land.
   Draining 5000 square miles of the country, the
Thames is probably the most carefully managed
river in the realm. Every one of the 45 locks has a
control weir attached, the banks through London
are raised and the surging sea is controlled from the
Thames Barrier at Woolwich. Flooding of upstream
fields eases the weight of water downstream, all
controlled by the Environment Agency at Reading.

   Literally a Royal River, that is until Richard II paid
for his Third Crusade by selling bits to the City of
London (1197). Magna Carta specifically guaranteed
rights of navigation although millers and bargemen
always quarrelled about fees.
   Oxford was just out of reach of heavily laden
barges so the first reliable improvements were three
locks upstream from Abingdon (1635). 'Navigation
Commissioners' (formed 1751) improved navigation
from Staines to the River Kennet at Reading (1773)
and then added further locks to Goring (1777).
   Four locks along the upper reaches to Lechlade
(1791) and 10 new locks added to Oxford (1795)
were tardy response to the coming of the canals to
Inglesham (1789) and Oxford (1790). Railway
competition affected river traffic as much as canals
and the opening of Brunel's Great Western Railway
was too much, even though eight more locks had
been improved from Teddington (1811) to Cookham
(1830). Management of the river then devolved to the
Thames Conservancy (1857, 1866), the Port of
London (1908), Thames Water Authority (1974) and
Environment Agency (1996).

Management and Restoration
Environment Agency Tel: 0118 953 5000
River Thames Society Tel: 01491 571476

Approach by modest causeways against winter flooding, Swinford Bridge is one of only two remaining toll bridges across the Thames. Built by the Earl of Abingdon (1769), it replaced an
earlier bridge commissioned by King Gearge III after an uncomfortable ferry crossing

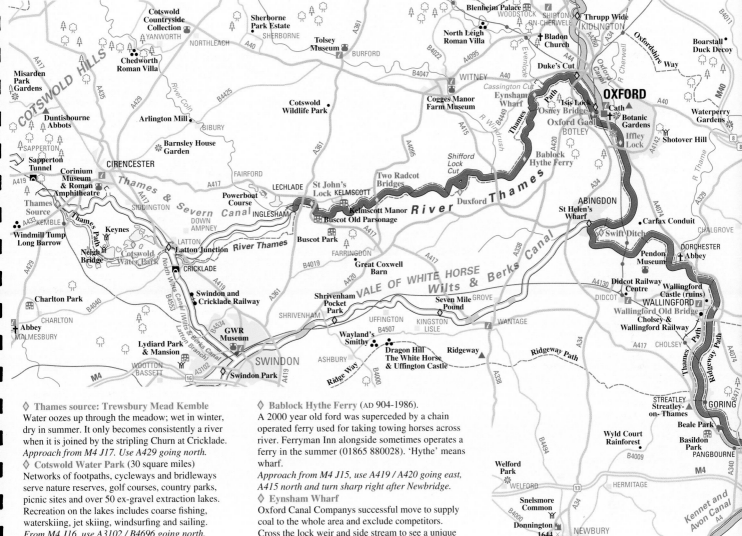

◊ **Thames source: Trewsbury Mead Kemble**
Water oozes up through the meadow; wet in winter,
dry in summer. It only becomes consistently a river
when it is joined by the stripling Churn at Cricklade.
Approach from M4 J17. Use A429 going north.

◊ **Cotswold Water Park** (30 square miles)
Networks of footpaths, cycleways and bridleways
serve nature reserves, golf courses, country parks,
picnic sites and over 50 ex-gravel extraction lakes.
Recreation on the lakes includes coarse fishing,
waterskiing, jet skiing, windsurfing and sailing.
From M4 J16, use A3102 / B4696 going north.

◊ **St John's Lock: Lechlade**
Father Thames overlooks the start of a series of
narrow, meandering reaches which avoid almost all
roads, tracks and habitation. Thames Path walkers,
wildlife and fishermen are all that follow the river.
From M4 J15, use A419 / A361 going north.

◊ **Two Radcot Bridges**
The oldest stone bridge on the river, three arches
were built by itenerant monks when fords were the
normal way of river crossing (AD958). A bone of
contention during the Civil War, the Earl of Oxford
won it once... and lost it once.

   Then a wider single span bridge was needed over a
new cut built (1787) to allow larger barges upstream
when the Thames and Severn Canal was opened.

   Nearby wharf sent Cotswold stone downstream to
build Oxford Colleges, Windsor Castle and, after the
Great Fire, Wren's St Pauls Cathedral, London.
From M4 J15, use A419 / A420 / A4095, going north.

◊ **Duxford**
Ford across the original course of the river, still
useable, but bypassed by Shifford Lock cut (1898).
From M4 J15, use A419 / A420 going east, near A415.

◊ **Bablock Hythe Ferry** (AD 904-1986).
A 2000 year old ford was superceded by a chain
operated ferry used for taking towing horses across
river. Ferryman Inn alongside sometimes operates a
ferry in the summer (01865 880028). 'Hythe' means
wharf.
*Approach from M4 J15, use A419 / A420 going east,
A415 north and turn sharp right after Newbridge.*

◊ **Eynsham Wharf**
Oxford Canal Companys successful move to supply
coal to the whole area and exclude competitors.
Cross the lock weir and side stream to see a unique
single gated lock (remains) which was filled by
channelling diverted river water behind the closed
gate. Former wharfinger's house is now a pub.
From M40 J8, use A40. Go west and B4044 south.

◊ **Osney Bridge** (7' 6" average headroom)
Limited headroom divides the boys from the men.
Only smaller craft can continue further upstream as
the bridge acts as head of navigation for larger craft.
Reaches upstream have a different character with
fewer craft and locks, mostly worked by hand.
Approach from M40 J9. Use A34 south / A420 east.

◊ **Iffley Lock**
Original lock chamber (1635) is now the by wash
channel to a modern lock (1924) and punt ladder.
College oarsmen start Eights Week races from here.
Approach from M40 J8. Use A40 / A4142 / A4158.

◊ **Swift Ditch: Abingdon**
Originally the main navigation (till 1790), original
'Oxford-Burcot Commissioners' lock (1635) was set
in the small channel and is proposed for restoration.
Approach from M40 J13. Use A34 north / A415 east.

◊ **Wallingford Old Bridge**
Seventeen medieval, ribbed stone arches span the

floodplain to the east of the castle earthworks of this
ancient city (1130 charter). Only five span water.
Open air swimming and other riverside recreations
flow under the others. Excellent museum.
From M40 J6, use B4009 west / A4074 south.

❋ *Boat Trips*
Oxford *Lady Ethel, Goring, Oxford*
Tel: 01865 248285

📖 *Suggested Guide Book:*
David Sharp *The Thames Path* Aurum Press, 1997

ℹ️ *Tourist Information*
Cirencester Tel: 01285 654180
Burford Tel: 01993 823558
Wantage Tel: 01235 760176
Witney Tel: 01993 775802
Oxford Tel: 01865 726871
Abingdon Tel: 01235 22711
Wallingford Tel: 01491 826972

Lower Reaches 112 B2 - 113 D2

Management
Environmental Agency Tel: 0118 953 5000
River Thames Society Tel: 01491 571476

◇ **Pangbourne Meadows**
Just downstream of the glorious Goring Gap in the Chilterns and not far from Mapledurham Working Mill, seven acres of river bank is held for the nation by the National Trust.
Approach from M4 J12. Use A4 west / A340 north.

◇ **Sonning Mill** (Tel: 0118 969 8000)
Eighteenth century timber-clad flourmill converted to a riverside theatre. A restored mill wheel (1998) is visible in the cocktail bar. A trio of watercourses are crossed by a narrow elevenarched redbrick bridge. Thames Path changes sides, traffic lights control cars.
Approach from M4 J10. Use A329(M) / A3290 / A4 going north-west.

◇ **Marsh Lock: Henley-on-Thames**
Backed by steep wooded hillsides, two long, timber boardwalks stretch out to the lock and weir. Further downstream the River and Rowing Museum sits quietly behind the meadow moorings. Royal regatta.
Approach from M4 J8 / 9. Use A404(M) / A4130 west.

◇ **Bisham Abbey** (1338)
Centre of excellence for sporting prowess. Lacrosse, football, tennis, sailing, rugby et al. Preceptory of the Knights Templar and graveyard of ancient aristocracy.
From M4 J8 / 9, use A404(M). Upstream of Marlow.

◇ **Flood Alleviation Scheme** (1989-2001)
Seven miles of variable width habitat for wildlife and an attractive footpath network for humans. Car parks, picnic areas, reed beds, osier beds and 'braided' channels. £45 million.
Approach from M4 J7. Use A4 west / B3026 south and east.

◇ **Windsor and Eton**
Thames Path crosses over Telford's iron bridge, now for pedestrians only. Walk upstream to a splendid new covered swimming pool, replacing the use of the backwater channel for hardy, river water swimming.
From M4 J6. Use A332 to Windsor Town Centre.

◇ **London Stone** (1285)
A few hundred yards upstream of Rennie's Staines Bridge (1832), alongside a small backwater, there is a replica of the stone that marked the tidal limit of the Thames when Richard I sold the right to levy taxes on river movement (1197). See plaque.
Approach from M4 J5. Use B470 west / B376 east. In the gardens south of B376 on outskirts of Staines.

◇ **Shepperton Weir and Ferry** (Tel: 01932 254844)
On the most southerly point on the Thames, fierce river flows over a weir create ideal swirls to test the skills of whitewater canoeists as they twist and turn to avoid suspended markers. Thames Path crosses by ferry. Ring the bell at the times stated.
View from Thames Street Car Park, Weybridge. Approach from M25 J11. Use A317 going east.

◇ **Cowley Sale: Walton Bridge**
Popular site with car park overlooking the water. Access to a much used section of the Thames Path.
Approach from M25 J9. Use A244 going north.

◇ **Kingston Bridge**
Timber traders line the banks, barges tied up beside the wharves… at one time up to three and four deep. But one severe winte,r in a time of flood (1928), cables snapped, 26 barges broke loose and charged

down the river on the swollen waters. Some formed a log-jam across the arches of Kingston Bridge. Chaos ensued, some sank but heroics limited the scale of the disaster. The bridge survived.
'Breasting up' is now limited to two craft.
Approach from M3 J1. Use A308 going east.

◇ **Teddington Tidal Locks** (Tel: 020 8940 8723)
Last three locks of the freshwater Thames; downstream are tidal waters. Three locks (rebuilt 1931). Old lock (1811, 1858), tiny skiff lock (1858) and the huge barge lock (640 feet x 24 wide) which can take a tug and six barges (1904). Footbridge and unusual cycle channel leads to Teddington.
Approach from M3 J1. Use A308 east / A310 north.

✳ **Boat Trips**
Caversham Bridge *Devon Belle* Tel: 0118 948 1088
Henley-on-Thames *Maratana* Tel: 01491 572035
Maidenhead *Bray Royale,* Tel: 01628 637880
Windsor *Lady Margaret Anne, New Queen of the Thames, Lucy Fisher* Tel: 01753 851900
Walton Bridge *Walton Lady* Tel: 01932 253374
Kingston upon Thames *New Southern Belle, Yarmouth Belle, Richmond Royale* Tel: 020 8546 2434

📖 **Suggested Guide Book**
David Sharp *The Thames Path* Aurum Press, 1997

ℹ **Tourist Information**
Reading Tel: 0118 956 6226
Henley-on-Thames Tel: 01491 578034
Maidenhead Tel: 01628 781110
Windsor Tel: 01753 852010
Kingston-upon-Thames Tel: 020 8547 5592

Tidal Thames 113 D2-E2

Management
Port of London Tel: 020 7481 8484
London River Association Tel: 020 8519 5127

◇ **Teddington Boundary Obelisk** (1909)
About 500 feet downstream of the tidal lock, this marks the beginning of Port of London jurisdiction.
Approach from M3 J1. Use A308 east / A310 north.

◇ **Richmond Half Tide Lock** (249 feet x 26 feet)
There is a small fee for passing through the last lock on the Thames but it is only needed half the time. Once the tide has half filled the river the sluices alongside are lifted and the whole river width is freely available for navigation. Does little business!!
Approach from M3 J1. Use A316 going north-east.

◇ **Lambeth Bridge**
Nearby wharves which specialised in pineapples are celebrated by the decorations on this bridge in the centre of London.
Approach from M1 J1. Use A5 / A4202 / A302 / A202 along Embankment, downstream of Vauxhall.

◇ **Pool of London**
Now home to HMS Belfast. The only place that goods could be legally landed under the eye of the Customs men. Twenty 'legal quays' between London Bridge and the Traitor's Gate of the Tower of London formed London's major port. Approval for off line docks behind tidal lock gates was only officially granted when congestion became unbearable. West India Dock (1802), Wapping Docks (1805) and St Katharine Docks (1828), all had high walls and armed guards to reduce the pilfering that was endemic on the open river wharves.
From M25 J3, use A20 / A2 / A100 going north-west.

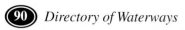

◇ **St Katharine Docks** (1828-1968)

Thomas Telford's bold, stark five storey warehouses are now converted to shops, restaurants, pubs and apartments. New apartments fill the gaps left by demolition and the whole quayside is accessible on foot and through a single renovated lock onto the Thames. Surrounding high walls muffle traffic noise; it is an unexpected experience, especially at night.
From M25 J3, use A20 / A2 / A100 going north-west.

◇ **Limehouse Basin**

Partly filled in by the underwater structure of the Limehouse Link Road Tunnel to Docklands, this basin started life as the terminus of the Regent's Canal of the Grand Union. Now occupied by new jetties to which all manner of boats are moored.
From M25 J30, use A13 / A1203 west to Docklands.

◇ **Thames Barrier** (1982) (0181 305 4188)

Tested every month and raised in anger 31 times so far. Twelve movable gates (3700 tonnes each) can stop the flow of water across Woolwich reach. Visitor centre, small fee.
Approach from M25 J30. Use A13 west / A102 south to Blackwall Tunnels then east along A206.

◇ **Woolwich Free Ferry**

Regular cross river service allows the public a taste of boating... free of charge.
Approach from M25 J2. Use A2 west / A205 north.

◇ **Queen Elizabeth Crossing** (1991)

450 metres (1475 feet) cable stayed bridge on the M25 is the longest in Europe and third in the world. The QE II cruise liner can pass under even at high tide.
Approach from M25 J30. Use A282 going south.

◇ **Thames Estuary: Tilbury**

Present day commercial dockland. Container shipping comes no further upstream than these wharves.
Approach from M25 J30. Use A1089 going south-east.

Jerome K. Jerome's 'Three Men in a Boat' tells of floating downriver in a camping skiff, a typical use of the river by Edwardians. 120 years after Boulter's Lock was built for commercial traffic and 40 years after the railway companies started promoting excursions upriver. E.J. Gregory's painting, 'Boulter's Lock on a Sunday Afternoon 1895', shows pleasure boat congestion under the watchful eye of the lock keeper, W.H. Turner. This picture was recreated in real life by the Thames Society on the centenary of the painting (1995).

❀ *Riverboat Piers*

London Transport River Services
Tel: 020 7222 5600

Barrier Gardens, City Airport, Dome, Greenwich, Canary Wharf, West India, London Bridge-Tower, City, Globe, Jubilee Gardens, Embankment, Westminster, Mill Bank, Peace Pagoda, Chelsea Harbour, Putney, Kew, Richmond, Hampton Court.

ℹ️ *Tourist Information*

Riverboats Tel: 020 7730 4812
London Tel: 020 7730 3488
City Tel: 020 7606 3030
Richmond Tel: 020 8940 9125
Tower Hamlets Tel: 020 8980 4831
Greenwich Tel: 020 8858 6376

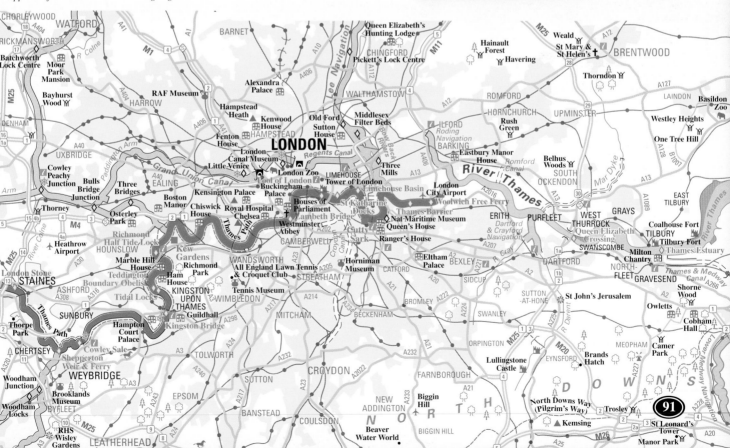

Thames

Kew Gardens
Parks, museums and boatyards on a tidal river.

A stroll either side of the river, but allow plenty of time to visit the canal terminus, steam museum and gardens. It could take all day to see everything along the Thames Path cross a footbridge at Richmond and back along the opposite bank.

Cross Kew Bridge by car and you see nothing of the river, but **stand on the pavement and look downstream.** There is space for a rain-swelled torrent to flow to the sea between firm river banks. When tides enter the Thames estuary at Tilbury in winter they can push against this stream to fill the river from bank to bank, but at low tide in summer there are mud banks and some boats left stranded. *Start the short stroll from the north end of the bridge, follow Strand-on-the-Green back towards the water, follow the Thames Path acorns downstream, up the short ramp over a low wall into:-*

1 Strand-on-the-Green at Riverside Gardens
Houses facing the river across the walkway are very conscious of the danger of flood. Glass screens protect and steel channels either side of doorways allow strong planks to be inserted when Authorities give 'Yellow' alert. Most days children and dogs take the air, welcomed by the toys in a house window. *Wander past* **2 Olivers Island** *as far as the railway bridge which takes tube trains to Richmond and resist, if you can, the splendid cafés and pubs along the way.*

Return upstream to follow the Thames Path **under** *Kew Bridge and after walking alongside moored Dutch Barges, etc for 100 yards, look for a tall Victorian chimney on the right.*

Walk up to the main road, cross carefully. This is:-

3 Kew Bridge Steam Museum (*entrance in Green Dragon Lane*)
Formerly pumped water to London and the Regent's Canal and houses many steam engines, including the largest working beam engine in the world. Exhibits in steam at weekends and Bank Holidays.

Return to bridge foot and use the traffic lights to cross over all parts of the South Circular Road. **Cross Kew Bridge** *to the south bank and:-*

4 Kew Pier
Supports boat trips in season which go as far as Westminster and Hampton Court.

At the end of the bridge, **turn left** (*away from the traffic*) *and move clockwise all around:-*

5 Kew Green
Pass the pond, an old coaching inn, the ancient church of St Anne and watch the cricket in summer. At the far end is Ferry Lane and the main gate to:-

6 Royal Botanical Gardens
Over 300 acres of botanical research to which the public have access (entry fee) including a restored Palm House (1840) the 'Princess of Wales Conservatory' (1987), the 'Orangery' and the former Royal Palace (1631). Over 40 000 species of plants are on display and all are labled, even within the lakes and woods.

Continue **around Kew Green,** *cross Kew Bridge and* **return to the start at** **1** *Riverside Gardens.*

92 *Kew Gardens*

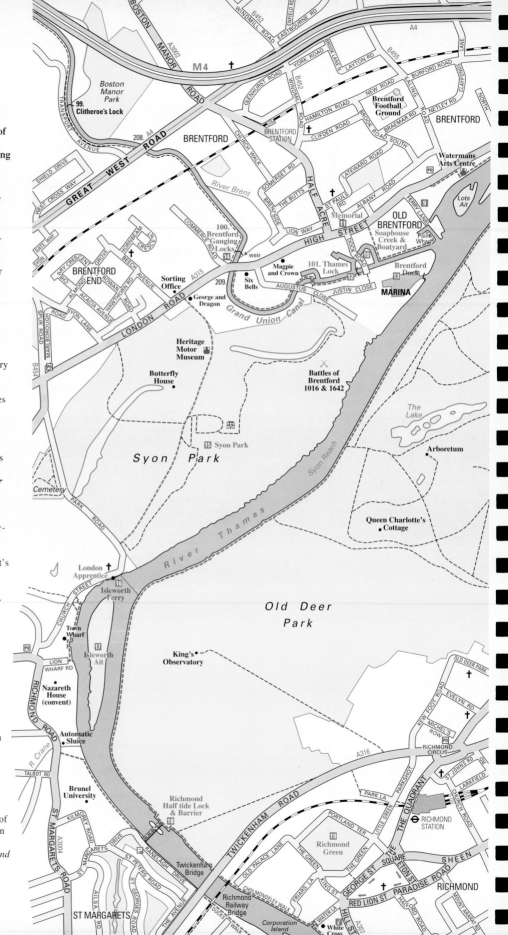

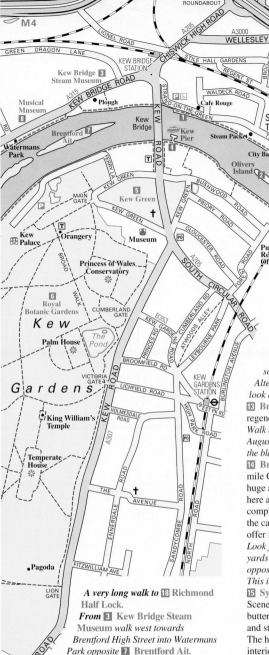

Kew Bridge Steam Museum contains five giant Cornish Pumping Engines, including the Grand Union Canal Company's Boulton and Watt (1820) moved here from Chelsea (1840-1943). All types of Pumping machinery are in working order - even a 72 bucket waterwheel.

10 Soaphouse Creek and Boatyard where huge sheds shelter the work of building and maintaining wide beamed river boats.

Outside the County Courts on the opposite side of the High Street the **11 Memorial Column** *reminds citizens of events in Brentford in 780, 1016 and 1642.*

Turn into Dock Road, pass the weir and look down on:-

12 Thames Locks. A pair of wide locks with a low bridge over, which are generally only open when high tide coincides with normal working hours. It can only open for two hours before and after high tide because, at other times, the Thames is likely to be too shallow for navigation.

At the far end of the bridge you can join the towpath and follow the way marked Thames Path, but the route is rather complicated and some of the direction signs appear to be missing.

Alternatively, go under the flats to Justin Close and look at:-

13 Brentford Dock and housing development, a regeneration of railway sidings and timber wharves. *Walk back over the Grand Union / River Brent via Augustus Close and cross over the main road. Lean on the black and white parapet over the navigation to see:-*

14 Brentford Gauging Locks at the start of the 140 mile Grand Union Canal walk to Birmingham. A huge area of water acted as a major canal terminus here and is still surrounded by a warehouse complex complete with cantelevered covers hanging far over the canal and its towing path, but currently (1999) on offer for redevelopment.

*Look for a modern Postal Sorting Office about 200 yards westwards along (A315) London Road and opposite is a small alley with a long high brick wall. This is where the **Thames Path** acorns lead into:-*

15 Syon Park

Scene of two medieval battles, contains a lake, a butterfly house, a Great Conservatory in gun metal and stone, landscaped gardens and courtyard. The house stands on the remains of an abbey, its interior was remodeled by Robert Adam (1760). *Pass out of the main (southern) Gate and turn left into Park Road, back to the river and to the:-*

16 Isleworth Ferry and London Apprentice Pub.

There is now a multiple choice.

On summer weekends, you could **cross the river by ferry** *and return to* **5 Kew Green**. *At other times you could follow Church Street upstream to the constriction where one of the two mouths of the River Crane (the Duke of Northumberland's River) swirls under the road. Just* **before** *the bridge, you could* **follow the Thames Path** *through an archway with swinging metal gate or, just* **after** *the bridge,* **turn left** *along an alleyway (unmarked). Both lead to Lion Wharf through a timber terrace in front of the Town Wharf pub opposite* **17 Isleworth Ait.**

Turn up Lion Wharf Road towards Old Isleworth shops and, keeping left along Richmond Road, follow

the long brick wall of the convent towards the back gates of **Brunel University Campus** and the river. *Within 500 yards you will come to:-*

18 Richmond Half-tide Lock and Barrier

A glorious Victorian structure (1894) formed of two pedestrian bridges with a huge set of gates swung between them. Unlike the more recent Thames Barrier at Woolwich, these are lowered at every tide and hold the river at a steady level. Like the Thames Lock they are only open for navigation for two hours either side of high tide. *After stepping across the river ⚠, again a choice.*

Turn right *along the towpath, under two major bridges carrying road then rail, via Cholmondeley Walk, to arrive at the White Cross pub and the waterfront square in front of Old Richmond Bridge, popular on summer Sundays. Then, to get home by public transport, turn away from the river up Friars Lane, cross* **19 Richmond Green**, *follow the railway station signs into The Quadrant for bus and tube services.*

Alternatively, **turn left** *for a long walk (¾ hour) along the riverbank to* **return to** **5 Kew Green**.

Getting there:

Approach from M4 J1. Use South Circular Road (A205) southwards to the river.

- 🅿 At the end of Ferry Lane off Kew Green. Join at **5**.
- ♿ Along Strand-on-the-Green near Kew Bridge. Join at **1**.
- 🚆 From Kew Bridge Station exit cross the High Road. Join at **1**.
- ⊖ From Kew Gardens Station walk to Kew Road. Turn north. Follow a long garden wall to join at **5**.
- 🚤 Arrive by boat. Join at **▢**.

Landranger Map 176 Ref TQ 19 77

Map labels

CHISWICK ROUNDABOUT
M4
M4
A205 CHISWICK HIGH ROAD
A3000 WELLESLEY
ROAD A4
OXFORD RD NTH
OXFORD RD STH
GREEN DRAGON LANE
LIONEL ROAD
KEW BRIDGE STATION
STILE HALL GARDENS
BROOK RD STH
REGENT ST
WALDECK ROAD
CHISWICK VILLAGE
STRAND-ON-THE-GREEN
STRAND ON-THE-GREEN
Kew Bridge 3 Steam Museum
Musical Museum 8
Plough
Café Rouge
Brentford Ait 7
Kew Bridge
Kew Pier
Steam Packet
City Barge
Thames Road
Watermans Park
Kew Road
Kew Bridge Road A315
Ferry Lane
Olivers Island
Kew Railway Bridge
Bulls Head
Public Record Office
Main Gate
Kew Green
Kew Green
Bushwood Road
Priory Road
Gloucester Road
Forest Road
Kew Palace
Orangery
Museum
P O
Princess of Wales Conservatory
A205 South Circular Road
Kew 6 Royal Botanic Gardens
Cumberland Gate
Broad Walk
B353
Kew Gardens Road
Princes Road
Atwoods Alley
Cumberland Rd
Leybourne Park
Burlington Avenue
Palm House
The Pond
Gardens
Broomfield Rd
Kew Gardens Station
West Pk Rd
Lichfield Road
Holmesdale Road
High Park Road
Victoria Gate
King William's Temple
Kew Road A307
P O
Temperate House
The Avenue
Ennerdale Road
Sandycombe Road
North Road
Pagoda
Fitzwilliam Ave
Lion Gate

A very long walk to **18 Richmond Half Lock.**

From **3** **Kew Bridge Steam Museum** *walk west towards Brentford High Street into Watermans Park opposite* **7** **Brentford Ait.** Through the park railings note the **8 Musical Museum** featuring automatic musical instruments from barrel organs to a cinema 'Wurlitzer' (a further 90 mins possible here).

Along the riverside terrace of the Arts Centre, down steps ⚠ through the 'back yard' and blue railings out onto the road for a longish (200 yard) stint... as far as:-

9 Ferry Lane which leads down to the mouth of the River Brent and the junction of the Grand Union Canal with the Thames. Huge developments are taking place which will allow direct access to the river bank and thus use the *existing* well landscaped Point Wharf footpath. It leads back to a small unmarked alley alongside red brick offices facing the main road (worth the detour *in reverse* even now). *From the Point Wharf footpath, you have excellent views of:-*

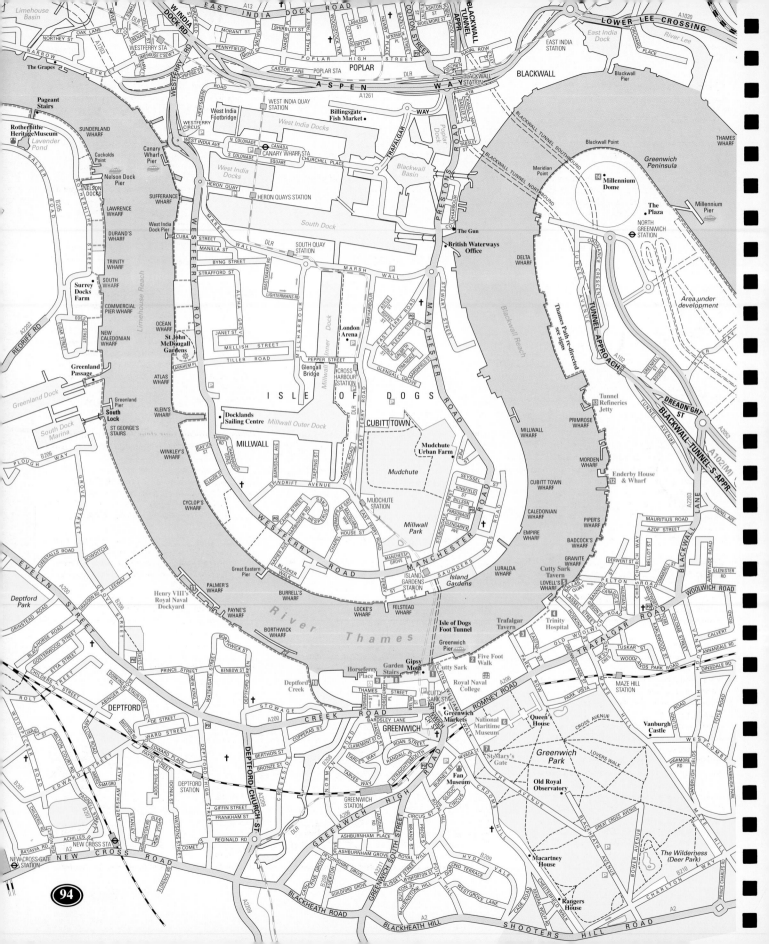

Cutty Sark
Clipper to tavern,
and a lottery-improved museum

Thames Path at its easterly end is windswept in
winter and weaves through old industry and
surprising survivors from the pioneering days of
Venetian Galleys, Antarctic whaling and
submarine cables.

Greenwich had a Royal Palace for 200
years from 1447. Henry VIII's home
and birthplace of Elizabeth I.
Sir Francis Drake's voyage around
the world started here. Sir
Francis Chichester's yacht
finished here.

MANHATTAN
WHARF

Bugsby's Reach

London
City Airport
Pier

Greenwich
Yacht Club

MUDLARKS WAY

Millennium Village
(under development)

Anchor & Hope

ANCHOR & HOPE LANE

Thames
Flood Barrier

Thames
Barrier
Industrial
Estate

Russian
Submarine

Barrier Gardens
Pier

Thames
Barrier
Visitor
Centre

BOWATER ROAD

HERRINGHAM ROAD

NEW UDENE'S
STREET

WESTMOOR
STREET

EASTMOOR
STREET

FARADAY WAY

WESTFIELD
STREET

A206

WOOLWICH RD

Start the stroll from:-
1 **Cutty Sark** (*only tea clipper to survive*).
Built on the Clyde (1869). Brought tea from China for
seven years and brought wool from Australia for
twelve years. Wooden hull, with iron frame and
copper bottom. Try to go down steps to see the ship
from within the dry dock. Her sleek lines meant she
beat records for speed. *Go east past the entrance to
Greenwich Pier, follow the Thames Path acorns to:-*
2 **Five Foot Walk and Royal River Gate**
Christopher Wren's grand design excluded the public
from the foreshore (1731) except for this narrow
footpath along the embankment. Excellent views of
Greenwich University buildings, aka Royal Naval
College. *If the tide is out and the path is crowded
go down the △ steps and enjoy the foreshore (you
can get out at the far end!). Stand at the top of the
landing stage steps, look through River Gate (1849)
up the grand vista to the Queen's House.*
3 **Trafalgar Tavern**
Sumptuous rebuilding (1837) of Dr Johnson 100 year
old watering hole. Host to Dr Crippin, Dickens,
Thakeray and to Ministerial whitebait dinners for 70
years. *Pass to the shore side of the tavern, through
alleyways between housing and towards the now
defunct huge iron jetty of the private Greenwich
Power Station. Built (1906) on the site of a
horsedrawn tram depot, (see tramlines in the path).
Now on 'stand-by' for London's Underground.*
4 **Trinity Hospital and High Bridge Quay**
Venetian Galleys were so high out of the water that a
special quay was built here in the 1400s. The warden
of Trinity Hospital (founded 1613 as an old people's
home for 21 'gentlemen'), marked tides for 1874 and
1928 on his (1817) riverwall. No longer a risk thanks
to the Thames Barrier two miles downstream.
Continue beyond the power station to the:-

5 **Cutty Sark Tavern and Ballast Quay**
Where empty ships took on ballast before they went to
sea. The Tavern (1695) supplies victuals on two internal
levels and to customers sitting on the riverwall. *Retrace
your steps along the Thames Path to* **1** *Cutty Sark.*

A longer walk from **3** **Trafalgar Tavern**
*Turn away from the river, up Park Row, right into the
main road. Use the crossing. Go along the railings on
the south of Romney Row to the central entrance (open
1000-1700hrs) and into the grounds of:-*
6 **National Maritime Museum** (Tel: 020 8312 6565)
*Walk up the line of the 'Grand Vista' to the Queen's
House (1616), up the left-hand steps and into the
colonnade. Follow the obelisk signs to the main
museum entrance or a*

children's playground outside the
'Bosun's Cabin' café. Continue to:-
7 **St Mary's Gate**
*A major pedestrian crossroads with signs easily
readable for a man on horseback. There are many
tourist attractions.* **Go left** *for the* **Old Royal
Observatory** (*arrive just before 1300 hrs to see the*
Time Ball *drop*), **straight on** *for Croom's Hill Gate,
or* **right down King William Walk to return to** **1**.

A short detour from **1** Cutty Sark *would be:-*
*Move along the concrete of Cutty Sark Gardens, past the
elegant dome covering the lift and stairs to the* **Isle of
Dogs Foot Tunnel** *(1902), past* **Gypsy Moth IV** *to:-*
8 **Garden Stairs**
Earlier landing stage, before the pier and tunnel were
opened. **Dock** is medieval in origin (enlarged 1850).

Views upstream of **11** **Henry VIII's Royal Naval
Dockyard.** *Views across river to Island Gardens and
Canary Wharf's 800ft (245m) Canada Tower and long
views downstream to* **13** **Tunnel Refineries Jetty** *as far
as* **14** **Millennium Dome.** *Turn south into:-*
9 **Horseferry Place**
A slipway stretched down to the low tide mark and
was used as landing place for horseferries.
Walk to A200 Creek Road, turn right and find:-
10 **Deptford Creek** (Tidal)
Mouth of Ravensbourne river. Watermills recorded in
the Domesday Book. Boatbuilding through the ages,
heavy barges still bring sand aggregates. *Return to* **1**
Cutty Sark *by going directly along Creek Road.*

A much longer walk from **5** **Ballast Quay:-**
*Continue downstream for 500 yards, past scenes of
industrial dereliction to:-*
12 **Enderby House and Wharf**
As mentioned in 'Moby Dick', the Enderby family
were whalers (established 1775) and made ropes at
this site for almost 100 years (till 1855). Until
recently (1979) this wharf served cable laying ships
of the Standard Telephone Co (1834). The House
(1846) has a substantial first floor bay window
looking downstream. *Proceed towards the smell of
maize emanating from the grain silos and arrive at:-*
13 **Tunnel Refineries Jetty**
Dedicated to 'the people of Greenwich' by Tunnel
Refineries, this jetty gives wide views of the river and
Canary Wharf... and is well 'worth the detour'.
**Return by retracing your steps, but also possible
by bus from Trafalgar Road... see Thames Path signs.**

Getting there:
*From M25 J2 use A2 west / A205, South Circular,
north to Woolwich. Train from Woolwich Arsenal Sta.*
P *Suggest away from Greenwich. Arrive at DLR
Cutty Sark, DLR and* ⊋ *Greenwich or*
⊋ *Maze Hill.*
⊋ *From Greenwich station exits cross the High
Road. Turn left and at the end cross South
Street. Go into Circus Street and Gloucester
Circus. Cross Crooms Hill into Greenwich
Park. Join at* **7**.
⛴ *Arrive by boat at Greenwich Pier from:-
Westminster Tel: 020 7930 4097
Embankment Tel: 020 7987 1185
Tower / St Katherine Tel: 020 7987 1185
Thames Barrier Tel: 020 8305 0300*

Landranger Map 177 Ref TQ 38 77

Practically unchanged since Canaletto painted it (1750). Cross by DLR or the Foot Tunnel to Island Gardens on the north bank.

Thorne

Trent and Mersey Canal:
The Grand Trunk   **118 B4 - 116 A1**
Opened: 1770, 1777
Engineers: Brindley, Henshall
Preston Brook to Trent Lock
93½ miles, 64 narrow locks, 9 wide locks, formerly 5, now 4, tunnels
Caldon Branch
Opened: 1779-1961, 1974
Etruria Junction to Froghall
17 miles, 17 narrow locks, 2 tunnels

Views over the Cheshire Plain, crooked buildings due to salt subsidence, the longest tunnel (1999), much evidence of earlier industry in the Potteries and wide rural valleys around the Burton breweries make using this canal a varied experience.

With increasing justification this canal was dubbed the 'Grand Trunk'. Branches were growing very quickly. Before it was completed the Staffordshire and Worcestershire linked to the River Severn (1772) and, after it was finished, the Caldon to Frogall limestone (1779), the Coventry Canal to Warwickshire coal and London (1790), the Derby Canal to Arkwright's Mills (1796), the Chester Canal to the Dee estuary (1833) and Macclesfield Canal to Derbyshire limestone (1851).

Management and Support
British Waterways, Marple Tel: 0161 427 1079,
Norbury Tel: 01785 284253,
Fradley Tel: 01283 790236
Trent and Mersey Canal Society Tel: 01543 255410

◊ **Runcorn Gap**
Start of a grand sweep of canals and improved rivers that passes the inland ports of Preston Brook, Shardlow, Gainsborough and Goole before arriving at the Humber port of Kingston upon Hull which is a shelter from North Sea storms.
Approach from M56 J12. Use A557 going north.
◊ **Preston Brook Tunnel**
Despite the fact that the Duke of Bridgewater's pioneering canal incorporated only one item of innovative engineering (the Barton Aqueduct) and at the time had no locks at all, the Trent and Mersey wished to have the Duke's backing for what was an

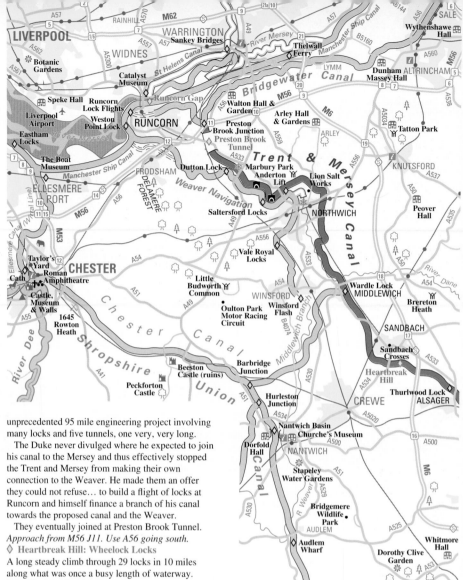

unprecedented 95 mile engineering project involving many locks and five tunnels, one very, very long.
The Duke never divulged where he expected to join his canal to the Mersey and thus effectively stopped the Trent and Mersey from making their own connection to the Weaver. He made them an offer they could not refuse… to build a flight of locks at Runcorn and himself finance a branch of his canal towards the proposed canal and the Weaver.
They eventually joined at Preston Brook Tunnel.
Approach from M56 J11. Use A56 going south.
◊ **Heartbreak Hill: Wheelock Locks**
A long steady climb through 29 locks in 10 miles along what was once a busy length of waterway. Paired locks reduced waiting time.
Approach from M6 J17. Use A534 south.
◊ **Red Bull Aqueduct**
Interesting walking around a sort of 'slip road' of the canals. Also see start of paired lock flight.
Approach from M6 J16. Use A500 going east then A34 north to A50 at Hardings Wood.
◊ **Two Harecastle Tunnels** (8778 feet)
Eleven years in the making (1766-1777) Brindley's narrow tunnel was duplicated by Telford (1827) to make a sort of dual carriageway of waterways. Subsidence took its toll and closed the earlier bore (1904). Now boats tie up at each end whilst waiting their turn to go through the fan ventilated tunnel.
Approach from M6 J16. Use A500 going east then local roads towards A50.
◊ **Etruria Bone and Flint Mill**   (Tel: 01782 287557)
On a short arm below the junction to the Caldon Canal, Shirley's Mill (1857-1972) contains 'Princess', the oldest steam bone-crusher in the country. Fine 'bone' china could only be made by including the powder from bones. This mill became the 'wholesale' supplier of the powdered bone… transported to its customers by narrowboat.
At M6 J15 use A500 north / A53 east / B5045 south

◊ **Hazelhurst Aqueduct: Caldon Canal**
Three locks start the drop down the Churnet Valley towards the target for the Caldon Branch… limestone quarries beyond Froghall. The later extension to reach up to the water in Rudyard Reservoir and collect trade from Leek, continues like a motorway sliproad and crosses back over the main line on a large aqueduct. Intriguing complexity.
From M6 J15 use A500 / A53 going northeast. East of Endon, turn south to Denford / Horse Bridge.
◊ **Great Haywood Junction**
Maybe by good luck or good judgement the canal was opened from Trent Lock to here (1770) and to Stone (1771) just about the time that the Staffs and Worcs was opened to the Severn and Bristol (1772). Thus did Brindley achieve two parts of his vision of joining the four main rivers of the land. He died (1772) before it was possible to get from here to the Mersey (1777) or the Thames (1790) thus creating the other two arms of his 'Grand Cross'.
From M6 J14 use A5013 / A513 going south then A51 north.

Wooden chutes transferred salt from narrowboats on the Trent and Mersey Canal directly into sea going ships on the River Weaver below. The engineers of the Weaver Navigation (Edward Leader Williams) proposed (1850s) a 50 foot boat lift to improve the connection. His design of two connected hydraulic rams, each supporting a huge (75' x 15'6") tank, worked well (1875-1882) but then slowly chemical pollution corroded the rams beyond repair.

In 1908 a completely new method of lifting the tanks was installed. Independent sets of cables and counterweights were driven by electricity and supported by 6 foot diameter pulleys on a new framework built around the existing mechanism. This worked for 78 years (1908-1986).

The original ram design (as shown here) is now to be reinstated but with oil hydraulics... not water.

◇ **Christina Collins: The Wench is Dead**

Colin Dexter's Inspector Morse solved a murder from his hospital bed which was based on a true story. A seamstress, who was an inventor's daughter, married a conjuror and then an ostler before being murdered (1839) by boatmen working a flyboat from Preston Brook to London. Ten thousand people saw the public hanging on 11th April 1840. Christina Collins' grave is in Rugeley Churchyard and her presumed place of death is still known as the 'Bloody Steps'. (see ISBN 0 95159 130 4)
Approach from M6 J11. Use A460 going north.

◇ **Alrewas**

River Trent mixes with the canal. Weirs between the two are traversed by long towpath walkways, giving walkers wide views of winter-flooded fields. Canalside sculpture near A513.
Approach from M42 J10. Use A5 west / A38 north / A513 west.

◇ **A38**

Cars travelling the 12 miles from Alrewas (A513) to Willington (A5132) have a good chance of spotting narrow-beam craft on the canal alongside. Bargees often wave in answer to a quick 'toot' of the horn.
Approach from M42 J10. Use A5 west / A38 north.

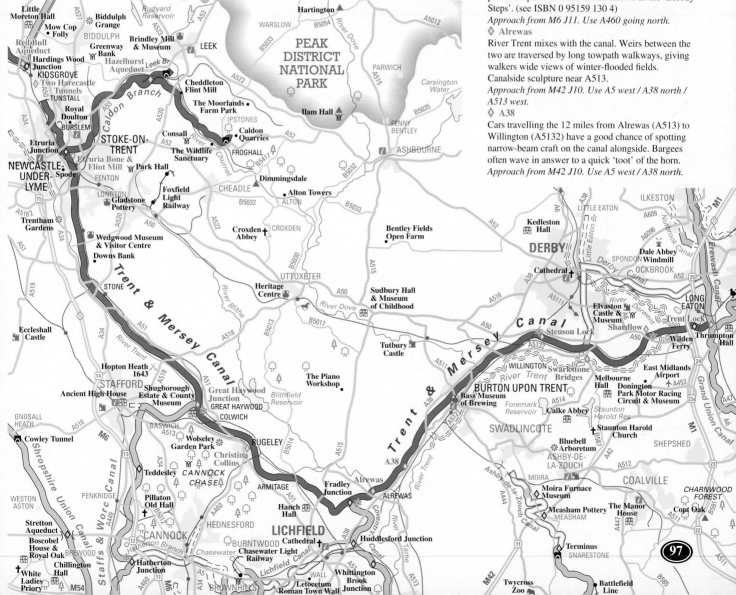

Josiah Wedgwood

Josiah Wedgwood was a self made man. He had an enquiring mind and tenaciuos will.
Although his business as a potter involved neither iron nor steam, he was a driving force in the Industrial Revolution.
He was the first to see the benefits of the smooth passage of his delicate products if sent by water and campaigned to create a public company to build the second major canal.
Without him and other visionaries like him, many of the engineering geniuses of the canal era would not have been able to show their skills.

Born into a family which had been minor potters for four generations, he was indentured to his brother until he was 20 and ended up in a partnership with a creative businessman, Thomas Whieldon, working with some of the best figures in the business - Spode, Wood and Greatbatch. He was experimenting constantly and, after 5 years, branched out on his own (1758), first renting premises and eventually building his own.

He was a man of boundless energy and vision. He:-
- fought for road improvements (turnpikes, 1763)
- improved quality of everyday china... Queensware
- invented a method of adding gold decoration
- invented a blue / black clay mix for 'Jasperware'
- opened 'manufacturers showrooms' in London
- courted the fashion for classical Roman designs
- named his new (1769) factory 'Etruria' after the presumed source of these designs
- organised his factory for quality mass production
- actively applied principles of the Enlightenment
- supplied a unique 952 piece table and dessert service decorated with 1244 views of England to Catherine the Great of Russia (1774)
- became an associate of the Lunar Society
- bought an early 'Boulton & Watt' engine (1782)
- invented the 'pyrometer' to measure high temperatures for which he was elected Fellow of the Royal Society (1783)
- created a 'seal' for Slave Emancipation Society (1786) which sought abolition of the slave trade

He also 'fathered' the Trent and Mersey Canal. The Bridgewater Canal had been financed by the Duke of Bridgewater personally, but this canal was to be very long (93 miles) and would benefit many. Wedgwood convinced his fellow promoters that it should be financed through shareholders rather than as a trust. He gave it a 'kick start' by himself partly financing James Brindley's early survey. He was part-author of the 'prospectus' pamphlet, supplying estimates of cost savings to potters like himself… i.e. earthenware products carried at less than half price and clay from Cornwall or flints from Kent carried at only one eighth of existing costs.

He then proceeded to convince landowners along the canal line of the advantages to them personally, obtaining permissions and shareholders in equal measure. He took advice on the politics of getting support from Liverpool from his friend and eventual partner, James Bentley, and obtained the patronage of Lord Gower and the Duke of Bridgewater.

He was so embroiled in the project that he once wrote "I scarcely know... whether I am a Landed Gentleman, an Engineer or a Potter". Preparation was so thorough that, despite the pioneering financial arrangements, the parliamentary committeee took only six days to complete hearings into the boldest engineering project of the time, crossing thousands of properties in its 93 miles.

When the Act was passed he was appointed Treasurer (unpaid!) and cut the first sod near his factory at Burslem on 26th July 1766.

i Wedgwood Visitor Centre
Tel: 01782 204218
Website: http://www.wedgwood.co.uk
Approach from M6 J14. Use A34 north to Barlaston
Trent and Mersey Canal: walk from Bridge 104.

◊ **Stenson Lock** (12 foot rise)
A last and a first. It is the *last* of the five wide locks up from the Trent which allowed river barges to serve the industries of Burton. It also has the *first* of a whole series of modern mileposts installed by the Trent and Mersey Canal Society. Over 175 years ago (1879) the Canal Company had replaced its 93 wooden mileposts with a unique cast iron design which counted the miles from both Shardlow and Preston Brook, but 46 were missing after WWII. The Society replaced them with a small variation on the original design starting here (1979).
Approach from M1 J24. Use A50 northwest / A5134 west. Turn north at Twyford.

◊ **Swarkstone Bridges**
Two spans across two channels of the River Trent are linked by an ancient (12th Century) causeway with flood relief arches. One bridge was swept away (1865) and replaced with tall graceful arches, but the causeway itself has slowly sunk into the flood plain under the weight of modern traffic.
   Southern limit of a Jacobite invasion led by Prince Charles Edward Stuart (1745).
From M42 J11, use A444 north / A514 east.

◊ **Shardlow**
Transhipment port between river barge and narrowboat. The Clock Warehouse (1780) which lifted goods from craft moored underneath its archway is only one of many. Others typically still have elegant cast iron mullions in all their topmost windows, helping this settlement to show how early industrial buildings were built to a neat 'country house' vernacular. A short walk leads to a new (1947) bridge which replaces one they made earlier (1759), that itself replaced Wilden Ferry which had taken north-south traffic over the river since Roman days.
Recently relieved of A6 traffic by the A50. From M1 J24 use A50 north, turn off at the first junction.

◊ **Trent Lock**
A veritable cross roads of waterways where the canal ends. The improved navigation of the River Soar to Loughborough and the man made Erewash Canal join the confluence of the Trent and Derwent.
From M1 J24, use A50 north and west / B6540 east.

✴ *Boat Trips*
Acton Bridge *Lapwing* Tel: 01606 852945
Great Haywood *Milford Star* Tel: 01785 663728
Stenson *Stenson Bubble (electric)* Tel: 01283 703113
Shardlow *Aquarius* Tel: 01332 792285

📖 *Suggested Guide Book*
Micheal Pearson *Four Counties Ring*
J.M. Pearson, 1995

i Tourist Information
Warrington Tel: 01925 442180
Altrincham Tel: 0161 912 5931
Stoke-on-Trent Tel: 01782 284600
Leek Tel: 01538 483741
Lichfield Tel: 01543 252109
Burton upon Trent Tel: 01283 516609
Derby Tel: 01332 255802

Trent (Burton) Navigation   **J16**
   Wilden Ferry near Shardlow to Burton upon Trent
   Bond End Canal Trent (Burton) Navigation to Shobnall

Trent Navigation

118 B4 - 119 E3

Improved: 1772, 1783, 1926
Engineers: Smeaton, Jessop, Whitworth, Rayner
Wilden Ferry to Gainsborough
67 miles, 13 wide locks, six over 160 feet long

Supplemented by the waters of the Soar, the Trent widens out to flow down a wide valley, through Nottingham, past Country Parks and Nature Reserves to become a commercial waterway.

Like all ancient navigations the Trent was a 'free' river with no organisation taking overall control. Apart from improvemnets from Trent Falls up to Burton (1699) and small improvements above Newark (1773), Acts for improvement only became urgent after the Trent and Mersey Canal was opened. An act to improve the whole to Gainsborough was passed (1783). Dredging and a horsepath (1787) were followed by locks at Sawley and a 2½ mile cut to bypass Trent Bridge in Nottingham (Beeston Cut). Other cuts were made at Snoball (1795) Cranfleet (1797) and Holme (1800).

This century deep draughted boats were catered for by raising water levels with weirs and new locks at Cromwell Tidal (1911), Holme, Stoke Bardolph, Gunthorpe and Hazelford (1926-7). The Trent can take substantial barges and is maintained to a high standard.

Management

British Waterways, Newark Tel: 01636 704481 and Long Eaton Tel: 0115 946 1017

◊ Wilden Ferry

A ferry no more but a major point on the Roman road network. In this area the Trent meanderings are controlled and smoothed out by flood gates and the locks of two cuts (Sawley and Cranfleet).
From M1 J24 use, A50 north and west / B6540 east.

◊ Lenton Chain

The wide Beeston and Nottingham Canals provide the alternative to the shoals and bridges that make the Trent un-navigable through Nottingham. This wide cut was always closed to navigation on Sundays to ensure boatmen's religious well being… a heavy chain was stretched across the water.
Approach from M1 J25. Use A52 / A6005 going east.

◊ Newark Castle (Ruined by Cromwell)

Dominating the river and its public gardens, the castle promises an attractive market town. Newark Lock, like most locks on the Trent Navigation, is of awesome scale, longer than most and capable of taking a 350 tonne barge. Resident keeper.
From A1 / A46 junction use A616 south to river.

◊ Cromwell Tidal Lock (1960) (Tel: 01636 821213)

A vast weir, huge lock capable of taking eight Trent barges at a time and the start of serious boating. Stone marks the site of an 8 span Roman bridge.
Approach from east of A1, 3 miles north of Newark.

◊ Torksey Lock (Tel: 01427 718202)

Entrance to the Roman Fossdyke Navigation set in a wide landscape. 72 hour pontoon moorings bring possible relief to boats unused to tidal waters. Just upstream are gravel pits that dispatch their entire product by water.
Approach from A1 / A57 junction. Use A57 east / A156 north.

✾ Boat Trips

Nottingham *Tamar Bell* Tel: 01602 586672
Newark-on-Trent *Sunny, River Prince*
Tel: 01636 706479 / 525246
Lock and Castle Tel: 01636 707939

ℹ Tourist Information

Derby Tel: 01332 255802
Nottingham Tel: 0115 915 5330
Newark-on-Trent Tel: 01636 678962

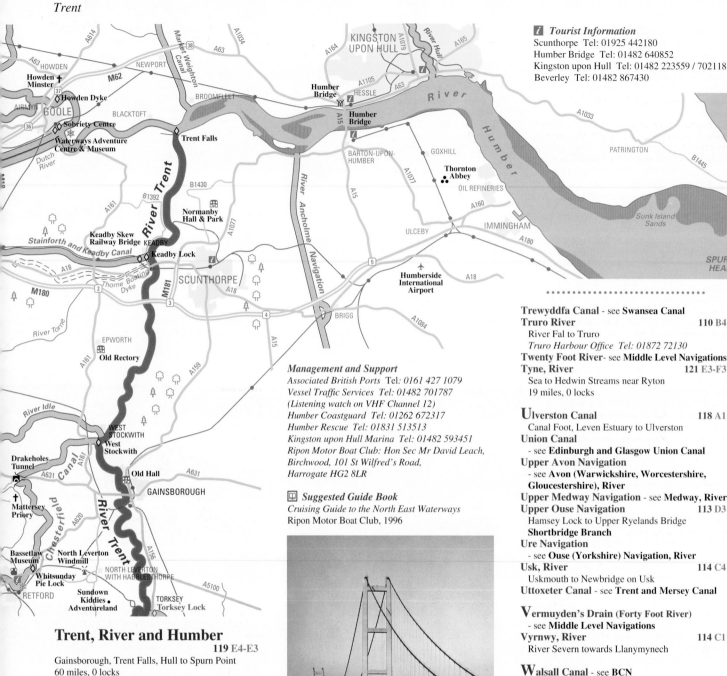

Within the map:

A614
A63 HOWDEN
NEWPORT
Howden
Minster
GOOLE
AIRMYN
Howden Dyke
M62
A1034
A63
A164
KINGSTON UPON HULL
River Hull
A1079
A165
BROOMFLEET
HESSLE
Humber Bridge
A63
A1105
Humber Bridge
River Humber
A1033
PATRINGTON
B1445
Sobriety Centre
BLACKTOFT
Waterways Adventure Centre & Museum
Trent Falls
River Trent
Market Weighton Canal
38
A15
BARTON-UPON-HUMBER
GOXHILL
Thornton Abbey
OIL REFINERIES
EASINGTON
Sunk Island Sands
Visitor Centre
Dutch River
B1430
B1392
River Ancholme Navigation
A1077
A15
A1033
ULCEBY
IMMINGHAM
SPURN HEAD
Normanby Hall & Park
A161
A1077
A160
A180
Keadby Skew Railway Bridge
KEADBY
Keadby Lock
SCUNTHORPE
Humberside International Airport
A18
Stainforth and Keadby Canal
A18
Thorne Boating Dyke
M181
A18
5
A18
M180
2
3
4
BRIGG
A1084
River Torne
EPWORTH
Old Rectory
A161
A159
A15
River Idle
WEST STOCKWITH
West Stockwith
Chesterfield Canal
A161
A631
Drakeholes Tunnel
Old Hall
GAINSBOROUGH
A631
Mattersey Priory
A620
River Trent
Bassetlaw Museum
North Leverton Windmill
NORTH LEVERTON WITH HABBLESTHORPE
A156
Whitsunday Pie Lock
RETFORD
Sundown Kiddies Adventureland
A5100
TORKSEY
Torksey Lock

Trent, River and Humber

119 E4-E3

Gainsborough, Trent Falls, Hull to Spurn Point
60 miles, 0 locks

All at sea. Associated British Ports is responsible for the shifting channels of the Humber as far as Spurn Head Lighthouse as well as this part of the River Trent. I think that says it all. But it is a useful link between calmer waters, if treated with respect.

Conversation is full of seafaring terms. Mooring lines are measured in fathoms, listening watches are on VHF Channel 12, progress against 6 knot tides, coastguards, comprehensive equipment, run up, duration of rise and talk of a mythical Scandinavian giant called Aegir.

i Tourist Information

Scunthorpe Tel: 01925 442180
Humber Bridge Tel: 01482 640852
Kingston upon Hull Tel: 01482 223559 / 702118
Beverley Tel: 01482 867430

Management and Support

Associated British Ports Tel: 0161 427 1079
Vessel Traffic Services Tel: 01482 701787
(Listening watch on VHF Channel 12)
Humber Coastguard Tel: 01262 672317
Humber Rescue Tel: 01831 513513
Kingston upon Hull Marina Tel: 01482 593451
Ripon Motor Boat Club: Hon Sec Mr David Leach, Birchwood, 101 St Wilfred's Road, Harrogate HG2 8LR

📖 Suggested Guide Book

Cruising Guide to the North East Waterways
Ripon Motor Boat Club, 1996

One of the longest suspension bridges in the world crosses the Humber Estuary.

Weaver Navigation
and St Helens (Sankey) Canal

118 B4

Improved: 1732, 1757, 1793, 1810, 1870
Engineers: Robinson, Berry, Pownell, Telford,
Leader-Williams
Weston Point Docks to Winsford Flashes
20 miles, 5 long, wide locks (220' x 42')

**Walk from windswept marshes to subsidence-
threatened buildings alongside the meandering
river that drains most of Cheshire. There are only
a few remains of a pioneering chemical industry.**

Salt preserves food, cures hides, glazes pottery and
is a basis for chemicals. It can be mined as rock or
obtained from underground as brine, but brine needs
coal to make salt. The tidal Weaver and tiny Sankey
were both 'improved' to bring the coal to the brine.

A huge waterborne business developed (1760)
bringing coal across the Mersey and up the Weaver,
taking salt away to the trawlers of Newfoundland and
the Baltic and bringing fish back to Liverpool.

Coal, salt and exotic imports were brought together
to form a chemical industry in Widnes and Runcorn.
Surplus revenue worth millions of pounds has been
paid to the Cheshire County Council to improve the
road system under terms of the 1791 Act.

Management and Restoration
British Waterways, Ellesmere Tel: 01696 622549

◊ **Frodsham Marshes**
The Weaver meanders through an abundance of wild
life whilst the navigation cuts a straight run to
Manchester Ship Canal's Weston Marsh Locks and
the huge Weaver Sluices into the Mersey (1891).
From M56 J12, use A557 to Western Point Church.

◊ **Pickerings Wharf**
The manager's house overlooks the former tidal limit
where goods were transhipped onto packhorses. A
footbridge and first modern lock are just upstream at
Duttons.
*Approach from M56 J10. Use A49 south and just
across Acton Swing Bridge / B5142 / B5153 to
Crowton and Crewood Common Lane.*

◊ **Saltersford Locks**
Locks at the head of Barnton Cut. The river takes a
meandering swing around the valley whilst, in the
hills, the Trent and Mersey rests between tunnels.
*From M56 J10, use A49 south to Acton Swing Bridge
then by towpath. Or by the towpath from:-*

◊ **Winnington Swing Bridge: A553**
Large sea going ships still use the navigation on a
regular basis. Just occasionally this main road bridge
has to be swung out of the way.
*Approach from M6 J19. Use A556 going south / A553
north to Barnton. Walk up to Anderton Lift which can
also be seen from the river around the next bend.(see
page 97).*

◊ **Winsford Flash**
Salt is the basis of prosperity of all the 'wiches' -
Northwich, Middlewich, even Droitwich alongside
the River Severn. Salt is also the reason for massive
subsidence as the uncontrolled underground brine
caverns collapse. Such collapses force buildings in
the towns to lean crazily and create many lakes in the
countryside. This is one of many that can be explored
by shallow draughted boats.
Approach from M6 J18. Use A54 going west.

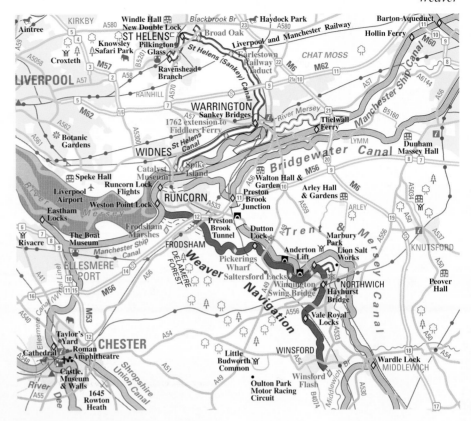

📖 *Suggested Guide Book*
David; Burkhill and Howarth *The Salt and Sails Trail*
Footprint Press, 1995

Sankey Brook Navigation (1755)

118 B3

(St Helens Canal: 1845)
Opened: 1757, 1762, 1833-1931 and 1963
Engineers: Berry, Eyes, Giles
Widnes Lock to Broad Oak Old Double Lock
15½ miles, 12 wide locks

**Much of the line is in water and can be walked
between bridges that once lifted and are now fixed.**

Presented to Parliament as an improvement to
Sankey Brook, this was actually built as a canal -
arguably the first of the Industrial Revolution. Coal
stopped flowing down from St Helens only after the
railways came but it was kept open for supplies of
raw sugar to Sankey Sugar Factory (till 1959).

Management and Restoration
British Waterways, Wigan Tel: 01942 242239
Sankey Canal Restoration Society Tel: 01744 739396
Website: http://www.scars.demon.co.uk/scars/index.htm.

◊ **Broad Oak: Old Double Lock**
Probably the first staircase lock in the country.
*Approach from M6 J23. Use A580 west / A58 south
for under two miles.*

◊ **Earlestown Railway Viaduct (1830)**
Nine arches (70 feet high over the water to allow
Mersey Flats to sail the navigation) have carried
loads way in excess of their design capacity for

almost 170 years.
*Approach from M6 J23. Use A49 south / A572 west
to Penkford Bridge (short of B5204).*

◊ **1762 extention to Fiddlers Ferry**
Sankey Brook lock was the entrance from the Mersey
for 5 years. The 1762 extension moved the Mersey
connection to a point where there was less silting and
longer tidal access. The canal is used as a haven for
yachts accessed through a restored lock.
*Approach from M62 J7. Use A57 east / A562 west.
Just beyond the roundabout look for Tannery Lane.*

◊ **Spike Island: Widnes**
Land between the canal and river where the canal
company successfully (1833) challenged a new
railhead by building large paired locks and a new
dock alongside the railway facilities. Now somewhat
restored with wrecks and rudders of Mersey Flats on
show.

◊ **Catalyst Museum** of the chemical industry
nearby.
*Approach from M62 J7. Use A557 south. Turn left
before A553 slip road.*

📖 *Suggested Guide Book*
Colin Greenall and Peter Keen *The Sankey Canal - A
Towpath Guide to England's First Industrial
Waterway* Sankey Canal Restoration Society, 1999

ℹ️ *Tourist Information*
Warrington Tel: 01925 442180
Knutsford Tel: 01565 632611
Runcorn Tel: 01928 569656
Nantwich Tel: 01270 610983
Vale Royal Tel: 01606 862862

Wednesbury Oak Loop - see **BCN**
Wednesbury Old Canal - see **BCN**
Welland Navigation, River   **116 B2-C1**
The Wash to Stamford Includes
Stamford Canal Market Deeping to Stamford
Environment Agency, Lincoln Tel: 01522 513100
Wensum, River - see **The Broads**
Wern Canal   **114 B4**
Copperhouse Dock, Llanelli to Wern Colliery
Weston Canal - see **Weaver Navigation**
Westport Canal   **111 E2**
River Isle to Westport
Somerset Inland Waterways Society,
Tel: 01278 652681

Wey and Arun Canal   112 C3
Opened: 1816-1868
23 miles, 26 narrow locks
Includes **Wey and Arun Junction Canal**
Shalford - New Bridge 18½ miles 23 narrow locks
Arun Navigation (part)
New Bridge – Pallingham 4½ miles, 3 narrow locks

**'London's Lost Route to the Sea' is in three parts:-
the River Wey, this canal, and the River Arun.
Permissive paths and rights of way are signposted
as the 'Wey South Path' from the North Downs
Way in Surrey to South Downs Way in Sussex.**

Restoration
Wey and Arun Canal Trust Tel: 01403 752403
Website: http://www.wact.nu/

◇ **Guns Mouth: Shalford**
Junction with the River Wey (1816) is in water and
used as off line moorings. Stonebridge isolated wharf
nearby was for loading gunpowder from the Chilworth
mills (1626-1920).
*Approach from M25 J10. Use A3 to Guildford / A281
south towards Horsham / A248 west to the Parrot.
Walk south on the towing path.*
◇ **Loxwood** (including Oxwood Pound)
Three miles of navigable waterway and towpath pass
two fully operational locks. Base for trip boats.
*Approach from M23 J11. Use A264 west / A24 south /
A281 west / B2133 south to 'Onslow Arms'.*
◇ **Newbridge Wharf**
Former limit of Arun Navigation.
*Approach from M23 J11. Use A23 south / on A272
west just beyond Billingshurst.*
◇ **Pallingham Canal Bridge**
A bridleway passes over the confluence of two
branches of the Arun to get to this bridge over the
start of a man made river channel. Barge building
dock and lock site. Tidal limit of the River Arun.
*Approach from M23 J9. Use A24 south / A283 west
beyond Pulborough. Then use a lane north for
approximately 4 miles from Fittleworth.*
◇ **Arundel Harbour**
Active since the Norman Conquest. Shipbuilding
centre (1575). Coasters brought coal round the coast.
Improved to Newbridge (1787, 1816).
From M27 J11. Use A27 east, beyond Chichester.

✳ *Boat Trips*
Loxwood *Zachariah Keppel* Tel: 01403 753991

Wey and Godalming Navigations
112 C3
Opened: 1653, 1764
Thames Lock to Godalming Wharf
15½ miles (9 miles of cut), 12 wide locks

Delightfully rural scenes in suburban Surrey.

Wey Navigation is 60% artificial cut, 40% river. It is
almost the earliest canal in the country (1653). Other
contenders tend to be short lock cuts on bigger
rivers:- avoiding weirs near Exeter (1566), on the Lee
at Waltham Abbey (1577) or on the Thames at
Abingdon, Iffley and Sandford (1635).
   The Stevens family operated barges on the Wey for
almost all the last 100 years (1840-1963) and ended
up owning the Navigation itself. They then gave it to
the National Trust who then acquired the Godalming
Navigation (1968), rebuilt many of the locks and
corrected the backlog of maintenance.

Management
National Trust: Dapdune Wharf Tel: 01483 561389
Website: http://www.nationaltrust.org.uk

◇ **Coxes Mill Pond**
Mill pond managed as a wildlife habitat. Mill itself
(now converted to apartments) obtained its grain by
barge from London Docks (1653-1969, 1981-1983).
*Approach from M25 J11. Use A317 east / B3121 west.
Turn right after level crossing.*
◇ **Grounds of Sutton Place**
Originally artificial water meadows of 'Richard
Weston Esquire' (1591-1652) who fed them by a
3 mile cut down from Stoke Lock (1618). 160 acres
of land were improved for hay. Sir Richard was also
the driving force behind making the Wey navigable
to Guildford (1651). Once Paul Getty's residence.
*Approach from M25 J10. Use A3 / A3100 west. Walk
the towpath north from Bowers Lock.*
◇ **Catteshall Lock**
Currently (1999) the southernmost lock on the
navigable connected system. Over 150 miles away is
the northernmost (2000) at the Tewitfield flight of
eight locks, abandoned in favour of the M6.
*Approach from M25 J10. A3 to south of Milford /
A3100 north. Turn east to Farncombe boathouse.*

✳ *Boat Trips*
Guildford *Harry Stevens* Tel: 01483 504494
Electric Eel (electric) Tel: 01483 561389
Godalming *Iona (horsedrawn)* Tel: 01483 414938

📖 *Suggested Guide Book*
Paul Rippingham and Brian Turner *The Wey South
Path* Wey and Arun Canal Trust, 1997

ℹ️ *Tourist Information*
Guildford Tel: 01483 444333
Petworth Tel: 01798 343523

Wharfe, River   **119 D2**
River Ouse Navigation to Tadcaster
9¼ miles, 0 locks
White Cart Water - see **Cart Navigation**
White House Farm Canal - see **Mundon Canal**
Wicken Lode - see **Ranch Lode**
Wilson House Canal Reach, near Lindale   **118 B1**

Guildford Boathouse
Mill, meadows and birdlife in the heart of a City.

Start the stroll from:-

1 River Meadows

The meadows flood every winter. They are between two parts of the river:- a **navigation channel** which follows a constant contour, whilst the **river water** tumbles over the upstream weir and weaves and splashes down the valley floor.

To the south (upstream) of the Jolly Farmer, get into the meadows by climbing ⚠ steps of a footbridge over the still waters of the navigation channel. Turn right (downstream), walk until opposite to:-

2 Guildford Boathouse (Tel: 01483 504494)

Rowing boats, canoes, restaurant boat and trip boats are all to be seen, sharing the water with ducks and swans. *Continue on the towpath to:-*

3 Millmead Lock (1760)

First lock of the extension of the navigation up to Godalming. Wide enough for River Thames Barges. *Cross the lock tail bridge, up the alleyway past the Yvonne Arnauld Theatre until, on the left, are the:-*

4 Mill Race and Mill Studio

Domesday Book recorded a mill here. Mill interests stopped navigation upstream to Godalming for 80 years after Sir Richard Weston had improved the river to Town Wharf (1653). The mill race drove a pump to supply town water (1701-1866). The mill building is now adapted as a studio theatre (improved 1998). *Bear left to the traffic light controlled crossing. Once across, go up to Quarry Street in one of two ways.* **Either** *go up the steps ⚠ directly ahead (Rosemary Alley)* **or** *go up the slope of Mill Lane.*

At the top go right along Quarry Street (beware of one way traffic when crossing) and turn left at the Museum, through the arch in the castle walls (1265), climb a little way up Castle Hill and through a metal gate into:-

5 Castle Grounds

A town park with excellent views back across the river valley, especially if you climb ⚠ the keep. *Exit the grounds, go down past the flower sellers under Tunsgate and into the cobbled:-*

6 High Street

Look uphill to coaching inns (1527), Guildhall Clock (1683) and shops.

Walk down to the bottom of the hill and turn right to the far end of Friary Street. Regain the riverside walk by passing left between shops through Friary Passage (under the A281 - on the level: **no steps***) and left again onto:-*

7 Town Wharf

Terminus of the original navigation (1653), the wharf has an 18 foot diameter treadmill used to work a crane. Two men inside could lift almost 2 tons from barges alongside (1726). At the end is Town Bridge (1200-1900), swept away by floods, replaced and now pedestrian only. *(There is a flood mark, 1968, on the north wall of St Nicolas' Church opposite). See the waterbus stop for the electric boat to* **9***.*

To return to the start at **1** *cross the bridge and turn left down to the riverbank. Go upstream along the towpath. Find 'Alice's rabbit hole' on the way.*

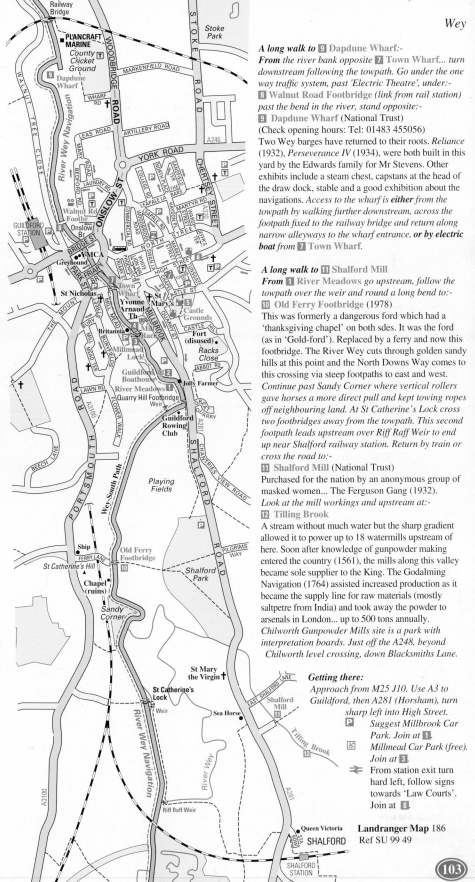

A long walk to 9 Dapdune Wharf:-

From *the river bank opposite* **7** *Town Wharf... turn downstream following the towpath. Go under the one way traffic system, past 'Electric Theatre', under:-*

8 Walnut Road Footbridge (link from rail station) *past the bend in the river, stand opposite:-*

9 Dapdune Wharf (National Trust)

(Check opening hours: Tel: 01483 455056)

Two Wey barges have returned to their roots. *Reliance* (1932), *Perseverance IV* (1934), were both built in this yard by the Edwards family for Mr Stevens. Other exhibits include a steam chest, capstans at the head of the draw dock, stable and a good exhibition about the navigations. *Access to the wharf is* **either** *from the towpath by walking further downstream, across the footpath fixed to the railway bridge and return along narrow alleyways to the wharf entrance,* **or by electric boat** *from* **7** *Town Wharf.*

A long walk to 11 Shalford Mill

From **1** *River Meadows go upstream, follow the towpath over the weir and round a long bend to:-*

10 Old Ferry Footbridge (1978)

This was formerly a dangerous ford which had a 'thanksgiving chapel' on both sdes. It was the ford (as in 'Gold-ford'). Replaced by a ferry and now this footbridge. The River Wey cuts through golden sandy hills at this point and the North Downs Way comes to this crossing via steep footpaths to east and west.

Continue past Sandy Corner where vertical rollers gave horses a more direct pull and kept towing ropes off neighbouring land. At St Catherine's Lock cross two footbridges away from the towpath. This second footpath leads upstream over Riff Raff Weir to end up near Shalford railway station. Return by train or cross the road to:-

11 Shalford Mill (National Trust)

Purchased for the nation by an anonymous group of masked women... The Ferguson Gang (1932).

Look at the mill workings and upstream at:-

12 Tilling Brook

A stream without much water but the sharp gradient allowed it to power up to 18 watermills upstream of here. Soon after knowledge of gunpowder making entered the country (1561), the mills along this valley became sole supplier to the King. The Godalming Navigation (1764) assisted increased production as it became the supply line for raw materials (mostly saltpetre from India) and took away the powder to arsenals in London... up to 500 tons annually.

Chilworth Gunpowder Mills site is a park with interpretation boards. Just off the A248, beyond Chilworth level crossing, down Blacksmiths Lane.

Getting there:

Approach from M25 J10. Use A3 to Guildford, then A281 (Horsham), turn sharp left into High Street.

🅿 *Suggest Millbrook Car Park. Join at* **1***.*

♿ *Millmead Car Park (free). Join at* **3***.*

🚆 *From station exit turn hard left, follow signs towards 'Law Courts'. Join at* **8***.*

Landranger Map 186
Ref SU 99 49

Wilts and Berks Canal   112 A2-B2

Opened: 1810, 1819-1914, 1977-
Engineers: Whitworth (Senior, Junior), Rennie
Semington Junction with the Kennet & Avon Canal
to St Helen's Wharf on the Thames at Abingdon
Branches: Chippenham, Calne, Longcot, Wantage
52 miles, 52 narrow locks

North Wilts Canal
Swindon to Latton Junction with Cotswold Canals
8½ miles, 11 narrow locks

eg Melksham, Swindon, and Abingdon.

Volunteer navvies gave the restoration project an early kick start. Over 1000 came (1991) and joined in a 'BIG DIG' weekend camp, which changed the face of stretches of the canal near Wantage.

A feasibility study was recently commissioned (1997) by the newly formed Trust which shows that, subject to slight variations from the original line, restoration is both feasible and of economic benefit to the area.

[Map of the Wilts and Berks Canal region, showing places including Cirencester, Oxford, Swindon, Chippenham, Abingdon, Melksham, Devizes, and the canal routes]

◊ Wootton Bassett
One mile of navigation. Site of the National Trail Boat Festival (1998). Over 70 craft were brought to the water… including coracles, canoes, inflatables and three pedal powered craft. Spring Bank Holidays will never be the same.
Approach from M4 J16. Use A3102 to south-west. In Wootton Bassett turn south-east along Station Road.

◊ Swindon Restorations: Moredon, Kingshill
With assistance from developers and the Heritage Lottery Fund, two lengths of canal within the River Ray Valley are under restoration (1999).
Approach from M4 J16. Use B4005 going south-east towards Wroughton, then back north over M4. Or from M4 J15 use A419 north then at the stadium use B4534 west to Elborough Bridge.

A considerable length of restoration needs to be achieved but there are already some pocket parks and picnic sites and towpath walking is possible alongside water in six localities.

The 1794 Act of Parliament was remarkably informal - the 'Wilts and Berks' is the correct name. Local Government reorganisation (1974) took the Vale of White Horse out of Berkshire and set it in Oxfordshire, so perhaps nowadays 'Wilts and Oxon' would be a better guide to the areas served.

The original line is rural and visible for much of the route. Exceptions are where urban developments have occurred since the canal was closed (1914)

Restoration
Wilts and Berks Canal Trust
Wilts and Berks Canal Amenity Group
Tel: 01628 544666
Website: http://web.ukonline.co.uk/dg.small/index/htm

◊ **Melksham Canal Walk**
Waymarked walk (1998) indicating the canal route that used to serve the town (now dry).
From M4 J17, use A350 south to Melksham.

◊ **Foxham Top Lock**
Restored and awaiting gates. Walk alongside water and see a typical lift bridge (also restored).
From M4 J16, use A3102 south to Goatacre. Turn west.

◊ **Daunsey Lock** (Tel: 01249 892289)
Lock and nearby wharf were restored using profits from the renovation of cottages overlooking them. Towpath alongside 1 mile of water (plus a further mile by end of 1999). A development led scheme with mutual benefits.
From M4 J16, use A3102 to Lyneham / B4069 west to Peterborough Arms.

Young fisherman making a catch from the waters of the Wilts and Berks Canal.

◊ **Cricklade Country Way** (Tel: 01793 751394)
Major initiative from Swindon to Cricklade and beyond. The corridor will have bridleways, steam railway and the restored North Wilts Canal.
Approach from M4 J15. Use A419 going north. At Cricklade B4553 south.

◊ **Shrivenham Pocket Park**
Car park, picnic site, trail boat slipway alongside restored canal (farm bridge limits navigation, 1999)
Approach from M4 J15. Use A419 / A420 going north-west. Turn south near the pedestrian crossing in Shrivenham.

◊ **Seven Mile Pound**
Part of this towpath is used by cycle commuters to avoid traffic on the outskirts of Wantage. Some fish!
Approach from M4 J13. Use A338 north / A417 west towards Faringdon. Flattened canal bridge on sharp bend north of East Challow.

◊ **St Helen's Wharf: Abingdon**
A splendid bridge, paid for by the Wilts and Berks Canal Company, spans a small brook at the riverside garden. The feasibility study acknowledges that the original canal alignment following the River Ock is now of ecological value and an alternative route is being sought… somewhat complicated by proposals for a new major water supply reservoir in the area.
From M4 J13, use A34 north / A415 east. Seek river.

📖 *Suggested Books*
Douglas Small *The Wilts and Berks Canal* Tempus, 1999
L J Dalby *The Wilts and Berks Canal* The Oakwood Press, 1971, 1999
Dr Eric V. Tull *Canal Days in Swindon,* 1993

ℹ *Tourist Information*
Melksham Tel: 01225 707424
Chippenham Tel: 01249 706333
Swindon Tel: 01793 530328
Wantage Tel: 01235 760176
Abingdon Tel: 01235 522711

· ·

Wisbech Canal   116 C2
Wisbech to Outwell
Wissey, River   117 D2
Great Ouse Navigation to Oxborough Hithe near Stoke Ferry

Witham Navigable Drains
(and Witham and Sleaford Navigations)
116 C1

Opened: 1598, 1807, 1826,
Engineers: Rennie
36 miles, 3 wide locks

Bell Water Drain Hobhole Drain to Thorpe Culvert
Castle Dyke Newham Drain to Howbridge Drain
Cowbridge Drain Cowbridge to Hobhole Drain
East Fen Catchwater Drain Northlands to Stickford
Fodder Dyke eastwards from Hobhole Drain
Frith Bank Drain Anton's Gowt to Cowbridge
Hobhole Drain near The Haven to near Toynton Fen Side
Howbridge Drain Newham Drain to Castle Dyke
Maud Foster Drain Cowbridge to Boston
Medlam Drain Anton's Gowt to near Tumby Woodside
Stone Bridge Drain Cowbridge to Northlands
West Fen Drain Cowbridge to Howbridge Drain
West Fen Catchwater Drain Revesby Bridge to Northlands

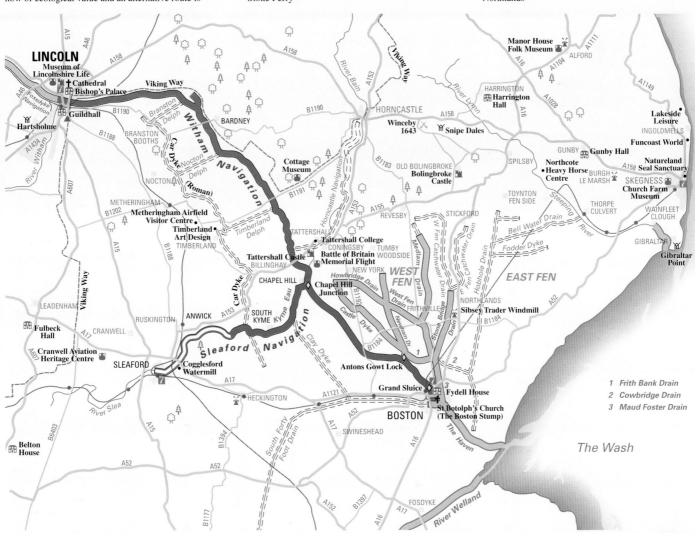

Management and Restoration
*Witham Fourth District Internal Drainage Board,
Boston Tel: 01205 310099*

Witham Navigation (see previous map)
116 C1

Opened: 1763, 1770, 1795
Engineers: Fortray, Edwards, Jessop
36½ miles, 3 locks
Lincoln to Boston
Branston Delph, Nocton Delph, Timberland Delph

The River Witham runs to the north-east of the
Roman Car Dyke and became the alternative
navigation route after the Fossdyke was improved
to new standards (1774).

Sponsored by Lincoln Corporation the works
started at the Grand Sluice protecting the river
from the sea at Boston (1763) and improved the
depth through three wiers and locks (1770).
Connection to the Fossdyke was under High Bridge
(which in reality was rather low and very shallow).
High Bridge was finally improved (Jessop 1795)
but the size of through traffic to the Trent was
limited by the relatively shallow Fossdyke (3'6")...
a fact that mattered less when the railways killed
off all traffic anyway.

Management and Restoration
British Waterways, Newark Tel: 01636 704481

Sleaford Navigation (see previous map)
(River Slea and Kyme Eau)   **116 B1**
Opened: 1794-1881, 1986
Engineers: Hudson, Jessop
12 miles, 7 locks
Witham Navigation to Sleaford

Romans had drained parts of the area and given
themselves waterways navigable to Lincoln
(Car Dyke). Later, a ford over the Slea on the
route from Peterborough to Lincoln gave rise to
the Town. After long discussions about the
heavy tolls on the Witham the proprietors
implemented a project to widen the river and use
an isolated medieval navigation (Kyme Eau) to
get to the Witham.
After a burst of prosperity lasting almost 50
years, the navigation was formerly abandoned
(1881) although the drainage channels continued
to be used... the more so since the reopening of
Kyme Eau Lock (1986).

Management and Restoration
*Company of the Proprietors of the Sleaford
Navigation Society, Steve Hayes (Sec), 10 Chelmer
Close, North Hykeham, Lincoln LN6 8TH
Sleaford Navigation Trust Tel: 01636 812572*

- -

Wombridge Canal   **115 D1**
Wombridge to Donnington Wood Canal
Later part incorporated into **Shrewsbury Canal**
- see **Shropshire Union Canal**
Woodeaves Canal   **118 C4**
near Fenny Bentley to Woodeaves Brook

Worcestershire and Birmingham Canal
115 E3

Opened: Tardebigge 1807, Worcester 1815
Engineers: Clowes, Cartwright, Woodhouse, Crosley
Gas Street Basin to Tardebigge Wharf
14½ miles, 0 locks, 4 wide tunnels
Tardebigge Wharf to Diglis Basin
15½ miles, 56 narrow locks, 1 tunnel

A broad canal fitted with narrow locks.
Excellent level walking through the leafy suburbs
of Edgbaston on the outskirts of Birmingham, the
only diversions necessary being over three tunnels.
After Tardebigge a long, steady, attractive desent
through countryside into the Severn valley.

The enabling Act of Parliament (1791) was only
passed after two false starts (1786, 1790) and after the
promoting canal company agreed to many restrictive
clauses forced on it by potential objectors. The canal
would be serious competition. It was designed to be
shorter than the existing connection to Stourport and
would arrive at the Severn where the navigation was
deeper and more reliable. So, as well as the usual
concessions to millers about their water supply, the
Birmingham, Stourbridge, Dudley, Staffordshire and
Worcestershire canal companies also had to be
appeased. It ran for 26 years but, after its salt traffic
from Stoke suffered competition from the railways
(1841), it went bankrupt (1868). All its liabilities and
assets were purchased by the Gloucester and
Sharpness Canal (1874) so that it could obtain full
control of a waterway route to Birmingham, subject
only to the vagaries of navigation on the Severn.

Management and Restoration
*British Waterways Tel: 01564 784634
Worcester and Birmingham Canal Society
Tel: 01527 402360
Lapal Canal Trust Tel: 0121 585 5878
Droitwich Canals Trust Tel: 01905 773289
Website: http://www.g4nzk.demon.co.uk/wbcs*

◊ **Worcester Bar: Gas Street Basin**
Birmingham Canal Company extracted the condition
that the new canal would 'come no closer than seven
feet' from its waters. Trade onto the new Worcester
and Birmingham canal could only start by
manhandling over this 7 foot bar. Only pierced after
20 years (1795-1815).
*From M5 J1, use A41 south to A4540 (Birmingham
Ring Road). Then anti-clockwise to A456 (Broad
Street). Turn north-east then south into Gas Street.*
◊ **Selly Oak Junction**
To avoid further dealings with the monopolistic BCN,
the Dudley Canal Company opened the Dudley No 2
Canal (1798) to link their system to this junction. The
major engineering challenge for the route was the tiny
bore (7 feet 9 inches) but very long (11 385 feet)
tunnel at Lappel (1798-1914) which originally took
four hours to 'leg' boats through. Later (1841) this was
reduced by 25% through the creation of an artificial
ebb and flow with a massive pumping engine.
From M5 J4, use A38 northeast. At A4040 junction
◊ **Bourneville**
A classic 'new town', sponsored by a responsible
employer and set in the countryside alongside a
transport artery... the canal. For over 80 years (1879-
1961) the Cadbury chocolate company used
narrowboats to transport milk from its Cheshire
factory at Knighton on the Shropshire Union Canal.
They also imported chocolate crumb from Frampton
on the Gloucester and Sharpness Canal to their
factory in Bourneville and used both to create 'Milk
Tray' and other high quality products.
Sadly, neither the 'Cadbury World' theme park
exhibition nor the museum in the basement of the
factory celebrate their 82 years of commitment to
splendid liveried narrowboats advertising chocolate
all around the system. (Tel: 0121 451 4180).
*Approach from M5 J4. Use A38 going north-east /
A4040 south to Bourneville railway station.*
◊ **King's Norton Stop Lock**
Stratford Canal increased traffic by opening up a
route to London (1802) but this guillotine gate was
necessary to stop water draining away from the

A few locks from the longest flight in the country at Tardebigge

Worcester and Birmingham's top (and at the time *only*) pound. Now fixed in open position.
Approach from M42 J2. Use A441 north as far as King's Norton Park.

◊ **Wast Hill Tunnel** (8178 feet)
Known also as the King's Norton Tunnel, this is the longest of four wide tunnels on the top level of the canal - Edgbaston (with towpath), Shortwood and Tardebigge are the other three. Horseboats used to wait at each entrance to be hauled through in groups by one of five steam tugs which worked a timetable (1876-1908). Self propelled boats now pass through without waiting (35 minutes).
From M42 J2, use A441 to Hopwood. Turn east.

◊ **Bittell Reservoirs**
Popular with fishermen. One concession extracted from the company by mill owners was that they should have a guaranteed water supply, if necessary by pumping water 425 feet up from the Severn.

The Lower Bittel Reservoir was devoted entirely to their needs and proved adequate. A top up to the canal's second reservoir (Upper Bittell 1832) was only allowed from the miller's reservoir when it was above a certain agreed water level.
From M42 J2, use A441 for / mile / B4120 west.

◊ **Tardebigge Wharf**
Famous amongst Inland Waterway Association (IWA) members as the spot where Robert Aickman first met the author Tom Rolt and his boat *Cressy* after travelling from London to Bromsgrove station and walking to the top lock of the Tardebigge Flight of locks. Robert had read Rolt's book (*Narrow Boat 1946*) and at the end of their meeting proposed the formation of a 'waterways protection body of some kind', soon to become the IWA.

The wharf is currently British Waterways workshops and offices, but for 8 years (1807-1815) it was the interchange point for cargo and passenger services to Worcester. This way the canal waited at the end of the top pound whilst the problems of descending the relatively steep sides of the Severn Valley were contemplated by its engineers.

Partly to save water, the company engineer John Woodhouse proposed 12 boat lifts instead of 76 locks. The first was built and used (without trouble) for six months but a nervous company asked for a second opinion and, on Rennie's advice, the idea was rejected as being unreliable. Extra water supplies were secured and the top lock was then constructed using the existing lift chamber. As a result it is one of the deepest narrow locks on the system (14 feet). (Now challenged by the modern Tuel Lock (1996) at Sowerby Bridge in Yorkshire.)
Approach from M5 J5. Use A38 north / B4184 east.

◊ **Stoke Pound**
A very short pound between two flights of locks… the Tardebigge *thirty* (rising 217 feet) and the Stoke /Astwood *twelve* (rising 84 feet). Some boaters consider the two as a single flight of 42 locks in 5 miles between the top pound (14½ miles) and the Oddingley pound (5½ miles). They prepare themselves accordingly.
From M5 J5, use A38 north to Stoke Heath. Turn south-east.

◊ **Droitwich Junction Canal** (1853)
Built from Hanbury Wharf to connect with the short (6½ mile), older (1771) Droitwich Barge Canal up from the Severn. Both canals are currently (1999) under restoration to create a short (22 mile) cruising

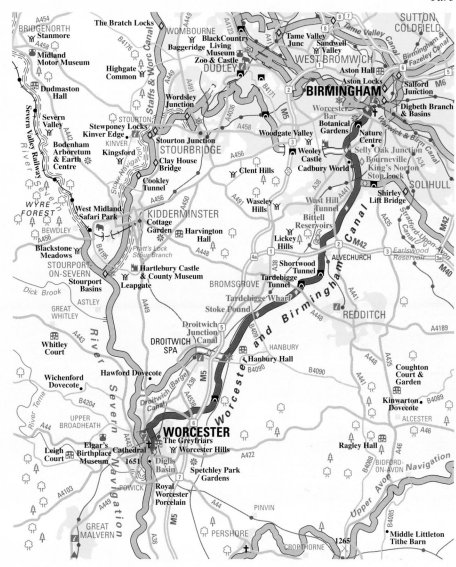

ring which would give a variety of waterway experiences... viz. a 700 foot tunnel and seven self service narrow locks on this canal, eight wide locks on the barge canal and pretty manned Bevere Lock on a four mile reach of the lively River Severn.
Approach from M5 J5. Use A38 south / B4090 east into Salt Way (Roman Road).

◊ **Diglis Basin: Worcester**
End of the canal and outlet onto the river. Two locks stepping down to the river are wide enough to allow Severn Trows to escape the river's lively flows. Two basins are surrounded by warehouses built for the interchange trade between river vessels and narrowboats. Downstream trade was in coal and iron, upstream in goods for the cities, including grain and wine. The Royal Porcelain Factory (established 1751) used waterways to bring china clay from Cornwall and coal from the Midlands. Exotic ingredients previously imported by boat are included in Lee & Perrins sauce.
From M50 J1, use A38 north to Diglis. Turn west.

✳ *Boat Trips*
Droitwich *Pamela May* Tel: 01905 776541

📖 *Suggested Guide Book*
Micheal Pearson *The Stourport Ring* J.M. Pearson & Son, 1992

i *Tourist Information*
Birmingham Tel: 0121 693 6300
Solihull Tel: 0121 704 6130
Bromsgrove Tel: 01527 831809
Droitwich Spa Tel: 01905 774312
Worcester Tel: 01905 726311

• •

Wreake, River- see **Melton Mowbray Navigation**
Wye, River   **114 C3 - 115 D4**
  River Severn to Aberdw
Wryley and Essington Canal - see **BCN**

Yare, River- see **The Broads**

Restoration

Once upon a time there were, broadly speaking, 4000 miles of navigable waterways in Britain consisting of 1000 miles of rivers and 3000 miles of canals.

An official study after WWII identified only 2500 miles available for navigation. Since then 300 miles have been restored and within three years a further 150 miles will be added. Although this still leaves 1000 miles still to go, it is a massive engineering achievement which has brought enormous benefits to people living nearby... ranging from the simple delights of walking through a corridor of wildflowers and wildlife to profiting from business opportunities presented by waterborne visitors.

Such an achievement has involved partnership between many organisations but was inconceivable without the practical help of volunteer navvies.

Navvies
The concept of voluntary work on the inland waterways was born in the early 1960s and has steadily grown. From the early days when very few volunteers worked on projects such as the Peak Forest and Ashton Canals near Manchester, the lower River Avon in Worcestershire and the Stratford-upon-Avon Canal in Warwickshire, the position has changed out of all recognition. Now there are over 30 voluntary groups spread all over the country, with an estimated workforce of over 3000 people.

From the Forth and Clyde Canal in Scotland to the Chichester Canal in the South, the Bude Canal in Cornwall to the Ipswich and Stowmarket Navigation in Suffolk, voluntary working parties exist attached to local canal societies, branches of the Inland Waterways Association and regional WRG Groups.

They either work regularly on some project in the immediate area or as a mobile task force, travelling up to 250 miles in a weekend to work where their help is most needed, thus giving a boost to local effort.

This mass of enthusiastic voluntary labour (known as 'navvies' after the original constructors) can present problems of organisation and the number of bodies involved can present problems of coordination. It quickly became clear that some central organisation was needed to overcome these problems, assist with financing, supply and loan items of large plant and advise on methods and technique. 1970 saw the formation of the Waterway Recovery Group.

The Waterway Recovery Group
The Waterway Recovery Group was formed in 1970 by enthusiasts who had been active in voluntary restoration work since the mid 1960s. Their aim was to be a coordinating force, not centred upon any individual project but backing up and assisting local groups on any worthwhile project.

Since then, considerable knowledge of restoration methods and a large pool of plant and equipment has been amassed. At present, the group has an excavator and transporter, a fleet of vans, a ten station radio network plus a bewildering variety of dumpers, pumps, mixers and other sundry equipment.

All of this is freely available on an 'expenses paid' basis and drivers / operators can be found too. WRG can also help with the supply of labour and has coordinated groups of volunteers visiting important

sites such as the Ashton and Peak Forest Canals, the Upper Avon restoration, the Droitwich and the Basingstoke Canals, resulting in a constant flow of labour and ensuring smooth operations.

Major projects
Perhaps the most spectacular early projects were the Big Digs. Undertaken as demonstrations of the staggering effectiveness of well coordinated voluntary labour, dramatic improvements were made to long derelict stretches of canal. Twice in the Manchester area and again in Dudley, Woking, Welshpool, Droitwich and Wantage, WRG organised mass working parties with work forces of between 180 and 1000 people.

In March 1972 came 'Ashtac' when some 850 people descended upon the Ashton Canal near Manchester. In one weekend's radio-controlled onslaught they removed over 3000 tons of rubbish from the canal. The project, officially estimated to cost £15-20,000, was completed for a total outlay of only £1800. (Map on page 8.)

In October 1991, over 1000 people reclaimed over two miles of canal in a single weekend at Wantage on the Wilts and Berks Canal. (Map on page 104.)

WRG's largest project to date has been the rebuilding of the four Frankton Locks, on the

Montgomery Canal at the junction with the Llangollen Canal and the three Aston Locks on the same canal. During 1993/4, a four acre wetlands nature reserve was also constructed on the Aston site. Built entirely by volunteers at a cost of just over £100,000, there was a saving on contract prices of over £200,000! WRG had long been a leading voice in the campaign for restoration of the canal and, financed by its parent organisation, the Inland Waterways Association and a Department of the Environment grant of £37,500 WRG undertook these works, on a canal that has been derelict since 1936. The work at Frankton was completed with an official reopening in 1987 and the locks were restored to a higher standard than that of their original construction! The success of this work and that undertaken in Welshpool some years earlier by

the Prince of Wales' Committee has brought local authority and central government investment in other schemes on the canal and plans for the complete restoration of the whole 35 miles of this unique and scenic waterway are well advanced. (Map on page 81.)

None of this would have been possible without the initial enthusiasm of volunteer navvies and much official funding is only forthcoming if matched by their valuable work.

Canal Camps

Most voluntary work must obviously be done at weekends, for even navvies have to earn a living. However, the exceptions to this rule are the Canal Camps, first organised in the early 1970s for a few weeks in mid-summer, and which have now expanded into a flourishing annual programme.

20 or so weeks of Canal Camps are organised each year which offer the opportunity to achieve a vast amount of work in a short time; it is not unusual for a

camp to achieve in a week or two what might take the best of local societies many months of weekend workparties.

Camps have due regard to an ever increasing list of legislation on health, safety, land contamination, wildlife, etc.. They are held the length and breadth of the country from long established restorations such as the Montgomery and Wey and Arun Canals to such new projects as the Hereford and Gloucestershire Canal, the Derby Canal and the Wilts and Berks Canal. Some camps also help out at the IWA's National Waterway Festivals, providing much of the back up and site organisation for events which attract tens of thousands of visitors in one weekend.

Camps attract a wide range of people, from young volunteers taking part in the Duke of Edinburgh's Award Scheme to waterway enthusiasts who wish to make a contribution to restoring and preserving the system which gives them so much enjoyment. On a Canal Camp age doesn't matter nor does previous experience as, although everyone is treated the same, no one is asked to work beyond their capabilities and any necessary skills will be taught. A Canal Camp is a worthwhile week in the open air with 20 or so like minded people with lots of hard work, fun and an enjoyable social life.

Future possibilities
Waterways attract many people for many purposes. Houses, restaurants and pubs overlook water. Families with pushchairs or walkers with dogs enjoy a quiet environment away from the hassle of traffic. The continuous hedgerows and undisturbed undergrowth harbour delicate flowers such as cowslips and primroses and support abundant wildlife such as otters and heron.

Movement of heavy goods by water is not quick but is a fantastically efficient use of energy. Currently most boats on the water are used by people seeking a week or fortnight's holiday. Circular tours or 'Rings' are popular, especially if they take about 14 days to complete. Existing examples are Cheshire Ring, Four Counties Ring and future possibilities include the Wessex 'figure of eight'

centred on Swindon, the 'Don Ring' via Chesterfield and Rotherham and shorter rings linking Leamington and Stratford-upon-Avon or Droitwich and Worcester.

Future possibilities are endless, and it is not necessary to afford an ocean going cruiser to enjoy the water. Most people live within 5 miles of a waterway; take a walk down there and enjoy it for free.

For further information contact:
WRG Enquires
PO Box 114
Rickmansworth
Hertfordshire
WD3 12Y

Tel: 01923 711114
Website: http://waterways.org.uk/index.htm

Regional Maps

Map Reference

Broad Canal (over 7ft wide)
—————— Navigable
—————— No longer navigable
—————— Under restoration

Narrow Canal (max 7ft wide)
—————— Navigable
—————— No longer navigable
—————— Under restoration

River Navigation
—————— Navigable
—————— No longer navigable
—————— Under restoration

Tidal River Navigation
—————— Navigable
—————— No longer navigable
—————— Under restoration

Other Navigation
—————— Canal with lock size unknown
- - - - - Proposed navigation

Other river

Built-up area

National boundary

4〈 Lock flight with number of locks

▣ Tunnel

◢ Inclined plane

◇ Feature of interest

⚠ Local hazard

○ 12M / 8L ○ Distance in miles/number of locks between markers

▴80 Height of waterway in feet above sea-level

Scale 1: 700 000

0 10 20 30 miles

0 10 20 30 40 50 kilometres

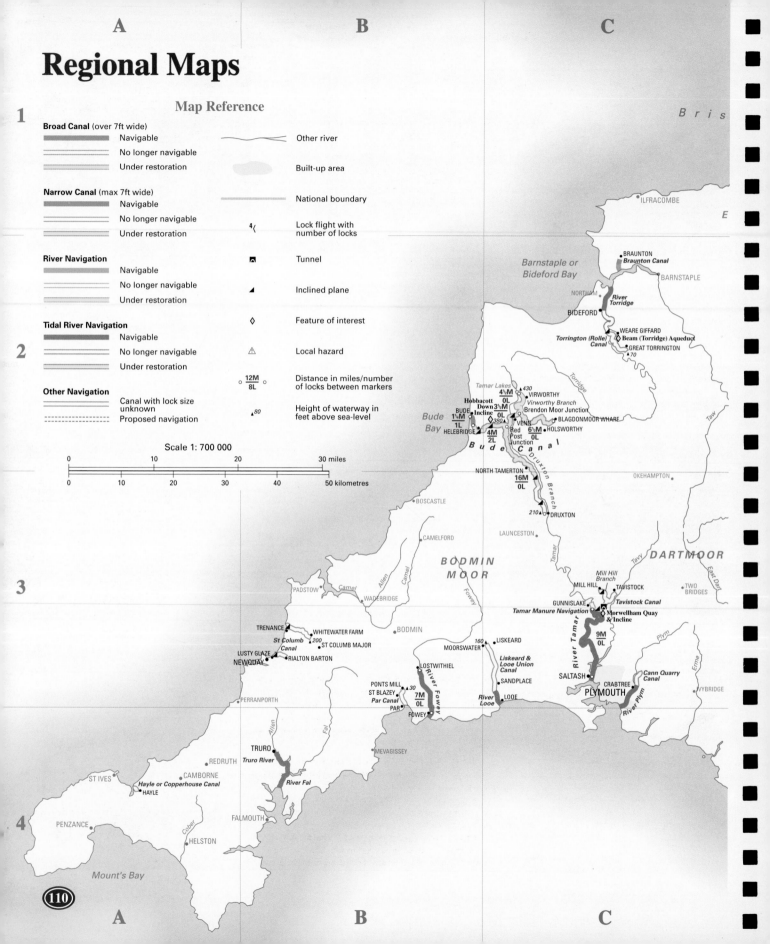

Bris

ILFRACOMBE

E

Barnstaple or Bideford Bay

BRAUNTON
Braunton Canal

BARNSTAPLE

NORTHAM

River Torridge

BIDEFORD

WEARE GIFFARD
◇ Beam (Torridge) Aqueduct
Torrington (Rolle) Canal
GREAT TORRINGTON
▴70

Torridge

Taw

Tamar Lakes 4½M / 0L ▴430 VIRWORTHY
Virworthy Branch
Hobbacott 3⅜M / 0L Brendon Moor Junction
Down Incline ▴380 BLAGDONMOOR WHARE
BUDE 1¼M / 1L ◇ VENN 6⅝M / 0L HOLSWORTHY
Bude Bay HELEBRIDGE 4M / 2L Red Post Junction
Bude Canal
Druxton Branch
NORTH TAMERTON 16M / 0L
210▴ DRUXTON

OKEHAMPTON

Tamar

LAUNCESTON

BODMIN MOOR

CAMELFORD

DARTMOOR
TWO BRIDGES

Tavy
East Dart

PADSTOW
Camel
Allen
Camel
WADEBRIDGE

Fowey

Mill Hill Branch
MILL HILL TAVISTOCK
Tavistock Canal
GUNNISLAKE
Tamar Manure Navigation ◇ Morwellham Quay & Incline
9M / 0L

BODMIN

Plym

TRENANCE
St Columb Canal ▴200 WHITEWATER FARM
ST COLUMB MAJOR
LUSTY GLAZE
NEWQUAY RIALTON BARTON

160 LISKEARD
MOORSWATER
Liskeard & Looe Union Canal
SANDPLACE

LOSTWITHIEL

River Fowey

River Tamar
SALTASH
Cann Quarry Canal
CRABTREE
PLYMOUTH
IVYBRIDGE
Erme
River Plym

PONTS MILL ▴30
ST BLAZEY *Par Canal*
PAR 7M / 0L
FOWEY

River Looe
LOOE

PERRANPORTH

Allen
Fal

Cober

TRURO
Truro River
River Fal

REDRUTH

CAMBORNE

ST IVES
Hayle or Copperhouse Canal
HAYLE

MEVAGISSEY

FALMOUTH

PENZANCE
HELSTON

Mount's Bay

A   B   C

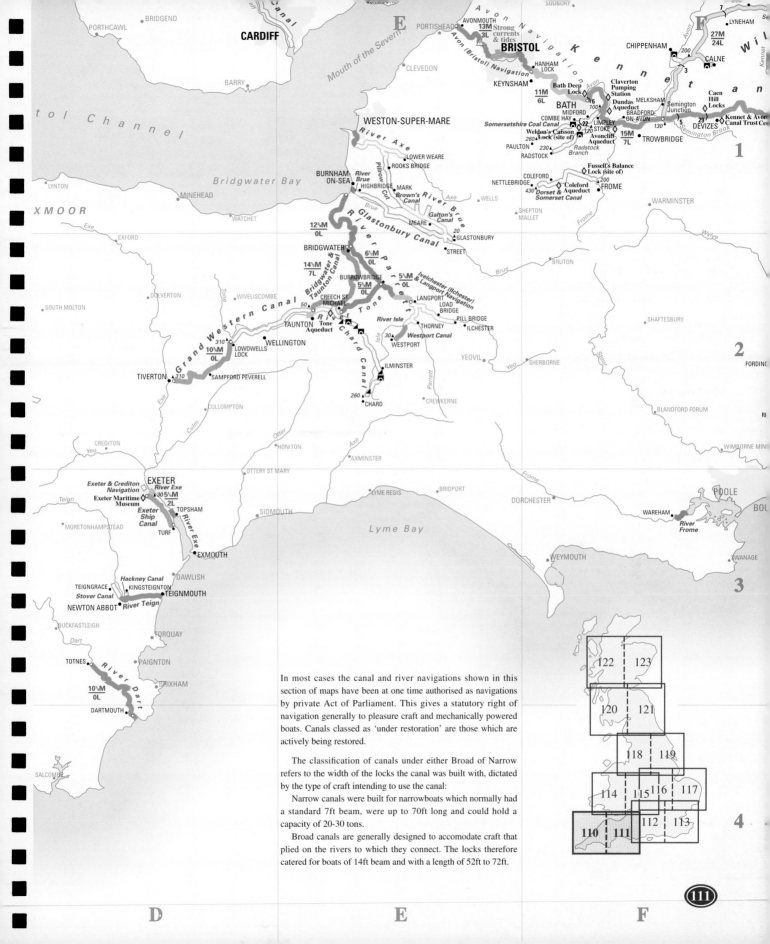

In most cases the canal and river navigations shown in this section of maps have been at one time authorised as navigations by private Act of Parliament. This gives a statutory right of navigation generally to pleasure craft and mechanically powered boats. Canals classed as 'under restoration' are those which are actively being restored.

The classification of canals under either Broad of Narrow refers to the width of the locks the canal was built with, dictated by the type of craft intending to use the canal:

Narrow canals were built for narrowboats which normally had a standard 7ft beam, were up to 70ft long and could hold a capacity of 20-30 tons.

Broad canals are generally designed to accomodate craft that plied on the rivers to which they connect. The locks therefore catered for boats of 14ft beam and with a length of 52ft to 72ft.

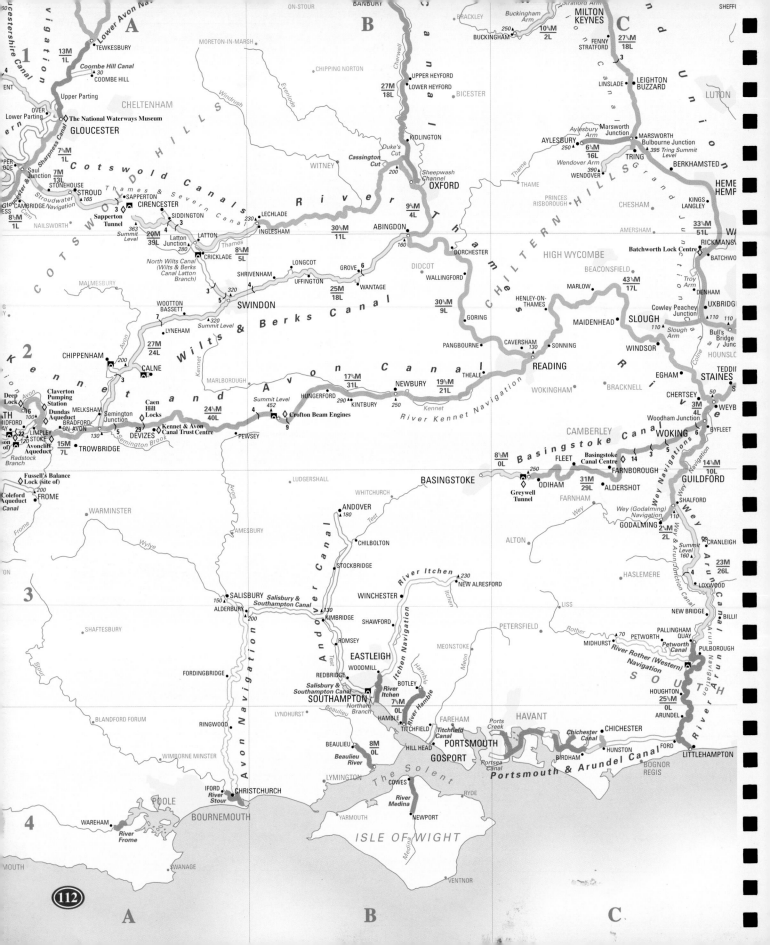

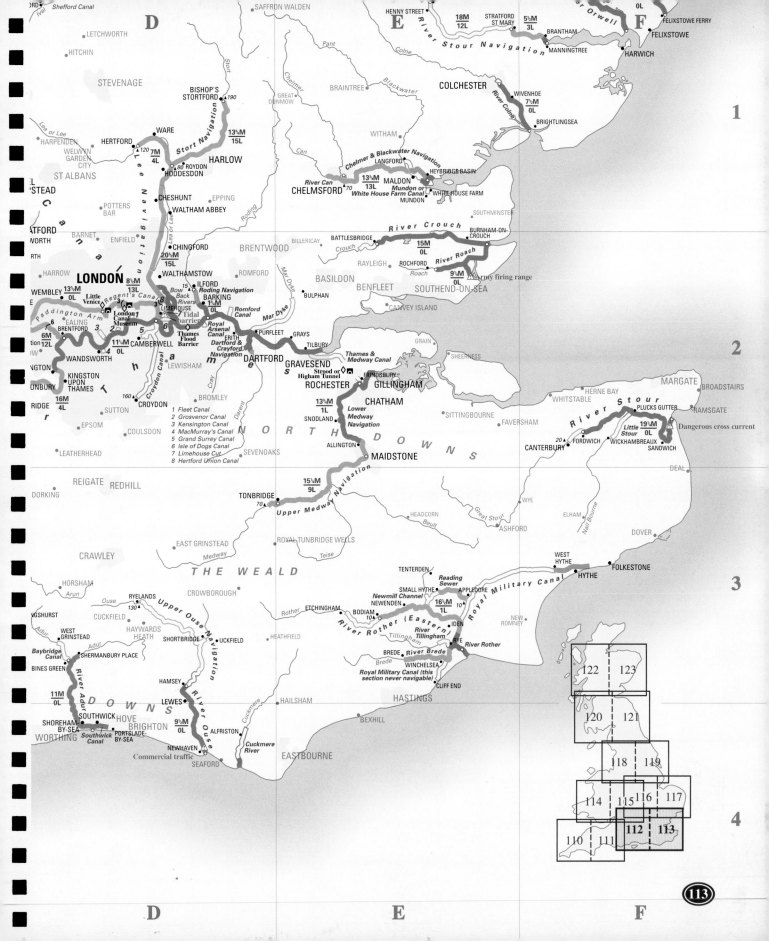

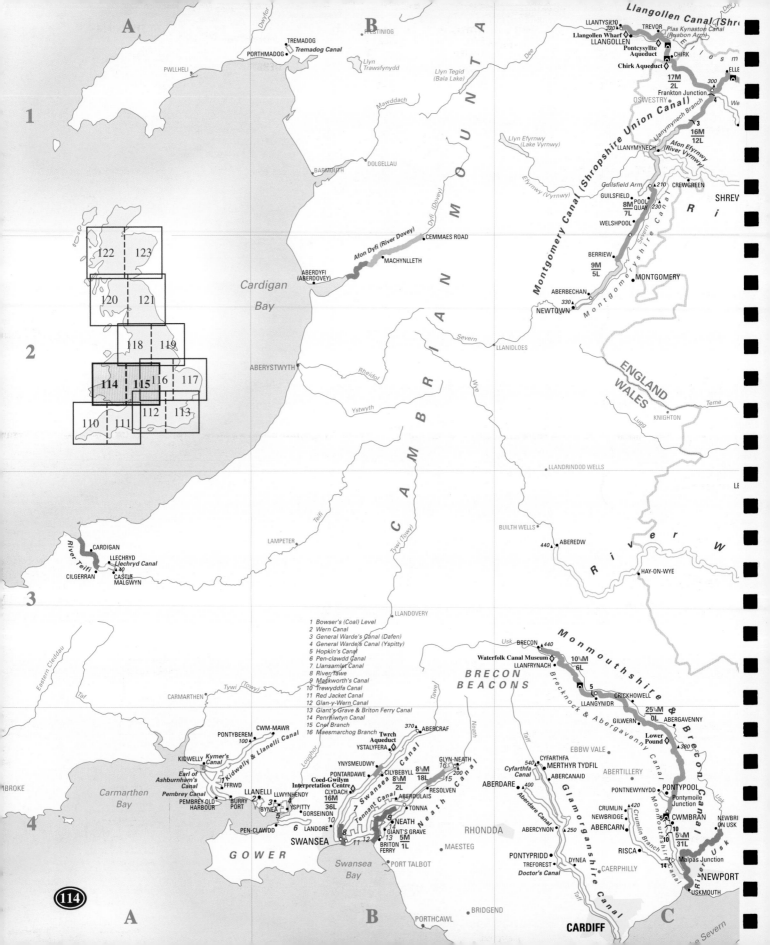

A **B** **C**

1

TREMADOG
PORTHMADOG
Tremadog Canal
FFESTINIOG
PWLLHELI
Dwyfor
Llyn Trawsfynydd
Llyn Tegid (Bala Lake)
Dee

Llangollen Canal (Shro
LLANTYSILIO
320
TREVOR
Plas Kynaston Canal (Ruabon Arm)
Llangollen Wharf
LLANGOLLEN
Pontcysyllte Aqueduct
CHIRK
Chirk Aqueduct
ELLE
300
17M
2L
Frankton Junction
4

Mawddach
BARMOUTH
DOLGELLAU
Llyn Efyrnwy (Lake Vyrnwy)

Montgomery Canal (Shropshire Union Canal)
16M
12L
LLANYMYNECH
Llanymynech Branch
Afon Efyrnwy (River Vyrnwy)
3
16M
12L

Efyrnwy (Vyrnwy)
Guilsfield Arm
210
CREWGREEN
SHRE
GUILSFIELD
8M
7L
POOL
QUAY
230
WELSHPOOL
Severn

Afon Dyfi (River Dovey)
CEMMAES ROAD
MACHYNLLETH
ABERDYFI
(ABERDOVEY)

Cardigan
Bay

BERRIEW
9M
5L
MONTGOMERY

ABERBECHAN
330
NEWTOWN

Montgomeryshire Canal

2

122 123
120 121
118 119
114 115 116 117
110 111 112 113

ABERYSTWYTH
Rheidol
Wye
LLANIDLOES
LLANDRINDOD WELLS

Severn

ENGLAND
WALES
Teme
KNIGHTON
Lugg
LE

3

River Teifi
CARDIGAN
LLECHRYD
Llechryd Canal
40
CILGERRAN
CASTLE
MALGWYN

Eastern Cleddau
Taf
Tywi (Towy)
LAMPETER
Teifi

BUILTH WELLS
ABEREDW
440
HAY-ON-WYE

River W

LLANDOVERY

1 Bowser's (Coal) Level
2 Wern Canal
3 General Warde's Canal (Dafen)
4 General Warde's Canal (Yspitty)
5 Hopkin's Canal
6 Pen-clawdd Canal
7 Llansamlet Canal
8 River Tawe
9 Mackworth's Canal
10 Trewyddfa Canal
11 Red Jacket Canal
12 Glan-y-Wern Canal
13 Giant's Grave & Briton Ferry Canal
14 Penrhiwtyn Canal
15 Cnel Branch
16 Maesmarchog Branch

BRECON
440
Waterfolk Canal Museum
LLANFRYNACH
10½M
6L
BRECON
BEACONS
CRICKHOWELL
5
LLANGYNIDR
25½M
0L
GILWERN
ABERGAVENNY
Lower Pound
380

Monmouthshire
Brecknock & Abergavenny Canal

4

Tywi (Towy)
CARMARTHEN
PONTYBEREM
CWM-MAWR
100
KIDWELLY
Kymer's Canal
Kidwelly & Llanelli Canal
Earl of Ashburnham's Canal
Pembrey Canal
PEMBREY OLD HARBOUR
FFRWD
1
LLANELLI
LLWYNHENDY
BYNEA
YSPITTY
GORSEINON
LANDORE
PEN-CLAWDD
2
3
4
5
6
BURRY PORT
Carmarthen Bay
PEMBROKE

ABERCRAF
370
Twrch Aqueduct
YSTALYFERA
YNYSMEUDWY
PONTARDAWE
CILYBEBYLL
Coed-Gwilym Interpretation Centre
CLYDACH
16M
36L
Swansea Canal
8½M
18L
8½M
2L
Tennant Canal
ABERDULAIS
TONNA
NEATH
GIANT'S GRAVE
BRITON FERRY
SWANSEA
Gower
Swansea Bay
PORTHCAWL
BRIDGEND
PORT TALBOT
MAESTEG
RHONDDA
GLYN-NEATH
16½M
200
15
RESOLVEN
Neath Canal
5M
1L
9
7
8
11 12 13
10
14
5

Tawe

CYFARTHFA
540
MERTHYR TYDFIL
ABERCANAID
EBBW VALE
ABERTILLERY
Cyfarthfa Canal
ABERDARE
400
Aberdare Canal
ABERCYNON
250
ABERCARN
NEWBRIDGE
CRUMLIN
420
PONTYPOOL
Pontymoile Junction
PONTNEWYNYDD
CWMBRAN
5
10
10
5¼M
31L
NEWBRI
ON USK

Taff
PONTYPRIDD
TREFOREST
DYNEA
Doctor's Canal
CAERPHILLY
RISCA
Monmouthshire Canal
Crumlin Branch
Glamorganshire Canal
Malpas Junction
NEWPORT
14
River Usk
USKMOUTH
Severn

CARDIFF

(114)

A **B** **C**

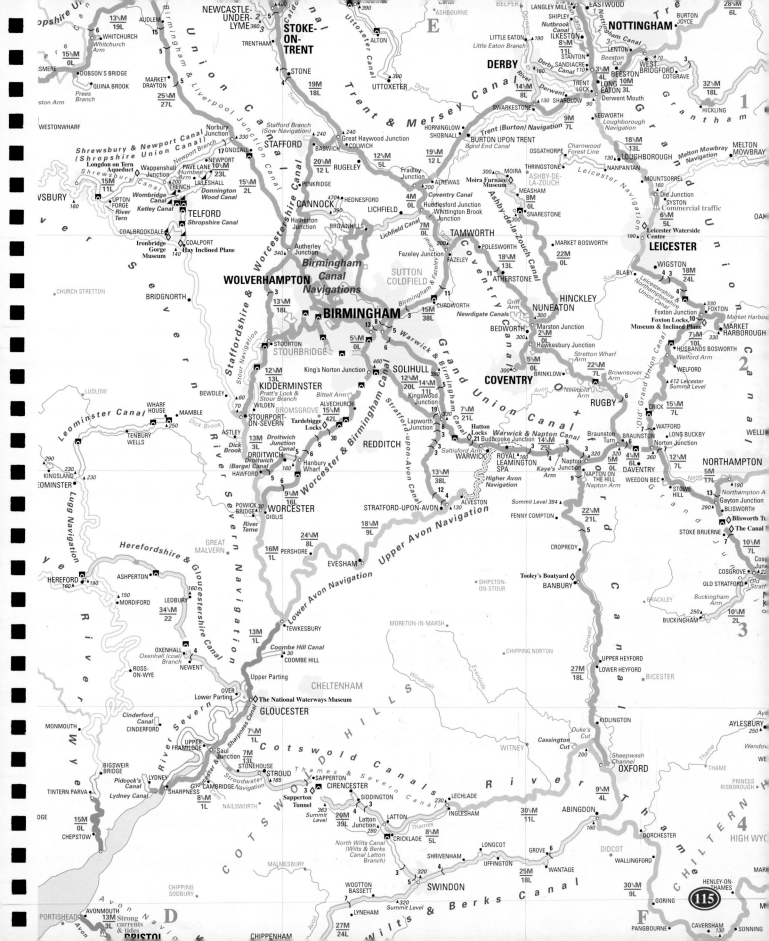

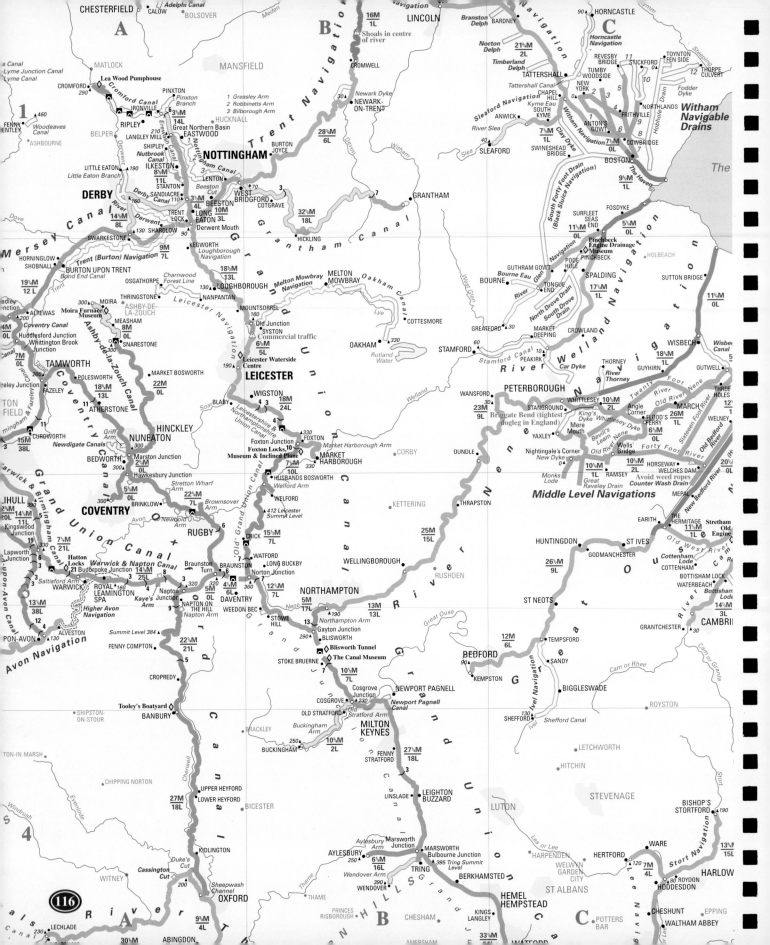

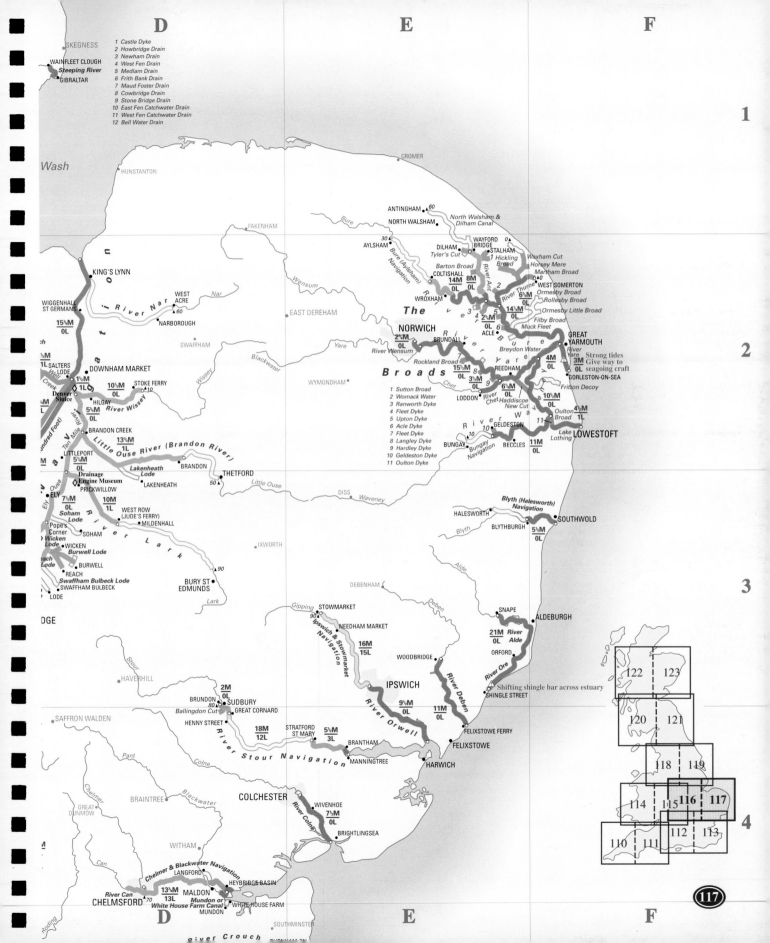

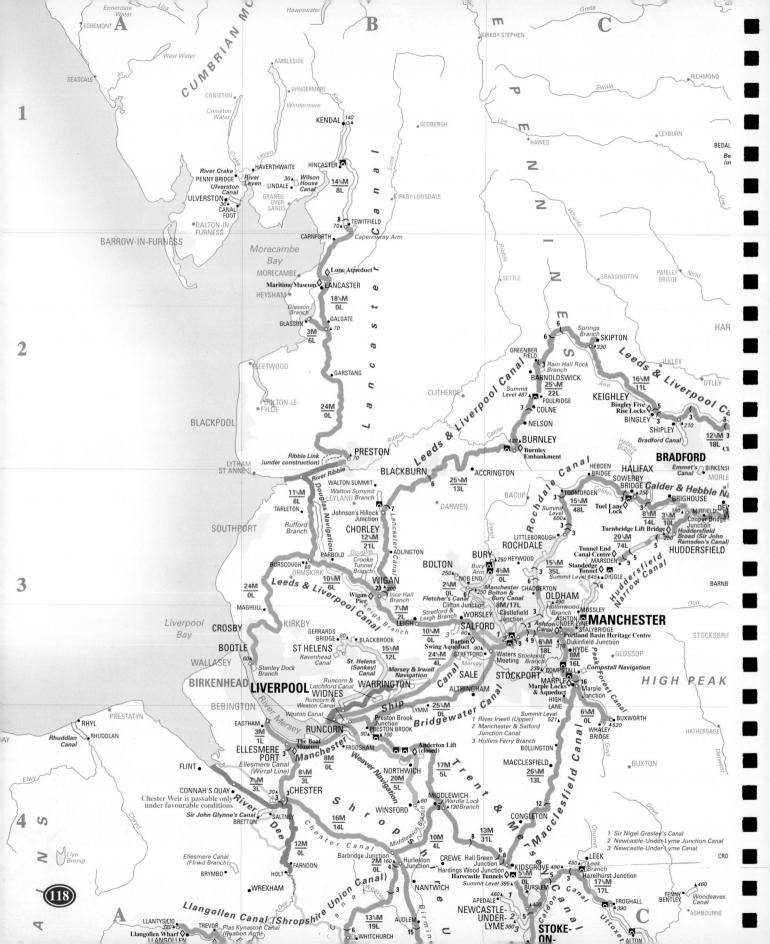

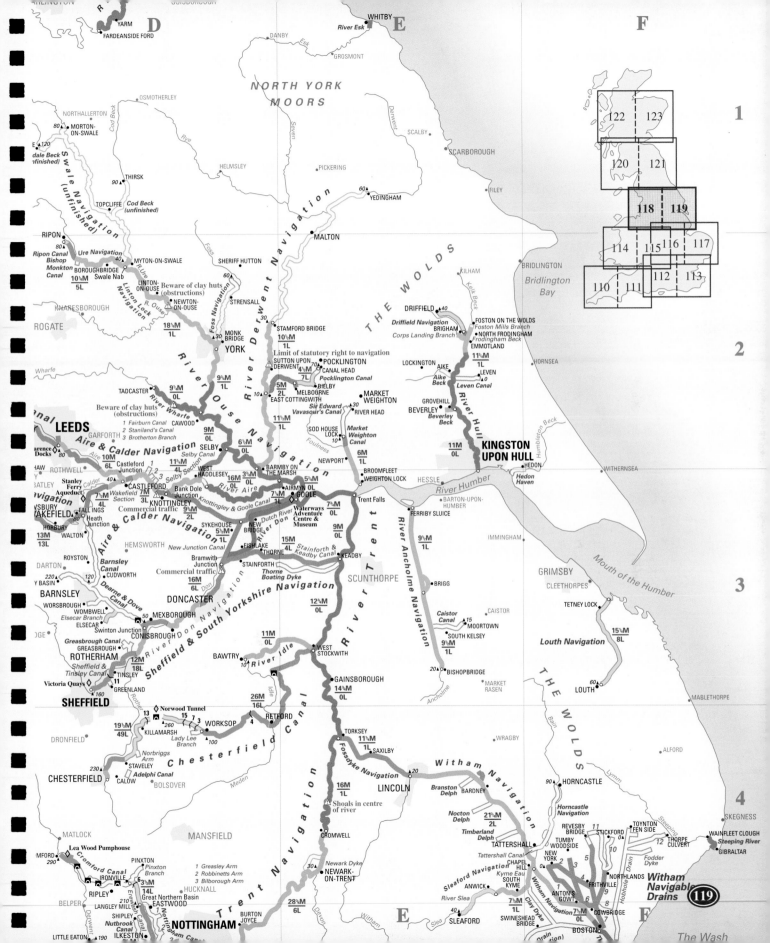

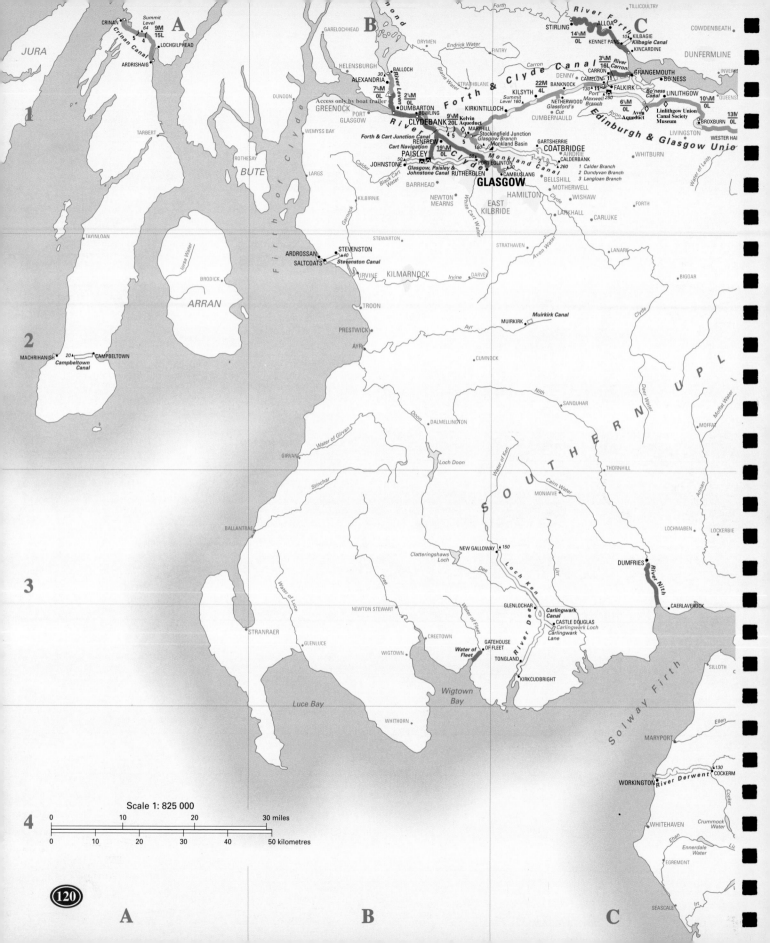

JURA

CRINAN
Summit
Level
64
A
9M
15L
Crinan Canal
4
LOCHGILPHEAD

ARDRISHAIG

1

TAYINLOAN

MACHRIHANISH
20
CAMPBELTOWN
Campbeltown
Canal

2

TARBERT

ROTHESAY

BUTE

BRODICK

ARRAN

Firth of Clyde

DUNOON
WEMYSS BAY

GREENOCK
PORT
GLASGOW

HELENSBURGH

GARELOCHEAD

DRYMEN

Endrick Water

FINTRY

B

River Leven
BALLOCH
ALEXANDRIA
7¾M
0L
2¾M
0L
DUMBARTON
BOWLING
Access only by boat trailer

30
0L

Forth & Clyde Canal

Blane Water
STRATHBLANE

KIRKINTILLOCH

KILSYTH
4L

Summit
Level 160
130
250
Port
Maxwell
Branch

CLYDEBANK
9½M
20L
Kelvin
Aqueduct
MARYHILL
Stockingfield Junction
Glasgow Branch

CUMBERNAULD

Forth & Cart Junction Canal
Cart Navigation
RENFREW
50
5
PAISLEY
19½M
0L
JOHNSTONE
Glasgow, Paisley &
Johnstone Canal

5
160
Stockingfield Junction
Glasgow Branch
Monkland Basin

GARTSHERRIE
COATBRIDGE
AIRDRIE

River Clyde
PORT EGLINTON
RUTHERGLEN
50
90
Monkland Canal
3
260
1
2
3

GLASGOW

CAMBUSLANG
BELLSHILL

BARRHEAD

NEWTON
MEARNS

EAST
KILBRIDE

HAMILTON
MOTHERWELL
WISHAW
Clyde

Calder

Black Cart Water
White Cart Water

KILBIRNIE

STEWARTON

ARDROSSAN
STEVENSTON
40
SALTCOATS
Stevenston Canal
IRVINE
KILMARNOCK
Irvine
DARVEL

TROON

PRESTWICK

AYR
Ayr

LARKHALL
CARLUKE

STRATHAVEN
Avon Water
LANARK

Cumnock

River Forth
TILLICOULTRY
STIRLING
ALLOA
KILBAGIE
14½M
0L
KENNET PANS
Kilbagie Canal
KINCARDINE

C

COWDENBEATH

DUNFERMLINE

3¾M
16L
Carron
River
Carron
GRANGEMOUTH
BO'NESS
CAMELON
11
104
6½M
0L
Bo'ness Canal
LINLITHGOW
10½M
0L
QUEENS

DENNY
BANKNOCK
22M
4L
130
11
FALKIRK
Forth & Clyde Canal

NETHERWOOD
Glassford's
Cut
6½M
0L
Avon
Aqueduct
Linlithgow Union
Canal Society
Museum
13M
0L
BROXBURN

Edinburgh & Glasgow Unio

CUMBERNAULD

LIVINGSTON
WESTER HA

WHITBURN
Water of Leith

MUIRKIRK
Muirkirk Canal

DALMELLINGTON

GIRVAN

BALLANTRAE

Stinchar

Water of Girvan

Doon

Water of Luce

STRANRAER

GLENLUCE

NEWTON STEWART

Cree
Water of Fleet

WIGTOWN

Luce Bay

WHITHORN

CREETOWN

GATEHOUSE
OF FLEET
Water of
Fleet

Wigtown
Bay

Water of Fleet
TONGLAND
KIRKCUDBRIGHT

Loch Doon

NEW GALLOWAY
150
Clatteringshaws
Loch
Dee
Loch Ken

GLENLOCHAR
CASTLE DOUGLAS
Carlingwark Loch
Carlingwark
Lane
Carlingwark Canal

River Dee

River Ken

Water of Ken

MONIAIVE
Cairn Water

THORNHILL
Nith

SANQUHAR

CUMNOCK

SOUTHERN UPL

Clyde

BIGGAR

MOFFAT
Moffat Water

LOCKERBIE

LOCHMABEN

DUMFRIES
River Nith
CAERLAVEROCK

Annan

Daer Water

SILLOTH

Solway Firth

MARYPORT

WORKINGTON
River Derwent
130
COCKERM

WHITEHAVEN
Crummock
Water

Ennerdale
Water
EGREMONT

SEASCALE

3

4
Scale 1: 825 000
0   10   20   30 miles
0   10   20   30   40   50 kilometres

A | **B** | **C**

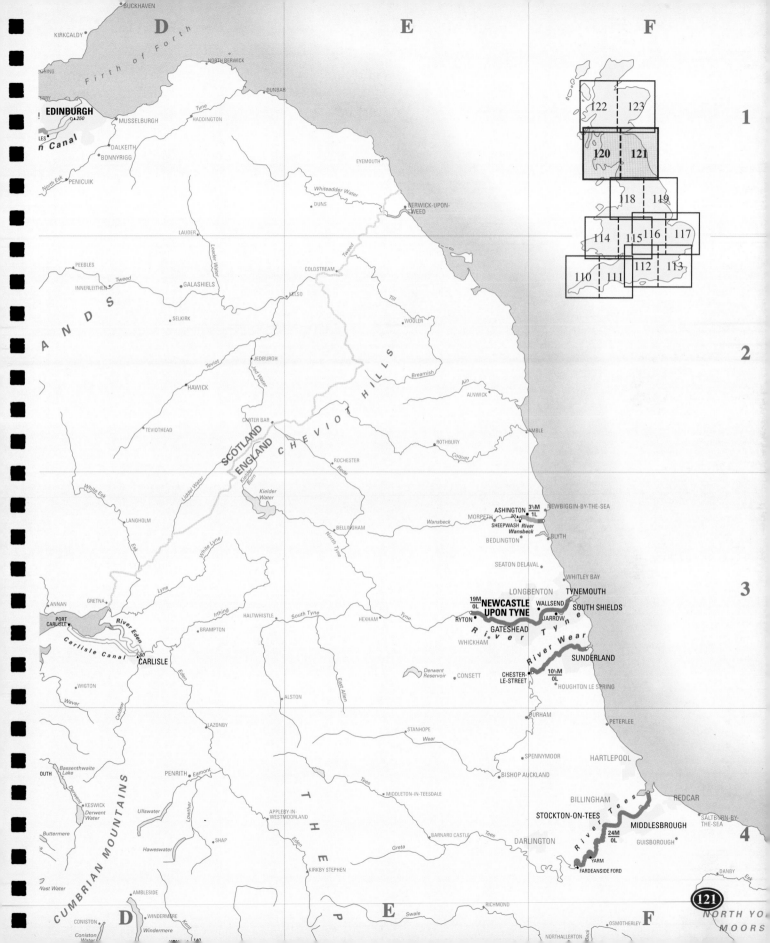

D E F

1

BUCKHAVEN
KIRKCALDY

Firth of Forth

EDINBURGH ▲250
MUSSELBURGH
HADDINGTON
NORTH BERWICK
DUNBAR

n Canal
LES
DALKEITH
BONNYRIGG
NORTH BERWICK

EYEMOUTH

PENICUIK
North Esk

Whiteadder Water

DUNS

BERWICK-UPON-TWEED

PEEBLES
Tweed

INNERLEITHEN

LAUDER
Leader Water

COLDSTREAM

GALASHIELS

KELSO

2

A N D S

SELKIRK

Tweed

Till

JEDBURGH
Teviot

WOOLER

HAWICK
Jed Water

Breamish

CHEVIOT HILLS

TEVIOTHEAD

CARTER BAR

SCOTLAND
ENGLAND

Ain

ALNWICK

ROTHBURY

AMBLE

ROCHESTER
Rede

Coquet

Kielder Burn

Kielder Water

NEWBIGGIN-BY-THE-SEA

LANGHOLM

White Esk

BELLINGHAM

North Tyne

ASHINGTON 3½M
20 1L
MORPETH
SHEEPWASH *River Wansbeck*
Wansbeck
BEDLINGTON
BLYTH

White Lyne

Liddel Water

Esk

SEATON DELAVAL

WHITLEY BAY

3

ANNAN
GRETNA

Lyne

LONGBENTON
TYNEMOUTH

PORT CARLISLE
River Eden
Irthing

HALTWHISTLE
South Tyne

HEXHAM
Tyne

19M
0L
NEWCASTLE
UPON TYNE
WALLSEND
RYTON
JARROW
SOUTH SHIELDS

BRAMPTON
GATESHEAD
River Tyne

Carlisle Canal
▲60
CARLISLE
WHICKHAM

River Wear

WIGTON
Eden

Derwent Reservoir
CONSETT
CHESTER-LE-STREET 10½M
0L

SUNDERLAND

Waver

Caldew

HOUGHTON LE SPRING

ALSTON

DURHAM

4

OUTH
Bassenthwaite Lake

PENRITH Eamont
LAZONBY

STANHOPE
Wear

SPENNYMOOR

PETERLEE

HARTLEPOOL

KESWICK
Derwent Water
Ullswater
Lowther

East Allen

T H E P

Tees

MIDDLETON-IN-TEESDALE

BISHOP AUCKLAND

BILLINGHAM

REDCAR

Buttermere
CUMBRIAN MOUNTAINS
Haweswater

APPLEBY-IN-WESTMOORLAND

SHAP

BARNARD CASTLE
Tees

STOCKTON-ON-TEES

MIDDLESBROUGH

SALTBURN-BY-THE-SEA

DARLINGTON
River Tees 24M
0L

GUISBOROUGH

Wast Water

Greta

YARM

FARDEANSIDE FORD

DANBY
Esk

AMBLESIDE

D
WINDERMERE
Windermere
Kent

E
KIRKBY STEPHEN
Eden
Swale

RICHMOND

F
NORTHALLERTON
OSMOTHERLEY

121

CONISTON
Coniston Water
▲140

NORTH YO
MOORS

122 123

120 121

118 119

114 115 116 117

110 111 112 113

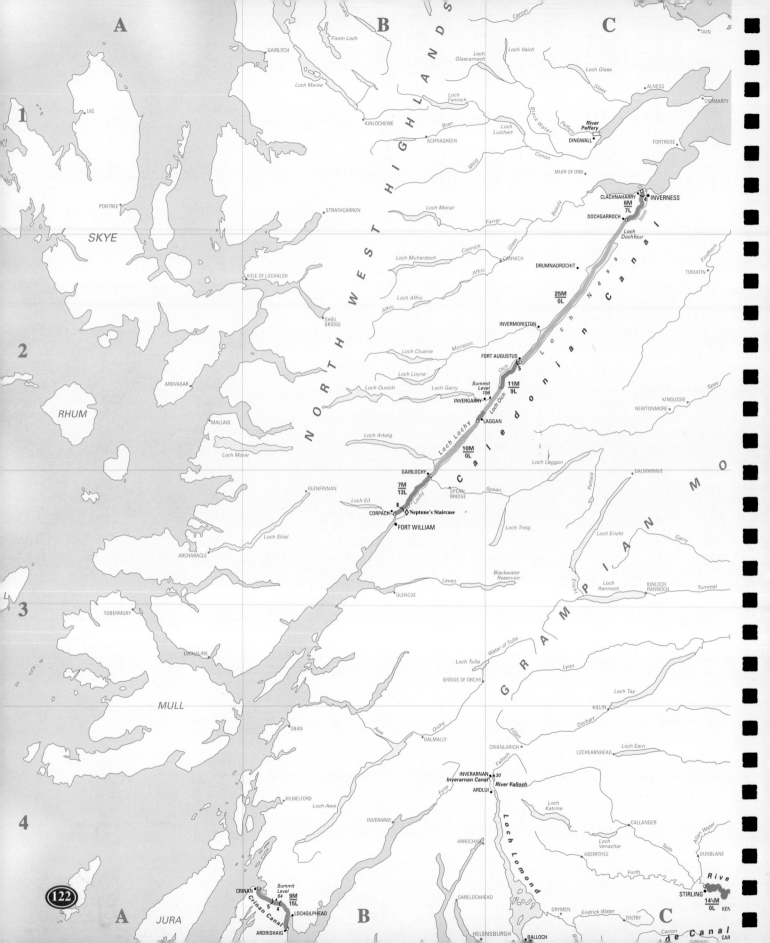

A B C

1

UIG

SKYE

GAIRLOCH

Fionn Loch

Loch Maree

KINLOCHEWE

ACHNASHEEN

Loch Fannich

Loch Luichart

Loch Glascarnoch

Loch Vaich

Loch Glass

Glass

ALNESS

TAIN

CROMARTY

Black Water

Peffery

River Peffery

DINGWALL

FORTROSE

MUIR OF ORD

Beauly

CLACHNAHARRY   INVERNESS
6M
7L

DOCHGARROCH

TOMATIN

Findhorn

N O R T H   W E S T   H I G H L A N D S

PORTREE

STRATHCARRON

Loch Monar

Farrar

Loch Mullardoch

CANNICH

Cannich

Glass

Affric

Loch Affric

Affric

DRUMNADROCHIT

Loch Dochfour

Loch Ness

Caledonian Canal

2

KYLE OF LOCHALSH

SHIEL
BRIDGE

Loch Cluanie

Moriston

INVERMORISTON

25M
0L

Ness

ARDVASAR

Loch Loyne

Loch Quoich

Loch Garry

FORT AUGUSTUS
5

Oich

RHUM

MALLAIG

*Summit
Level
106*

INVERGARRY

11M
9L

Loch Oich

KINGUSSIE

NEWTONMORE

Spey

Loch Arkaig

LAGGAN

Loch Lochy

10M
0L

Loch Laggan

DALWHINNIE

Loch Morar

Lochy

GAIRLOCHY

7M
13L

SPEAN
BRIDGE

Spean

Pattack

GLENFINNAN

Loch Eil

8

CORPACH   ◇ **Neptune's Staircase**

FORT WILLIAM

Loch Ericht

Garry

G R A M P I A N   M O

Loch Treig

Loch Shiel

ARCHARACLE

3

TOBERMORY

Leven

GLENCOE

*Blackwater
Reservoir*

LOCHALINE

Water of Tulla

Loch Tulla

BRIDGE OF ORCHY

Lyon

Loch Ericht

Garry

*Loch
Rannoch*

KINLOCH
RANNOCH

Tummel

Loch Tay

MULL

KILLIN

Dochart

OBAN

DALMALLY

Awe

Orchy

CRIANLARICH

Fillan

Loch Earn

LOCHEARNHEAD

CALLANDER

*Loch
Venachar*

DUNBLANE

Allan Water

KILMELFORD

Loch Awe

INVERARAN
Inverarnan Canal

INVERARAY

30

River Falloch

ARDLUI

*Loch
Katrine*

ABERFOYLE

Teith

Forth

4

Falloch

Fyne

ARROCHAR

Loch Lomond

R i v e r

STIRLING

14M
0L

KEN

122

CRINAN

*Summit
Level
64*

9M
15L

Crinan Canal

5 4

LOCHGILPHEAD

GARELOCHHEAD

DRYMEN

Endrick Water

FINTRY

HELENSBURGH

BALLOCH

de Canal

CAR

ARDRISHAIG

A   JURA   B   C

Carron

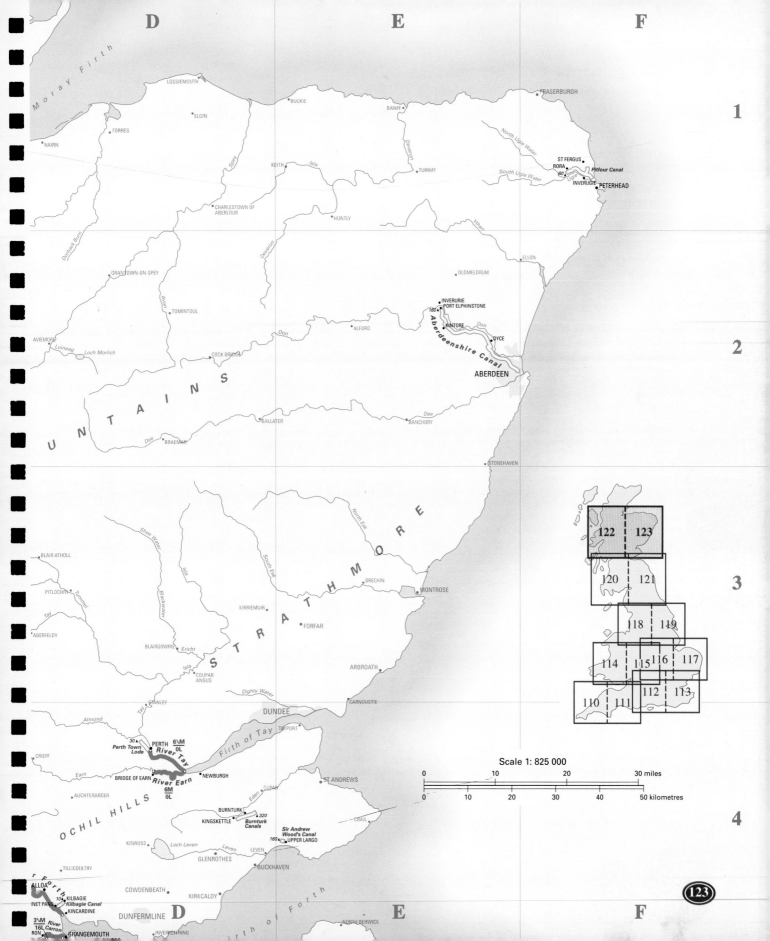

D   E   F

Moray Firth

LOSSIEMOUTH

FRASERBURGH

1

ELGIN

BUCKIE

BANFF

North Ugie Water

ST FERGUS

RORA

FORRES

NAIRN

KEITH

Isla

Spey

TURRIFF

Deveron

South Ugie Water

60

Pitfour Canal

Ugie

INVERUGIE

PETERHEAD

CHARLESTOWN OF
ABERLOUR

HUNTLY

Dorback Burn

Ythan

ELLON

GRANTOWN-ON-SPEY

OLDMELDRUM

INVERURIE

PORT ELPHINSTONE

160

AVIEMORE

Luineag

Loch Morlich

Avon

TOMINTOUL

Don

ALFORD

KINTORE

Don

DYCE

Aberdeenshire Canal

2

U N T A I N S

COCK BRIDGE

ABERDEEN

Dee

BALLATER

Dee

BRAEMAR

BANCHORY

STONEHAVEN

BLAIR ATHOLL

Shee Water

North Esk

S T R A T H M O R E

122 123

120 121

PITLOCHRY

Tummel

Isla

Blackwater

BRECHIN

MONTROSE

118 119

3

ABERFELDY

Tay

BLAIRGOWRIE

Ericht

KIRRIEMUIR

South Esk

114

115 116 117

Isla

COUPAR
ANGUS

FORFAR

112 113

110 111

STANLEY

Dighty Water

ARBROATH

Almond

Tay

CARNOUSTIE

CRIEFF

Earn

30

*Perth Town
Lode*

PERTH

6½M
0L

River Tay

DUNDEE

TAYPORT

Firth of Tay

Scale 1: 825 000

BRIDGE OF EARN

River Earn

NEWBURGH

6M
0L

Eden

CUPAR

ST ANDREWS

0   10   20   30 miles

AUCHTERARDER

BURNTURK

320

O C H I L   H I L L S

KINGSKETTLE

*Burnturk
Canals*

CRAIL

0   10   20   30   40   50 kilometres

KINROSS

Loch Leven

Leven

*Sir Andrew
Wood's Canal*

160

UPPER LARGO

4

Leven

LEVEN

GLENROTHES

BUCKHAVEN

TILLICOULTRY

r Forth

COWDENBEATH

KIRKCALDY

ALLOA

104

KILBAGIE

Kilbagie Canal

NET PANS

KINCARDINE

DUNFERMLINE

INVERKEITHING

NORTH BERWICK

3½M
16L

*River
Carron*

RON

GRANGEMOUTH

Firth of Forth

D   E   F

(123)

Acknowledgements

This book is dedicated to
Ella Alexandra
who started it all.

My family will tell you I am a sucker for books.

I have more coffee table books than coffee tables to put them on. For the last six years in particular the only problem at Christmas was whether an intended purchase of a 'waterway' book was already in my collection. I thank the authors of all of them for their original research and the excitement and perceptions they have passed on to me. Together with the guide books suggested in each section, they have been the main sources for the text but any misinterpretations or mistakes are mine.

There are many books. Some were expensive because they are thick and full of photographs, others because not many people want to read an academic tome with millions of references. Some were cheap but were supreme examples of succinct writing, such as the Ladybird Book on Canals. But if you wish to go beyond the thoughts of this 'introduction' I suggest you ask your library service to find one or more of the following:-

Barrell, Emrhys et al. *Getting Afloat,* Romsey Publishing Co., 1998
Blaygrove, David *Braunston... a canal history,* Braunston Boat Show, 1994
Bolton, David *Race Against Time,* Methuen, 1990
Burton, Anthony *The Great Days of the Canals,* Tiger Books International, 1995
Cumberlidge, Jane *Inland Waterways of Great Britain Seventh Edition,* Imray, Laurie, Norie & Wilson, 1998
Defoe, Daniel *A Tour Through the Whole Island of Great Britain (1724-6),* Penguin Edition, 1971
Dibneh, Fred and Hall, David *Fred Dibneh's Industrial Age,* BBC Worldwide, 1999
Gladwin, D.D. *Passenger Boats on Inland Waterways,* Oakwood Press, 1979
Hadfield, Charles *British Canals,* David & Charles, 1984
Hutchings, Carolyn *Canals,* Ladybird Books, 1975
Mare, Eric de *The Canals of England,* Architectural Press, 1950
McKnight, Hugh *The Shell Book of Waterways,* David & Charles, 1974
Paget-Tomlinson, Edward *The Illustrated History of Canal & River Navigations,* Sheffield Academic Press, 1993
Paget-Tomlinson, Edward *Waterways in the Making,* The Landscape Press, 1996
Ranson, P.J.G. *The Archaeology of Canals,* Worlds Work, 1979
Ranson, P.J.G *The Archaeology of the Transport Revolution,* Worlds Work, 1984
Ranson, P.J.G *Waterways Restored,* Faber & Faber, 1974
Reilly, Robin *Josiah Wedgwood,* Macmillan, 1992
Richardson, Christine *The Waterways Revolution,* Self Publishing Association, 1992
Rolt, L.T.C. *Narrow Boat,* Eyre & Spottiswode 1944, Alan Sutton Publishing, 1994
Rolt, L.T.C. *Navigable Waterways,* Longman, 1969
Rolt, Sonia *A Canal People,* Sutton Publishing, 1997
Smith, Peter *Canal Barges and Narrowboats,* Shire Publications, 1975, 1986
Stewart, Shiela *Ramlin Rose,* Oxford University Press, 1993

And of particular attraction to me the huge amount of research and cartographic skill in the series of historical maps prepared by Richard Dean in association with M & M Baldwin.

Books still in print can also be obtained from your local bookseller or order from:
IWA (Sales) Tel: 01923 711114

The many Canal Societies and Organisations noted within the text have been very generous with their time in answering our queries but both responsible officers and telephone numbers will change with time. There are also three monthly magazines which provide us all with news and stimulating articles:-

Canal Boat and Inland Waterways Tel: 0118 977 1677
Website: http://www.systemD.net/canalboat
Canal & Riverboat Tel: 01372 741441
Website: http://www. canalriverboat.enta.net
Waterways World Tel: 01283 742970

As noted in each section, there are also many *web pages* maintained by canal groups, some with startling designs, some not updated often enough. There are also official sites and chat rooms. Some of more general interest are listed below:-

From the British Tourist Authority
http://www.visitbritain.com/activities/waterways
A fast acting gateway to sites http://www.ukwaterways.net
Searchable listing of waterside events
http://www.waterways.org.uk/iwa/diary/index.shtnal
George's: an enthusiasts' much respected site http://www.canals.com
Inland Waterways Association: campaigning charity http://www.waterways.org.uk
British Waterways: official site for 3000 miles http://www.britishwaterways.co.uk
Environment Agency: keeper of rivers and fens
http://www.environment-agency.gov.uk
Some boats offer holidays: hotel style http://www.canal-cruises.com
Some offer self-drive holidays afloat. Booking agencies include:
http://www.blakes.co.uk   *http://www.drifters.co.uk*
http://www.holidayuk.co.uk/afloat   *http://www.hoseasons.co.uk*

And last, *but by no means least,* I thank all my family and waterway friends who have been supportive throughout this process, with special mention for those who 'tested' the short strolls and suggested ways of making them clearer. I hope we succeeded.

http://www.Brian:Roberts@cwcom.net

Thanks must also go to all those at GEOprojects (UK) Ltd and Garnet Publishing for all the hard work which has gone into this publication. Particular thanks to:

Mary Spence General Manager Cartography
Karen Tait Senior Cartographic Editor
David Edwards Cartographic Draughtsman
Jo Adams Picture Researcher
David Rose Jacket design

Photographs supplied by kind permission:
© Harry Arnold pp 37, 39, 86, 108 *top left*
© Bath Tourism Bureau p 52
© British Waterways pp 34, 80, 106
© Alex Gillespie p 26
© Judy Gray, Linlithgow Union Canal Society p 33
© Kew Bridge Steam Museum p 93
© David Lee Photography Ltd. p 100
© Lincoln City Council p 35
© Ian Meredith *cover - centre, centre left*
© National Waterways Museum p 36 *centre right*
© Den Phillips Photography p 1
© Derek Pratt pp 27 and *cover - top right*, 48 *bottom right*, 68, 88 *bottom*, 108 *bottom right*
© Brian Roberts pp 20, 30, 48 *left top, left bottom*, 59, 104.
© Robin Smithett pp 9, 23, 25, 36 *bottom left*, 64, 84, 88 *top*, *cover - top left*
© Royal Armouries Museum p 7
© Waterways World pp 11, 12
© David Wedd p 109 *top left, centre left top right*
© Stella Wentworth pp 108 *top right, bottom left*, 109 *bottom right*

Old images and drawings:
© Hulton Picture Library p 2 *left* © T.T. Burys 'Coloured views on the Liverpool and Manchester Railway' p 2 *right* © Herbert Simpson 'Lambton Staithes' courtesy of Tyne and Wear Museums p 3 *top right* © Eric de Mare p 3 *centre* © Blakes Holiday Boating p 22 © Sonia Rolt p 31 © Barbara Jones p 38 © Pickfords p 43 © Rochdale Canal Historical Society p 48 © G.N. Williams p 51 © Trustees of the late Dennis Watkins-Pitchford p 67 © Ordnance Survey, Alan Godfrey Maps p 72 © Rochdale Metropolitan Borough Council Local Studies Library p 73 © Ironbridge Gorge Museum p 76 © Science and Society Picture Library p 83 © Board of Trustees of the National Museums and Galleries on Merseyside p 91 © The National Maritime Museum p 95 © Harley Crossley p 97 © Trustees of the Wedgwood Museum p 98

Index